Andrew Tow

Andrew had his first Jake Dillon adventure thriller published in 2006 - The Chimera Code is fourth in the series. His writing is a reflection of his extensive travels and inherent interest in national security and covert operations. Andrew lives in Dorset, where many of Dillon's tours take him. Andrew lives with his family and is currently completing the fifth Dillon novel, due for publication in 2013.

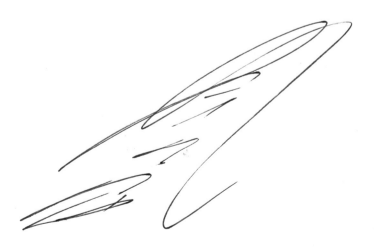

The Chimera Code

Andrew Towning

© 2012 Andrew Towning

Cover photography by Jennie Franklin Photography, modelled by Harriet Towning

ISBN: 978-1481200868

Published by Andrew Towning
www.andrewtowning.co.uk

This novel is dedicated to the memory of my Father 1939 - 2012

ACKNOWLEDGEMENTS

My thanks to L and S, two very talented IT Social Engineers who, after a chance meeting in a bar and many conversations later, were unwaveringly generous with their technical advice, interest and most of all their patience during the writing of this novel. You both know who you are!

Also, my special thanks to Zoe Wilson whose professionalism, energy and zest is truly inspiring.

Prologue Assassins

My name is Legion: for we are many.
St Mark ch.5, v.9

Carpathian Mountains - Ukraine

The old winch-house jutted defiantly out from the jagged cliff top. Sections of the stonework had fallen away far below, revealing toothless gaps in the sheer elevations - the dark smile of an old Ukrainian revolutionary. The two-storey building, that had endured hundreds of years of the harsh mountain elements, had once been the only route up and in to the fortress that over - lord the entire valley for as far as the eye could see. This had long ago been defended against marauding invaders but now and for centuries past, had only been smashed and bombarded by wind, rain and snow intent on a gradual stripping away of its outer defenses.

Something - a quick stealth-like movement - the only sound the rushing of air as it skimmed easily, almost fluidly across the mountain face on the end of the high-tensile line. A figure shrouded by darkness, protected by the night and its moonless sky of brooding black clouds. It landed lightly on the aged timbers of a narrow walkway. And, through the glass of a narrow window, dull light shone out into the gloom.

The figure emerged from the shadows and moved forward with the light-footedness of a stalking cat. Then it paused, listening, a static outline against the night, before sliding once again into the darkness and vanishing: a ghost; mist; a black dream.

* * *

There was a deep oppressive silence in the dimly lit corridor, at one end of which was a solid oak arched door, the single portal for the protected sanctuary.

Seated, three heavy-set Ukrainian guards, full beards and their hair grease-smeared and lank, were armed with GRACH MP-443 pistols and shoulder-slung Nikonov AN-94 'Abakan' assault rifles. One of them, sitting with the earphones of his MP3 player firmly plugged into his ears, was rocking back and forth on his wooden chair against the stone wall. The other two were playing cards across a small makeshift table by the warm light of an oil-burning lantern; their brutal scarred features softened temporarily by the amber glow, a bottle of cheap vodka their only shared release from the boredom of duty.

There was a soft clatter, muffled, from back along the shadowed corridor and the two men, who were playing cards, exchanged bloodshot gazes over the smeared bottle. One man, the leaner of the two, removed the American cigarette from his lips and discarded it on to the flagstone floor.

"Your turn, *Comrade*."

The larger of the two men shook his head. "It'll be a fucking bear again. They come down here looking for food."

"Not at this time of night. They don't like the dark - or the bullets. Go on, you stinking good-for-nothing, go and check who's there." He grinned, baring rotten and heavily tobacco stained teeth. "Anyway, we're safe. If they'd got this far they would have triggered the perimeter sensors. *And* there are Special Forces bodyguards in there with the *Comrade* himself," he sneered. "We have nothing to be afraid of."

Cursing, the other man stood and checked his pistol and Nikonov. The magazines were both full and he flicked the safety off. "I used to enjoy shooting bears" he muttered, and with his bloodshot eyes as alert as they could ever be in the gloom, he left the friendly glow of the lamp.

The other Ukrainian guard sat, shuffling the cards with the expert hands of a man practiced in guard duty. His eyes shifted right to the digital display of the monitor on the wall, its black plastic surround and LED warning lamps out of place against the rough stone work. It registered normal. Nothing. No intruders. Nothing to worry about. But the hi-tech electronics made him nervous. He was a guard trained with traditional weapons: guns and bullets. He did not rate fancy gadgets…

There was a sound somewhere in the distance - almost inaudible - like the air being let out of a tyre.

The seated man frowned, his brow furrowed, his eyes darting over to the LED monitor, then back to the gloom of the empty corridor. He kicked the other guard, who woke with a start and, who instinctively brought the Nikonov, that had been resting on his lap, up in a menacing arc. The other man stood up and with a fluid sweeping action of the back of his large hand, struck the man heavily across the face, knocking him off the chair and across the stone floor. Blood trickled from the corner of his mouth, but he knew better than to strike out against his superior officer, instead he picked himself up and stood to attention.

The lean Ukrainian soldier moved towards the gloom of the corridor. "Mikhail, are you there, *Comrade?*" His words echoed, alone, through to the other end. When no reply came, he picked up the Nikonov and switched it to fully automatic. He moved with a smooth military precision that indicated a history of violence and, despite his sleazy appearance, a cold precise professionalism kicked in; he motioned for the other man to stay on guard at the door, as he crept forward close to the wall, suddenly alert, all senses buzzing with a sudden rush of adrenalin. He reached a junction in the corridor and glanced tentatively to the left, gun muzzle tracing an imaginary arc of fire. The half-open distant iron door showed only a beam of faint moonlight breaking briefly through the clouds and spilling over the walkway. There was no sign of Mikhail.

The guard started to back away - and was slammed off his feet, flung against the wall, a tungsten tipped arrow shaft protruding from his forehead. His Nikonov AN-94 clattered deafeningly on the granite slab floor. Blood trickled from the tiny wound, running across his face, and onto his chin and over his fatigues. His eyes, open and lifeless, stared unseeing at the ceiling as his legs and arms continued to twitch, while blood pooled around him from the smashed skull and formed a slowly growing viscous puddle on the floor.

* * *

Scorpion 7: One of ten elite units, supremely proficient and lethally effective in the violent worlds of; counter-terrorism, protection of government and political VIPs and covert operations worldwide. This was supposed to be an easy gig. Protection: close quarters, waiting for one of the British Government's many top-class analysts to arrive in order to verify certain information carried - *stolen* - by Valentin Vladimirovich Ivankov.

Ivankov, Russian born, lately of Venice, Italy, and before that involved with some nefarious desert activity in Libya. He was a man with a unique profession. He was an internationally renowned and highly respected archaeologist, but had since his university days been a spy for the former soviet KGB. In the corner of the fortified living quarters sat an aluminium case containing the tools of his trade. The metalwork had been handcrafted to a very individual and precise design: the case had been created with an inner and outer skin with concealed X-Ray proof compartments in between for the sole purpose of smuggling. On this occasion Ivankov was carrying encoded documents stored on an SD (secure digital) memory card, which looked just like the one in his professional Nikon digital SLR camera. He knew the British Government would pay a high price to get their hands on the information that was stored on the card.

The safe room in this lonely fortress had been designed, appropriately enough, first and foremost for the safety of its occupants. The only window was glazed with a high-grade bullet-proof glass that was unusual and expensive for such a remote location. The walls, although weather beaten on the outside were solid stone, two feet thick, the ceiling and floors solid concrete, the door heavy oak with a bomb-proof core and controlled by biometric and two digital locking systems.

The occupant, obviously, was paranoid.

Valentin Vladimirovich Ivankoff slept lightly on his back, a pillow covered in the finest silk beneath his cropped blond hair. The silk sheets had been thrown free in favor of the heavy bear skin due to the extreme cold seeping in from the mountain. The old wood burning stove in the corner of the room had long gone out.

A *click* sounded. Valentin's eyes instantly opened in the darkness.

He lay perfectly still staring up at the ceiling for a while, his breathing almost inaudible with a steady and even beat. Then he scanned the room, glad that he was no longer subject to the severe headaches that he had been recently suffering due to the high altitude. Just outside of his private suite, on the other side of the solid door sat three guards, courtesy of the Ukrainian army.

Inside the room with him were two of his most trusted personal bodyguards and the three members of the Scorpion 7 protection squad. All were waiting for the British Government's expert analyst and the money that he would bring with him. Ivankov relaxed a little more as he watched the Scorpion squad; they were rated among the best and Valentin Vladimirovich Ivankov had had dealings with them on a number of occasions over the last two years since their inception. They were good. No, he thought, they really were the best of the best.

Hawk was cleaning his Heckler & Koch MP5 submachine gun, while Jules sat with her head resting against the wall as she rubbed at her eyes. Big Fitz, was on his feet by the bullet proof window. The big man tilted his head sideways, and there was a cracking sound of released tension as his neck vertebrae clicked back into alignment.

From outside there came a distant muffled sound of a helicopter's rotor blades cutting through the thin mountain air. Hawk and Jules exchanged meaningful glances. "What is it?" said Ivankoff, suddenly - skittishly - nervous. He sat up in bed, quickly glancing down at where his own personal and concealed sawn-off shotgun nestled under a heavy oak chest: the *last line* of protection should Scorpion 7 and the bodyguards outside fail.

Yakov moved towards him, black-clad, menacing and yet, to Valentin, reassuring. He set his own weapon to fully automatic and grinned a mouthful of gold teeth. "Don't worry yourself, Valentin," he rumbled. "We are all here. You have nothing to fret over, you'll be fine." He reached out to pat Ivankov on the back.

A shrill noise cut through the air and then a metallic *clack*.

Both digital locks failed.

The heavy oak security door burst open.

"I wouldn't be so sure about that," came the calm controlled voice.

The figure was of average height and slight build and dressed in a single-piece black body-hugging garment. The face was concealed by a tight black balaclava that revealed only the eyes, which were as blue as the ocean.

The voice was quietly spoken, carried no accent and the figure appeared not to be carrying any sort of weapon.

Everybody in the room froze...

"Who the fuck?"

"Save your questions for your God."

The figure moved with awesome speed as the three members of Scorpion 7 and Ivankov's two personal bodyguards opened fire. Rounds screamed across the room as the black clad figure leaped high into the air, somersaulted, twisted, and connected, booted feet first, with the large bulk of Yakov. The big man fell, and before he had crashed to the ground a long gleaming knife had been run across his throat.

The black-masked figure looked up - a quick glance. Yakov's gun was lifted without preamble from the floor. "You *bastard!*" hissed Jules, her feminine mouth open in disbelief. She had moved with exceptional agility and speed, her gun spitting its lethal payload, shell casings ejecting, but the black clad figure was - gone.

The gun muzzle felt cold against Jules' temple. There were two dull thuds as the rounds exited and slammed into oak panelling before Hawk got his MP5 submachine gun trained on the black-clad figure from across the room.

But it was too late, "No," Hawk mouthed silently.

The black intruder squeezed the pistol trigger and, even as Jules' blood and brains were oozing from the side of her smashed skull, kicked off from her slumping corpse and somersaulted in a tight ball, somehow avoiding the screaming 9mm rounds from Hawk's weapon, hit the ground and rolled towards a heavy oak chest. From nowhere a sawn off shotgun appeared and there was a heavy bass *boom*. Hawk was lifted from his feet and blown across the room. He left a trailing smear of blood against the stone wall, then slid down onto his haunches and remained quite still.

Suddenly everything was awesomely silent. The smell of cordite hung heavy in the air, only the flickering of a damaged light illuminated the cowering figure of Valentin Vladimirovich Ivankov. He looked up slowly, glanced around at the carnage, and let out a long-drawn shuddering sigh. He was fully aware that he was lucky to be alive, realised that he was extremely lucky not to be a corpse sprawling beside the five carcasses on the floor.

The black clad Assassin was standing with the sawn-off shotgun in his or her hands.

The figure said nothing. Made no move - no sound.

Valentin, who had good cause to feel nervous, was uncomfortable sitting on the hard floor as trickles of sweat crawled down his neck and back.

He looked at the figure as he stood up and dusted himself off, "Shit man, I can't believe you've just taken down a Scorpion unit," he croaked. There was no response - physical or oral. "How the fuck did you move so fast around this room? What are you a fucking acrobat or something? And are you here for what I think you're here for? You don't need to worry, I've still got it and it's safe. I was on my way to him when I was snatched by this lot." Valentin looked around the room.

The sawn-off shotgun swung up and the double barrels blasted Valentin across the room and into a twisted bloody heap in the corner. There was a clatter as the shotgun fell noisily onto the flagstones and landed in a pool of congealing blood. Soft black boots left crimson imprints across the floor while footsteps pounded down the darkened corridor towards the scene of carnage. The Assassin threw a small round ball at the center of the bullet-proof glass which attached itself by tiny suction cups.

The figure approached the aluminium case, hurled aside in the recent confusion. Crouched down behind the oak chest and hands moved swiftly to open the two outer combination catches, revealing the contents, which were hurriedly tipped out onto the floor. The pressure release was found and the inner metal lining came away easily to reveal the secret compartment holding the memory card. This was stowed away inside the tight black clothing.

The Assassin turned the outer dial on its watch face and instantly the small explosive device attached to the glass detonated. It leaped up to the opening and glanced down at the valley far below. Fresh morning sunlight bathed the scene and then the figure was gone, leaving only bloody footprints outside on the stone parapet.

* * *

There was the distant rattle of Russian-made sub-machine gun fire.

The guards who had come running in from their sentry posts outside had all exchanged worried glances as they surveyed the five corpses in the room.

"How did he open the digital locks? I was told that they were foolproof. Infinite fucking combinations or something."

"Over here, *Comrade.*"

The two other guards lumbered towards the gaping window, saw the footprints in congealed blood and glanced down into the sprawling valley below...

* * *

Within the damp dungeons, deep beneath the mountain top fortress, something barely visible had been attached to the constantly dripping stone ceiling. A single red light, glowing faintly, an omen of death and devastation.

The bomb detonated. The explosion, savage, fire and destruction screamed white heat through the passageways up to the building above, wrenching it apart with the force of unleashed chemical annihilation.

In the valley below, there was a spattering of small stones into the fast moving river, followed by thunderous splashes of heavy chunks of granite and timber cascading down through the early morning mist.

Black smoke billowed up towards the sky, blocking out the new dawn sun.

* * *

South China Sea - off the coast of Hong Kong: The tropical rain storm beat violently across the South China Sea; heaving, beating waves towards the dark rusting hulk of the grounded oil tanker, unlit and abandoned, pounded and abused by the elements. The tanker had run onto the jagged rocks that lurked just below the surface of the water many years before. Had been left to rot by one of the world's largest petroleum corporations. The huge engines, that no longer thundered and beat with life, had long ago been dismantled and taken for scrap, as had anything else of any value including the bridge, stripped of everything and was now just a shell, empty and devoid of life. The bow was a tangle of fused rusting steel being gradually eaten away by the sea spray, and the enormous ship was a cast-off - discarded, abused, raped, bled dry and forgotten.

The ship was a ghost, deserted. Almost...

The figure moved out into the twilight from somewhere in the bowels of the ship, wearing a tight-fitting black garment and a rolled-up balaclava. Gloved hands wrapped around a rusting rail and the man looked up, gasping as the wind rocked him almost off his feet and over the side of the rail.

He grinned and revelling in the wild roller-coaster ride feeling, pulled out a cigarette and shouldered his MP5 submachine gun as he searched for his lighter.

"You've got more chance of falling over that rail, than you have of lighting that thing."

"You may be right - but then again you may be wrong, my old son." The accent was broad east end of London. Pulling free the Zippo lighter, he cupped the cigarette in an attempt to defeat the torrential rain that was beating down. Miraculously, the end of the cigarette glowed, a bright spark against the gloom. White smoke swirled around the young man's face and he inhaled deeply, closing his eyes and enjoying the nicotine rush.

"Pete, this is the most shite gig, man."

Pete merely nodded, turning his back on the stocky muscular man with the heavily scarred complexion and gazing out into the black churning waters. "Go get us some strong coffee, mate? And check on our North Korean friend while you're at it."

The thick-set man - recently recruited to Scorpion 4 - stomped off down the gangway to the lower level which had been converted back to sleeping and living quarters as well as the galley for the duration of their stay.

Pete took his time smoking his cigarette, gazing out over the rolling waves of the South China Sea that hid the bright lights of Hong Kong. He wondered idly what it would be like, working on a tanker, living on a ship so big that you need a scooter to get from one end to the other. His mind drifted; he pictured the tanker carrying many thousands of tons of crude oil, the speed and force that it would cut through the ocean and the vast amount of distance needed to stop a ship that was so big. And he thought about himself: Pete; twenty-five year old Scorpion veteran; two tours of Afghanistan and then head hunted by a spook from MI6 to join one of the Government's most secret and elite units and given one of the softest gigs ever devised by the shadowy Scorpion planners. To protect Zhu De Chung, anti-communist rebel sympathiser and professor of mathematics at the Peking University, Beijing, China. Zhu De was a hunted man - he was hunted because of the highly classified secrets he held. Pete was simply tired; and he wanted to go home. Wanted to be far away and preferably out of this game. He had been killing people far too long and just wanted a quiet life.

Pete laughed to himself, and leaned out over the rail. It moved under his weight, the metal creaked, the noise lost in the wind as he gazed down into the black water far below. His fear of drowning, close at hand.

The quiet life. I thought only old men got tired, his inner voice taunted him.

I thought you were a professional soldier. A fighter - not a quitter - you wussy.

He had seen enough blood and gore in Afghanistan to last most men a lifetime and then some.

Levi was right; he thought as he moved to the stairwell and braced himself against the wild wind. This really is a shit gig; a full five man team locked away on this cursed rusting pile of scrap metal for a whole ten days with Zhu De, a slightly crazy North Korean professor. He had defected from the communists and now wanted sanctuary in Britain, but while this was being organised, he had to be hidden away and baby-sat.

Pete flicked his cigarette butt over the rail and went down the stairwell to the lower deck gangway. The howling wind and rain beat against the slab side of the tanker and the emergency lighting that had been rigged and hung untidily from the low ceilings swayed and thrashed around with each fearsome gust. He sauntered on towards the galley and canteen, his boots hammering the metal, his torso twisting and turning to fit through the narrow watertight doorways.

"Wakey, wakey, you lazy bastards. You got that coffee on?" Pete grinned as he stepped into the canteen. The smile was immediately wiped from his face. There were dead bodies strewn across the floor, blood pooling on the rusting metal. Blood was spattered up and across the walls, across the stainless-steel worktops, dripping from the low ceiling. Levi was sprawled on his back over a table, mouth slack, dead eyes staring as the flickering fluorescent tube above him flickered over his corpse.

Pete didn't move; slowly, very slowly, he unslung the MP5 and flicked off its safety. He quickly scanned the room, first to the left. His breathing had become unconsciously labored through clenched teeth and he could taste bile in his mouth.

What the fuck screamed his brain.

Gavin was dead, trailing backwards off a bench, blood covered fingers clasping the webbed strap of his MP5. Chris lay face down against the iron-studded flooring. And Slider, arms fully outstretched, face contorted in wretched agony, a wide gash across his throat, looked unseeing up at the ceiling.

Come on - focus. You must think...

There had been no sound of gunfire; the Assassin - Assassins

- had used silenced weapons. The poor fuckers - Levi and the others - hadn't even known what had hit them. And that meant the Assassins were - quick!

Something raced across the edge of Pete's vision and he instinctively pulled back. Silenced bullets sprayed through the open doorway and up the iron wall, splashing white hot sparks that burnt his face. Pete hit the deck, rolled onto his front and squeezed the trigger of his own weapon. The gangway on the other side of the doorway was filled with a deafening roar of gunfire, and ricochets peppered the stairwell with hot bright metal flashes as Pete picked himself up and sprinted for his life in the opposite direction.

His booted feet pounded along the gangway and the blueprint of the oil tanker flickered back into his brain; gangways, ramps, stairwells, containment tanks, derricks - all now seemed a blur and Pete halted, slowed his breathing, and took a quick glance behind him. He stepped sideways behind a doorway and waited, his breathing suddenly calm, his professionalism kicking him into - reality.

Nothing, no sounds of pursuit, and… the black-clad figure glided into view, its attention focused on something ahead, it sensed rather than saw Pete at its side. The head, no more than twelve inches from the levelled MP5 submachine gun, snapped left - and Pete found himself staring into the ocean blue eyes of a killer…

He squeezed the trigger.

Everything happened at once; the world seemed to explode as the Heckler & Koch MP5 submachine gun hammered in the confines of the gangway. The Assassin was snatched and thrown up against the iron wall and drilled with the entire magazine of bullets whose impacts held the body upright, dancing and twitching, until the 'dead man's click' reverberated in Pete's brain and abruptly brought with it a sudden echoing silence. Pete pulled out a fresh magazine from his jacket with gloved hands covered in brain and gore, trying not to look at the pulped goo that covered his arms, trying not to gag on the cordite reek that filled his nostrils and throat.

The corpse slithered to the metal deck and lay in a crimson pool of its own blood.

He firmly clicked the fresh magazine into place, and then breathing slowly and heavily through blood spattered lips - looked left and then right. He was temporarily deaf from the thunderous roar created by the weapon and could only hear a ringing in his ears.

What the *fuck* is going on, he thought.

He stepped over the corpse, then headed towards the steep stairwell ahead. Warily, firmly gripping the rail, he climbed towards the night. Outside the rain was still pounding, driven by the high winds off of the South China Sea. Above, Pete could see nothing but darkness and the diagonal slashes of sheeting rain.

Carefully, and with all his senses on full alert, he pulled free his Matrix G8 communicator and, placing his forefinger on the biometric reader to activate the device, initiated the emergency mayday signal. But instead of the usual flicker of blue lights the G8 failed to respond. Pete stared at the futuristic looking device in disbelief. Since joining the Scorpion unit a G8 had never failed him. Unlike conventional civilian devices the Matrix G8 had been developed by Government boffins exclusively for the Scorpion units. These compact devices encased in titanium do not conform to normal rules of physics; signals can bypass electromagnetic interference, and the devices allow nearly always instantaneous communication at the most extreme distances from any point on the planet without the need for satellite links.

"Bollocks."

He drew in a deep breath. *Calm*, whispered his racing mind. Focus.

Zhu De Chung: Pete knew that he had to reach the North Korean. Had to protect him; save him. Get them both off this desolate rusting graveyard.

The only escape craft that the squad had were inflatable ribs, moored at the stern of the tanker on the starboard side. But the most pressing question now was:

How many Assassins were onboard?

Had he killed the only one? Or were there more waiting for him?

However many there were, they had killed five members of a Scorpion Unit. It had to be more than one. *Had* to be. Which meant - the game was not yet over.

Pete gingerly peered over the edge; the tanker, at eye level, was a rusting bucket of twisted metal, slippery like ice, stretching away into apparent infinity. Pete glanced along the gangway, towards the forward deck and the storage tanks, which seemed to descend into nothing.

It's not far.

But not far is always *too far* when someone is firing hollow point bullets at your heels.

What to do? Run or sit tight?

Pete crept up to the open doorway until he was crouching on the platform; the rain stung his face and the wind howled as it drove into him, finding its way into his tight military clothing, and soaking him to the skin. His eyes followed every contour that the weak gloomy light could reveal. He searched for every possible sniping position. He racked his jangling brain for the best place to lay an ambush.

He decided it would best to move around to the other side of the ship. This might allow him the time to sneak down to the lower deck where Zhu De's quarters were located. Hopefully, the fucker would be there, waiting, ready to sprint to the safety of the boats... Pete smiled to himself, craving the nicotine hit of a cigarette.

He suddenly froze to the spot, more out of instinct than anything else.

And then it was there, his worst nightmare.

Cold metal, pressing against the back of his skull.

"Fuck," he whispered.

He started to turn, but a hard warning jab stopped him. Slowly, he crouched and placed his MP5 on the deck.

"Get up and move."

Pete started to walk... everything ahead of him was starting to blur and he realised that he was weeping - not from fear, fear was no longer an option, but from sheer frustration. Of all the ways to be caught, of all the fucking ways to die.

The *crack* echoed dully against the howling wind.

A limp lifeless figure toppled over the rail and disappeared into the black boiling cauldron of sea far below.

Ocean blue eyes watched coldly as it fell.

And, in the next instant, the Assassin was gone.

* * *

Buenos Aires - Argentina: The air was so still and the heat so intense it felt as if it were pressing down with a force that was almost physical. The robust contours of the scarred government building glittered in the sunshine. It stood defiant and majestic against the elements themselves. The recent bombing had left one of the front wings between floors six and thirteen now exposed, water cascaded down the side of the building from the sprinkler system, and trailing cables hung from what used to be service shafts. The Argentine Ministry of Defence building was wounded, torn, betrayed. To the people of Argentina it was a symbol of their world gone berserk.

Flint squatted, the heat from the mid-day sun pounding his tropical fatigues; he listened to the radio and glanced at the Matrix G8 in his hand. Blue LEDs flickered. A voice in his ear said, "They're on the move."

Flint crawled forward, then glanced down, checking the magazine of the AMSD OM 50 Nemesis 12.7mm sniper rifle. He repositioned himself, peering from the rooftop of the building towards the other side of the harbour. The government building was hazy in the heat, the harbour spread out before him like the stage set of an enormous theatre. Flint reached out and steadied himself on the narrow parapet - he felt the usual tension flowing through every muscle and sinew of his body. He felt alive. He pushed a small electronic button just above the trigger guard of the rifle and placed his forefinger over the large touch-screen of the G8; a tiny red light illuminated and a click as the rifle synchronised with the device. For a brief moment Flint watched the scope automatically rotate and focus; then he placed his eye against it and the world seemed to become very clear.

The building had been evacuated except for a small number of officials who had been taken hostage by the terrorists. The scene was rendered in a blue purple tint; he zoomed the scope quickly forward, until he could see even the finest details of the building, each bullet hole and shrapnel scar. Then he pulled back and swept round to the right along the harbour front, searching for the 4x4s and power boats that he knew were coming.

"You in position, Flint?" said the gruff Yorkshire accent in his ear.

"In position - all systems synchronised and itching to go, Gordie." Flint said smiling, picturing the small wiry man who had the fiercest looking crop of red hair he'd ever seen. He shifted his weight, sighting on a distant skyscraper and a rooftop position that he knew Gordie had secured for himself. He raised a thumbs-up, and he returned the signal. "Is Jacko synchronised?"

Jacko only spoke over his comm-link when he had to. From his position on board a motor launch belonging to the Argentine Navy, which was conveniently moored directly opposite the Ministry of Defence building, his reply was self-evident as he stuck up two fingers in the V sign. Flint's comment was a derisory blow below the belt.

Flint moved his own sniper sight back to focus on the Ministry of Defence building. Jacko was there, all in black, ready and steady. He had opted for the most dangerous position out of the three, on the water itself, and despite being well concealed Flint still shivered involuntarily. But then, he thought, Jacko was a wild fucker, untamed. Some said he was mentally unstable; Flint decided that you had to be to do the job and that Jacko probably was more than most.

"Game on, boys."

The words came from the ground support soldiers, Argentinean Anti-Terrorist Special Forces led by a swarthy captain named Santiago, who were waiting in the wings as the scene unfolded. They were monitoring the suspected terrorist vehicles from vantage points around the Puerto Madero area. The Scorpion 3 Unit was positioned as sniper support.

"Three target vehicles on route: Range Rovers, three occupants. ETA zero three minutes. Over."

Flint waited. Every few seconds he glanced at the army issue chrono watch strapped to his wrist.

* * *

Jacko spent the limited time going through his drill, checking his weapon, scope focus, Matrix G8 synchronisation. "Fucking heat," he muttered as he wiped away the sweat from his forehead, and shifted his weight slightly to ease the cramping in his muscles. The boat was gently rocking with the swell from a passing craft, this meant that he would have to rely on his expertise and experience when aiming.

Gordie swept the area with his scope. Through the audio link he was listening intently to the ground soldiers tailing the suspect vehicles.

The tip-off had come from an extremely reliable source: an ex CIA agent turned international techno-weapons dealer who was in the process of negotiating his way out of a firing squad for crimes against the Argentine regime. He had given them masses of information about terrorist funding activity in South America - he had contacts all over the planet and was well positioned to know about such things. So far everything had checked out fine and the Argentine Government was feeling confident about the outcome of this latest outrage. Eight terrorists of South American origin had taken over the building and taken hostage a senior computer systems analyst and his personal staff of four assistants who had been working for the Argentine Government on a top secret project. They appeared to have got hold of a full set of blueprint plans of the entire building and, had known exactly where and when to plant the bombs for maximum damage. At least one hundred people had been instantly killed by the first explosion which had torn out three entire floors and another seventy when the second and third charges had detonated, taking out another three floors and completely destroying them. Shortly after the explosions, the terrorist leader had come on-line and had made his demand. Three Range Rovers to be left outside of the main entrance to the building, each to be loaded with twenty-million US dollars in gold bullion. There was to be no negotiation and if the demand was not met, they would blow up the rest of the building and kill the hostages, one by one, live on the Internet for the entire world to witness.

"Fucking terrorists," snorted Gordie, and swept the area with his scope one more time.

No Range Rovers approaching.

Come to think of it, no ground support soldiers, either.

"GS leader, confirm status. Over!" Gordie was using the standard issue radio comm-link to raise, Santiago.

No response.

"GS leader, come in. Over!"

Again, no reply.

"You there, Flint?" This time he spoke into the G8.

"Yeah, I'm here."

"You see anything?"

"Not even a fly having a shit."

"Something's very wrong," came the quiet West Country accent that was Jacko's rarely heard voice; both Flint and Gordie felt the tiny hairs on the back of their necks stand up and a shiver run down their spines. And yet their G8s were still picking up the chatter of the pursuit vehicle that was following the three Range Rovers. *"Heading south towards the harbour area, down La Rabida Norte, heading towards-"* Gordie scanned the area once more through the rifle scope. He sensed rather than felt a movement of air beside him, a mere fanning of the intense heat - and then the garrote was around his throat before he knew what was happening. His gloved hand, instinctively and with a lightening quickness, came up under the cheese-cutter wire as his eyes suddenly widened and searing pain sliced into both sides of his neck, he felt blood flowing freely down under the collar of his fatigue jacket and body armour as his rifle clattered noisily onto the concrete rooftop.

Gordie was heisted into the air, his legs kicking. He slammed his head backwards, once, twice, three times, hearing a crunch each time. The grip slackened but did not let go. "Flint!" he managed to shout into the G8 Bluetooth earpiece, then rammed his elbow back into the solar plexus of his assailant with all of his remaining strength. The garrotte loosened and Gordie stumbled to his knees, coughing, scrabbling at the fine wire that was biting viscously into his flesh.

Flint sighted his rifle on the rooftop of the building that he was positioned on, could see Gordie struggling, but his attacker was far too close for a clear shot and the heat haze was fuzzing the whole scene and obscuring his aim. Then Gordie struck back. The assailant stumbled backwards and Flint squeezed off a shot, and then two more in quick succession. He grinned nastily just as the silenced machine pistol touched the back of his head and blew his brains and most of his face over the rooftop.

Gordie heard the hiss of the bullets as they flew past him. He spun round, crouching low as he drew his Glock 9mm automatic pistol. The black-clad figure moved forward towards him with lightning speed, kicking the gun out of his grip and out over the edge of the skyscraper. Dazed and confused about what was happening - he heard three dull thuds, knew that Flint's bullets had hit their mark. *Kevlar?* The question flashed through his mind as reflexes took over. Punch, left kick, right kick, punch - he blocked each with his arms, then smashed a straight left that the figure dodged with ease as it moved around him. Gordie came close up and personal with his assailant - the eyes were ocean blue, focused, sharp - and he brought his knee up hard into the crotch of the Assassin. The figure twisted, went down onto the concrete and immediately spun round to take out Gordie's legs from under him. He hit the concrete with sudden shock, the back of his head cracking against the edge of the rooftop. The whirling blackness of semi unconsciousness flooded his vision - he struck out wildly, but hit nothing. He realised with horror that he was being manhandled closer to the edge. "No!" he yelled his arms and legs scrabbling for some sort of hold on the concrete rooftop. But wind rushed up past him as his eyes widened in terror and despair. The sound of his scream remained silent. Then he hit the ground and it was over.

Jacko was considered a total loner by those who worked with him. He appeared to have no friends and was - emotionally and socially inept. He was however, dedicated, professional - and almost the best long range sniper in the business. Rumour had it that he could part the hairs on a target's head from over a mile away with a single shot without them even knowing about it.

He was angry with himself that he not seen them coming. Three figures in black had climbed on-board the boat without being seen. "*Impossible!* " screamed his mind as they closed in for the kill. He swung his rifle and shot the first figure between the eyes - there was a crack as the bullet ripped open the back of the Assassin's skull, a spray of blood and brains, and it fell back limply and fell over the side and into the water.

Jacko grinned malevolently at the other two figures.

They drew silenced pistols in fluid movements and then everybody started shooting at the same time. Another dark-clad shape fell, hurled backwards onto the deck like a rag doll by the 12.7mm round. Then Jacko was hit by a bullet in the shoulder, spinning him round as a second smashed through his side and a third into his stomach. He could feel the blood rising up into his throat and mouth. He groaned and through crimson lips the blood spewed out over the white of the deck. He could feel himself starting to drift away, "Bastards", as he started to loose consciousness. Blood dripped from his limp corpse. The only remaining Assassin crept closer and put three more bullets into Jacko's head. Ocean blue eyes stared down for the briefest moment. Then the black-clad figure dived over the side, into the harbour and disappeared.

* * *

The heavy military truck screeched to a halt on the hot tarmac. Kody stared hard past the shimmering heat haze, then barked, "Out." Six men from the Argentine Special Forces leaped out from the rear of the truck and moved around to the side where he was standing. They spread out, American issue machine pistols covering each other's arc of fire. Kody looked through binoculars towards the high rise skyscraper and then at the rooftop of the building opposite the Ministry of Defence. He then trained them on the power cruiser in the harbour and on the dead body of Jacko. His head riddled with bullets and he assumed that Gordie and Flint had met their ends in a similar way. "What the fuck has gone down here? Three of you take the truck and head over to where the sniper on the roof of that high-rise was positioned, you three get over to that rooftop on the other side of the harbour - bring back their bodies. I'll go and take a closer look inside that building - we will re-group back here in fifteen minutes. Xavier, have we got comms back yet?"

"Sorry Boss, the whole network is down including the Scorpion Squad's G8 link."

"Fuck. Well, let's get on with it boys."

Kody was shocked at the devastation caused by the terrorist's bombs, but there were no terrorists, dead bodies or anyone inside the building. It didn't take him long to realise that the whole thing was looking decidedly odd. Kody knew - could feel it - had been at this game for far too long.

They had been well and truly shafted - but to what purpose? Had the terrorists planted the explosives, set them off remotely, and then from some elaborate studio played out their demands - without actually being in the building?

Fifteen minutes later, Kody was leaning against a wall, a Cuban cigar between his teeth, smoke spiraling around his face. At his feet, on stretchers, lay the dead bodies of the three Scorpion unit personnel, Flint, Gordie and Jacko. Flint's face was completely missing from the bullet in the back of the head. Gordie's body was so smashed that there wasn't one single bone that wasn't broken. And Jacko lay face up with unseeing eyes from his multiple bullet wounds to his body and head. Kody stared at the bodies and shuddered, bent down and gently closed Jacko's eyes before zipping up the black body bags.

Xavier approached. "All comms are back on-line, Boss. But, the G8 network is still out. We've scanned the entire area and there are no other bodies. Hell man, what went on here?"

"Smoke and shadows. They were brought here on a fool's errand."

"What? But, what about that fucking big hole in the Ministry building?"

"This was never about the building or the gold bullion demand," said Kody. Reluctantly, he took the cigar from between his lips and tossed it into the harbour below. He faced Xavier and their stare met.

"Somebody wanted those Scorpion snipers dead."

"So you think this was a hit?"

Kody nodded. "Oh yes, my old friend. And of one thing I am absolutely certain of: whoever did this, whoever killed this Scorpion unit - I'm sure as hell glad they're not looking for me."

"How do you know they're not?" whispered Xavier.

Kody shrugged. "Because, I'd already be dead," he said simply.

* * *

GCHQ Transcript 1. CLASSIFIED HQ1/FYEO-289 SPECIAL SERVICES SUPPORT UNIT. Hacked: GLOBAL TERRORIST MONITORING INTERCEPT.

Transcript of encrypted email: They call them Scorpion Units and belong to the British Government. They are constantly undercover - have no official department and are acknowledged as 'not existing'. They are sent into situations where, like a surgeon's knife, a quick and effective result is required. These clandestine groups have more expertise, training and experience than any other fighting force in operation today and can operate in any terrain and climate. They are considered more covert than any other global government organisation or secret service agency. To any head of state, president or world power who even suspect their existence, they are the ultimate weapon in the fight against global terrorism.

Our agent in Paris has made contact with a member of such a Scorpion Unit, code named Alektra. She has made herself known to us. We have already authenticated her association with Scorpion. Alektra claims that the British Government, in its battle to wipe out terrorism, stabilise corrupt governments and erase the evil and scurrilous profiteers who trade in; human life, drugs, prostitution and terrorist funding wherever they are found, has developed a highly sophisticated and self-thinking prototype computer system - named - Hydra - which is supposed to be impenetrable from attack and has been developed to help with their mission. This information is highly classified.

Prior to Alektra's assassination she claimed that something was very wrong with Scorpion and in particular at the highest level of government. In her own words: there is a traitor within their midst. Alektra mentioned a word: 'Thanatos.' Taken from Greek Mythology this means, the personification of death. We suspect that this indicates an Assassin or Assassins of some considerable skill.

The female Alektra was pulled out of the River Seine near to the Eiffel Tower embankment earlier this month. The subject had been garroted.

GCHQ Transcript 2. CLASSIFIED AQBL/FYE048902 SPECIAL SERVICES SUPPORT UNIT. Hacked: GLOBAL TERRORIST MONITORING INTERCEPT. Transcript of encrypted email: Our programmers have made significant breakthroughs in the virus and worm programme development; the new codes self-replicate at the fastest speeds ever and that Denial of Service occurs within seconds of the host CPU becoming infected. The anti-virus programs tested were not able to stop the spread of the new virus because of enhanced armouring virus scripts that have been written into the codes. Both Microsoft Windows and Macintosh Apple operating systems were effectively shut down and all data erased from the host hardrive. During initial testing the hardware targeted was physically killed within three minutes of being infected with the virus. The speed at which it works its black magic is truly incredible. When it goes live the effects will be instant at all levels and on all aspects of computing, from military applications to world commerce and economics. We predict a total meltdown across the planet within 24 hours. Attached are the encoded data files for you to proceed with when the time comes... TRANSFER OF DATA TERMINATED - HACKER INVOLVEMENT SUSPECTED. Intrusion detected at level 5 - GCHQ building. Initiate lock-down protocol...

Chapter 1

Dillon watched the row of six monitors on the opposite wall of the oak lined study. Hidden CCTV cameras picked up the driver of a Mercedes AMG 55 wheel spin the luxury sports car up the narrow snowbound lane and park precariously and at an obscure angle in the sweeping drive. The driver's door swung open and the woman climbed from the warmth and comfort of the interior. She glanced up towards him, towards the shield of glass and waved through the lightly falling snow.

Dillon moved from the study, across the great hall, walking barefoot over luxurious Persian rugs to one of the day rooms. He threw more logs and coal on the fire and then went back through to the study, picked up the handheld control unit off his desk and, remotely opened the front door, went back to the living room and crashed out on one of the large sofas with a large single malt whisky.

He heard her, stamping snow from her boots and quietly cursing the weather, the location and, most of all, him. He smiled wryly, swirling the whisky and taking in its silky smooth flavour as the attractive woman came up the stone steps to the front door.

As she appeared in the doorway he raised his arm over the back of the sofa and remotely closed the heavy oak door. "How's life, Tats?"

"It's Tatiana, not Tats."

"Bit tense, aren't we. Whisky or wine?"

"What wine?"

"White. Italian - very cold. Does it really matter?"

"It matters, Dillon. Why the fuck did you buy a castle in the middle of fuck knows where?"

"It's the Scottish Highlands, and I happen to like it here."

"But it's in the middle of nowhere!"

"That's just it, Tats. There's not a living soul within fifty miles. Unlike London, which has become so congested it's almost suffocating." Dillon shook his head as he walked off to the kitchen to pour a glass of wine. A moment later he returned and handing her the glass and said, "I moved out of the city because it's not a pleasant environment. Up here the air is fresh, what you might call conducive

1

to relaxation and hopefully a long life."

Tatiana gave a short laugh, her gaze moving around the spacious living room. "I can't believe you gave up everything you've ever worked for to come and live the easy life. Christ, you even sold your Porsche Carrera S4 in favour of a fucking Landrover, and an old one at that."

"To be honest, Tats. A Porsche wouldn't be much good to me up here." Dillon frowned. "I don't have to go out much. I have everything I *need* right here."

Tatiana stopped, took a deep breath and counted silently as she summoned patience. She removed her coat and threw it over the back of a nearby leather armchair, closed her eyes for a moment and then took a long gulp of her wine, followed by another, emptying her glass. She held it out for a refill. Dillon picked the bottle out of the ice bucket and poured her another generous glass full.

"I hate Scotland," she said.

"There's nothing to hate, Tats," Dillon said softly. He drained his glass in one and immediately poured himself another. "It feels right to be here, it's just so beautiful. You won't understand, but I've discovered that I like my own company. The solitude has given me a rejuvenated inner strength and vitality for life once again. All of those years, killing to survive and having to constantly watch my back, drained me to a point where I felt that if someone had put a bullet in my head, they would have done me a favour. Just to escape from all the shit. All I've done, Tatiana - is to step off the merry-go-round for the sake of my own sanity." He watched her slim and athletic form. He thought back to better times - long days and endless nights, making love, laughing, talking, drinking...

He topped her glass up. She ran a hand through her long naturally blond hair, using a small elastic band to tie it into a pony tail, the way she knew from old, was how he liked it. He smiled, downed his whisky in one gulp and threw the cut crystal tumbler into the fire where it shattered: for a brief moment the flames flared, the light dancing across the walls and over the high vaulted ceiling.

"You always were melodramatic," said Tatiana thoughtfully, staring down into her wine glass. She moved in front of the fire, sitting on the luxurious rug in front of it and gazing into the flames, seemingly lost in thought.

"Why are you here?" He said finally when he realised that she

2

was not going to break the silence without prompting.

Flames crackled for a while and Dillon wondered if she had heard him.

"Why has there got to be reason, Jake?"

"Well for starters - it's been well over a year since I left London," Dillon sighed. "Are you still working for Ferran & Cardini?"

"Of course. The firm grows more important to the British Government with each passing day. LJ sends his regards, by the way."

She smiled softly.

"That old slave-driver should be retired by now."

"Well, that as may be. He has a job for you."

"Ah." Dillon sighed, climbed to his feet and walked to stand in front of the large bay window. The snow was falling much more heavily now and he could see, dimly through the swirling flakes, the mountains on the other side of the loch, blue-grey and sheer - exhilarating. The wind howled through the woods outside and whistled in through odd gaps in the wooden window casements, lifting the edge of the heavy drapes as it passed by. Dillon shivered, despite the fire's heat in the room. He felt a twinge of disappointment that he could not see the frozen mountain peak in the distance.

"Would I be working alone?"

"On your own. A protection job."

"I don't know, Tats." Dillon said softly, still gazing out of the window - his mind playing back vivid images of events he would rather forget, nightmares he would rather not relive. She stood, a fluid and graceful action, and moved to him, draped her arms over his shoulders and rested her cheek on his broad back.

"I know you've turned down the last two assignments that LJ has offered you - as is your prerogative. But this has come from the very top of Government. It's really important, Jake."

"It always is," said Dillon bitterly.

"It's something big, and it's going to happen soon. We don't know when - where - or how. But it's got the weenies in Whitehall very twitchy, indeed.

"What's new? Nothing you've told me so far, Tatiana, has grabbed my interest."

"The world is changing, Jake, and you're fucking *hiding* up here..."

She tailed off as she saw the look on his face and cursed herself inwardly. That had been a blow way below the belt; Dillon was good.

3

No, he was the best. And after the stolen painting assignment... he had the right to live and rest any way he pleased...

Tatiana took a deep breath.

"Look, I want you to do this," she said. She moved around to face him very slowly. Her lips touched his and he allowed her to kiss him for a few moments. Her breath was sweet, her lips soft and inviting.

"Why?"

"How long is it since Isabella left you for that stockbroker?"

"You're evading my question, Tatiana. Just over a year ago - and you knew that anyway, it's in my file."

"The girl in question is young, vulnerable, alone and afraid - someone who I can empathise with. Damn it, Dillon. You're the best in the business and she needs the best there is."

"Crap." He kissed her again, anyway, tasting the lightness of the wine on her lips. When he pulled away, he was frowning. "Why not one of the Scorpion units, they're more than capable of protection duties. Surely they would be first in line?

There was a long pause. Tatiana averted her gaze and looked over at the fire as though she was having a tussle with her conscience. Dillon caught a glimpse of something then, in her face, in her eyes. There was something that Tatiana knew, a secret she didn't want to divulge.

Dillon smiled tightly and reached up, stroking her hair. She turned back to him, she had regained her composure.

"The partners asked for my recommendation and I said *you*, Jake," she said the words softly. "Don't turn me down. Don't let *her* down."

"Who is she? Why should I give-a-damn?"

"Zhenya Tarasova. She's twenty-two. The niece of Professor Kirill"

Dillon pulled away for a moment. He noticed a mischievous sparkle in Tats' blue eyes as he searched her face - he shook his head, unsure of the unspoken signs he sought.

"Kirill? Where the hell is LJ sending me?"

"You really shouldn't let me manipulate you, Jake," said Tatiana, turning and walking away from him.

Dillon watched the hypnotic sway of her hips. He sighed inwardly. How long has it been since I've had the pleasure of this woman's company? He thought. How long without soft lips to kiss and so-soft skin to caress...

"I can't help myself, Tats." His voice was a little hoarse. "Where am I going?"

"Castle Drago, Cornwall. One of my favourite counties in England. A place where you can step off the treadmill for a couple of weeks and recharge the old batteries. Unspoilt sandy beaches and wild surf. Absolutely blissful."

"Kirill is based at the Government's secret establishment here in Scotland, isn't he?"

"Yes, but he's come out of his bunker up here to give a series of lectures to the Scorpion Unit top brass and selected unit commanders, and for a celebration of his achievements working on several major breakthroughs in software development. Many of those involved in the project have been based in Cornwall for - shall we say security reasons..."

Dillon sighed and shrugged. He rubbed at his suddenly weary eyes, then met Tats' gaze. "Will you stay?"

There was a brief pause. Tatiana put her hands in her pockets and looked at Dillon steadily. She tilted her head, touched her lips with the tip of her forefinger, her beautiful blue eyes unreadable. Dillon realised that she had aged - matured - wonderfully in the year or so since he had last seen her. And in that instant, he realised too that he wanted her more than anything in the world.

"*And you left her for Issy, didn't you, you cock?*" Mocked his subconsciousness, a distant whisper in his head. "*You cock. You sent her away.*"

Dillon shifted his weight and stood up to his full 6'2" height. Then he smiled and looked up to see the tenderness in Tatiana's expression.

"Not tonight, lover boy," she said in a whisper. She smiled. "But we'll make a date. When you get back from this assignment, maybe."

"You mean, maybe never. Well, I can't say I blame you after the way I treated you. But thanks for the cheap kisses, though. At least they were enough to entice me to give Ferran & Cardini the benefit of my skilled services once again."

Tatiana moved forward and placed a finger against his lips. "Not another word. When you return from Cornwall - we will meet up."

"Promise?"

"I promise. Here catch this."

She tossed Dillon a new mobile phone. It was much lighter than the previous models, and he turned it slowly; similar in size to the one he had before, the dull black alloy shone as it fitted neatly into the palm of his hand. "New model?"

Version 6. LJ has had them designed and made specifically for our own field agents. It also allows you to connect with the majority of government agencies should the need arise. The technology has moved on since you last worked for us, Jake."

"Really? Same basic functions?"

"Yes and a few little enhancements."

The device was loaded with an ultra-fast operating programme, was solid-state - no moving parts - and quite robust; it responded verbally to commands - if activated - and had biometric fingerprint recognition facilities; it was automatically logged into the Ferran & Cardini main computer system using advanced GPS - constant web access gave world maps at the touch of a button. It also had a few hidden and very ingenious little tricks within its alloy casing.

Tatiana turned to leave, gathering her coat and gloves and moving out into the great hall and the front door and the severe cold outside. "When are you coming back to the real world, Dillon? It's missing you - and so am I."

"I've needed the time to get myself back together."

"That wasn't the question."

"Then, when I have a good enough reason to. Does that answer it?"

She held his gaze for a long time, then turned and left. He stood listening to her leave, then moved back into the living room and stood by the window and watched as the Mercedes AMG moved off in a plume of exhaust fumes and angry spinning wheels. The expensive sports car cut a swathe through the fresh snowfall and was gone in an instant, tail lights flickering into nothing.

Dillon felt suddenly alone. Something had been stirred in him for the first time in over a year.

For a while he watched the snow falling, and then stared down at the phone nestling in his palm. He switched it on, and it immediately came to life. A series of encrypted symbols appeared across the large touch-screen. He looked from the phone to the roaring fire - and for a moment was in two minds...

He could simply throw into the flames. Walk away and forget his conversation with Tatiana had ever taken place.

He had vowed the last time that he was through with LJ and Ferran & Cardini International.

Because, when he was truly through with them, then he would be at peace with himself. Dillon shivered, staring into the flames. Ferran & Cardini did not know about what was going on inside his head - his self-loathing of what he had evolved into over the years. But then *nobody* knew about it. Not even the firm's shrinks. He had fooled them all at each and every assessment interview that all field agents had to undergo every six months. He had effectively hidden a dark and psychopathic slice of his personality that had gradually surfaced from the deepest recesses and now perched menacingly, always waiting to prove itself again as it had before in Jersey and Dorset. A blood demon ready to feed at any time...

Dillon sighed.

He turned from the flames and slumped into the embrace of the deep and comfortable antique leather sofa.

Protection, Tatiana had said. Dillon's head was thumping and his mouth dry and he realised that she - and LJ himself - understood him perfectly. No more killing. No more racing around the countryside with someone chasing him... Those days were over. Gone. Thrown into the ocean, just like Charlie Hart's Brinks Mat gold bullion bars had been. But he knew where to find them all the same...

Protection.

The protection of Kirill's niece - the British Government's most coveted communist defector since the cold-war and one of the world's foremost authorities on military computer software programs.

No killing, no bombs, no more collective violence...

He placed his forefinger on the biometric fingerprint reader and told the device his name. Instantly it locked onto the Ferran & Cardini mainframe. A moment later the information he had requested appeared on the screen.

Kirill; Russian professor, born Kiev, educated Moscow and Prague. Born to parents of aristocratic ancestry, who were accused of treason and murdered by the KGB. Kirill brought up by aged aunt - attained honours degrees with distinctions in applied mathematics and quantum physics. On leaving university he was enrolled on a Soviet space programme and under direct supervision of the Kremlin.

Expert in computing systems, specialising in advanced

programming scripts and artificial intelligence scripts for military applications. Assisted to defect to UK after approach from MI6 double agent inside Kremlin. Currently developing the 'Chimera' military software programme for the British armed forces - Scorpion Units testing prototype model. Kirill based in underground bunker facility - exact location top secret, but Highlands of Scotland most likely. The technologically advanced research facility has been set up with the utmost security in what is largely inhospitable and inaccessible terrain. The facility is fitted with a stealth mode and therefore is virtually untraceable from the ground - air - or space.

Kirill has been the target of various death threats; suspect terrorist activity, most likely Middle Eastern influences with attention fixed on the 'Chimera' Programme which is still in the development stage. British SAS units are involved with protecting Kirill while in Cornwall. One weak link could be his niece, only child of his late brother who died of cancer three years ago; she lives and travels everywhere with him and could be a target for kidnapping, or possibly murder in order to blackmail Kirill to obtain information on the new programme.

* * *

Dillon peered out of the glass cockpit as the rotor blades above picked up pace with a rhythmic whooshing sound. He grinned like a young boy - unable to contain his pleasure - as he felt the power of the machine around him wind-up to take-off speed.

The Bell-Robinson R22 Beta II, lifted off from the snow-covered heli-pad, located on the west lawn of Dillon's castle, and rose up into the crisp morning air of the Scottish Highlands. Snow tumbled off the helicopters skids as Dillon banked it around to the right and he watched the mountains drop away beneath him. Exhilaration filled him as the nose of the Bell dipped and the helicopter increased speed as he eased forward and the Bell's air-cooled four-cylinder engine pitch changed with the adjustment. He had always felt alive from the thrill of flying and ensconced in his specially adapted HIDSS - a Helmet Integrated Display Sighting System - Dillon could execute any procedure with the blink of an eye.

The intercom in Dillon's helmet came alive as a familiar voice filtered out through the tiny speakers.

"Hi, Jake, you hear me up there with the birds, mate?"

"I hear you loud and clear, Vince."

"I thought those choppers were for millionaire playboys, not roughnecks like you?"

"They are, but they made an exception in my case."

"Is it fast?"

"Tops out at around 102 knots and climbs at a rate of 1000 feet per minute. I'm currently cruising at two thousand feet, heading due south down the coast towards Cornwall."

"Taking the scenic route, I don't blame you. Let me know when you're nearing your destination. And remember to stay on this secure channel."

"Roger that. Over and out."

Dillon settled back in his seat as the Bell hummed at its cruising speed of 96 knots. He activated the stealth mode, one of the extras he had fitted by the manufacturer before it had left their factory, and cruised down the coastline of England. He checked the mobile phone that Tatiana had given him and noticed that he had one new email. It contained the operational instructions for the assignment. Protection duties in support of British Special Air Service and MI6 operatives. That's all he needed, these boys would not welcome him in Cornwall with open arms and smiling faces. These boys would resent him being there at all. This was LJ's way of easing him back into the Ferran & Cardini fold... and then he would feel the dark side of his psyche spread its wings and wait in abeyance for the killing to start...

He felt a cold shiver run up and down his spine.

He returned the mobile device back to his jacket pocket. "I should have stayed in Scotland," he mused, settling deeper into the helicopter's padded seat; the original had been structured in hard polycarbonate, very uncomfortable, so Dillon had it replaced with something more luxurious.

Dillon had engaged the auto-pilot system which was now flying the compact two-man helicopter at low altitude down the east coast of England, the cold dark waters of the North Sea a few hundred feet below him as the Bell's stealth system worked seamlessly to automatically adjust its course so as to evade detection by radar stations and other more sophisticated probing detection equipment. He continued on down the coast, only stopping once to re-fuel at a small private airfield just outside Ipswich. He then set a course inland over Oxfordshire, and then headed due south towards the Isle of Wight, picking up the southern coast of England and passing over Bournemouth on his way down the rugged Jurassic coastline towards Cornwall and his final destination - Castle Drago. The further west he flew the worse the weather became; rain and wind buffeting the small helicopter.

The speakers inside his helmet crackled and the next moment Vince Sharp's voice was being piped into his ears. "You okay, Jake?"

"If you call high winds and torrential rain okay, then yes, I'm doing just fine."

"I've estimated that you should be at Castle Drago in approximately ten minutes. LJ has asked me to thank you for undertaking this assignment and wishes you all the very best."

"Sounds ominous. Couldn't he have said that to me personally?"

"Sorry mate. He's currently in Argentina - some sort of government crisis thing..."

"What's Castle Drago like?"

Nice little pad they've got hidden away in the middle of nowhere, mate. We've been given strict instructions that you're not to land anywhere near to the main building. There's a Heli-pad in the middle of a wooded area due south of the main residence - that's where you put down and they'll send a reception party to meet you."

"Nice."

"Do I detect the return of that legendary surly contemptuousness, Mr Dillon?"

"Vince?"

"Yes mate?"

"Fuck off."

"Okay. Before I forget, de-activate that stealth mode you've got fitted before you get within three miles of them. They'll want to track you on their radar screens as you approach."

"Roger that. Over and out." Dillon grinned; flicked two switches and the Bell swooped down from the sky towards the undulating and heavily wooded landscape below. He watched the treetops as he headed inland from the coast and eventually spotted the clearing with a large 'H' in the middle of a concrete hard-stand. A few moments later he had touched down and had shut down all on-board systems. At the edge of the clearing a black Range Rover was waiting for him. He stepped down from the cockpit, the wind and rain hitting him with all its might, closed the cockpit door and armed the security system. Should the Bell be tampered with or stolen, Dillon was able see what was going down on the small LCD screen on the remote key, which was wirelessly linked to the Bell's on-board camera. The remote operated a small explosive device that would detonate inside the engine compartment. The end result was the same whether the helicopter was in the air or on the ground - instantaneous death to anyone in or close to the machine at the time of detonation - the remote had a range of one hundred miles.

Two black clad soldiers got out of the 4x4 as he approached them, one took charge of his canvas holdall, and the other ran a handheld security scanner over his clothing. He got into the rear seat and a moment later was being driven along an unmade track towards, Castle Drago. High trees were moving past on either side and the vehicle soon drove through the gloomy sanctuary of the woods and out into the rugged Cornish landscape.

Dillon wound down the window and breathed in the pleasant fresh scent. Rain spat through the gap and he revelled in the shocking coolness on his face. He saw himself imposed over the image of the rolling countryside: Dillon, reflected in glass - unruly dark hair, heavy stubble, dark brooding eyes. A somewhat weathered face that had taken one too many punches. A strong chiseled chin - he thrust it forward, and then grinned weakly at his reflection.

Ugly bastard, he mused, and subconsciously pulled out the packet of cigarettes and lit one, reminding himself that he really should quit.

The castle was impressive. Completely restored. Very expensive.

Dillon went through the usual security scans and check-in rigmarole and was then shown up to his room by one of the uniformed orderlies. He immediately unpacked, showered and shaved, and then spent twenty minutes thoroughly searching the room for bugs and cameras. Satisfied that his room was neither bugged with listening devices or cameras he then went and familiarised himself with every aspect of the castle. He walked around, smoking, checking out entrances and exits. He sat for a while in the main lobby, watching the people coming and going, and being eyed himself by two of the security service guards armed with Heckler & Koch MP5 machine carbines. A waiter approached and asked him if he required a drink. He asked for a single malt whisky and then shook his head, telling himself off.

You've got one day left before Kirill and his niece arrive, he mused. The last thing you need is alcohol to blur your thinking.

Ignoring his own advice, he ordered a bottle of the best single malt from the castle's cellar to be sent up to his room. When the waiter had disappeared he went outside and stood under the high covered portico and smoked a cigarette. The rain was still falling heavily and the wind was not giving in - blowing a gale from the west. He finished his smoke and went back up to his room for a drink and to watch TV for a while before dinner.

He sent an email to Vince Sharp in London, to which the reply was almost immediate. *Keep off the booze!* He laughed, and downed the glass of whisky in one gulp. He felt the tension he had been feeling since his arrival at the castle temporarily leave him - he refilled his glass, but again the guilt of having even a single drink nagged at him. It was always the same thoughts that returned with the booze - was he going mad...

"I don't know what's wrong with you, Jake. Your mind is all over the place and running a-muck everywhere you go." Issy had shouted this at him as she'd walked out of his apartment and out of his life for good. And her words had haunted him ever since.

He had let Issy walk out without a proper farewell and had thrown a long friendship into oblivion. She had known there was a problem - a needle in his mind, a splinter through his soul - and had begged him to tell her what was wrong. But he could not. How could he describe the feeling he got when he killed in mere words? How could he define the torment and torture, his misery - that came afterwards?

He could not - would not - expose that part of his psyche to anyone...

Dillon laughed drunkenly at that and refilled his glass, spilling whisky over the back of his hand. He could remember when the black beast had first manifested itself and, how he had to admit to himself, that without it he would almost certainly be dead many times over by now. This part of his mind, that he could neither understand or get away from in his life, had pushed him on to murder without mercy or compassion.

Dillon felt weakness and this enigma inside his head was untroubled by fear or doubt or even consequences and had *maimed* and *slaughtered* with precision and yet.

Dillon couldn't help wondering if he would rather be dead. What it would be like - to be normal, without the killing? What life would be like - if he had chosen a different path to walk along? Dillon fell into a fitful and uneasy sleep, images of the people that he had murdered in the line of duty floating up from the depths of his mind. They accused him, fingers pointing, silent dead mouths open and screaming at him.

* * *

F&CI Com-intercept. <u>Transcript of recent</u> <u>Reuter's news article.</u>
Reports have been flooding in from all of the major banking institutions around the globe of a potentially malicious computer virus attack - so far unnamed - which has apparently indiscriminately entered tens of millions of machines in quick succession and within thirty seconds of even the most powerful network systems booting-up.
From America to Iceland, from London to Sydney. No country or major city is unaffected. According to IT analysts and experts, the suspected virus has been placed at the highest level of threat and enters the network through a back door using Port 7597. Once in, it detects and installs itself in sectors of the operating system where it then remains in what appears to be a dormant state and with no apparent detriment to the infected machines. Because of the speed at which the virus replicates itself, the hard discs are being urgently examined by a number of anti-virus software organisations who are already estimating that should the virus become malicious it is likely to cause upwards of US$6.5 billion damage.
IT experts predict that there is a secondary script hidden within the main body of the virus and that this is likely to contain the real threat. This element of the virus will deliver the payload - with devastating effects. The banking world is still coming to terms with this massive global security breach and is now on high alert. However, there is no way of

knowing when the real attack will take place or whether anti-virus software can be written fast enough... The question is why has this virus been released on the world of high finance - and to what end?

Chapter 2

Dillon woke early the next morning, got out of bed and immediately wished he hadn't. The pounding in both his temples made him wince, like hitting your thumb with a hammer, that sort of pain. He made a mental note to quit the cigarettes and the booze just as soon as this assignment was over. Outside it was still raining persistently, as it had been when he had arrived in Cornwall the day before, heavy thunderous skies painted a dreary and miserable picture for the day ahead.

He phoned down to housekeeping and ordered a full English breakfast with coffee and toast to be brought up to his room. Ten minutes later there was a knock at the door and a uniformed orderly stepped into the room and placed the tray down onto a circular oak table by the window.

As Dillon was finishing breakfast; the mobile phone that Tatiana had given him in Scotland, started to vibrate on the table. He picked it up and was not surprised to have been sent an email from Edward Levenson-Jones. It simply outlined the timetable that he would be working to for the next few hours and gave him the location address for Professor Kirill's lectures. Dillon was somewhat surprised that Kirill was not giving his talks inside the well equipped conference center at Castle Drago. His thoughts were interrupted by the ringing tone of the bedside telephone, the sergeant major at the other end informed him that his transport and escort detail were waiting outside the main entrance.

* * *

The Range Rover swept through the heavy iron gates and up the gravel drive, went through a stone archway and parked in a large walled courtyard at the rear of the impressive period house. Dillon checked the mobile phone for any messages and then accessed three coded menus; the phone flickered at him with red digits. Dillon smiled - the wonders of technological advancements would ensure that the anti-bug mode jammed or scrambled any listening devices that were within its range.

15

Dillon got out of the luxurious interior, light-weight running shoes crunching on gravel and lit a cigarette. He looked up at the two hundred and fifty year old home of Professor Kirill, a magnificent, yet pretentious structure with its giant classicism, almost awe inspiring with its dressed stone dominated by four turreted corner towers. The windows were tall and narrow with leaded light panes of glass and set back into stone. Visually, Dillon thought as he walked back through the stone archway and around to the front of the building; this was a tense and formal place, almost emotionless. The spectacular open portico, sitting atop broad layers of steps, only endorsed what he was thinking.

The rain had eased a little, but the heavy clouds were still rumbling around almost directly above. Dillon walked back into the courtyard and across to what would have been originally a kitchen service door. He was met by one of the MI6 suits who were crawling all over the place.

"You Dillon?" The surly spook snarled at him, the flash of gleaming white teeth in the process.

"That's me." Dillon took a heavy pull on his cigarette and smoke plumed around him. He coughed. "Must remember to try and give these frightful things up."

"We don't need you here; we're doing just fine without you, hard man."

Dillon held up his hands. "Wow, tiger. I'm simply here to observe, my friend. Now, I'd appreciate it if you would get the fuck out of my face before I decide not to be so friendly towards you." He smiled and blew smoke into the young spook's face.

Holding eye contact, the agent used a comm. to confirm Dillon's identity and stood aside to allow him to enter the building. With a glance over his shoulder, Dillon noted the sniper on the roof of the garage block opposite as he moved inside.

His stomach groaned at him. He reached the door. At least a dozen men in the grounds, he thought. Good. He wasn't meant to have seen half of them: *even better.*

He walked through the kitchens and along semi-darkened corridors until he came to the service stairs that led up to the main house. Outside, the sound of rolling thunder made him look up as he climbed the stone steps.

* * *

Dillon watched Zhenya Tarasova enter the richly decorated room. She was much more beautiful than her photograph on file. Her beauty stunned him. She wore her auburn hair mid length just below her shoulders, a soft shimmering silken fan; she moved with elegance and grace, and a light smile danced across her face when she saw Dillon. She crossed to him, the only sound was high heels clicking as she walked over the highly polished marble floor, and Dillon felt himself irresistibly gazing into those beautiful Cossack eyes.

"You know why I am here?" he said softly.

"I know why you're here, Mr Dillon," she replied in near perfect English. "And I am very grateful for you accepting to look after me. Tatiana wasn't being truthful when she described you. You're much more beautiful."

Her voice was husky, something that Dillon had always found attractive in a woman. He stood, smiled, and without speaking motioned to her necklace, bracelets and rings. She looked at him quizzically and Dillon made gestures for her to remove all of the jewellery. He walked around her, checking the clasps on her elegant deep red dress. Taking all of the items from her, he placed everything on a low maple occasional table, and then motioned for Zhenya to take off her shoes and follow him outside to the formal gardens.

She did so without question, and Dillon led her barefoot out into the grounds. The rain had stopped and the clouds had started to drift away to the east, the gardens scent, fresh, after the heavy rain of the past two days.

"Where are we going?"

"Bear with me, Miss Tarasova. Down these steps and through the stone arch, if you would, please."

She laughed then, and Dillon heard the chink in the laughter; the fear was there, well hidden - especially considering the girl was only twenty-two years old - but still there.

They walked - Zhenya a step or two behind Dillon.

He stopped abruptly and turned round. He took her hand.

"You should be afraid. Especially as your uncle has received a number of death threats and he considers them to be very real. Not a hoax - but directly linked to this new software programme that he's developed for the military. Your uncle fears that those making the threats may turn their attention on to you, as a soft alternative target while both of you are down here in Cornwall, either to kidnap you or

17

to... well, I'm sure you understand the situation as well as I do. Now, there are many agents here whose job it is to protect you and your uncle. I am merely here to look out for you and to give back-up to them - if required. To be your personal bodyguard, shall we say? But I would like you to agree to one thing."

Zhenya had gone white. Dillon could feel the clamminess of her palm, against his own.

"Yes, Mr Dillon?"

"I want you do everything I ask - without question or hesitation. I want your absolute trust - and never forget that I cannot be bought. I'm wealthy enough in my own right and money does not interest me. But I must know that when I say jump, you'll jump without hesitation - if you want to stay alive that is. Will you agree to this?"

She paused, and then smiled softly. "Yes. I will do what you ask. But I too have a question."

"Okay. Fire away?" Dillon was looking around the garden.

"Why did I have to remove all of my jewellery and shoes?"

"Bugs. Almost certainly put there by the MI6 guys here, they're only doing their job - but I wanted a little privacy. This little device," Dillon held up his mobile phone, "is particularly clever and very effective at blocking and jamming, but I hate surprises. I trust myself far more than technology. I have a little motto - better to be cautious than *dead*." He let the word hang in the air.

"Oh, I see."

"So tell me, why do *you* think you've been threatened?"

"Since the death of my father, my uncle has treated me like his own daughter. I have my own private living quarters at the establishment in Scotland and we always eat dinner together every evening. My uncle works extremely hard - he is a genius. All I know is that we suspect terrorists want to get the new programme destroyed because it almost certainly means that governments and agencies around the planet will be able to locate and destroy them with extreme ease."

"Why are *you* here in Cornwall?" asked Dillon. "Your uncle knew before he left Scotland that your life could be in danger. After all, you are his only living blood relation - the daughter he never had. You should have been sent somewhere safe, away from the possibility of extreme danger."

Zhenya turned away from him, then stopped and picked a brightly coloured flower. She held the small delicate petals to her nose and, her eyes lowered, said softly; "My uncle is a man of unbending principles and I admire that. He will not be intimidated and will always stand by what he believes in. The truth is, he didn't want me here at all; but I also, will not have my life dictated by madmen who may or may not carry out their loathsome threats. I am my own person, Mr Dillon." She met his gaze then said. "I will do what I wish. And to be honest - if they can get to us here, then they can get to us anywhere we choose to hide." She said with contempt.

Dillon said, "I want you to know that I've never failed on a protection assignment. He squeezed her hand gently. "If you do what I say - when I say it, we might just stay alive if the bullets start flying. Okay?"

"Okay." Zhenya smiled a beautiful smile. She placed the flower in his lapel button hole. "I want you to have this flower as a mark of my friendship." Dillon was touched by the girl's gesture and followed her back up towards the house. He watched the agents in the bushes and, as clouds gathered once again overhead with the threat of more heavy rain, did not envy their position. A smile crossed his face as he walked over the gravel path that led back to the main house.

* * *

"Professor Kirill."

Dillon stood up and watched the older man approaching him. He was of small build, with sandy coloured hair, soft grey at the temples and a neatly trimmed goatee-beard. His eyes were sharp and intelligent, his dress smart and expensive. Dillon shook the offered hand - a remarkably powerful grip.

"A drink, Mr Dillon? Dillon was about to accept when Kirill continued. "No, don't tell me. Let me guess. Straight single malt whisky without ice. Am I right?"

"Absolutely right, Professor. But, not while I'm working. Just water will be fine."

"It was extremely good of you to agree to this assignment. As I understand it, you are virtually retired, yet you come, shall we say, with the very highest of recommendations."

"I've had many years to perfect my talents." Dillon smiled wryly. He took the glass and watched Kirill go and stand in front of the fireplace and light a cigarette. The man fixed his gaze on Dillon who sat back down and glanced over at Zhenya, who was seated on an antique leather chair by one of the tall windows.

"In your opinion, Mr Dillon. Are we in great danger here?" Asked Professor Kirill.

Dillon sipped at the glass of iced water. Placing it down on to a small round side table at the side of his chair. He looked up at the Professor and shrugged. "From what I've been told and the reports I've read. I would say most definitely, yes. If I understand correctly, you have been working for the British Government, and it would seem that your work has gained you a few enemies."

"The people you are referring to, Mr Dillon. Are nothing more than cowards, they have heard rumours about a new programme that I have developed - their fear is justified - it means the end for them. But I must tell you that whilst I believe them to be cowards, that in reality, they will try and fight back as sure as adversity stares them in the face.

"Can you tell me about the new programme?"

"Even with your security clearance, that is still too highly classified," said Kirill softly. "All I can say is this, and I know that you are fully aware of the Scorpion units. They exist to combat against the terrorist threat wherever it may be found and my new programme will be of tremendous assistance in their task. It is incredibly powerful and is able to gain access and interact with any programme or database - whether encrypted or not - in the blink of an eye. I have created a programme that can locate computers being used by organised crime syndicates and terrorist cells globally by accessing their every available on-line resource. It then up-loads a tiny piece of mal-ware which eventually destroys the hard drive. But not before taking control of the system and downloading every single piece of data on it... Ahh," he sighed, relaxing slightly, the look of excitement in his eyes fading to a more guarded unreadable expression. "But I'm getting ahead of myself. As you pointed out earlier, this is still at the field trial stage and very much only a prototype - it is not quite ready to be set free - yet."

"It must be uniquely powerful and light years ahead of anything else currently developed to evoke such interest... and a threat to your life, Professor?" Dillon said, almost casually. "Maybe there are some people who would prefer not to see it ever become operational?"

Kirill merely nodded, smiling, and sipped at his drink.

"This threat to Miss Tarasova - you do realise it could be merely a double bluff? *You* could be the target." Dillon said matter of factly.

"Of course, that possibility was the first thing that came to mind. However, should the need arise - rest assured that I can handle myself, Mr Dillon. I worked for the KGB for many years as a field operative. Like you, I am very capable of staying alive. It is my niece who needs protection now, I cannot watch over her twenty-four hours a day. Edward Levenson-Jones will have sent you the schedule of events, I will be giving lectures throughout the day and then there is the party this evening." He looked across the room at his niece. "I'm afraid her stubborn nature will not keep her away and well..."

"I can only advise you to cancel, professor."

"I will not cancel. And, I will not cower because of something that might or might not happen." Said Kirill, his face hardening. Anyway the MI6 agents have said they will draft in more men if needed. And of course, you're here." He smiled without humour, showing tobacco stained teeth. "Zhenya will be safe. She can stay out of the day's proceedings..."

Zhenya turned to face them from where she was sitting. Her eyes bright. "No I most certainly will not. I won't hide myself away either." She sounded indignant.

"If that's the way you want to play it."

Dillon stood up and left the room. Rain was falling again and he delved into his jacket pocket and pulled out the mobile phone, turning it over in the palm of his hand. After a moment he connected to the security services and checked that all of the agents assigned to the protection unit were present and correct, but most importantly stationed at their positions at various locales inside the building and outside in the grounds. He set the device to automatically check and update him every fifteen minutes until the day's events and party that evening were over.

Dillon cursed Kirill's stubbornness. A party! For work colleagues and Government dignitaries to celebrate a 'milestone achievement'.

"Bloody hell, Kirill. Why couldn't you just stay in Scotland?" Dillon said aloud to himself.

Dillon had to admit to himself that he was annoyed. He hadn't realised that LJ had drafted him in on what he had thought was a simple VIP protection assignment. Kirill was a top dog - a former KGB operative, Government researcher and world renowned computer program developer - and Dillon knew that he would therefore have

21

made some very powerful enemies along the way. That meant the game was far more important than Dillon had been led to believe; more important than Tatiana had led him to believe.

Dillon moved through the house, checking security points and his own weapon and ammo stashes.

With this preamble came the electric feeling he always felt, the excitement of the imminent danger and the promise of killing - that was surely to follow.

* * *

The three black long wheelbase Landrover Defenders pulled over onto the roadside, powerful diesel engines idling with a promise of almost limitless torque. Heavy raindrops continuously rolled down the blacked out windows and in the heavy woods to either side a quiet stillness prevailed.

The police car that had been following, a dark blue BMW M5 sporting full police livery, slowed to a crawl as it passed the Landrovers. The two armed response officers inside taking a close look, before moving on, tail lights glowing. It disappeared over the brow of the hill up ahead and was immediately swallowed by the rain and dense woodland.

Still, the Landrovers remained at the edge of the road with their engines idling.

Heavy thunderous clouds continued to roll in with ever increasing persistence, the rain still ferocious as it pounded against the blackened glass of the Landrover's windows and sent streams running down the narrow strip of tarmac.

In the gloom up ahead, bright headlights glittered through the downpour. The blue lights in the front grille of the BMW flickered into life and the fast German car returned to a halt beside the three Landrovers. Windscreen wipers swished, sending splashes of rain dancing onto the slick road. One of the patrol car's doors opened, and a muscular man wearing a bright yellow waterproof over-jacket over his body-armour, climbed out. He walked warily forward, his hand on his holstered pistol. Behind him, the other officer remained standing by the BMW, wedged between the door and the car's body, eyes alert, Heckler & Koch MP5 machine pistol held across his chest body-armour.

The lead policeman tapped on the driver's side window of the lead Landrover and said in a raised authoritative voice. "Please open the door and step down from the vehicle."

Nothing moved; the lead Landrover remained still, engine rumbling, the rain running in rivulets down the dark windscreen and bonnet. The police officer repeated his request.

Still nothing happened.

A moment later, the driver's window slid down on smooth electrics; the police officer took a step backwards and at the same time slipped the leather safety strap off of the holstered Glock. The officer peered inside the Landrover to be confronted with the muzzle of a silenced pistol.

The bullet hit the middle of his forehead with a dull thud. The officer was hurled backwards, dead before he had had time to shout a warning to his colleague. Through the gloom came a shout of - "*No!*" - as the second officer brought the MP5 up and began to fire. Three bullets slammed against the side of the Landrover before a stream of automatic gunfire cut through the BMW and into his body, spun him off his feet and left him lifeless and bleeding on the tarmac.

All three Landrover Defenders moved off in unison. The last one swerved a little and ran over the body of the first police officer to have been killed, leaving wide tyre tracks across his crushed chest.

They roared off into the gloom, leaving a ghostly scene of carnage, and the flashing blue lights of the police car, in the mist.

* * *

Dillon watched the convoy of luxury Mercedes limousines sweep up the drive towards the house. Standing outside Zhenya's room as she dressed for the party that evening, his attention drawn to the small window out of which he gazed. Rain was still falling heavily from black murderous clouds directly overhead and an oppressive gloom had settled over Cornwall.

Dillon half listened to the live orchestra tuning-up, guitars, keyboards and percussion sounds floating up the wide sweeping staircase at the end of the lavishly carpeted landing and coming from the huge ballroom - and the rhythmic sound of Beyoncé from Zhenya's bedroom. Dillon un-holstered the automatic pistol from under his right arm. He passed the Glock from hand to hand, feeling its perfectly weighted balance, checking that there was a full clip in and one round in the chamber then checked the six other clips he carried about his body. Ninety-two rounds in total. Dillon had learnt over the years to always be prepared. As he had always told the younger members of the Ferran & Cardini - Special Projects Department: "Who wanted to die because they ran out of bullets."

The door opened. Zhenya appeared - stunning in a small black cocktail dress that showed off her pale complexion and auburn hair.

"You ready?" asked Dillon, immediately sensing her nervousness, and added. "Don't worry, I'll look after you."

Zhenya took a deep breath. She knew - as well as he did, as well as the MI6 agents around the house and in the grounds - that tonight was a golden opportunity for an Assassin to strike. If the threat were for real and not just a hollow blackmail attempt. A *hoax*...

"I want you to stay close by at all times. Do not leave me for one moment."

"So you'll be coming with me to the toilet?" She laughed at her own joke.

"Of course."

"Really?"

Dillon smiled. "Yes. Easy location for a hit - it's the one moment when, shall we say, a person's guard is well and truly down."

They decended the extravagantly wide sweeping oak staircase, the walls lavishly decorated with contemporary abstract artwork. Working for a secret research department funded by the British taxpayer obviously paid well.

Dillon had been very specific with his instructions to Zhenya Tarasova earlier that evening: to stay inside the house, no alcohol, and definitely no wandering off without him. If Zhenya wanted to survive this potential threat then she had to minimise the opportunity.

Damn this party, thought Dillon.

Damn Kirill! Stubborn bastard.

A hundred and fifty guests. Dillon had almost shot Kirill himself when Mark Palmer, head of the MI6 security operation, had handed him the slip of paper.

Guests mingled. Waiting staff with trays of drinks and canapés circulated and Dillon's gaze swept across the large, glitteringly decorated suite. Rich velvet drapes hung to the floor, obscuring the view of any outside observers - and more importantly from any long-range snipers.

Dillon stayed close to Zhenya. She knew many of the people who had come to the party and Dillon allowed the conversation to wash over him. If anybody approached or spoke to him he was dismissive to the point of being rude, and had no intention or interest engaging in conversation with them - it only distracted him from his job at hand.

He watched. Zhenya socialised and, as she had promised, stayed off the booze.

Kirill, obviously suffering from a little stress, was well on his way to a serious hangover and was holding court with a small group in a corner. Dillon checked the security units status and found everyone where he or she should be. Everything was okay.

* * *

The many hundreds of acres of woodland and moor surrounding the Castle Drago estate rose and fell, following the slopes and dramatic contours of the land - spread out for many miles. Several rough tracks, littered with fallen trees and branches, crisscrossed the estate, but on this dark and rain-filled night everything except the thick branches swaying in the wind high above, was still. The rain ran in violent rivulets down the nobbled bark of the oak trees - a deep rumble cut through the gloom, and three dark blue long wheelbase Landrover Defenders crept smoothly over the moor and through the woodland. Heavy wheels crushed branches and negotiated fallen trees with 4x4 ease... slowly the all-terrain vehicles came to a halt in a small clearing, one behind the other.

All three engines died - and a silence crept back.

Doors opened, and black clad figures climbed out of the Landrovers. They moved stealthily forward and crouched, peering through night vision goggles towards Castle Dago, its lights glittering with promise in the distance.

The many shadowy figures bristled with weaponry.

There were various clicks as magazines were slotted home. Commands were given through concealed earpieces; and slowly, with an infinite and precise care, the unit of armed killers moved off through the undergrowth, untroubled by the rain and the threat of death to come.

* * *

25

Stevenson squatted beside the old garden potting shed listening to the commands being issued by Mike Palmer. He hoisted the sniper's rifle up and rested its tripod atop the rough stonework of a low wall just in front of him. It was late and he had been positioned there for a number of hours, he glanced up at the rolling clouds obscured by the driving rain.

"Damned weather," he muttered. "Sent to torment a man".

He sighted down the high velocity rifle's scope, and swept the grounds in front of him, rotating the rifle on the smooth-action tripod. He could see nothing through the rain, even with the night-vision intensifier switched on. Stevenson stretched his arms and rolled back his shoulders to relieve the tension in them and craved a cigar and a cup of hot tea. Yes, he could almost taste the richly satisfying tobacco and steaming brew.

A sound behind him made Stevenson glance over his shoulder. Despite knowing that the other members of the security unit were posted at the rear, protecting his back from infiltration, Stevenson nevertheless felt that something was not quite as it should be. He scratched at his short trimmed beard and frowned, eyes trying to pick out any movement in the gloom. Then he brought round the rifle and sighted down the scope. There - he definitely saw something... A figure darting behind a tree? Or a trick played by the swaying branches in the shadowy gloom fuelled by the desire for tobacco?

He adjusted the scope slightly, but could see nothing more between the tree's dense foliage. He shifted his aching muscles in the rain, feeling trickles run down the back of his neck.

"God, will this effing rain ever give up?" Stevenson muttered. He lowered the rifle for a brief moment to wipe his face dry, and in the same instant the black cross-bow bolt hissed through the darkness and slammed into his forehead, disappeared into soft brain tissue and on exit lodged itself in the timber cladding of the potting shed. Stevenson hadn't had any time to close his eyes or even shout a warning to his colleagues. He had been pinned silently backwards against the side of the timber building that he had been crouching next to, his unseeing eyes now staring straight ahead. Blood and gore mixed with rain seeped out from the exit wound of his smashed skull, congealing in his hair and soak into the timber at the back of his head. There were soft footsteps; four figures crouched by the corpse. One of them lifted the weapon from the ground and ran a black gloved hand over the cold metal.

"Leave it. We don't need it." The words were spoken in a clipped military fashion. The weapon was dropped onto the soft earth beneath their feet and the figures disappeared into the night.

* * *

Ninety minutes had passed. Dillon could feel himself growing weary and motioning to Zhenya he followed her into the relative calm and cool of the glasshouse located just off one of the many sitting-rooms. He took a small pen-like cylinder from his pocket, twisted the top off to reveal a short needle, and stuck it decisively into his neck and then replaced it back in his pocket.

"What was that?" asked Zhenya.

"A stimulant. Made specifically for me by our chemists at Ferran & Cardini. Allows me to keep going and stay alert, but more importantly it takes my primary senses to a higher-level. Lasts about twelve hours, but I'll pay for it tomorrow."

Zhenya smiled, and shivered. "It's cold in here."

Dillon looked at her, then turning, walked back inside the sitting-room and through to the hall, Zhenya was only one step behind him. His gaze moving up the sweeping staircase. "Do you feel that cold air?"

Zhenya nodded.

"Well, it wasn't there earlier."

"One of the guests have probably just opened a window, said Zhenya, as Dillon discreetly withdrew the Glock and with his free hand waved Zhenya to keep close behind him. He pulled free his mobile phone and opened the channel that the security service was using.

"Palmer?"

"Yes?"

"Can you come to the foot of the main staircase? I think we have uninvited company."

"Okay."

Mark Palmer was there within twenty seconds, a small black Berretta pistol in his hand. "Stay with Zhenya for a moment or two," said Dillon. "I have a really bad feeling about this..."

"Wait, I'll get some of my men to back you up."

"No time."

Dillon followed the cold air, his running shoes silent on the thick carpet. He felt adrenalin and the recently injected stimulant kick his system and with this surge of energy and heightened awareness he climbed two steps at a time to the first floor landing. The music drifted into the distance, a surreal ambience. He checked the security service interface screen - ten minutes since all members had checked in with Mark Palmer. Dillon frowned. An awful lot could happen in ten minutes.

He moved into a darkened doorway that was located directly opposite a nearby window on the wide landing and, crouching low, peered out into the darkness. He couldn't see any of the positioned snipers - but that didn't mean they were not there.

He moved cat like along the landing, keeping low and moving fast, all the time keeping his free hand outstretched following the gentle breeze.

Stopping in front of a broad oak door, he rested his hand against the polished wood.

His senses were alive; the thought of what might be on the other side, excited him.

He pushed gently and stepped aside; the door swung free. Dillon peered in, and then with the Glock held outstretched in front of him, slid in. The room was pitch-black and he swiftly turned on the main light...

Empty.

Dillon moved towards the window, which was open, no more than a four inch gap. He looked out, then down, immediately spotted the muddy scuff mark on the wooden sill - and suddenly realised that he was an easy target against the window. He moved fast, as the hollow-point round smashed through the glass and embedded itself in the ceiling.

Dillon rolled away from the window, was up and running.

He shouted into the comm, "We have uninvited guests, I repeat, uninvited guests - first floor entry."

He flew out of the doorway and into the path of a startled black-clad figure; the Glock kicked twice in his hand and the intruder was hurled backwards off its feet, its hands groping around its throat in a futile attempt to stem the flow of blood pumping out of the bullet wounds as it hit the carpeted floor, hard.

Dillon looked left and right. From somewhere in the house came the sound of distant screams and rapid automatic gunfire. He ran to the top of the stairs and a stream of silenced bullets slammed into the surrounding woodwork, sending splinters and chunks of balustrade in all directions. He dived, rolling up against the far wall with a jarring thud. His gaze fixed on the bullet holes in the woodwork, judged the angle of entry and determined where the shooter was positioned, rolled over twice and fired off six rounds in quick succession. Then, scrambling to his feet, he ran across the landing.

The silenced machine pistol devoured the wall behind him as Dillon reached the top flight of stairs and started to descend them two at a time; his Glock kicked in his hand once more, four rounds that picked up the Assassin and sent it spinning down the remaining stairs where it lay crumpled at the foot, blood soaking into the plush ivory coloured carpet.

The hall was quiet - no guests - no security service.

How many of them were there? Dillon thought as he crept down the remaining stairs and over the dead Assassin's body. The comm. in his ear crackled. "Dillon, Palmer. I have Zhenya in the kitchens. There are eight of them in the main ballroom - they've rounded all of the guests up and are holding them in there. Oh and, Dillon. They're heavily armed with some nasty little toys."

"I know. I've already taken down two of them," said Dillon softly as he put home another full clip into the Glock. "You stay there, I'm coming to you."

Dillon moved quickly along the wide hallway towards the ballroom, stopping momentarily outside to listen. Everything was quiet apart from the occasional whimper from some of the guests who were otherwise silent. Dillon slowly eased his head around the corner; a black-clad Assassin stood guard with a silenced 9mm Micro UZI SMG. Dillon fired two rounds and ran off in the opposite direction towards the courtyard. As he burst through the outer door, bullets tore the wood and plaster only inches behind him. Outside in the courtyard he ducked and darted in between large pillars, returned fire as he ran, taking down two more of the Assassins, before he'd made it to the door. Glass and wood splintered as he dashed through and down the stone steps to the main kitchen, all the time the tirade of bullets kept coming. He made it to the bottom of the steps and launched himself onto the tiled floor, sliding between stainless steel cabinets on his belly until he came up against the far wall.

"Palmer?" he yelled.

"Over here, Dillon," came the shout from one of the adjoining rooms.

Dillon looked around the stainless steel cabinets - all clear - he then peered over the tops, pans sat atop gas burners, their contents bubbling and simmering with half cooked soups and vegetables. There were no cooks to be found and, as he moved between the cabinets and around the room, the hairs on the back of his neck bristled with anticipation.

"Hold your fire - I'm coming in."

He stepped into the large brightly-lit room; a long overhead fluorescent light hung from two short chains in what appeared to be the kitchens main walk-in larder cold-room. There were sacks of vegetables and crates of produce stacked against the walls. Dillon looked around and saw Palmer, not more than five feet away, standing beside an ashen-faced Zhenya.

Dillon turned and, met Palmer's stare and he knew - knew that something was definitely wrong - the Browning in Palmer's hand rose and was now pointing at Dillon.

"I am very sorry, my friend. But it's now time for you to really retire - permanently.

Dillon looked Palmer in the eye, and nodded gently. "I hadn't figured..." He brought the Glock up in a blur, and fired a round directly into Palmer's throat; the bullet entered the throat at the Adam's Apple and made an explosive exit through the back of Palmer's head across the wall and ceiling. Palmer was thrown backwards landing against wooden crates, as if in slow motion, sliding down them until sitting almost upright on the tiled floor.

"...on having to kill so early in the evening," Dillon finished.

"Dillon," Zhenya ran to him and fell into his arms. He hugged her briefly, and then closed the door - sealing them inside the storage room. He sat the girl down onto one of the wooden crates and moved to Palmer's blood-drenched body and checked through his pockets. He took the dead man's Browning, pushing it into the waistband of his trousers in the small of his back and collecting the spare magazine clips.

"What's happening?" said Zhenya.

"Bad shit, that's what. Something very dark." Dillon said with malice. "The question is. How the fuck did they get past MI6 and all of their security sensors that are placed throughout the grounds and inside the house? Either a very large sum of money has changed hands, or something is at play. Something that I don't understand."

"What about my uncle?"

"The guests have all been herded to one end of the ball room and there's the possibility that the Professor is with them. There are at least eight gunmen..." Palmer's word's came back to him again. Was this whole thing a set-up? Something didn't feel right - everything was too easy - too neat.

Like attempting to unravel a puzzle with some of the pieces missing, Dillon's brain grappled with the implications.

"Trust me about this, Zhenya, and don't ask questions. We've got to get out of here and away from the main house."

The mobile phone vibrated in his hand. "Yes?"

"It's Vince. I hear you have company down there. I've secured the use of an American satellite that's passing over. I'm now your eyes, old son. There are at least twelve of them. They came in from the woods - and have already killed the three MI6 boys who were stationed in that sector. Where's Palmer?"

"Dead," said Dillon. "We now have at least eight Assassins in the main ballroom. Two were on the first floor and I've already taken care of them. Two were taken out as I crossed the courtyard. Are you sure about there being twelve to start with, Vince?"

"Absolutely. I'm using the thermal imaging on-board the satellite and I've used the electronic guest-list to calculate how many people should be inside the house - the numbers tally perfectly."

What do you suggest?"

"You are currently inside the main kitchen on the lower ground floor. Is this correct?"

"Yes."

"The girl is with you?"

"Yes."

"Okay. Stay right where you are. I'll liase with MI6 and get them into position outside in the courtyard to cover you both as you come through the door."

"Well be quick. I don't know how much time we have."

A few seconds later, Vince Sharp was talking to Dillon again.

"Jake, make your way up to the top of the stairs and wait just inside the door. Roth and his men will be there to escort you both out. Good luck, old friend."

"Thanks - we're going to need it."

Dillon closed the cover on the phone and slipped it into his jacket pocket; he looked at Zhenya. "We are in deep shit. You need to follow my every order if you want to survive. Understand?"

The girl looked at Dillon, not comprehending what he was saying.

Dillon grabbed hold of her arms and shook her, hard. "You understand what I'm saying?"

"Yes - I understand. Let go of me, you're hurting."

Dillon released his grip. "This is what we are going to do. They think we're going to leave through the back door; they don't know that I've killed Palmer."

There was a sound. Dillon moved smoothly to the door he had originally entered through and opened it - fast, the barrel of the Glock moving, scanning.

"My God," hissed Dillon, removing his finger from the trigger.

Professor Kirill had been severely beaten. Blood covered his face and had spilled down the front of his white dress shirt. By the look of it he had a broken nose and his lips were badly swollen and split from the repeated blows upon him. He staggered forward, the reek of alcohol surrounding him like some sort of cheap cologne. Dillon helped him into the kitchen and checked the stairway outside; he could see the door sensor flickering and he checked the phone's touch-screen once more. He scrolled through and found the security application, tapped the screen once and it immediately lit up with a complex looking grid system. He activated the function: anybody else entering the kitchen or stairway would now trigger the silent alarm.

"Uncle!" Zhenya ran over to Kirill, hugged him, and helped him to sit down as he winced with pain. His bloodied nose was dripping onto the tiled floor, as he stared in horror at the pool of blood surrounding Palmer's corpse slumped on the floor of the storage room.

"You killed him?"

"Let's just say that he wasn't up to the job and his contract has been terminated - permanently."

Dillon, the Glock still in his grip, crouched in front of Kirill. "What's happening here?"

"There are eight of them. They have imprisoned the guests at one end of the ball room. They have sent me to give you a message..."

"*Me?* But they think -"

Dillon paused. the only way that they could know that Mark Palmer was dead was if they had the kitchen bugged for sound and vision - or had access to and were listening in on the MI6 comms-network. That meant that the entire MI6 protection unit were in on the assassination. But why wait for Kirill's party in Cornwall - why not take Zhenya out in Scotland with a snipers bullet?

Dillon's phone started to vibrate in his jacket pocket - the alarm warning him that movement had been detected. He moved quickly to the doorway; his Glock went around the door and sent a warning shot up the stairway leading in from the courtyard. There was no return fire and no more movement detected.

Dillon turned sharply.

Kirill was now on his feet - but now held a gun pointing directly at Dillon. Dillon's stare met that of the older man. There was coldness in his eyes - a steely hardness that Dillon had previously seen. The hardness was that of a cold blooded killer.

"What is you want from me?" Dillon spoke softly and with total calmness.

"What indeed you bastard," hissed Kirill in a spray of spittle and blood. "Drop the Glock - now!"

Dillon glanced across at Zhenya; and she had changed, a change that was so dramatic that it actually shocked him. The tears had dried, the frightened young girl - gone. She was standing, a small Russian handbag pistol in her hands. The lethal looking weapon was pointing at him.

"I don't get any of this," growled Dillon. "I thought you were working for the British Government?"

"I told you to drop your fucking weapon!" Screamed Kirill, the pain of his beating was showing as each word was heavily laced with an edge of urgency.

Something cold and sinister inside Dillon's head - came alive.

Zhenya smiled at him and gave a small shrug.

"Don't act so surprised, Dillon. It's not as if you're a blood relative."

Dillon knew then: knew that he would die. There were two targets, both brandishing guns and the odds were against him dropping them both in the blink of an eye... He was surely going to die, in that kitchen under the bastard's country castle. Murdered and so obviously betrayed by... By who? And for what reason? What game was being played here? And why was *he* the centre of attention all of a sudden? *"Because you were always the target - you cock,"* whispered the stony voice deep within his mind. A sudden calmness took over Dillon's mind - excitement made his finger-tips tingle - adrenalin pumped into his heart - and Dillon knew exactly what he had to do...

Kirill was still standing a few feet away. He dabbed at his split lip with a fore-finger and it came away flecked with blood. He waved the heavy looking Browning in his right hand, his face a contorted animal snarl. "I said drop your fucking weapon now!"

Dillon held both hands in the air as a sign of surrender, and then began to stoop, as if to place the Glock on the ground.

Dillon blinked and the world changed from Technicolor to the harsh black and white tones of a 1960's film set. His brain screamed at him; *"Do it now..."*

And, slowly, the merciless killer inside the darkest recess of Dillon's mind opened his eyes.

Chapter 3

The scene was a stark colourless black and white picture. He smiled at the blood smeared Kirill; the Glock felt good in his left hand, reassuring, like an old friend. It had become a part of him, his body and soul. It was held low as he stooped, at an angle. All it took was a twitch.

Dillon flicked his wrist - faster than thought - and squeezed the trigger.

Kirill was blown backwards, folding in half with a grunt of expelled air, and he slumped, sprawling to the ground with a look of sudden horror on his face. He dropped the gun. He looked down to where his hands clutched a widening patch of crimson at his belly. Dillon, in the same movement, spun on his heel, the Glock flashing up sideways and, again, he pulled the trigger - the bullet smashed into Zhenya's shoulder, spinning her back to rebound from a tall stainless steel cabinet. She hit the ground hard, moaning, blood splashing down onto the cold stone floor, her small ornate Russian gun forgotten. "Fucking devious woman," snarled Dillon, and moved forward to kneel beside Kirill.

"It takes a very long time and pain like you've never before experienced to die from a stomach wound," he said with malice. "It really is going to hurt - a lot." He smashed the butt of the Glock across Kirill's already broken nose. Kirill screamed out in pain - and another two heavy blows silenced him, reducing his scream to a foaming gurgle.

Dillon moved back across the room to the door at the rear of the kitchen. He flicked open the mobile phone to scan the area for anyone in the small preparation room on the other side. The device was being jammed and every application; including normal phone functions had been disabled. No scans. No location finder. Nothing. Confusion wrenched his face as he realised that he was totally alone - not even Vince Sharp could contact him.

Dillon searched the recesses of his mind - it took the blink of an eye - then, opening the door, he ran across the room, vaulting the stainless-steel worktop and toward the far wall, diving head long into the rubbish chute, he pushed his way into the tight hole, kicked at the stainless-steel base, and allowed himself to slide down and out the other end into a large commercial size wheelie-bin that had, thankfully, been emptied that morning.

The sound of rapid automatic gun-fire came from above.

Dillon climbed out and landed softly and looked around. He was standing in an underground service area. He moved past pallets and wooden crates towards the back of the room and a solid looking door. He pushed it open, waited a few seconds, and when nothing happened he crouched down low and rolled through the opening; coming up to a squat with the Glock held out in front of him. He checked left and then right, shifting his position to the cover of a large upright pillar. The underground garage. He moved past various cars covered with tailored protective covers. He halted, looking sideways at a gleaming black Porsche 911 Carrera 4S - it took a second or two for Dillon's brain to register this. Then he ran forward to the ramp and the wide Aluminium security roller shutter door leading from the garage. He peered through the crack into total darkness. Dillon looked down at the mobile phone in his hand, rolled it over gently in his palm a couple of times and as if by magic the LED's flickered and glowed from the device. The app's menu appeared and rotated around the screen, Dillon tapped the screen twice and the colour of it changed from blue to red and two spikes appeared at the base of the device. He pressed the spikes against the electrical access panel to one side of the roller door and the next instant the screen colour changed to green and there was a sharp *click* and then a little smoke spiralled out of the top of the casing. Silently, he eased the aluminium door up a fraction.

Running back to the Porsche, he tried the door - locked. He used the spikes on the phone, once again, to disarm the alarm and override the vehicle's locking system, then opened the driver's door leant in and felt for the ignition wiring. A few cuts. A few twists to bypass the immobiliser and he was sitting behind the wheel gunning the 3.6ltr flat-six engine, clutch dipped, into first, depress the throttle to 6,000 revs.

Dillon settled back into to the leather sports seat and popped the clutch.

The Carrera rear tyres gripped the tarmac and it shot up the ramp and under the roller shutter door with barely six inches to spare.

Machine pistols on full automatic turned on Dillon as the Porsche shot like a bullet down the gravel drive, the Glock thumping in Dillon's right hand. Skidding around the water fountain, Dillon blew a hole in an Assassin's head, that you could have driven a bus through, with a single shot. He kept the revs high in second gear and the rear wheels kicked up gravel as he drifted around the fountain one more time before shooting off straight down the drive and away from the three figures that ran from the gate-house with their machine pistols blazing.

Bullets slammed into the side panels of the Porsche and Dillon stamped on the throttle as the car hit 165 m.p.h. He held onto the steering wheel like a limpet, an incredible grin across his face, the Glock forgotten in the joy and concentration of controlling this screaming insanity machine as the rev needle flickered on the redline.

Behind him, perhaps eight or ten black-masked figures swarmed forward, and then suddenly halted. They watched the Porsche disappear into darkness. Men were shouting - they jumped into 4x4s and the black-clad Assassins leaped apart as the power of the V8 vehicles roared past in pursuit.

In the Porsche, Dillon had the audio system wound up to near maximum and The Artic Monkeys blasting the night air. He spotted the headlights far behind him, and another smile hijacked his face as he drove the sports car even harder down the unlit lane surrounded by thick woodland. He suddenly slowed, ventilated discs being gripped and the nose of the car dipping under the harsh braking, and flicked off the vehicles lights as the Porsche's engine throttled back and the rev needle flickered as he dropped down a couple of gears.

The V8 Range Rover engines approached at high speed. The Glock kicked in Dillon's hand as he emptied a full clip into the windscreen of the lead vehicle. The Range Rover veered right and slammed head-on into a large oak tree: a figure was flung through the windscreen, a pulped corpse. Dillon blipped the accelerator pedal and watched the rev counter dance. The rear wheels gripped as the clutch was let out sharply; within seconds he had hit 100 m.p.h. and again he switched on the lights as he took a slow left-hand bend. As he came out the other side he opened the throttle again, his grin broadened and the chase was forgotten as the Porsche was pushed to the twitching 160 m.p.h. plus limits of the powerful engine's ability.

"I just love fast cars," Dillon said aloud.

Far behind, Kirill's country residence blazed briefly as several explosive devices located throughout the large building detonated one after the other. Fire roared, ate, consumed - billowed up into the night sky, causing Dillon to lock the Porsche's wheels into a long broadside skid, finally to halt and to glance back with an intense frown.

The explosions lit up the night - a vivid purple red in an otherwise black sky.

Dillon selected first gear and let the clutch out with enthusiasm, accelerating up the narrow road, leaving two streaks of burned rubber. He disappeared into the blackness of the Cornish landscape.

* * *

Dillon sat in the ancient woods, listening to the rustling of leaves in the light breeze and the gurgling of a small stream running nearby. He was smoking a cigarette leant up against the twisted knurled trunk of a three hundred year old oak tree. Nearby, well hidden, was the scraped, scratched and mud-spattered Porsche behind a screen of dense bushes.

Dillon wearily toyed with the mobile phone. He activated the emergency homer, a bank of red, green and blue lights danced across the touch-screen and, he felt it vibrate in the palm of his hand as the state-of-the-art device started to send out its powerful signal to the Ferran & Cardini International receiver in London. The longer he sat there, the more effect the tranquil environment had on him. Dillon felt the tension leave him and the sound of the running water was having a soothing effect on his soul. But too many questions were running around his head with no apparent answers to any of them.

The only thing that was obvious now - was that he had been elaborately set-up.

Dillon felt a shiver run through his body; someone wanted him dead - what was new about that. Somebody had wanted him dead real fast. But why go to the trouble of inducing him out of his self-enforced retirement to undertake such an assignment? Of course - to get him away from Scotland and into an environment where he had little control... Somewhere he was totally on his own. If he was supporting MI6 then he could not have been assigned to any other Ferran & Cardini job.

And Zhenya.

Dillon shook his head. She had fooled him; and he had shot her. She may be wounded or even dead and buried, and all to what end? To kill *him*?

Kirill and Zhenya. They were both British Government... and yet they had both tried to kill him. And it would seem that some of the MI6 protection squad had been in on the betrayal... and those explosions. What the fuck was that all about? And what in God's name had been going down back there?

After Dillon had started killing, events had taken on a dullness, not dissimilar to a dream, without colour, or realness. The fury with which he had automatically cut down anyone in his path had left a sour feeling in his belly, and an empty void in his soul.

Dillon stared at the Glock in his hand. It had done its job - had saved his life again as it had done many times before. But he was angry at how he had been protecting his own would-be Assassin... and now was she dead? Lying with Kirill in a cold freshly dug grave?

Dillon stood up and paced around the thick trunk of the oak tree, stretching his back and rolling his neck, which cracked as it realigned itself with the release of tension.

Why hadn't they killed him earlier?

Dillon pondered. Maybe the explosions had been intended - not just for him, but for the guests as well? But something had obviously gone horribly wrong with their plan and he had messed it all up for them, and so it had been left to Kirill and Zhenya to carry out the kill. Maybe.

Dillon rolled the mobile phone in his palm, and then sent his report to Ferran & Cardini.

What the hell, he thought. Let them figure it out! Maybe Vince Sharp could discover what had happened when the signal to the phone had disappeared as well...

Twenty minutes later, a low whomping sound made Dillon look up through the canopy of the trees. The sound pounding over the ancient wood.

Dillon held his position, safely concealed, while he patiently waited for the helicopter to come into view. It hovered directly overhead and then veered away to the right towards the clearing and touched down. The *whump, whump,* of the rotors sent branches and trees swaying and Dillon ran the hundred metres or so to the cockpit and the serious face of Ferran & Cardini's most experienced pilot,

Tony Brown.

"Come on, Dillon - hurry up," he shouted. "We've got company close by."

"Company?"

Brown nodded as Dillon climbed into the cockpit of the modified Bell Robinson four-man helicopter and belted himself in. "Put on the spare helmet, will you. I may need your help. Whatever the hell you've been up to down here, you've certainly stirred up a bloody hornet's nest. Ever used a helmet with a heads-up display before?"

"I had one in my own helicopter."

"Why use the past-tense?"

"Because those bastards back there blew it up. That's why you're here."

"Oh. Well, let's get this thing back in the air and as far away from this place as possible."

The Bell-Robinson's powerful twin engines screamed and the helicopter launched up into the total darkness of the night. Brown veered left, the nose dipped and the next instant he was heading south-east, following the coast at an altitude of five hundred feet above the white capped waves below.

Chapter 4

The twin hulls of the American Navy *Sea Predator* stealth ship cut through the tumultuous waters of the Barents Sea, pushed forward at forty-five knots by its nuclear powered turbines. A vessel alone in dark waters, seventy-five miles west of the Russian island of Ostrov Kolguev.

John Taylor, Commander of the stealth ship and many times decorated special forces veteran, drummed his fingers on the arm of his seat and stared at the charts and information displayed on the large glass screen in front of him. The bridge was buzzing with activity and anticipation as the order was given to bring the one hundred and seventy foot vessel to a stop. The turbines wound down and the sinister looking black painted hulk came to rest on the swell of the sea. Taylor glanced across at his second-in-command, Steve Kramer who had been on the bridge for a straight twelve hours and had a worried expression on his unshaven face as he studied the charts and data stream running across the glass display panel. The Commander smiled warmly, and dismissed the man.

For the past six months the Americans had been working alongside the British Government and Ferran & Cardini's research department in an attempt to erase a glitch in the new Kirill-Chimera seek - retrieve - and destroy programme. The *Sea Predator's* computer system had been loaded with the prototype and while undertaking trials on a number of Russian mafia targets - had momentarily become visible to them. Kirill had written the programme in such a way for it to constantly alter its script, once it had infiltrated the target's hardrive and operating system - allowing all data to be extracted remotely and sent back to the *Sea Predator* - Kirill had then created a deletion protocol that was activated after releasing a death virus onto the target's hardrive.

A young rating by the name of Zak Ryan had immediately spotted the glitch. Had informed Taylor, who barked the order to get off-line and shut down the programme. He was now hoping that their invasive snooping had not been noticed by any eagle-eyed nerds working for the Russian Mafia... The border of Kazakhstan with Russia had, in

41

recent times, seen a hundred fold increase in drug smuggling activities by the Mafia cartels, who were using the inhospitable terrain of the Ural Mountains to transport raw opium all the way up to the coast of the Kara Sea. The opium would then be processed in laboratories and distributed throughout Europe by a sophisticated network of transport routes. From the same labs came the latest designer drug - peddled to the higher end of the market and only available to the wealthiest of addicts with the promise of a never before experience. What they found was narcotic hell. This drug, Red Horse as it had been nicknamed, had made the Mafia-led cartels billions of dollars and even more powerful, but was costing the government financially, politically and, of course, socially. Ferran & Cardini had asked the American Navy if they could have the assistance of the *Sea Predator* in an attempt to locate the labs that were producing and distributing the Red Horse drug and erase them with her lethal payload of missiles.

A day earlier, the *Sea Predator* had been tracking an unnamed vessel that was under suspicion of drug trafficking; the vessel was the size of a container ship, of unknown origin, and had been making slow progress from the north-east, close to Russia's Artic coast. Its heading had been on a direct course towards the island of Ostrov Kolguev.

Now however, the vessel had disappeared.

Taylor used every resource that the *Sea Predator* had to find it, to no avail. As a last resort he dispatched two tracking torpedoes, these did not have warheads, instead they were equipped with the latest satellite navigation and tracking systems housed in the nose cone. The torpedoes had a two hundred mile range and had never let the commander of the stealth ship down before. If the mysterious ship that had so far evaded their state-of-the-art searches was there, then they would find it.

For now, though. They were playing the waiting game.

Taylor shook his head and sighed, running a hand through his fair coloured hair. He stood up, and paced around the bridge, if for no other reason, than to stretch his legs and relieve the tension he was feeling in his neck and shoulders. He went and took his seat again. "Anything back from the torpedoes?"

"Negative, Commander."

"What about the satellite video stream?"

"The same Commander, negative. We currently have three

satellites passing over this sector, and according to the data they're sending back down to us. There are no vessels visible to them."

Taylor cursed.

"What is the position of the torpedoes?"

"They've separated, Commander. The first is ninety-five miles due north of us, the other due east approximately seventy miles. If there's *anything* out there, they will find it and report back." Taylor moved across the bridge to where the young Navy rating was sitting in front of his monitor screen. He looked up and said, a little nervously.

"Commander, they've never missed a target."

Taylor nodded, rubbing wearily at his temples. "Have you informed command HQ or Ferran & Cardini of this?"

"No Sir, I haven't."

"Do so. They may have further intelligence relating to this vessel. What did we find out before it - vanished?"

"Only that the vessel is approximately four hundred and twenty-five feet in length. That there is a possibility of some sort of weapons system on board. *Predator's* system has also calculated that the vessel's speed and distance it covered during the time we were tracking - is much faster than any ship of that size has a right to move at."

They waited, watching the torpedoes progress on the display screen. A tense silence filled the entire bridge with the glittering glow of computer monitors displaying data feeds and map co-ordinates. Blue light scattered like sapphires across Taylor's haggard unshaven face, and his eyes narrowed as his gaze fixed on one of the torpedoes.

He pointed, "What's that?"

There was an instant where the screen went completely blank, resuming a moment later - minus both of the torpedoes.

"What information was sent back by the torpedoes and can you confirm that they have been terminated?"

"Zero information, Commander. And yes both torpedoes have been destroyed."

"That's impossible! They're supposed to relay data back to us on a constant stream. Could there have been a system failure - are you positive that they have been destroyed?"

"Affirmative, Commander. Both torpedoes have definitely been terminated."

Taylor continued to stare at the blank monitor screens, frowning. And then like a tiny Sun exploding from a central black pinpoint, they turned white and then in reverse action - went black again. The Commander turned his attention to the two torpedo-linked scanners before them. A stream of encrypted data started to appear on the screens at lightning speed - lasted for approximately fifteen seconds - and then, like a visual tidal wave, the lines were swept out and into a virtual darkness and *death*.

Taylor stared, numbed, at the scanners. Both were now black. Both torpedoes had been destroyed.

"Report status." he asked, his voice a dry croak.

"Negative, Commander. All information relating to both torpedoes - appears to have been deleted from our system."

"Deleted?"

"Affirmative, Commander. Deleted."

Both torpedoes destroyed; and not a single shred of information left to give the *Sea Predator* a clue to their attackers, had been registered; not a single warning given. Nothing.

Taylor could taste the sweet Bourbon on his tongue and he longed for a drink.

Then, his common sense shouted at him.

"Contact Command HQ and Ferran & Cardini, again. Tell them we have an *emergency* situation."

"Transmitting, Commander."

They waited fifteen seconds - a very long fifteen seconds of tense wondering filled with uneasy sweat and thoughts about death as every man on the bridge waited for a reply, looking out of the stealth ship's windscreens into total darkness and the black waters of the Barents Sea below their craft. Imagining their enemy with incredibly superior technology - the sort of technology that could make a container ship disappear, the sort of technology that could evade their most sophisticated scanning systems, and the sort of technology that could seek and destroy two fast moving torpedoes that were also equipped with a stealth mode - without giving away any indication of their location or weapons used.

The reply came back...

"Two Ferran & Cardini tech officers and one CIA station officer will be with us in approximately three and a half hours from Bergen in Sweden. They're being flown up by helicopter; we are to deploy one of our mini-predator jet boats to meet them on the Finnish coast. They recommend that we sit tight and do nothing - merely to report any change in our status."

Taylor nodded, deep in thought - and then he started to pace across the bridge.

The ship's perimeter scanners and monitors remained dark, still and without life; this was not helping when you had started to believe the enemy to be *invisible*.

* * *

The *Sea Predator* received the *Mini Predator* jet boat back into its huge labyrinthine hull. Winches whirred, and within a few seconds the outer doors were watertight, ramps engaged and one uniformed woman and two civilian-suited men walked down the ramp towards Commander John Taylor.

"I believe you have a problem, Commander, said the tall, blond-haired female. She had cold blue eyes and high cheekbones that highlighted her incredible beauty. She looked at Taylor, assessing the legend that stood before her, as they shook hands. "Major Deborah Armstrong at your disposal, Commander. I have a master's degree in marine engineering and my expertise is covert marine surveillance and tracking systems. I was part of the design team that invented the stealth torpedoes and I'm currently working with the CIA."

Taylor nodded. "Your reputation precedes you, Major Armstrong."

"Thank you, Commander. But in these emergency situations - my reputation is of little consequence. Let me introduce to you, from Ferran & Cardini, Simon St Vincent, weapon's expert, and Tim Greenwood, who has an incredibly detailed working knowledge of warships utilised by most world governments."

Formalities were speedily dispensed with, and Taylor led the trio straight to the bridge.

"We have all the data from the ship's computer system for the last twelve hours, as sent via the upload link at Langley. This shows that no malfunction occurred, at any time, with any of the torpedoe's systems. It also confirms that no data survived - at all, about any ships or other craft within one-hundred miles of them. At the time of their termination, not one scanner showed anything out of the ordinary?"

Taylor nodded.

Deborah Armstrong seated herself in front of one of the

monitor screens, and began to type; she merged with the ship's computers and for a few moments all was silent as data flashed across the main screen located at the centre of the bridge. Eventually, she clasped her hands together, as if she were about to prey, eyes distant. "Gentlemen. I think we are in extreme danger."

"You've found something, Major?"

Armstrong nodded. "It was hidden within the data flow; you did receive the reports back from the torpedoes, but they were *scrambled* so that the *Sea Predator's* computers would not recognise the codes."

"What destroyed the torpedoes?" Asked Taylor slowly.

"I don't know. But they were tracking an extremely large ship, is that correct? Much larger than your run-of-the-mill container ship."

"Yes."

"But now it's tracking you, Commander. And it is closing fast."

"That's nonsense. How is it possible to track a stealth ship?"

"I think it's obvious, Commander. You are up against a much superior vessel with far superior systems."

"Weapons?" Asked Taylor.

"Oh yes. You're going to need every weapon you've got, Commander."

* * *

The *Sea Predator's* twin hulls cut through the dark waters of the Barents Sea with ease. Turbines roared, all need for stealth thrown off as the sleek craft surged forward towards the protection of the nearest Finnish naval base. A distance of three hundred and sixty-seven nautical miles.

As the stealth ship increased its speed, so it increased the heat signature in its stern; nose raised, it powered through the water, cloaked only by darkness. Something thumped against the starboard side hull and then another a moment later. On Deborah Armstrong's instruction they slowed their speed and she analysed the boat's perimeter scanners, calling for Greenwood's assistance in quickly disassembling the data. She looked up at Taylor, who was standing off to her left, and said, "The hull sensors are confirming that we haven't hit anything sinister, like a mine. That it was much more likely to be some sort of floating debris."

Suddenly, a siren sounded and a constant flow of data started flashing across all the screens on the bridge simultaneously; Taylor moved forward to the main control console as his second in command looked round and informed him that they were being tracked. A moment later the radar operator shouted in a panicked voice, "They've locked on to us, Commander."

Taylor snapped; "That's impossible." And then immediately gave his crew a string of commands. The *Sea Predator* was fitted with the latest anti-detection systems, and a state-of-the-art predictive combat analysis programme. The *Sea Predator* was supposed to be completely hidden from its enemy - the enemy was not supposed to be able to see the stealth boat - at all.

"Arm and lock-on the Venom IV missiles!" snapped Armstrong as the bridge exploded with activity. Every man and woman present knew their jobs and knew them well; this was what they had been trained for - and now they all knew what they had to do and were doing it well.

"There it is," snapped Taylor.

Suddenly the ship uncloaked itself from out of nowhere, it was directly in their path and had them firmly locked in its sights; it had caught them by surprise in its trap with every exit covered.

The stealth ship rocked with the explosion, a scream of steel and a rumbling like distant thunder. The whole boat started to judder, vibrating, and Taylor looked helplessly across the bridge at Deborah Armstrong as it dawned on them that there was a strong possibility that they were going to sink.

"The missile hit us amidships." Taylor's face was ashen white as he met the stare of the crew present on the bridge. Armstrong was screaming orders at the seamen, who were carrying out her directives without question or hesitation. They knew what she wanted and understood the urgency required of them. The implications of ending up in open water and being gunned down was plainly written across their faces, which were bleached with shock and horror, at this terrible thought.

Every man and woman on the bridge stared at the monitors in disbelief and horror as some form of advanced self-drilling missile had penetrated the supposedly unsinkable multi-compartment hull, and then had started to gouge its way through inch thick plating, wreaking havoc and allowing ice cold water to flood in to the starboard hull. The stealth boat, as yet, had not launched its own lethal payload of missiles. Armstrong consulted the data stream on the monitor, assessed the best possible course of action and then told Taylor. "I suggest you access and authorise every missile we have on board to launch immediately, Commander. We do not have the luxury of time on our side - but - we do now know where the enemy ship is. I have already loaded the command sequence."

"Thank you, Major."

"Arm all of the missiles, and then sound the alarm to abandon ship Lieutenant." Taylor picked up the mike to address the crew, "Attention. This is Commander Taylor. In a moment you will hear the alarm to abandon ship. I want every member of crew to make sure they are armed before leaving *Sea Predator*. Good luck and may God be with you."

Deborah Armstrong grasped Taylor's arm. "The *Mini Predator* jet boat; we can still get away and make the Finnish naval base!"

Taylor shook his head sadly. He had been at sea far too long; he knew the dangers, accepted the dangers; "Only a miracle would even allow you to reach that section of the hull, and then the chances of escaping..."

Armstrong, closely followed by St. Vincent and Greenwood, the Ferran & Cardini tech officers, fled the bridge, boots stomping metal grilles, pushing past panicked seamen who were also trying to get off of the stricken vessel.

Sea Predator suddenly lurched sideways as the starboard hull, now completely filled with water, disappeared beneath the water. The crew were thrown like dolls; bodies smashed into screens and bulkheads and sparks showered the steel decking. Taylor hit the wall with incredible force and lay still, staring into the unseeing eyes of his second-in-command. The man had broken his neck and his limbs were now in some bizarre contortion.

Water was pouring in; sirens wailed; blue lights were flashing all around, and the only thing that Taylor could think about was his wife Sarah and their two young sons Aaron and James playing happily in the garden.

The water was cold around him, sloshing over his legs, a heavy and suddenly powerful swirling, remorseless. He was unable to move, the jagged piece of steel protruding out of his torso, pinning him against the mesh grille of the deck. Sparks showered him but he did not flinch. And then the power surged as the pre-programmed missiles were launched one after the other from their silos on the back of the stealth ship. Moments later, all power failed and only darkness prevailed.

More groans began, as if the *Sea Predator* were a dying animal in immense pain; Taylor was barely conscious, but he could *feel* and *sense* the sea - powerful and without compassion - rushing hungrily throughout his vessel.

Those final moments, in the pitch black, with ice cold water shocking his system into an uncontrollable spasm - those final moments were the most intense moments of Commander John Taylor's life. He dreamed of Sarah and the boys and how they would mourn at his grave side. Tears ran down over his cheeks. How did that ship find them - and why did they lose sight of it. What the fuck was it?

* * *

Deborah Armstrong strapped herself in at the controls of the *Mini Predator*; both St. Vincent and Greenwood were dead. Explosions erupted throughout the vessel, the steel grille of the gangway had become a writhing mass of metal flipping St. Vincent off of his feet, high into the air, and down onto a split steel girder, the razor sharp edges cutting him in half at the waist, his entire blood supply flushed from his torn flesh in the blink of an eye. Greenwood had been alongside his colleague as they were running to the *Mini Predator*, and had been thrown head first down a stairwell as an explosion had erupted directly above them. His neck snapped as easily as a twig under foot. Armstrong had been left dangling over an abyss as she watched the two Ferran & Cardini tech-officers disappear under a few feet of ice cold water. It was a miracle that she had made the docking area in the centre of the cavernous hull, an even bigger miracle that the *Mini Predator* was still intact and all of its controls still functioning and fully active.

As the *Sea Predator* was in the last throes of death, the fast nuclear powered *Mini Predator* was ejected from the docking station and spat out from between the twin hulls at high speed, foam spewing from its quad-exhausts. Armstrong, tasting blood from the wound to her forehead, watched in horror on the craft's monitors as the stealth boat went under the water and sank to the bottom of the Barents Sea.

49

Tears rolled down over her cheeks, streaking the blood there, and she armed the mini-predators weapons systems with a nervous glance over her shoulder.

Something very bad was happening.

Something so incredibly bad that she did not understand or comprehend.

She increased the *Mini Predator's* speed, skimming the water at a high rate of knots and navigating using sensors alone; outside the carbon-fibre hull the sea was an uncompromising and deathly black.

She glanced down at the radar monitor; squinting, she realised her worst nightmare. Something was tracking the *Mini Predator* - even though the stealth-mode was engaged.

Armstrong moved as if to lock her weapons - and realised that there was nothing on her scanners on which to lock. Swallowing hard, she switched to manual mode and flicked off the safety on the joy-stick. On either side of the *Mini Predator* missiles and torpedoes slotted neatly into place. And then, suddenly, a missile shot out of the darkness and there was an insane explosion of carbon-fibre and titanium and the sea rushed in towards her as she struggled to release the harness that held her fast in the seat. The more she struggled the tighter it became until the water was all around her and she was screaming. An intake of breath and the world descended into total blackness and cold and what was left of the *Mini Predator* disappeared and spiralled down into the deep of the Barents Sea, lost and *dead...*

Chapter 5

The London evening traffic, as usual, was busy and frenetic; horns blaring, engines spewing out their noxious fumes, lights cutting the darkness into fine slices of white and red, shimmering under the amber street lamps. Cars, lorries, buses and taxis winding their way across the city like giant snakes to all points of the compass. Past imposing landmark buildings standing majestic and towering skyscrapers pointing like metallic fingers towards the heavens. Piccadilly Circus was alive with activity, people from every culture rubbing shoulder to shoulder in this major European city. As the snakes wound on, they would pass deprived run-down areas, where buildings were so derelict that some had been raised by fire, others had windows blown out and now only gaping black-holes existed. Where pavements were littered with rubbish and dog-crap, people trod carefully and did so warily, eyes watching one another with unease, guns and knives concealed under coats.

The tall man stood on the pavement of the bridge, long black overcoat pulled tightly about him, silk scarf around his neck. His eyes were dark chestnut in colour and brooding, his face freshly shaved hair short and spiky, dampened by the light rain. He pulled hard on the cigarette, one last time, drawing the smoke deep into his lungs and then flicked the butt over the edge of the parapet and into the Thames below where it was swept along on the surface by the strong current. He waited for a gap in the heavy traffic and then weaved his way across the road, picking his way between Range Rover Sports, Porsches, Fords and Renaults. Once on the opposite kerb he halted, momentarily, looking west, back up the river towards the Houses of Parliament and the decaying Government that it gave shelter to.

The chill wind whipped at his face as he scratched the imaginary itch on his right ear, dark eyes glinted under the light of a street lamp. His hand brushed down the side of his long coat, and then he turned and walked briskly off the bridge and down the street, finest handmade Italian leather shoes fell solidly on the pavement. He passed a gathering of tourists who were intently listening to their tour guide, who looked up and stared at him as he passed by. He turned left down the steps that led to the Embankment and the smell of the river.

The rain fell, cooling his face, making the black overcoat sodden. As he walked, he undid the buttons down the front and made sure that his hand could easily delve inside the jacket he was wearing; underneath to the cold metallic of the Beretta secure in its side-holster.

Alix Knew.

Knew, that he was being followed.

The footsteps were almost inaudible behind him and he increased his stride. He blinked, raindrops falling from his eyelashes. When he reached the steps, he sprinted to the top and momentarily paused to get his bearings by a large metal wheelie-bin overflowing with rubbish and stink, turned right and after a short distance, darted into a narrow alleyway.

Alix halted, listening, the hairs on the back of his neck bristling.

He stepped backwards into the dark shadows of a goods entrance and lit a cigarette, hands cupped against the wind and rain. Smoke plumed above him, and as the slim platinum lighter was replaced in his jacket pocket so the Beretta found its way into his grip. He pulled the lethal weapon from its holster and immediately screwed the silencer in place, and then shoved it into an outside pocket of the long black overcoat.

Still hidden by the gloom - he turned.

A casual glance back up the alley.

Nothing.

Alix stepped out of the shadows and walked on down the alley, under metal fire escapes, under heavy drips from a dark and brooding night sky that looked down upon this over populated struggling city with malevolence. In the distance the bright sleazy neon lights of Soho glittered in the rain and Alix felt his smartphone vibrate and buzz, relaying a signal from the Scorpion Unit's main-frame computer system. The state-of-the-art system that was running a predator detection programme that was locked onto Alix's data-chip inside the smartphone, and was scanning a fifty metre perimeter around him, had picked up at least four assailants following. He glanced at the screen; "Shit."

Somebody wanted him *bad*...

Alix increased his pace again, flicking the cigarette aside and taking a right, down another narrow alleyway. He moved quickly with the minimum of effort, his eyes moved up, checking, scanning and adjusting. He reached the end and moved out into a quiet side street, and singled out a parked BMW, silver with blacked out windows, almost new and standing out from the other city-scarred vehicles. He crouched behind it, sighting the Beretta down the side of the highly polished bodywork, using the door mirror to steady his aim.

Four - maybe five...

Damn it, thought Alix. Who was it after him? Was it an organisation, or, was it a terrorist group?

Either way - he was in the shit and the gravest danger... If it was a terrorist group after him, taking them out would have to be quick - and would not be that easy - even though he was better trained and he had the benefit of surprise.

Or maybe it was just a just random gang, heavily armed and out looking for an easy target to rob? If it was the latter - then the problem would be erased in a matter of a few seconds.

Or maybe it was a rogue government dept...

The rain continued to fall.

Alix waited...

A noise, firstly from the darkened doorway of a nearby shop on the opposite side of the road. The second, much louder from the alley, alerted him. He turned, eyes still watching the entrance to the alley, some twenty metres away. The noises were too loud to be made by these secret followers. There was no element of stealth...

A group of five or six big eastern European men appeared from out of the alley, wearing the latest designer label suits and shoes. Their gazes turned towards Alix, who was by now casually leaning against their Silver BMW X5. Their faces took on a hardened expression of annoyance and anger.

They came out of the alley and while still walking towards Alix, one of them shouted. "Get the fuck off of my car." He had a heavy accent reminiscent of a heavy weight boxer having gone several rounds.

"Chill out, mate. I'm not doing any harm." Alix smiled easily.

The response was anything but chilled - a fusillade of bullets screamed and slammed into the side of the BMW, and Alix hit the ground hard, rolled over once and fired the Beretta from under the vehicle. The first man who had spoken; went down with a shattered knee, the bullet had gone right through his knee cap - blood started to ooze down his leg as he was hit by a second round to the groin - he went down hard onto the ground screaming in agony. There were shouts, the other men produced small Uzi machine pistols and a small scale war ensued with the BMW X5 taking the full force of the frenzied fire-fight.

"Bastards..."

Alix backed away from the vehicle and into one of the shop doorways, back-kicked, the heavy looking door with as much force as he could muster, and spun into total darkness.

Screams and the thwack of bullets ripping through flesh followed him as he continued to fire the Beretta at his pursuers.

One of the followers had got so close behind him, that blood had spattered across the back of Alix's overcoat from the bullet that had ripped his throat open.

Alix ran, dodging display stands and mannequins that loomed suddenly from the gloom. The Beretta felt heavy in his hand now as he moved through to the back of the building. He glanced down at the smartphone in his other hand, the screen displayed four followers, had logged their exact position on the grid and was now plotting Alix's escape route for him...

A thought crossed his mind - perhaps one of the local gangs would hear the gun-fight and come running to take out these mysterious Assassins?

No. He should assume the worst scenario; that the four left would follow; and that all four were heavily armed and under orders to seek and destroy their target - him.

He burst out through the back door and into an alleyway. Long powerful legs pushing him forward until he came to a solid metal door that must have led out into the street on the other side, and which had a digital lock securing it. His only chance was a fire escape directly above him. Pulling down a steel first-stage ladder he took the metal plates two at a time up to the first floor; pulled the lower section up after him and continued up towards the roof of the five storey building. At the fourth floor he looked back down into the alley - there was no one following - he entered the building through a window and found himself standing in a brightly lit hallway. Residential apartments over the ground floor shops. He ran on, producing a small silent chemical detonated death grenade from his pocket, which he tossed over the edge of the stairwell. If the four men had not pursued him into the ally, it was only because they had known it to lead nowhere. This meant that they were still inside the building, and most likely closing in on him from below.

He pulled the pin on the dull black coloured grenade and tossed it over the edge of the stairwell, Alix heard the metallic click as it hit the tiled floor of the lobby below and bounced once.

There was a muffled crack, and then a hiss.

A moment later, a bellow of angry hot air came back up the stairwell, rushing past him like the approach of a fast moving underground train through a tunnel. He didn't wait around to see if the grenade had created death and carnage: if nothing else, it would make his pursuers much more cautious. His head snapped around to his right at the sound of a group of people, laughing as their party spilled out through the doorway of the flat.

He started walking towards them, while all the time he was looking around for a way out, and then spotted the doorway to the fire escape stairwell.

This is good, very good.

People - they make brilliant cover...

As dreadful as that might seem.

He went to move past the revellers, and a young woman grabbed him playfully by the arm in her drunken state, and dragged him inside the flat to dance with her. Alix felt a little out of place wearing the long black overcoat in a room full of scantily clad university students, he removed it and managed to detach himself and decided to leave through a door on the other side of the room. He passed through another door, and into some kind of sparsely furnished smoke stinking back living room, which was in desperate need of re-decorating. An untidy mess of dirty dinner plates were stacked on a low coffee table, together with a number of discarded beer cans, errant tangles of party-popper streamers and general mess. The distant music interrupted Alix's pause for thought. Student's party? He quickly discarded the overcoat onto a hook on the back of the door he'd just come through, made sure the Beretta was properly holstered and concealed. And went back to the party again.

What better place to tread water for a bit - and give his pursuers time to get fed up and leave...

Dim lighting, strobes and the flicker of cheap disco-lights in time to the latest girl band music mixed with cigarette smoke and the aroma of Ganja filled the air in the hot stuffy room.

Alix picked up a can of lager from a table and pulled the tab off, taking a long swallow, while all the time his eyes surveyed the room and the group around the front door. Several girls gyrated into his path, bodies writhing in time to the beat of the music.

Alix swiftly sidestepped groping hands, glancing behind to see the group at the front door move aside. Hard faced men, battle scarred, cold eyes displaying their utter professionalism, appeared: dark-haired and well dressed in their Italian designer suits.

Alix stared, lips suddenly dry and the need to leave thumping in his temples.

Who were these people? Shouted his brain, searching the archives of his mind without success. He did not recognise these pursuers; but then, this information was an irrelevant factor...

Alix reacted by pushing his way back through the crowd towards the back living room. Bullets tore through the party, plaster and woodwork exploding as they slammed into the walls; Alix rolled, darted through the doorway and into the other room. The soundtrack had changed to one of panic and hysterical screams. He grabbed his black overcoat and ran through another doorway that opened into a small bedroom.

Trapped! Only a window. He opened it and peered over the edge - nothing but fresh-air for two floors and then a flat roof.

No thought was required. He stepped up to the window sill and jumped.

He landed heavily, rolled once and crouched on his haunches. Rapid gun-fire rang out from above, and a moment later bullets were screaming past him, slamming into brickwork off to his left. Alix slipped over the edge of the flat roof - released his grip and dropped twenty foot onto a stack of cardboard boxes below. He scrambled out from the crushed stack, and leaped lightly to the ground below.

Ignoring the shocked looks of passers-by, Alix ran up the street, gun in hand, approaching a man sitting astride a shiny black and red Suzuki Hayabusa sports motorbike. Without time for polite niceties, Alix grabbed the man by the collar of his leather jacket and pulled him backwards on to the wet tarmac, jumped aboard the powerful machine and, with the clutch in, he kicked down. The Suzuki screamed, fumes exploding from the exhaust... The bike's rear tyre spun furiously in the middle of the street, smoke billowing off the hot rubber as it reluctantly tried to grip the tarmac as Alix accelerated up the street. He kept his head down as bullets hailed down from the small window above, that he had just jumped out of, slamming into the bodywork of passing cars as the Suzuki's rear wheel attempted to grip the wet tarmac.

"Damn these people - whoever they are..." Alix said aloud.

At the end of the street, cars were grid-locked queuing to get out of a junction blocked by road-works. The bike screamed as Alix braked hard and spun the machine around, he let out the clutch and the bike lurched forward, mounted the pavement and started back along the route he'd just come from. He used parked cars for cover as pedestrians screamed and jumped out of the way as the powerful bike accelerated at high speed. Wheels spun, Alix slung the bike to the left, off the pavement and back onto the road again, the suspension dipping as he braked hard again to miss pedestrians who dived for cover.

Alix opened the throttle and the bike surged down the road. He braked hard at the entrance to a large building site, the rear wheel slewed round and a moment later Alix was racing through the gates and over rough ground, churning mud and heading for the exit on the opposite side of the large site. He hit the brakes, ending in a long mud-slew skid, and jumped free at the last moment as the Suzuki collided with a large earth moving machine. The fuel tank impacted against the heavy metal and exploded into a fireball. Alix looked around and spotted a black Mercedes Sprinter van parked just outside the exit of the site, ran across and climbed casually in through the side door.

"Step on it, Lola - it's time to leave." Bullets slammed into the rear door panel from behind as the Mercedes wheel spun and joined the late evening traffic, and then the glass of the rear windscreen exploded into millions of tiny fragments. In the back of the van Alix ducked low onto the floor as bullets ripped through the side panels. Ragged holes appeared and the hi-tech surveillance equipment and weapons held in the metal racks were being destroyed.

"Fucking hell, Lola! Get this pile of junk moving?" Alix growled, adding. "Get us out of here - now!" Alix eyes were wide, mouth dry as he eyed the bullet holes.

Lola veered the van to the left, mounted the kerb and smashed into oblivion one parking meter after another all the way to the end of the street; the van's engine roared and the bullets faded behind.

They drove through back streets and through deserted industrial estates.

Alix, sweating now, slumped in his seat and ran a hand over his spiky hair.

"Was I right?" Lola asked bluntly.

Alix met the woman's intense gaze in the rear view mirror, and nodded. "You were right. They definitely wanted me to lead them to you. Bad enough to kill anyone who got in their way."

"What now?" asked Lola, her sultry South American tones for once edged with a kind of panic so unlike her usual well-trained stability that it brought a frown to Alix's youthful face?

He shrugged. "We have to warn the partners of Ferran & Cardini and whoever is running the show at the Ministry of Defence."

"I can't use my Scorpion G8 unit - I'd say that's how the bastards have been tracking us," said Alix with a snarl. He checked that there was a full clip in the Glock and switched the safety to off on the Heckler & Koch MP5 machine carbine in his hands and grinned - that nasty grin he made just before the shooting started.

"We could of course just try this Pay as You go phone, that I carry around for such emergencies?" Lola called back.

"Well, I'll be damned. You're a tricky one."

"Comes with experience - lots of experience." Lola said amiably, and then added. "We've got no other choice than to use it. I'll send a message to Ferran & Cardini. Let them know that we've got a leak somewhere inside Scorpion HQ or at the Ministry Of Defence, and that they were laying in wait for us."

"That'll stir things up. There's no way they could have just happened upon us. Bastards knew exactly where we were."

"It'll be like waving a red rag at a black bull." Lola said, and laughed.

"Those bastards messed up my trousers *and* my new overcoat. The *bastards*. Lola, get us out of this shit-hole city. Then we'll see if we can dump this van - it'll almost certainly be tracked."

Lola pulled free her phone. Tapped in a number of digits and the device came to life and as quickly it went blank and died. She frowned - and tried it again.

"Damn thing won't work, Alix."

"Let's take a look at it."

"Bloody gizmos - never was very good with technology," complained Lola.

Alix smiled. "You're a prize technophobe, girl. They warned me about you and gadgets, and how you have a nasty habit of destroying them."

"That's a lie," Lola was smirking, "They only sometimes break. Otherwise they just break-down..."

Alix played with the phone, and frowned again. "I thought these things were practically bomb-proof?"

"They are," Lola called back from the front seat. "I very much doubt whether it has been damaged."

Alix looked at a loss, as Lola handed him her Scorpion smartphone. He attempted to bring the device to life, but it refused to boot-up. He shook his head, "Where to next?"

"We need to contact Ferran & Cardini, and we need to find out what the hell is going on. We need to be alert and remember that a number of Scorpion units have been assassinated."

Alix looked perturbed, answering. "No I haven't forgotten."

"Didn't you think it a little odd that Scorpion made a point of requesting that they brought Dillon in to protect Kirill and his niece - and not us?"

"A little." Said Alix, lighting a cigarette and laying back, staring at the panelled ceiling, smoke spiralling upwards and escaping through the torn bullet holes making him feel a tad wary. Tension, spinning bullets and a lack of sleep did not fuse together to well. A cold draft whistled in through the holes. Alix started to dismantle and clean his Glock.

He closed his eyes, thinking back to his last tour of Afghanistan and the random suicide bombers.

And the bullets...

And the killing...

"We need to pay a visit to an old friend," said Alix. He shivered. And welcomed the darkness of sleep as the van rumbled through the rain swept streets of the city.

* * *

59

REUTERS NEWS RELEASE. <u>GCHQ</u> <u>INTERCEPT</u> <u>CLASSIFIED HQ1/FYEO-457 - D NOTICE APPLIED</u>. At 7.30P.M.today London city suffered a total loss of electricity - telecommunications and mobile satellite coverage. The black-out lasted for approximately 15 minutes.

Millions of residential homes and commercial businesses, including Government departments and agencies, hospitals and the police, were left in total disarray as the lights went out and computer systems crashed.

There have been no reasons given for this failure by the Government or the power companies. Although, one theory is that it was caused by an explosion at a sub-station, which in turn generated a power surge to the grid network.

GCHQ Transcript 3. <u>CLASSIFIED HQ1/FYEO-457A</u> <u>SPECIAL SERVICES SUPPORT UNIT</u>. MI5 intelligence confirmed that a Cyber-Terrorist attack occurred today. The target: Electricity power supply - telecommunications and mobile telephone satellite coverage. The Home Office immediately issued a D-Notice press black-out order. The attack was made by, as yet unknown, terrorist or organised crime syndicate, was registered at 7.30P.M.today for a 15 minute duration.

All Scorpion and associated personal should go to **Code Orange** until further notice.

Chapter 6

It felt surreal, like a million light years had passed, as if he was on another planet. Dillon lay in the steaming hot Jacuzzi bath, water flowing over his body, massaging his back, easing the tension from his muscles, washing away the spatters and smears of blood. His eyes closed, his head resting on the roll-top bath, his fingertips massaging his temples ever so gently; round and round in tiny circles. It had been a long journey and his weariness had all but consumed him, devoured him whole and spat him out on the other side of the universe.

Too much had changed in the world since he had opted for the quiet life in the Highlands of Scotland.

He stepped out of the bath. The towel had been warming on the heated rail, and he dried himself in slow-motion, automaton movements. Then naked, he walked through to the master bedroom and collapsed onto the richly coloured, thickly opulent duvet. Sleep claiming him immediately into its embrace.

Dillon tossed and turned, sleeping a restless and sweaty sleep...

Zhenya - the look of utter disbelief. And then the silenced spit of the gun - everything in slow motion. A bullet spinning through the air, slamming into her shoulder, cloth tearing as the hollow-point bullet bore through skin and muscle, smashing bone. Kirill, face covered in blood and saliva, eyes unfocused as he lay in a state of shock - dying. But it was Dillon who took the bullet, felt his flesh tear and the searing heat as it entered his body and looking down, watched blood soaking through his shirt. Could see Kirill's face staring down at him as he was lowered into the shallow grave and Zhenya throwing flowers on top of him as they started to shovel the soft earth in and he wanted to shout, shout; "I'm still alive. I'm not dead..."

* * *

He awoke suddenly in the darkness, a cold sweat covering his body, shivering with flashbacks of his past cascading through his mind. Dillon pulled the heavy duvet up around his neck, groaning with tired and aching muscles. A moment later he rolled from the bed and pulled on navy blue jogging bottoms and a thick woollen pullover, much too large but really soft and comfortable, just the way he liked it. He went barefoot down to the kitchen and made himself a cup of tea as the first weak rays of sunshine were filtering over the summit of the mountain range on the far side of the loch.

Dillon went through to the living room and stretched his spine, then unlocked the French doors and stepped out onto the terrace. The cold hit him like a slap in the face and he gasped, revelling at the shock. Wind lashed his unruly hair and he leaned over the stone balcony, gazing out across the snow covered lawns. In the distance he could see woodland, snow-laden and picturesque. The lane snaked into the distance, between hills, and beyond it all; the mountains over lording the valley and watching over mere mortals far below.

God, this is such a beautiful place, he thought. The phone rang. He stepped back inside and picked up the handset. "Hello."

"Dillon, its Tatiana." She sounded serious.

"Tats - I need a *servere word in your ear*, my lovely. Have you any fucking idea what happened to me in Cornwall?"

"No time, Dillon. There's something very bad going down, here in London. I just wanted to let you know that I'm coming up."

"Here?"

"Yes. I'm on my way now, should be with you in about three hours. Do not use the mobile phone that I gave you. In fact, I doubt whether it is even connected at present."

"Why"

"It's the Scorpion units. It looks like three of them have been assassinated - wiped out. Look, I'll be there as soon as possible."

The line went dead. Dillon went back inside and picked up the mobile phone. He checked the signal strength, which was usually strong, nothing, not a single bar; the screen showed that the satellite network was temporarily de-activated. Tats had called him from the secure phone system built into the Mercedes SL55 on-board computer system. She had obviously not wanted anyone to listen into her call...

Dillon ran open fingers through his hair, her words troubling him. He shrugged to himself, pushing this worry from his mind temporarily. He would just have to wait until Tatiana arrived and wonder in the meantime what the hell was going on - and what her words of warning really meant - but it wasn't that simple. Why had he not heard from Vince Sharp or Edward Levenson-Jones at Ferran & Cardini? What the hell *was* going on?

He changed into a dark blue tracksuit and pulled on a battered old pair of Nike running shoes and trotted down the stairs and out through the front door. Dillon stood in the middle of the drive already feeling the invigorating effects of the bitterly cold morning air and fresh snowfall under foot. A moment later, he set off across the vast lawn leading down to the water's edge, and at a steady pace followed the contours of the shoreline around the Loch, as wariness and bad images of the assignment down in Cornwall flickered through his mind with each stride.

The early morning sunshine and the silence welcomed Dillon into its embrace and he groaned internally at the effort of such vigorous exercise and yet he felt the need. The need to work, to be doing something, to feel the exhilaration and power that only came with hard exercise; to feel the trail beneath his running shoes, to feel the burn of lactic acid, the strain of muscles, the tearing of strained lungs...

Soon, with leg muscles burning, he turned in-land and headed up a hill towards woodland. He crested the first rise and entered the woods. Frozen gorse crackled and snapped under each heavy footfall as he pushed himself to the limit and five minutes later he cleared the woods and was heading up to a rocky out-crop that offered a spectacular view across the valley right back to the modest size castle he now called home.

The distant engine noise indicated a large vehicle. It could just be passing by but Dillon had a bad feeling about it as no one ever came in his direction unless invited. Ever since the events in Cornwall only hours before and the low flying race back home to Scotland... The pursuit had ended without event but Dillon still felt drained after those bloody unexpected events at Kirill's country residence

The powerful diesel engine changed pitch. Dillon ran back down through the woods, staying just back from the tree line as he heard the vehicle turn up towards his property. He reached the rise just in front of the imposing building and gazed down at the battered Mercedes van, pumping diesel fumes from an engine that had run its last mile.

A Mercedes van? It had to be...

Alix and Lola, Dillon smiled.

He ran down towards the main gate and, ever careful, paused to watch the van pulling up outside the front doors of the castle and the visitors disembark. Alix and Lola stepped down from the Mercedes, both grumbling and stretching after the obvious effects of a long journey. Dillon stayed where he was for a moment longer - nobody following - then jogged slowly up the drive to greet his two old friends whom he had served with during his army intelligence days.

"Dillon!" Yelled Alix, and embraced the sweating man. They clasped hands, patting one another on the back. Lola smiled warmly. "I hope you've got whisky, Dillon? Lots of it..."

"You Lola, have a wicked mind, and at this time of the morning. I still haven't forgotten the last time the three of us started on the whisky!"

"It wasn't my fault Alix got thrown into the Thames! And it's never too early for a *wee* dram..."

"Lola, it was *you* who threw him in the river!"

"It was nothing, just a little fooling around! It's great to see you again, Jake."

"Come on in", said Dillon smiling. "I'm just about ready for a cooked breakfast, if I can entice two of my oldest friends to join me?"

"I'm up for some of that." Alix said, as he followed Dillon inside.

"And me," Lola called as she stepped down from the back of the van with a holdall full of weapons.

"It must be two or three years since we all got together. And with so many holes in that van. I assume there is a reason?" Dillon's eyes were hooded, his mouth a grim line. Recent events having removed much of his humour, and this unannounced visit felt somehow ominous.

"I'm afraid there is," said Alix softly. He lit a cigar, rested his head back and rubbed at tired eyes. "Something bad is going down, old buddy. Have you logged on with the Ferran & Cardini server recently? Checked out the encrypted fodder on your adventures down in Cornwall?"

Dillon shook his head. "No, not since I got back, I'm not really interested to be honest."

"Something just doesn't add up, Jake. Scorpion HQ has no answers as to how the security was breached at the facility in Cornwall and how the SAS and MI5 protection squads were eliminated with such ease. And Kirill - our friendly Government computer nerd and creator of the all-powerful new programme - has disappeared and is presumed dead. They pulled the char-grilled corpse of his niece - along with the bodies of *all* the guests from the party - from the burnt out ruins of his mansion once the fire service had managed to get the blaze under control. But mysteriously, no sign of professor Kirill. Strange that, considering you put a bullet in the fucker? I'm finding it just a little disconcerting that no one is able to answer the simple question of what the hell is going on - after all, their surveillance and technology budgets must exceed all the others put together."

Dillon shrugged. "Have you thought - just for a moment - that they might not know what is going on? After all, it might not be so bizarre to think, that what happened to me and from what you're saying has happened to you - may have something to do with someone trying to obtain or destroy Kirill's new software programme? After all Kirill seems to be the common denominator here."

"You're dead right, Jake," Alix said tucking into a plate of eggs and bacon. "Go on, Lola, tell him about the other Scorpion units."

Lola sighed, and took a swig of her whisky, and Dillon caught the resignation in the young woman. Strange, for sure, because they had survived some of the worst and most dangerous hot-spots on the planet together as serving officers in army intelligence. They had infiltrated terrorist networks throughout Europe, assisted humanitarian relief agencies in the most devastated areas of Africa and South America, and partied from dusk to dawn in a few dubious bars and clubs from London to Cuba.

Lola's face was stern. "Scorpion 7, was wiped out while they were on a babysitting assignment in the Carpathian Mountains in the Ukraine."

"I know," said Dillon softly. "But these things *can* happen. Anyone involved in this kind of work - knows fully well that it could happen to them. Good men and women *die*. Life's a bitch, *yeah?*"

"Yes, but what is even worse is that Scorpion HQ has not said one word about it. I found out from a friend of mine. A former Russian special forces sergeant who is now working inside the Kremlin for their equivalent of the cyber monitoring and crime squad. He came across the report on a Russian news agency website and called me. So, Alix and I set out to find out a few things, keep a few tabs on several other Scorpion units, including members of Scorpion HQ. Two more units are missing, 3 and 4."

"The Sniper unit and the Southern Asia close protection unit. God, all those good men?"

"Hmmm," nodded Alix, filling the room with cigar smoke.

"Coincidence or just very bad luck? I thought to myself. Then we get this real bad gig in London. You know the sort, Dillon. One of those jobs that you just wish you hadn't been given. But you still sign the insurance waiver form and pledge your allegiance to the Crown for ever and after eternity. And guess what..."

"Smoke and mirrors - a set-up?"

"Too bloody right." Alix finished his cigar, and immediately lit another. "They were waiting for us. I went in on foot to check ahead; there were five of them, almost got me and all. Very professional: well-armed, eastern European and as hard as fuck, intelligent, quick thinking, moved like greased lightening."

"And you also think that I was deliberately set-up?" Said Dillon softly.

"Certainly looks that way, doesn't it?"

Dillon pulled gently on one of his earlobes, and accepted a cigarette from Lola. "It's funny... I had a phone call from Tatiana earlier this morning. She's on her way up here. She sounded a little freaked out."

"Be careful with her, mate. She's turned into something else since you were with her. You know that the partners made her up to their personal liaison officer with the Government and Scorpion HQ. And don't forget, she's Old School. Crafty as a fox."

"I've known her for years - slept in her bed for a few of them. We're still good friends..."

Alix shrugged and gave Dillon a knowing look. "Tatiana is street wise - and don't you forget it." Alix said, and then immediately added.

"No offence meant, Jake. But you know what I mean, and you always did think with your dick. Trust no one, my old friend. Not Tatiana. Not even us. There are Scorpion Units that have been wiped out and others that are missing. You've been close enough to this thing to know what's what, and we had enough fire power used against us, back in London to have been able to start a small war. Why do you think we came up here? Looking for some lively night-life? Our telecom has been compromised and Scorpion HQ is not responding to any communications... and if our Matrix G8 encrypted comms. are down, then nothing is safe. We know that something is terribly wrong and think it started at Kirill's project establishment up here in Scotland. As you know there had been death threats against him and his niece. The main threat came from al-Qaeda. You sure this place

66

isn't bugged, Dillon?"

"I'm sure. I have the latest scanning equipment installed throughout the entire building. I don't believe that Ferran & Cardini or Scorpion HQ have anything sinister to do with any of this. But the ministry - well they're an entirely different can of worms... I reckon that Scorpion and my lot will have people working around the clock to sort this out."

"Maybe," said Alix. "But then, we're employed to think. Because we trust nobody. And, because we get the job done with the minimum of fuss. We don't have blind faith, Dillon old mate. There are people inside Scorpion HQ and Ferran & Cardini who are corruptible, they live in the real world, where they have real problems. Where a large sum of money would make their dreary little lives a lot more comfortable. As you found out yourself. Listen, the last email from Scorpion HQ was informing us of a special unit they are putting together to shut down the Taliban - permanently. Things are that close, Jake. The apparent betrayal by Kirill in Cornwall is being played down and kept very quiet. Don't want to give the fuckers any warning, do we now?"

Dillon scratched at the back of his head, then his tired eyes. "Kirill. That bastard got exactly what he deserved."

There was an uncomfortable protracted silence. Outside, snow had started to fall heavily again, large flakes falling straight down to earth through the absence of any breeze. Alix shivered, then grinned over at Lola. "You gonna keep me warm tonight, my South American beauty?" He winked, a cheeky boyish grin on his face.

"Alix, you couldn't afford me."

"Oh, don't be like that Lola. I'm sure I could scratch together a fiver."

"You cheeky bugger. I'll cut it off if you even try to wave that weener at me."

"Well, perhaps another time, another place, then. But enough of this banter - come on, we've been well fed and have warned our old friend of the impending danger. Time to get the hell out of here."

"Where to now?" asked Dillon as they both got up, leaving a pile of dirty plates and pans.

"Not telling," smiled Alix. "The less you know. You know the routine. And remember not to use your Ferran & Cardini mobile phone. It's linked to our G8's and most likely useless. Listen, Dillon. I have a bad feeling about all of this. A real bad feeling."

"Alix, your bad feelings usually turn out to be sheep in wolves clothing," said Dillon.

Alix shrugged. "I'm just saying man. Take it or leave it - but watch your back and lock up your doors and windows securely."

Dillon nodded, then led Alix and Lola outside into the heavy snowfall and towards their van. They thanked Dillon for breakfast and, with Alix's grinning face mouthing the words; "See ya around big man," from the window of the battered Mercedes van, within seconds, and through a plume of thick black exhaust fumes they disappeared out of the main gates through the snow.

Dillon watched them leave and went back inside. He sat, gazing out at the snow. He toyed with the mobile phone, but no matter how many times he tried he could not get the device to activate. The screen remained black and lifeless as he tossed it from one hand to the other, as you would a soft ball.

A roaring fire burned, crackling occasionally, the glow warming the room and contrasting the inclement snowy wilderness on the other side of the large bay windows.

Dillon stared at the mountains, their peaks invisible through the low cloud and heavy snow. On the coffee table in front of him sat his Sony Vaio laptop computer, the page blank, the cursor blinking in the top left hand corner. He flipped the mobile phone onto the floor, and remained staring at the bright screen deep in thought for a moment. He wrote:

> The problem is far worse than it appears: Scorpion units assassinated while on assignment. Kirill... and Zhenya's involvement? SAS and security service possibly in on betrayal in some way - bribery or other incentive at the highest level?
>
> The question is - who was the real target in Cornwall? Jake Dillon? Or the delegates/party guests? Or both? Most probable that Dillon was target. But why? And by whom?
>
> Kirill - expert in software development - Russian born - Kiev, of independent wealth, with properties in UK and Italy. Defected USSR during mid-1987. Creator of the Chimera military software programme. Developed at Kirill's top secret establishment in Scotland for the British armed forces, and currently undergoing

```
field trials with a number of Scorpion units.
   Who is the enemy?
   Scorpion HQ? Ferran & Cardini? Unlikely on
both counts.
   Where is Kirill now? How did he get out and
possibly survive the explosion at his country
residence in Cornwall?
```

Dillon stared at the words on the screen. Ferran & Cardini knew that he was alive. He had spoken to Tatiana. And, he had sent his report to LJ direct from the helicopter that had picked him out of Cornwall. They had okayed his return to his home in Scotland and told him to wait for Vince Sharp to contact him. If it had been the firm or someone in the ministry who had wanted him dead, he was sure as hell he would already *be* dead. Unless it was a rogue element *within* Scorpion working their own agenda. Perhaps it was a situation of biding time, waiting for the right situation to arise... Like Alix and Lola turning up on his doorstep? Or Tatiana making an appearance? Had Alix and Lola's van been tracked?

No. He shook his head. Scorpion stood for everything that was good; the global fight against terrorism in whatever form it took, cutting away the cancer of modern society with the precision of a surgeon's knife. Every detail always thought through, there were never mistakes... Not usually...

Dillon followed the premise: if whoever it was *did* want the Scorpion units out of the way for good, why the elaborate set-ups? If it were Scorpion themselves; why spend billions of pounds in recruitment of the most experienced field operatives - only to kill them off?

Something just didn't add up.

And where did the Chimera Programme fit into this jigsaw? This puzzle? Kirill was in charge of its development, programming and refinement of the software that the Scorpion units were now field testing. Dillon knew very little about the project or the programme, except what Kirill had told him, but Tatiana had obviously been involved from the start as liaison officer between Ferran & Cardini and Kirill's department and subsequently knowing more than most about it. Three years ago, when they had shared much more than just sex, she had trusted Dillon implicitly; she would talk to him long into the small hours after the warmth and lust of their love making, her features softened by candlelight... She would talk endlessly about the advancements in computer aided warfare, which would inevitably go straight over Dillon's head, and always surprised him that she had such an avaricious appetite for technological knowledge. And despite Dillon's extensive experience with military techno-systems the jargon had flown way above his head. Tatiana's involvement with the Chimera project was also something that had many questions attached to it...

And what now? Now?

Dillon wrote:

Assassination - How to assassinate the world's most highly trained specialist anti-terrorist units? Scorpion units are the ultimate weapon against the global terrorist in the twenty-first century - the best of the best. Each operative chosen for specific skills - Assassins, snipers, explosive/demolition experts, tech-weapons/computer experts, and a whole array of other covert and military expertise.

How to assassinate the assassins?

And why?

Scorpion Matrix G8 Comms and Ferran & Cardini mobile smart phones no longer secure: In Cornwall the smartphone and G8 network died, only reactivating when clear of site. Possibility of some kind of jamming device or power drain on both Scorpion and Ferran & Cardini mainframes in London? Somene is remotely accessing system? Possible internal betrayal???

Kirill.

Everything revolves around Kirill. He was the one who tried to kill Dillon, therefore he was willing to throw away his position and the multi-billion pound research and development facility...

Leave the British Government - leave the embrace of such a world-active country, who strives for global peace, which genuinely set out to fuck-up the bad guys?

The British Government, Scorpion, and Ferran & Cardini were betrayed. Set up.

Who better than someone involved with the Chimera project? Kirill, obviously... but he is merely a puppet; he cannot be the one pulling

```
the strings.
   So, who else?
   And Tatiana... Tatiana knew Kirill; She set
up the protection gig in Cornwall in the first
place. Sent Dillon to his own execution. How
perfect.
   Whatever this game is, it's much bigger than
I first thought.
```

Dillon got up and started to pace up and down the living room carpet; pondering the questions he had thrown in to the hat. Like the most frustrating maze, just when he thought he was heading in the right direction, a dead end appeared, and he would have to retrace his footsteps. And so it went, until he slumped down onto one of the sofas.

I don't know, he thought, closing his eyes.

Outside, the wind howled and Dillon, almost absentmindedly, threw a log onto the fire. It was Kirill who concerned him more than anything - the cold hate filled look in the man's eyes as the unwavering gun muzzle was pointing straight at Dillon's head. Something in Kirill made Dillon's soul go cold. There was something different about the man. Something *very* strange.

And Tatiana...

Tatiana had pleaded with him to take on the assignment in Cornwall. She had known Kirill a long time, worked closely with him in her capacity as Ferran & Cardini's liaison officer on the Chimera project.

And if they had wanted *him*, Dillon, dead, then Tatiana had to have known.

Dillon felt suddenly depressed, and immensely lonely. A sense of vulnerability washing over him, attacking his confidence.

He still loved Tatiana; and knew deep down that she still loved him. But the facts were staring him in the face.

She was part of it. Integral. A cog in the machine. Whatever that was... She *had* to be...

Dillon knew; he would have to be extremely careful. He would have to be prepared. And he would have to watch Tatiana's every move - and if she stepped out of line?

Then she would have to be dealt with.

* * *

71

Dillon went to his study. Entering the book-lined room, he moved to his desk and pushed the button located just under the edge of the oak top. Panels slid silently back to reveal the bank of six HD monitor screens behind them. A screen saver moved from one monitor to the next almost seamlessly and then changed theme every twenty seconds.

He sat down at the master keyboard and initialised the operating system. Entering the central hub, he typed in the password and accessed the main house and land defence security systems, and logged in.

Everything looked normal.

He scanned all hidden cameras for a three mile radius and then a one mile radius. Nothing had been tripped or tampered with, the power and voltage monitoring meters had not been broken or hacked into. The system had been built to his exact specification and the software programme written by one of the best hackers in the business, Vince Sharp.

He finished running the scan.

Nothing. He looked at the screens for a moment, and lit a cigarette. The CPU's purred inside their housings and he decided to randomly flick through a number of other concealed cameras located higher up on the mountain-side, but could see nothing suspicious.

Dillon knew that just because it looks normal, doesn't mean that there's not something there.

He was tempted to go and physically check the cameras, which would serve no purpose and be completely unnecessary, given that he had gone round all of them just before he had flown down to Cornwall. He checked his watch. Tatiana would be arriving in a few hours and he would need to be ready.

He walked through the hall and pulled on his boots, lacing them tightly. Then he moved down the stairs to the cellar and placed the palm of his hand on the biometric reader panel; a section of the wall slid smoothly back and he stepped into a brightly lit room.

The armoury smelled of gun oil, and he opened the Armourlite glass fronted security cabinets using a remote control unit. He moved to the first cabinet and pulled free the Glock 9mm automatic. He checked all the magazines and strapped them about his body. Then he picked out a Heckler & Koch MP5 submachine gun, and then from the next cabinet the AMSD OM 50 Nemesis 12.7mm sniper rifle, to which he attached an infrared scope to the weapon with a precise *click*. He checked the magazine, placed a couple of spares in his pockets, then with the rifle slung over his shoulder, he locked the room, and as he walked away the wall panel slid silently back into place.

Dillon locked the front door and using the remote control, armed the security trip monitors and the CS Gas modules that were located at strategic points around the property. He had a bad feeling about Tatiana's impending visit and wanted to check that she wasn't being followed by any big men in suits with submachine guns. Then he set off across the grey-lit fields towards higher ground, so free of violence in this far flung part of Scotland, and up past the edge of the woods towards the beautiful view point of Cairn bluff, a craggy outcrop of rocks.

* * *

Dillon felt cold to the bone.

His hands, protected by gloves, clasped the stock of the AMSD OM 50 Nemesis sniper rifle and he sat covertly amongst the outcrop of rocks, staring down at the lane. He had a clear view down the hillside for at least a mile straight ahead of him, he targeted the high powered scope, picking out snow laden branches on the trees, and the fluttering of snowflakes falling: and he stole a moment to smile to himself. From his vantage point, he had given himself the best possible advantage, and had chosen the best killing ground, and one reason why he had purchased the small castle in the middle of nowhere. If there was going to be trouble - then he had chosen his spot well.

He heard the engine, drifting up from the valley, before the vehicle came into view around the bend. And when it did come, it was slewing left and right with churning tyres, and then it slammed into the low embankment with metal scraping against the frozen snow, bouncing the back of the vehicle violently around and slamming it across the lane as the engine screamed and tyres eventually found grip, shooting the Mercedes AMG 55 forward at speed.

Dillon lifted the scope to his eye.

Tatiana was coming - and it appeared that she was in trouble.

The Mercedes accelerated madly down the narrow lane.

A black Range Rover Sport spun around the corner, gripping

effortlessly with its four wheel drive and winter tyres. It must have been laying in wait for her, ready to attack; it accelerated down the lane and started to gain ground on the Mercedes.

Dillon sighted smoothly. The auto-focus gave the Range Rover instant clarity. The six occupants became pin-sharp images inside the luxury 4x4. He could see them clearly - large men in dark clothing, some were wearing dark glasses. One window was down, allowing snow to blow into the vehicle - an automatic weapon appeared and began firing.

The *cracks* echoed up the hillside a moment later.

Dillon trained the Nemesis on the driver; the Range Rover slowed, immediately slewing to the left and then right, under heavy footed braking as it negotiated a large snowdrift and Dillon cursed, the figures inside the vehicle being thrown around, unsteady targets...

He closed his eyes, opened them and breathed out slowly. Squeezed the trigger gently - once - reloaded and squeezed again.

The rapport would have been deafening, had he not been wearing ear protectors, the stock punched his shoulder with a sharp kick, and he saw the windscreen shatter and disappear into a billion tiny pieces; the first round had missed the driver and hit the shooter, hanging out of the rear window with the automatic, in the neck, severing the main artery and spraying blood across the interior. The second shot, had slammed into the forehead of the man sitting next to him, blood, brain matter and fragments of skull turned the rear windscreen a bright crimson. With a scream of gears and engine, the Range Rover swerved left, smashing into the embankment and then violently righting itself; the rear bumper was hanging off, split and dragging noisily along the ground.

The lane, and Dillon's advantage, was fast running out.

"Bollocks," Dillon said out loud.

He repositioned the Nemesis and squeezed off a round. The bullet slapped into the front wing bursting the tyre, the heavy 4x4 veered, Dillon reloaded round after round, and bullets continued to slam into the door panels.

As the last round was fired, Dillon left the rifle in the snow and sprinted down the hillside for the castle and the cover it would afford him - if he could make it in time. Every muscle in his body felt alive as he powered forward down the hill, he heard the Range Rover's engine pitch change as it spun into the private lane that led up to his property, and then pass by him far below. More gunshots ricocheting as the 4x4 flashed from view and Dillon pushed on, arms pumping as he pushed on through the snow, the Glock automatic in his left hand, a cold sweat covering his body, stinging his eyes.

More gunshots rang out from up ahead.

Dillon came over the ridge at a full sprint and the world opened up before him, his home in the foreground with the stunning mountain range as a backdrop on the far side of the loch, snow falling in an idyllic postcard scene. Punctuated with the harsh full stop of; *savagery and destruction.*

Tatiana had swung the Mercedes around in the turning circle to form a barricade behind which she was crouched, gun in hand and resting on the edge of the bonnet.

As Dillon appeared, the Range Rover howled straight for the Mercedes, Tatiana darted out of the way as the heavy 4x4 ploughed into the sports car amidst the devastating noises of screaming crunching metal; the Mercedes was shunted into the front of Dillon's home, buckled and twisted, the windscreen exploded under the pressure and the Merc's boot popped open as the vehicle was pushed into the main steps. The Range Rover's doors were opening even as the collision took place and men tumbled from the 4x4, automatics and sub-machine pistols drawn.

Tatiana had taken cover behind Dillon's Landrover, at the right moment she came out, firing - in seconds bullets smashed across space. One of the men was spun sideways with a bullet to the shoulder, ripping apart clothing and flesh, and dropping him spinning to the ground in a flurry of snow and a spattering of blood.

The sound of automatic gun-fire echoed around the valley, as a fusillade of bullets scythed across the clearing. Four bullets smacked into the large oak tree behind Tatiana in quick succession, their impact making dull thuds in the bark.

The fifth bullet found its mark, catching Tatiana, puncturing her flesh and knocking her backwards off her feet, legs and arms flaying wildly as she went down hard onto snow covered gravel. She landed awkwardly in a heap, wedged against the trunk of the oak tree, face to the ground, legs twisted in a macabre abstract.

"No!" shouted Dillon.

Chapter 7

Ministry of Defence - Whitehall London. The highest level military headquarters in the UK, providing political control of all British military operations around the planet. The central staff is made up of integrated service and civilian personnel who are responsible for, amongst other things, planning strategy for the three principle services - and now the Scorpion units. They control the monetary budgets and financial deals, from buying and selling land, weapons and military hardware to the masterminding of stock market economics. Battles have been won, and some lost from within the inner sanctums of this austere Whitehall building...

Those who knew of Scorpion, or who worked for them, would often wonder about finance: how had this clandestine organisation, part of the British military war machine against terror, become so important? And how did it fund such impressive worldwide schemes and plans?

There were no simple answers. But Ferran & Cardini International was never very far away and always on hand to guide and advise the top-brass at Scorpion. They now had fingers in many pies - Scorpion held the controlling shares in some of the largest PLC companies and financial institutions, owned a myriad of businesses from matchstick making factories to oil corporations, worldwide. If there was money to be made - big money - then Scorpion would in some way be involved. And sitting in their eyrie, high-up in the atrium of their Docklands' headquarters. The partners of Ferran & Cardini stroked their egos and congratulated themselves for being such clever chaps...

Scorpion HQ was not visible from the air; it was hidden deep underground, deeper than even the London tube lines, a massive self-contained complex linked by hundreds of metres of labyrinthine tunnels leading to rooms housing an array of hi-tech surveillance equipment, canteens, satellite interface terminals and the main servers that linked the worldwide Scorpion G8 network. Along with two hundred highly trained Government men and women. Above Scorpion HQ was a busy London high street; all normal and oblivious to what lay beneath the pedestrian walk-ways, the bustling shoppers and camera-toting tourists. Below the heavily guarded London Underground... Scorpion HQ *existed*...

Deep down; an underground base, an underground world.

The entrances were disguised; hidden from the casual passer-by; only the elite few knew of these access points, and where they were located. One of them was located within the reception area of a travel agent's building. On this particular afternoon, the automatic sliding door opened silently to reveal a stunning looking young woman. She was smiling as she emerged outside, her expensive designer suit looking sharp and business-like, and her company name badge concealing a high-tech security access device to allow her to enter Scorpion's underground HQ.

She gazed up at the tumultuous clouds rolling overhead, watched by a small group of workmen across the busy road, their eyes and wolf-whistles admiring her long legs and immaculately groomed mane of auburn hair.

Her gaze shifted, and a moment later she raised her hand to hail a nearby taxi.

And then she was gone and replaced by a raging ball of gas and flame that roared up from hundreds of feet below ground, like a rocket racing up to the heavens screaming so loud it was beyond anything natural. Buildings were vaporised in an instant. Concrete, glass and steel disintegrated. Rooms and furniture and everything in them were pulped and pulverised along with the occupants of the buildings, and *below ground level* the heart of Scorpion, its central nerve centre, all were vaporised within seconds as the WMD explosive device was detonated - and the entire landscape of that part of London was changed forever...

First came the booming concussion as the device detonated, followed by the invisible but devastating shock-wave and in the wake came dust, billowing up in a huge cloud that mushroomed above the city, all generated by the small but high-tech nuclear device...

The explosion could be heard ten miles away.

With the aftermath came - silence.

Soon after, the screams and pitiful sounds of brutally injured men, women and children could be heard.

And this all went on for an eternity.

* * *

Kirill laid semi-conscious, dark waves of pain washing over him. In fact, he was sure that he could hear the ocean; struggling, he forced his head to the left and could see what he was convinced were crests of gleaming white on the rolling surf, crashing and foaming to a natural death on a beach of pure white sand. Kirill groaned, his whole body shuddering. It took every ounce of energy that he could muster to lift his head, gazed down at himself. He was completely naked - an angry looking wound, marked the bullets entry low down in his belly.

What happened? He thought sombrely.

And then the voices, the words; the words drifted to him as if they were a very long way away, tiny sounds in his brain, merging with the sounds of the sea, hissing and rolling, surging and retreating across the sand.

"He must be in great pain..."

"We have removed the bullet, but there are still many fragments of shattered bone lodged inside; the hollow-point bullet caused immense internal damage. This man should be dead; I am amazed we're looking down at him in a bed and not a coffin..."

Kirill groaned. He closed his eyes.

A cool breeze blew in from the Indian blue ocean.

He was aware that he was in a bad way, but also knew that by some freak of fate, he was still alive and that his body was repairing itself as he lay there. He could feel his blood racing through his veins, along with the sedatives and other drugs to take away his pain.

He thought back, Kirill thought back across the long span of his life - those long hard years.

Searing pain lanced him.

He concentrated on the wound; he could feel the drugs being fed into his body, racing through his bloodstream, making him stronger; could feel his body repairing the damage wrought by the bullet.

He drifted off for a while, the pain coming in wave after agonising wave.

He listened to the ocean.

Voices.

"Give him another ten mils of morphine; there, that should ease the pain for a while; or at least keep him going for another day or two. How the hell did he survive? Has he spoken?"

"Yes, he called out in his sleep"

"What did he say?"

"He called out for Zhenya. Who is Zhenya?"

"The young woman who was found dead at his country residence in Cornwall; she was his niece and only living relative. They brought in her charred corpse - what a mess she was in. She's in one of the chillers down in the morgue awaiting an autopsy, although I'm really sure what part of her they intend to use... Because there's not much left."

"Were they close?"

"I believe that she lived with him and accompanied him on every trip he made. He apparently treated her like a daughter."

Kirill felt the anger and rage well within him.

He remembered: remembered Dillon - remembered the bullet... and he remembered the gun, cold steel pointing at Zhenya, blowing her backwards against the tall stainless steel kitchen cabinet. Her small Russian pistol clattering on the floor, her skull cracking against the stone, a pool of blood forming around her...

Zhenya; my beautiful Zhenya.

He remembered a time, from years earlier: sitting outside at the long oak table. The sun gleaming, shimmering through the leafy canopy of a one hundred year old oak tree, casting strips of bright light across the table top. He could smell the lavender and the trees from the apple orchard. Zhenya had only been young then; nine, maybe ten. The two of them sitting next to each other eating freshly picked strawberries and a generous helping of double cream - both laughing at the moustache of cream across Kirill's top lip. Zhenya's eyes wide and gleaming and beautiful, her face a picture of delight.

Kirill closed the door of the memory.

The bitterness instantly returning to his mind, a cold and clinical hold taking over.

He knew; knew he should feel something amazing for Zhenya; he knew that his emotions should flow fast and furious, and there was anger there and a hatred for Dillon so intense that it held the promise of many long hours of torture to come. And he warmed to this thought, because he would be able to indulge his passion for the ancient art of Shackra torture... but he knew he should be weeping at her death. His intelligence told him he should be.

But something strange had happened.

Kirill could not bring himself to cry.

His face turned to a grimace now; the bullet wound to his gut was healing, his flesh knitting together; in this drug induced dream state it all seemed to be happening so quickly, almost instantaneously, strands of skin and muscle joining together, cells repairing and replicating in the blink of an eye.

It burned. It hurt real *bad*.

Kirill remembered his brother. It had been a shame, but the order had come from the highest level to kill him. To murder his own brother, to murder a man he loved, knowing that he would leave an orphaned child.

But he had carried out the order, with a single shot to the head.

And he had cried afterwards; Zhenya had not been there when Kirill had carried out the execution, but when she had returned, had come to him, asking why he was so sad. She had hugged him and sat with him, and Kirill had wept long and hard and had vowed then, that he would look after her forever.

Things had changed since then, he realised.

And then, bitterly; *I* have changed.

Now there were no tears. And he understood why - he understood that he had become as emotionless as those he served. He had thought that he could be immune from such changes; after all he had always had a philanthropic view about life. He thought that he would be able to make sacrifices for the good of the future; for the good of all things.

I am doing the right thing, he told himself.

The sacrifice *will* be worth it in the end.

The ocean crashed against the white sand shore; and Kirill realised that the surf, the rolling crashing waves and the hiss of the foaming spray were nothing more than voices once more, distant voices drifting in from the infinite darkness of the horizon.

"He appears to be stable and his temperature is almost normal again... Hey, who are you, you can't just barge in here, you've got no..."

"Shut-up. My security clearance gives me the right to be here. Now take this... And make sure you inject it straight into the wound."

"Good; now tell your men to put their guns away."

* * *

Kirill awoke suddenly. His eyes were still shut, and he waited for a while, listening to his own rhythmic breathing. His senses were all on high alert, though; he could hear breathing from at least another two people in the room with him. He could smell sweat, a hint of cheap stale aftershave, whisky, and somebody's odorous feet. Kirill inwardly checked his own body: it felt weak, the muscles stiff, taut with cramps, ravaged by fatigue. And his stomach: it was nothing more than a dull throb where the wound was still healing.

He slowly opened his eyes, sticky and crusted from days of sleep. He could see a white suspended ceiling. Clinical, harsh white light, made him flinch. The room was quite new; a private ward perhaps?

Kirill's hand moved down his body; he felt the fresh scar where the hollow-point bullet had recently smashed into him; he probed it gently but there was no pain. He smiled to himself, then attempted to prop himself up on one elbow.

There were three men; they were all watching him intently. Two were obviously bodyguard types, large street-brawlers, carrying mini-Uzi submachine guns concealed badly within their jackets; they were unshaven and looked weary. The third was a small frail looking man, somewhere in his late fifties, with a gaunt face and long crooked nose. What little hair he had, was smarmed, his hands small almost effeminate. He wore the long white coat of a hospital doctor and a stethoscope draped around his neck. A small aluminium attaché case was by his side and Kirill knew exactly what items were in it.

"It's very good to see you, Mendoza. How long have I been out?" he asked.

"Five days, sir. A little longer than we anticipated, but you were very nearly dead when we got to you. And you must appreciate that the bullet that Dillon shot you with, was designed to cause maximum amounts of damage on entry."

Kirill nodded. "I would like a cup of strong black Colombian ground coffee and one of my finest Cuban cigars. I feel like I've been unconscious forever!"

"That is a side effect of the serum, sir."

Mendoza waved away one of the bodyguards to fetch Kirill's coffee and cigar, who slid from the room. Outside the automatic sliding door Kirill caught a glimpse of a white sterile corridor, with several trolleys and more stark white lights.

"Does Ramus know that I'm okay?"

81

"He does, sir."

"Is this a private facility?"

"Yes. As you can appreciate; you were losing blood and your body had gone into shock, but with a slight boost of the new regenerative serum, we were able to stabilise you just long enough to get you to this private hospital. The drug will stay active in your system for another three or four days."

"Any side effects?"

"Mostly fatigue, sir. In some cases, it has been known to cause short-term depression and severe paranoia."

"Fatigue - paranoia!"

"But we also have drugs to combat these." Mendoza added quickly.

"Good."

Kirill sat up. "There are still bits of metal inside me."

"Yes, we ran the scans and determined that attempting to remove the fragments still inside your body, would have been too dangerous with the limited facilities that they have here. Also, Ramus said speed of recovery was of the utmost importance because of the critical state of the Chimera Programme. He said to tell you that we have had developments regarding the whereabouts of the stolen blueprints."

"And..." A pause. "Dillon?"

"After the incident in Cornwall, he has now been traced."

"Tell me."

"He killed many of our Assassins; very nearly killed *you*."

"He's far better than I thought - much better. Could almost be a fucking Assassin himself!"

There was laughter; cold laughter; it contained little or no humour.

"Another unit of Assassins has been sent to remove him."

Kirill nodded. The street-brawler returned and Kirill lit his cigar.

"Tell me, Mendoza. My niece, Zhenya Tarasova: I am right in thinking that she is dead?"

"I'm afraid that she is, sir. Nobody is sure what happened in that room... we were waiting for you to wake. The surviving Assassins got you out of there just ahead of the explosion designed to eliminate the majority of the Chimera development team along with a whole net-full of MOD top brass and mask your disappearance, but Zhenya... well, the bullet had nicked a main artery - she bled to death. There was

82

nothing that they could do for her and didn't have any time to make a snap decision... you were obviously the main priority."

"Priority?" Kirill said coldly, a dark intelligent glint in his eyes.

"Yes, I suppose I am."

"One other thing, sir."

"Yes?" His eyes sparkled.

"It appears that Scorpion had set up a special unit to search and destroy our operation."

"And?"

"Scorpion HQ and the special unit have both been successfully dealt with, sir. Scorpion HQ no longer exists, and many of this unit along with a large majority of the other operatives and networks are now dead."

"Exemplary, Mendoza." Kirill smiled nastily in satisfaction, and closed his dark eyes and allowed the pain to wash over him and take him away to a calmer place.

* * *

Tatiana lay, broken and torn on the frozen ground.

"No!" hissed Dillon. His own Glock started to kick in his hand as he ran out from behind his cover, both hands clasping the weapon. The man who had shot Tatiana was lifted off his feet and slammed backwards, bullets boring into his flesh, blood exploded from his mouth, staining his chin and nose in a crimson shower. Dillon landed, rolling across the ice crusted drive, grunting, his Glock magazine empty and his body sliding out of control against the twisted buckled Range Rover Sport with a dull *thud*. He changed magazines in an instant - checked inside the 4X4.

Two men were still standing, retreating towards the woods: two were dead inside of the vehicle from Dillon's sniper rounds; another had been shot by Tatiana, and one lay dead, face down, in the snow with his face blown away, Dillon's bullet in his brain.

Dillon popped his head around the car's protective shell; bullets screamed past from the edge of the woods, slamming into the stone and metal behind him with showers of dust. Dillon dropped down onto his belly and slid along to the edge of the Mercedes which ticked and hissed with the sigh of cooling metal.

A shoulder and arm exposed from behind the tree.

Dillon squeezed off three rounds in quick succession, heard

screams, and saw blood erupt from the shoulder, the arm fall away onto the ground.

One last assailant left .

Dillon looked to the right and left of the man he'd just shot but could not see the Assassin. Where was he? He had been crouching by a tree to the right, just back from the tree line, down near the low dry-stone wall that needed serious repair work which Dillon kept putting off until the long awaited summer...

Heavy boots thudded on the Mercedes roof and Dillon looked up - too late - as the man leaped forward on top of him with a growl. Dillon caught a glimpse of tanned Middle Eastern features and jet black cropped hair and three or four day's stubble growth on his chin. He smelled the stale body odour before he was grabbed, his Glock knocked easily aside. He brought up his knee, but missed - the large attacker rained down heavy blows on Dillon's head and face and he was momentarily stunned, blinded by the multiple impacts.

The weight lifted. Dillon lay on his back, on the snow, tasting the metallic tinge of his own blood. He glanced up, into a boot. His vision blurred and he was smashed backwards against the Mercedes, grunting, blood flowing freely down his chin, his nose broken. He might have even whimpered, he couldn't be sure - as he tried to push himself up off of the snow.

"Now, you're going to die," came the heavily accented voice.

Dillon's eyes flickered open - everything seemed to reach his brain in slow motion, and then something deep within his subconscious came to the surface and he knew what he had to do. The excitement rising, adrenalin started to pump through his veins to every part of his body - "*Drop this bastard like a stone,*" came the whisper.

Dillon rolled away to his right as the military style boot struck where - a split second before - his face had been. Dillon's fist smashed a heavy curling blow into the man's testicles and then the man screamed like a girl!

Dillon dragged himself to his feet, his senses heightened to a higher level, every nerve ending tingling in anticipation of what to come; the man on the ground was still wreathing around on the snow in excruciating pain.

Dillon staggered against the Mercedes. He gave a quick glance across to Tatiana - she was down and completely out of the game. He looked around for the Glock but could not see the weapon in the powdery snow. He felt a warm stream of blood running down over his cheek from an open gash above his right eye and he wiped it away with the sleeve of his jacket.

He moved forward and kicked the man in the head several times, until he was sure that the killer was unconscious. Then he knelt, and slammed his fist into the man's nose, breaking it in a return favour and making doubly sure that he wouldn't get up.

Covered in blood, Dillon skidded across to where Tatiana was laying. Gently, he eased her over onto her back. Remarkably, she was breathing, raggedly, her eyes rolled open, her jacket soaked in blood.

"Can you feel your fingers and toes?" he asked.

"You look like a fucking mess," she smiled, her voice hoarse.

"You're not so beautiful yourself."

"I can't move..."

Dillon gently lifted Tatiana into his arms and staggered despite her lack of weight. His head was spinning, pounding after the blows from the big man. She was still as light as he remembered... from better, happier times...

Dillon lurched towards the front door of his home.

Tatiana's eyes rolled back into their sockets and her fingers clawed at his arm.

Dillon cursed, and dropped to his knees in the snow, droplets of blood turning the ground pink. Tatiana was in deep shock, the colour had drained from her face, and beads of sweat had formed across her forehead.

Her eyes blinked, and then closed again. She did not speak.

Dillon lifted her, limp now in his arms, and climbed wearily over the wreckage of the Mercedes which was partly blocking the entrance to his home. He went up the steps and kicked open the front door. He was suddenly weary as he went inside, suddenly aware of the pain he was feeling through his battered and bruised body. Stars danced in front of his eyes and he had to pause for a moment, leaning, heaving and panting against the wall. He moved into the living room, and felt elation when he saw the fire he had lit earlier was still burning.

He gently lowered Tatiana on to one of the large leather sofas, pushed it nearer to the fire, and threw a few logs onto the smouldering coals, the flames flaring reassuringly. Tatiana's clothing was soaked in blood, seeping through the fabric.

There was a repetitive *blipping* coming from a remote control unit on the low coffee table: perimeter-sensor alerts triggered by the Assassins. Dillon reached over and picked the small device up, resetting the alarms with the push of a button and welcomed the silence.

Dillon threw a few more logs on the glowing fire, and then moved into the ground floor wet-room. He removed his jacket, groaning, and then his hoody. Cuts and bruises appeared across his body and shoulders, across his face and when he glanced into the mirror, an aging, battered shell gazed back. It grinned through blood stained teeth.

Dillon went through to the kitchen, and ran off a bowl of hot water, grabbed a knife from the teak block and returned to the living room. He knelt, and carefully started to cut away Tatiana's clothing, her blood soaked silk blouse and bra. Her flesh was pale and cool to his appraising touch. He realised that she had, thankfully, taken only a single bullet but he still cursed, leaning over her to take a closer look at the wound. It had entered high through her shoulder - tearing flesh, just missing bone and exiting in a tight hole from the back of the muscle. An inch lower and it would have caused *serious* damage... the wound was angry looking and inflamed with fluid.

"Bollocks."

Dillon went through to his study and grabbed a medical box; he returned to Tatiana and pulled out a syringe, injecting her intravenously with a morphine based sedative. He checked her pulse and blood-pressure, using a small hand-held monitor. Then he pulled free a sterile solution and cleaned the wound's entry point and then, rolling her over onto her belly, the exit hole, using a scalpel to cut away any alien particles of metal and clothing. Using sterile wire, he finally stitched the fresh sliced skin together.

Rolling her onto her back again mumbling, he stitched the entry wound, Dillon checked Tatiana's pulse and blood-pressure once more, then applied a dressing to her tightly stitched flesh and also to the cut above her right eye. Then he pressed tiny monitor pads onto her chest, which checked on heart rate and blood saturation levels. He pulled down her trousers, checking for any other wounds he might have missed.

Content with his work so far, Dillon considered wrapping her in more blankets, but used the fur throw-over instead. He piled on more logs, and gave her a final shot of antibiotics and another dose of sedative before limping to the wet-room himself.

He removed the remainder of his torn, blood soaked clothing, turned on the shower and stepped into the steam, wincing as the hot water lashed his battered and bruised skin like a bull-whip. Slowly, he felt the tension start to leave him as he lathered his body, washing free the dirt, sweat and congealed blood - his own and that of others.

His mind and body hurt - hurt bad, his mind a whirlpool of confusion.

There were far too many unanswered questions, and a broken nose did nothing to rationalise his thoughts.

He stepped out and towelled himself gently, his movements slow and laboured as the adrenalin left him. He looked at himself in the mirror and cursed. Heavy bruising, cuts, and abrasions. His nose was a mess, twisted bone and split skin. He dragged the medical box over and, with some difficulty, injected himself with a strong morphia based painkiller and waited for its numbing soothing effect to take hold. He went up to his bedroom and pulled on tracksuit bottoms and a T-shirt, feeling a little light headed as the drugs got a hold of his system.

He went back downstairs to the wet-room and stood in front of the mirror. Then, without preamble, he placed his two thumb-heels either side of his nose, counted to three and wrenched bone and cartilage back into some semblance of order. Everything went black and he yelped with the pain, despite the painkiller. He threw-up in the sink and stood leaning over the bowl, drooling and feeling decidedly fragile.

Dillon looked up.

His nose was still a little crooked but almost straight once more, like it had been hit with a cricket bat but not by a lorry! He smiled weakly at his reflection, brushed his teeth gently and swilled with mouth wash - to remove the sourness of the vomit, and splashed cold water on his face to carry away his pain-filled sweat.

He went through to the living room and checked on Tatiana who was still out for the count, her breathing was now regular and the sweating had subsided a little. He gently placed his hand on her forehead, her skin soft to his touch, the colour having returned to her face. He pulled on a heavy coat and thermal gloves, and a pair of boots unstained by blood, and went outside and down the front steps.

Dillon stood in the middle of the drive, looking at the carnage, feeling even more light-headed as the cold air hit him.

He stepped through the snow. Flakes were falling, much heavier now, from a dark brooding grey sky that cast silver shadows across the landscape. The world was silent, a watercolour of stillness and serenity; which had been broken briefly by the unwelcome intrusion of the assassins sent to kill him.

Dillon searched the area for his 9mm Glock, located it, checked the magazine and condition of the weapon, and used a rag to wipe it free of blood and dirt. He checked the unconscious man, and then moved around the battered vehicles that were now littering his drive and up towards the edge of the woods. There was deep red blood spatters and staining on the ground where the man whose arm had been shot-off had been standing. The blood led away and Dillon followed for a hundred or so metres until he found the man face down on the ground, dead. Dillon checked him and then went through his pockets, before dragging him deeper into the woods and rolling him over a steep slope down into the dark waters of the loch.

The effort was almost too much as he worked methodically, but slowly. He pulled one of the corpses out of the Range Rover, and gathered the other bodies, dragging them all into the woods and laying them to rest in a line, like a macabre scene from a TV police drama. He wiped the blood from his hands and returned to the only surviving man, who was making low moaning sounds. Dillon rolled him over onto his belly and pulled garden wire from his jacket pocket, binding the man's hands and feet so tightly that the wire cut into the exposed flesh. Then he dragged the tanned man to the tree where he had found Tatiana, propped him against the thick trunk and, taking his coat off, placed it over him.

"There, we don't want you dying of exposure now, do we?" He muttered.

Night was closing in and the snow falling fast, the heavy flakes tumbling through the darkness like leaves in winter. Dillon moved to the cars and stood, hands deep in pockets. Deep in thought about his next move.

He walked through the arch to the inner courtyard and the garage block, and pulled open the first double set of wooden doors. Jumped into his Landrover and drove it out into the drive. The wire was attached to the rear tow hook of the Mercedes. He selected the lowest gear ratio and then gently started to pull the wreckage away from the front steps of his home. Dillon shivered at the icy breeze and flakes of snow peppering through the open side window. He eased back on the accelerator, the twisted, buckled metal of the Mercedes groaned as he dragged it over the frozen ground and then he stopped suddenly.

Dillon got out and unhitched the tow-wire, reversed around the Mercedes and shunted it into the mouth of the lane and exiting Dillon's own private domain. The front of the Merc was smashed to oblivion; no headlights, no grille, only an exposed engine bay and a badly leaking radiator. Dillon went back to the Range Rover, eyes scanning the battered and hole riddled bodywork. The windscreen and driver's side window had been smashed, a headlight shattered and bullet holes had peppered the bodywork. The rear of the vehicle was okay, and Dillon climbed in and started the engine. The powerful turbo diesel kicked into life, fumes pluming from the exhaust pipe. Dillon eased it into drive - then drove away from the castle and out onto the snowbound road. The 4x4 ran reasonably well, only the excessive wind noise from the open windows betraying its recent abuse. Dillon turned the vehicle off the road and into the entrance of a field, turned, and drove straight back to the castle, revelling in the power of the damaged luxury motor.

Satisfied that the Range Rover would be able bodied to use if the need arose, he parked the 4x4 out of sight. The central locking system was inoperative - probably a stray bullet. He pocketed the keys and walked back to the Land Rover, he shunted the Merc further into the lane, completely blocking the only visible access to Dillon's property. He drove the Land Rover back through the arch and parked it inside the garage, locked the doors, and limped back to the large beech tree. Staring down at the would-be Assassin; he saw properly for the first time, just how big he was, much bigger than Dillon and quite fearsome-looking. He was dark-skinned, almost Arabic in appearance. He had a thick black moustache, and was looking up at him in immense pain - Dillon gazed down at the man - not compassionately - not with any feeling or emotion at all. His nose was well and truly broken and the wires that Dillon had tied around his wrists and ankles were biting deep into his flesh. Dillon crouched down. "Who are you?"

The man's eyes narrowed, the gaze hardened.

"Were you sent here to kill Tatiana, or me?"

Silence. He continued to stare blankly at Dillon.

Dillon's fist slammed into the man's already broken nose, and he screamed, saliva and blood drooling from his mouth. His head fell forward, and then lifted slowly to stare at Dillon. He spat into Dillon's face and grinned nastily, deep red staining his teeth.

"If that's the way you want it old son." Dillon whispered, wiping blood from his face.

Dillon grabbed the collar of the man's jacket and dragged him across the frozen lawn and down towards the loch, wailing and attempting to kick out. He had to stop halfway to get his breath back, but moved on a moment later and dragged the man the final distance to the water's edge. He took another length of wire from his pocket and tied it around a sturdy looking tree trunk, then attached the other end to the man's ankles with the same over-zealousness as before. He crouched down and said, "Now you listen and you listen good, you piece of scum. By the morning you will be frozen dead. But, I'm not unreasonable. I'll be back in a while, so I hope that the time you're going to spend by this magnificent lake will enable you to reflect on the error of your ways."

Dillon limped back to the warmth of the castle's interior and Tatiana. He slumped down by her side. Her breathing was deep, her colour had returned to normal. He threw a few more logs onto the fire, and armed the house security defences with the wireless remote control, and then went and slumped in one of the leather easy chairs opposite Tatiana. His head suddenly felt heavy and every bone in his body ached from the recent beating, he wearily flicked on the TV. Keeping the sound low, he watched without interest as images danced in front of him. Dillon hated the TV; it was brain numbing. But he acknowledged that it had its uses as he flicked through the news channels, eyes searching, brain working overtime even though he was almost falling asleep.

And then he saw it, like some incredibly bad coincidence...

The camera panned through one hundred and eighty degrees, showing in graphic detail the destruction and carnage in London, sweeping across the explosions' ground-zero where Scorpion HQ had once nestled in its secret enclave. Dillon wasn't interested in the reporters hysterical sensationalism, because he didn't need to hear his commentary, and he did not care what the man had to say; instead his widened eyes watched the amateur camera-phone footage, taken from a London Eye pod. The sudden rush of smoke, followed by chunks of concrete, twisted pieces of steel, and millions of fragments of glass emanating from the small nuclear device that had erupted hundreds of feet below the ground. The instant annihilation of every building and life-form within its effective striking distance of one hundred metres. Then came the small mushroom shaped cloud that rose up into the darkened sky.

Dillon remained sitting, totally shocked, and rubbing his eyes. What the hell is going on, screamed his confused mind? He pulled out the Ferran & Cardini mobile smart-phone; the screen was lifeless; except for a network error message. Not surprising as the network it was linked to, had just been vaporised in a single violent act of terrorism.

Dillon was suddenly thirsty, the game was getting bigger, the stakes getting higher, the unknown enemy becoming nastier.

The alter-ego that slept deep within Dillon's sub-conscious surged to the forefront of his brain like a black brooding monster emerging from the deepest darkest depths of the ocean. *"I've had enough of this shit, playing by somebody else's rules,"* snapped the voice inside Dillon's head.

"You're not the only one," Dillon's tone was gruff and thoroughly hacked-off.

For a while he dozed, drifting in uneasy sleep. When he awoke with a start the fire was still glowing warmly, but outside he could only see pitch-black, highlighted by the heavy snow drifting up the window panes. Dillon looked over at Tatiana. She was still sleeping deeply, her breathing regular. He checked the sterile dressings, and replaced them with fresh ones. Dillon poured himself a large tumbler of single malt whiskey, and re-took his seat opposite Tatiana, sipping at the smooth fiery amber liquid and staring into her face. She looked so serene, her skin so young looking.

And yet he would have to wake her shortly; not knowing if, or when, more Assassins would be sent after them? Highly trained and intent on murder?

He got up and went and knelt beside her, pushing some stray hair from her forehead. She murmured in her sleep, Dillon stroked her cheek, enjoying the warm flushed skin under his fingers; his mood had shifted to one of reminiscence, of years gone by. This was only moderated by the hard outer casing of the Glock against the small of his back.

More of them will come, he thought.

They will already know that they failed.

Tatiana moaned in her drug induced sleep; she turned, sighing, then her face twisted in pain - stitches pulling tight. She coughed, settling back against the cushions. Dillon held back from waking her, to question her. She had lost a lot of blood, was weak from her ordeal and injuries, the shock of what had happened to her. She needed to rest... but not for long. They had to leave; and leave soon. How long did they have? Twelve hours? Thirty minutes? Dillon caressed the Glock.

He would be waiting.

And he would be ready.

F&CI Com-intercept. Transcript of recent Reuter's news article.

Sources within the Kremlin have confirmed that two Russian nuclear-powered submarines have gone missing.

These long-range underwater vessels were both armed with the latest nuclear warheads when they went missing while on training manoeuvres in the Barents Sea. Early reports indicate that five surveillance satellites were overhead at the precise time the submarines vanished.

A rescue operation led by military craft in the immediate area was ordered, and since the disappearance of the subs, three high-speed search and seek submersible drones have been searching the deep water at the last known fixed position, but with no success.

The leaders of many countries have already been in contact with the Kremlin to offer their support during this tragic time...

Chapter 8

The small launch cut a foaming wake through the black water of the harbour, the deck rolling gently beneath his sandals. He stood looking back towards the shore as the wind caressed his long curled hair and thick beard, he could see the darkened buildings of the harbour side, embraced by the heat of a tropical summer. Seagulls flapped and squawked, like squabbling children, around the fishing boats as dusk descended upon this exotic part of the world.

A lone eagle soared high above the shoreline, backlit by the full moon, searching out its next prey. The one-hundred and fifty foot black twin hull stealth cruiser sat rocking gently in the deep calm waters of the bay. The eagle dived and disappeared beneath the trees.

The launch reached the stealth ship, bumping against the rubberised hull. The access door slid back and the man stepped up and into the vessel. He moved through the gloom and reached the watertight door, heavy steel, and it swung open on well-oiled hinges. Giving a final look over his shoulder towards the access door and the freedom of the ocean beyond - he was now trapped with nowhere to run...

Ducking to enter the confines of the ship's lower corridor, he moved up the broad steps, his silver tipped walking cane clicking as he made his way through the ship; his limp even more pronounced on the mesh walk-ways.

Despite his age of sixty-five, he was still an imposing figure of a man, huge and tanned, his head covered in traditional Middle Eastern head-wear, his face hidden under the large grey-streaked beard.

Moving down the corridor, he paused as he reached another door; he wanted to enter, *needed* to enter, and yet still he hesitated. He considered knocking, but realised it was not necessary... Ramus already knew he was there.

He pushed, and the heavy door swung inwards.

He stepped forward, into a room of low atmospheric lighting, that was pure opulence; fitted furniture of the highest quality and an array of high-tech computer equipment, and wood-panelling; long rows of unevenly sized books lining the walls and through a tiny porthole the last remnants of daylight spilled in. The room was awash with warm light and colour. Strategically placed throughout the space was some extremely high-tech equipment; binary codes flickered on the High Definition monitor screens, except for one, which remained black. Reminding the man of the darkness, that will fill and consume the new world.

"Ramus?"

"I am here, my old friend." A figure was standing beside a stack of old leather-bound books; tall and thin, the suit he was wearing, hand-made of the finest cloth that money can buy and concealing an ever present Browning automatic. The voice was rich, had strength and an almost melodious tone.

"Come my friend - speak - we are completely alone for the moment."

"They have failed," said the big bearded man in Arabic. "We thought that he might have gone soft after nearly a year and a half out of Ferran & Cardini. We thought him an easy target; retired, lacking rigorous and regular training."

"Even after the events in Cornwall with... Kirill?"

"He was merely lucky."

"Your naivety astounds me. You placed him low on the list of priority terminations, when in fact he should have been at the very top." The smooth voice had a razor sharp edge to it and the bearded man shivered.

"What would you have me do?" Came, the deep voice of the Arab. The voice was starting to crack under the immense pressure. His cane remained firmly at his side, as he waited for a response from Ramus. Who used this to his advantage, allowing the silence to build up the tension. He knew the other man well, knew his fear was a tangible thing, physical, an aura which surrounded him like a cloud.

"Send in just one Assassin, but this time, make sure that it knows just how dangerous the quarry is," came the soft voice.

"Why? What makes just one so special?"

"There is an elite group who are waiting for such an opportunity to demonstrate their unique abilities. Sending just one to our friend Dillon in Scotland, will reap success this time. And don't forget, these very special individuals who share our ideals, have been waiting patiently for many years, preparing - harbouring their grudges - for a war! Soon this stealth ship will be at the centre of our activities... Yes, my friend you are living through exciting times of immense change - on a global scale. The likes of which, no-one has ever seen before and it is good for you that you are a part of this - integral, shall we say."

The Arab gazed at the suited figure in front of him, seeing the smile, the show of teeth. His mouth was dry, his eyes filled with tears. His knuckles were white where they gripped the silver-tipped walking cane.

"You may go," said Ramus softly.

The large man turned, and stepped out from this private room deep within the heart of the stealth ship - Ramus listened intently as the walking cane clicked down the corridor, the noise finally disappearing into the bowels of this vast vessel.

The stealth ship rocked gently on eddies of sea current that caressed her twin prow and black flanks, and the moonlight shimmered across her decks, which were deserted and motionless.

Seagulls cawed outside the room's porthole as Ramus stood gazing out across the bay and cold eyes glittered in the mixed light of the room and the moonlight. A hand stretched out and opened the porthole, allowing the sultry South American night air to invade his air-conditioned sanctuary.

Pain gripped him, but only for the briefest of seconds. As his twisted face returned to calm, he drank from the tumbler the last remnants of brandy that burned all the way down to the pit of his stomach. "Soon, Mr Dillon - very soon..." came the soft words.

* * *

He stirred the coffee slowly, the headache crashing against the shores of his mind and leaving him battered and bruised. Dillon carried the coffee through to the living room, knelt down in front of Tatiana and looked up into her eyes. She had sat up on the sofa, her face drawn, her eyes hooded. Every movement brought a little grimace of pain and Dillon sipped his coffee, drums thumping in his head, rippling across his temples.

"You okay?" Came Tatiana's voice, weakened, jagged, almost a whisper and unheard.

"Yeah, I'm fine." Dillon opened his mouth to speak again, and Tatiana whispered; "Shh," with a finger against her lips. She met Dillon's gaze. There were tears in her eyes and she smiled warmly at him.

"I'm very sorry for bringing such trouble to your life and home."

"They came for me," Dillon said slowly.

"Both of us, surely?" said Tatiana. Tears rolled down her cheeks, and she abruptly brushed them away. "Thank you for saving my life. I don't know what would have happened, if it hadn't been for you."

"You would be *dead* - that's what would have happened, my lovely." Dillon said matter of factly.

Tatiana coughed, her face a grimace, her hand coming up to the sterile dressing covering the stitched bullet wound in her shoulder; she smiled wryly.

"You are a brave strong and honourable man, Jake Dillon. I have come up to this God forsaken place in the middle of nowhere, to warn you." She laughed softly. "Your life is in grave danger... Yes, I know, a little bit too late." Her gaze met Dillon.

"You do know that Scorpion HQ has been completely annihilated?"

Tatiana's eyes went wide. "Scorpion HQ... are you sure?"

"It was on the TV news; and part of Alix's encrypted message first thing when he came to visit was how the British Government had sanctioned Scorpion to assemble a strike task unit with the sole function of searching out major terrorists and assassinating them. How's that for a coincidence? And now the whole Scorpion headquarters is - gone!"

"Completely destroyed?" Her voice was a hushed whisper. "How?"

"The media is speculating that it was a Weapon of Mass Destruction, possibly a small nuclear device. There's nothing left. The images on the TV left little doubt in my mind that it was a nuke warhead."

"So LJ was right, after all." She whispered, horror lining her face like battle scars.

"Right about what?"

"This is even bigger than he imagined."

"What the fuck are you twittering on about?" Dillon's patience had run out...

The fire crackled. Dillon finished his coffee, and Tatiana, head bowed, deep in thought, looked up, her face pale, lips trembling.

"Listen, we need to leave here, Dillon... We need to get as far away from here as fast as we can. They will come - they will come soon!"

"If we move you now, the wound might start bleeding again. Then you could die."

"That's a chance I'll have to take, Dillon. Because if we stay here, we'll both die."

Dillon smiled, and then it turned to a nasty grin. "They will have to send a legion of killers," he said the words softly, his hand brushed against the Glock and something stirred deep within his subconscious that made him shudder with the anticipation of dealing out death.

"You're not listening, Dillon," said Tatiana sadly. Her hand reached out, stroking Dillon's cheek. "If LJ is right, and his informant is telling the truth, then they will send Assassins."

"Assassins? You mean like those sent to Cornwall to kill me?"

"No - these will be very different. All I know is that Scorpion had always known that a secret society of killers existed. It was thought that they had been destroyed a long time ago, and that the society had simply faded into obscurity. But it would appear that these ruthless killers are very much active, and linked with terrorist groups around the planet, paid for by the major drug cartels in Latin America. They have... somehow *returned*." The word hung in the air like a bad smell.

"Why is this happening to me?" Dillon's voice was cold as reality sunk in and he remembered what Alix had thought was happening to the Scorpion units. They were being assassinated, one-by-one... The possibility that this was happening passed like a chilling breeze over his soul, the certainty walked like a grim-reaper over his grave.

"You remember professor Kirill?"

"How could I ever forget him?"

"The partners of Ferran & Cardini believe that what took place in Cornwall was all about Kirill, and that it was the work of a group of individuals who are involved in terrorism, extortion, murder and just about anything that goes against the establishment. You think of me as your ex, and also as a tactical liaison officer between Ferran & Cardini and Scorpion - but appearances can be deceiving, Dillon, very deceiving."

Dillon met her gaze.

Tatiana licked her lips.

"My role at Ferran & Cardini has always been a *façade* for the work that I actually undertake on behalf of HM Government. I am part of a Government department that has no name and are accountable to no-one except the Prime Minister. We work within the Scorpion network to root out and eliminate anyone who co-operates with terrorists. We look for the enemy - we find them - we erase them. Permanently." She sighed.

"You're the bloody secret service?"

"Something like that," said Tatiana, smiling wearily. "But the enemy has hit hard and fast; we had only just discovered that Kirill was one of them... Our intelligence source was reliable, but we never thought that they were anywhere near ready to make their move... I unknowingly sent you on an assignment that could have led you to your death - but thank God you survived. Others were not so fortunate."

"And Kirill?" Dillon's voice was as cold as Arctic ice.

"Kirill is one of the group; as is another man known to us, Ramus. We think that they've struck now because Kirill's new Chimera Programme is almost ready, and with its awesome power they can use it to take over virtually every banking and governmental computer installation, satellites, and God knows what else. It is so powerful, Dillon - I can't even start to explain just how dangerous this software could be in the wrong hands."

"But I don't understand," said Dillon softly. "Why have virtually all of the Scorpion units being assassinated? And why has Scorpion HQ been destroyed? After all, no-one ever knew the exact location of the units and HQ was one of the Government's best kept secrets. I thought that Kirill was a good man?"

"This group, headed by Ramus and Kirill - believe that both the British Government and the current American administration to be weak, corrupt and riddled with decay and complacency. They also believe that Scorpion had become far too powerful - financed, controlled, governed by the upper-most echelon of the House of Commons and Lords. We both know that Scorpion was never meant to be like that - it was supposed to stand alone, incorruptible and untouchable. A worldwide organisation feared by terrorists and organised crime syndicates alike. Ramus and Kirill think that with Scorpion out of the way - they can rule the world. They think that they are way above the law of the land - any land. With Kirill's new Chimera Programme and the Assassins, they think they can bring down anyone - governments, banking, absolutely anyone they choose. Their beliefs are firmly rooted in the Illuminati, and their vision is to bring global peace... a New World Order... but..."

"The but is, that they will have to fight a pretty big war," Dillon snapped. "Before their New World Order can be achieved, there will come death, and lots of it. We've both encountered a few psychopathic egomaniacs in our time, and some, who have been involved with the Illuminati. Evil bastards, every one of them."

Tatiana nodded.

"We definitely need to get the hell out of here, Dillon; they will be coming for us even as we speak."

"Yes."

Dillon leaned towards her and kissed her gently on the lips. "We do need to get the fuck away from here, and there is only one person I can think of, one person who has the resources and the considerable knowledge to be able to help us."

Tatiana pulled back a little, her stare meeting Dillon's. "No," she said, shaking her head.

"Yes," said Dillon. "The world as we know it is about to be torn apart, Tats. The British Government will not know how to combat this threat when it breaks, and with Scorpion HQ destroyed, we have to assume that there are no operational units left either, except for Alix and Lola. Ezra used to be the one who Kirill went to for inspiration and advice. If anybody knows what Ramus and Kirill are up to and where they are, then it is Ezra. If we can find them, then we can find the server location of the Chimera programme and destroy it. At least that will even the odds up - and if we can take out Ramus and Kirill on the way, then so be it. Ezra is going to point the way to Chimera, and the bastards who want to abuse the trust and power that has been given to them."

"Dillon. We simply can't go to Ezra," said Tatiana.

"But he's the only one who knows!" hissed Dillon.

"Yes, but he's also a suspect, he could even be involved with Kirill and Ramus, which is why he is under twenty-four hour surveillance by the security services. To meet with him - would mean our death."

Dillon stood up. He withdrew the 9mm Glock, checked the magazine, and rammed it back home as he looked up and took a deep breath. "If Ezra is batting for the other side, the only death will be his own," said Dillon with grim finality.

* * *

Dillon had cleaned and re-dressed Tatiana's wounds. Her face was incredibly pale and Dillon helped her to dress, wincing with her in her pain as she struggled into fresh clothes.

"Tell me what you know of these Assassins that will be sent?"

Tatiana shrugged. "All I know, Jake, is that Ramus has them and that they have the same extreme skill and ruthlessness as their ancient predecessors - some say that they derive these abilities from a drug induced hypnosis. Which is ironic as the term assassin is derived from the Arabic and translates literally as *hashish-eater*, or one addicted to hashish. There is one Assassin who is supposed to be the teacher, or master of all others - no one knows who it is, because they all dress in the same black skin-hugging outfits that are hooded. Even the eyes are concealed behind dark lenses that must act as image intensifiers and night vision. But this one took out an entire Scorpion squad."

"Alone?"

"Oh yes, alone."

"Without any help whatsoever?"

Tatiana nodded. "That's what the MI6 encrypted files stated, when I read them prior to driving all the way up to this dissolute dump of a place to warn you, and to ask for your help. This thing is escalating and is totally out of control."

"The last time you asked for my help, Tats, I almost got myself killed. I'll go and get the hardware, check the surveillance monitors and arm the perimeter weapon systems. That'll just leave time to throw a few things into a holdall, and then we can get the hell out of here. Anything you need?"

"Just my overnight bag, thanks."

Dillon smiled. "Okay, I'll go grab it out of what's left of your Merc." He turned his back on Tatiana and walked out of the room, across the great hall and to his study beyond and the estate's monitoring system. He could sense her gaze boring into his back.

"Dillon?"

He stopped midway through the great hall. Turned.

"I still love you."

"Really?"

Tatiana nodded. "Really."

Dillon smiled warmly. "Get your ass in gear. We leave in five minutes."

* * *

Dillon stared with a heavy frown at the row of computer monitor screens.

Something was amiss.

Badly amiss.

Something was happening.

There was silence in the castle, apart from the distant ticking of a clock. Dillon watched the screens. A light started to flash, blinking with a proximity warning. By the north shore of the loch. Dillon activated the digital video cameras; fresh snow greeted him. And then he felt it... ...a ripple of a shockwave from the explosive device. Dillon felt a cold trickle of sweat run down his spine as the PCs instantly shut down... followed a second later by the lights to the whole castle. Everything was plunged into a murky half-light, long shadows being cast by a fine Scottish dawn. The computer cooling fans whirred to a halt.

"Bollocks." Dillon shot across the great hall at a sprint.

"What's happened?" Asked Tatiana.

"The main power has gone. And the back-up generators haven't cut in automatically as they should have."

"Give me a gun," said Tatiana.

Dillon unzipped the holdall and pulled out a Walther PPK from his personal armoury, and tossed her the black automatic. He drew a narrow knife from a hidden sheaf sewn into the lining in his jacket, then slid it carefully back. It always felt good to know he had this old friend as a back-up. Dillon moved to the window, and staying out of sight, scanned the area outside for any movement.

"What now, Jake?" Asked Tatiana

"We get as far away from this place as we can. It's too dangerous to stay here."

"You believe me now?"

Dillon picked up the Landrover keys from a side table, and put them into his jacket pocket. "All I know is that it takes a hell of a lot of tech-knowledge and know-how to knock out the type of sophisticated monitoring set-up and the three-stage back-up generators that I have here. And at the same time remain virtually undetected."

"Did your system pick up anything before it went down?"

"North shore of the loch."

"Don't trust your sensors - trust your instincts. The Assassin is out there, and is most likely much closer..."

Dillon shivered, and flicked the safety off the Glock. He moved back out into the great hall and positioned himself in the shadows... a good place to defend, he thought. He knew the building intimately - but to cut and run now? To use the half-light of dawn?

Dangerous and extremely foolhardy. He had no idea who was outside, or how many of them there were. Most importantly - he had no idea where they were.

We should have left hours ago, under the cover of darkness, he thought.

These lost hours could be the death of us.

He calmed his breathing. He forced his heart rate to slow. He blinked a number of times and licked his lips, then walked back into the living room and moved to the side of the window and peered outside and into the snow covered landscape.

Nothing.

Entry point? he mused.

The front door - unless the Assassin was high up on the roof?

Dillon's instincts told him that the Assassin was already inside the castle walls - every nerve ending in his body tingled with anticipation, and then he felt the breeze wash across his soul, like a ghost seeping deep into his bones. His head snapped around. The shadow moved quickly at the head of the wide staircase.

As his arm came up, he slid the safety off the Glock, and squeezed of three rounds in rapid succession. Bullets screamed, smashing into the landing wall and spitting sparks from the metal shields mounted on the granite. Dillon moved quickly, keeping low as he rolled across the open doorway to the other side of the living room, he dropped to one knee and glanced sideways.

"Tut tut, Mr Dillon. That was an erratic move, at best," came an emotionless voice. The tone was curiously flat and Dillon blinked sweat from his eyes and tried to pinpoint the voice. He moved slowly sideways, the Glock a close extension of his body - until he was crouched beside Tatiana, who was laying on her belly behind one of the large leather antique sofas - an automatic reaction, to get out of sight, and to minimise being hit by the gunfire.

With the gun still outstretched, he reached down with his free hand and handed her the keys to the Landrover. He pressed them deep against her palm and she nodded an acknowledgement.

They moved together, out into the great hall, keeping low and using the shadows for concealment. Towards a secret door in the oak panelling, that would lead them through a narrow passageway out into the snow.

A movement.

Dillon opened fire.

Bullets howled across the magnificent open space, slamming into the door on the other side, and wood splintering in all directions, the Glock kicking in Dillon's hand with each round fired, right up to the point when the only sound was that of an empty magazine and the dead-man's click...

The black clad figure sprang at him from out of the shadows and he instinctively ducked sideways, twisting to the right; the figure landed lightly and - without time to re-load a new mag Dillon thrust the Glock in its holster, and at the same time was close enough to reach under a long oak table and rip-off the masking-tape securing a Beretta from its hiding position under the top.

A kick came from behind, smashed into his back with such force that he was thrust violently forward, toppling over the back of a chair and landing in a heap, unable to breath, eyes wide, pain searing through his torso.

The figure leaped again with incredible speed and agility.

Dillon spun, was on his feet, leaping to meet the Assassin head on; they collided and Dillon's hands grasped spandex clothing and his head smashed forward, connecting with flesh and bone. They both hit the ground and Dillon threw a heavy punch to the figure's kidneys, then another and another - there was a deep grunt, they rolled twice into the middle of the great hall, and then the figure was - gone!

Dillon scrambled up as the soft leather of a boot slammed into his ribs, but his hands found their mark around the Assassin's foot and he twisted hard, flipping the figure over. Instead of landing heavily, the Assassin spun like a gymnast and grabbed Dillon with both arms. They were both thrust backwards and ended up against the heavy front door in a tangle of limbs. Dillon kicked the figure hard behind the knee, sprang up and wrenched open the door with both hands.

Outside, Dillon started down the front steps, and was instantly flung forward into the snow, tasting blood.

The Assassin rolled, coming up in a rigid poised crouch.

A cold wind blew off the loch, ruffling hair, cooling skin.

Dillon blocked, and backed away, shaking his head to clear the fuzziness. Blood was running freely down over his cheek. He grimaced, realising that he had a long gash over his right eye. He felt his bones crunching, *age was creeping up on him*, but he was careful to show no reaction, no indication of injury.

The black clad figure circled.

Dillon caught the shocked face of Tatiana to the left. Get in the fucking Landrover, his brain screamed, why don't you get in the damned car, just get in the car? He watched her level the gun and fire off two shots, but even at that distance he could see her hand shaking...

Powder snow kicked up and bullets whined.

Dillon calmed his breathing. The Beretta was still in his pocket, and he now had to *focus*.

The Assassin approached. The figure was of slim build, tall, clad entirely in black and wearing a black balaclava. Tight black boots were on the Assassin's feet.

Dillon could see no visible weapons.

The Assassin launched forward - Dillon blocked a series of four punches, dropped low and delivered a powerful left hook to the Assassin's jaw; he stepped in close, and was kicked hard in the chest, sending him scrabbling backwards gasping for breath, hands and arms held in front of him defensively.

Dillon's mind was racing, thinking of his next move, all the time aware that the a Assassin was much faster and more agile than he was.

The attacker leaped; instantly Dillon twisted and rolled to his right, hooking his left foot in a wide arc, and as the Assassin landed, knocking him or her off its feet. The figure landed heavily on its back, instantly sprang back into a standing position, and charged.

Blows were exchanged left and right. Dillon blocked, received another kick to the chest and a series of rapid punches that sent him spinning into the snow. He tasted blood and looked down at the frozen ground, which was suddenly cool and soothing to the bruised and battered flesh of his face. It would be so easy, so easy to lay there and never get up again...

Dillon tried to get up, but his body screamed at him. A rainbow of colours flashed before his eyes.

He pushed, heaved, but finally fell back onto the snow exhausted.

Behind, he heard the Assassin approach, soft crunching footsteps on the snow, but he did not have the strength, could not move, could not bring himself to turn, to roll over.

Was this it, the end…?

He could do nothing… his body was not responding…

"Fight, Dillon, fight. Don't let this fucker kill you like this…" Dillon's subconscious screamed from the dark recess of his mind.

But Dillon was unable to move.

Chapter 9

The small chapel at the university stood some fifty metres from the west wing, half obscured by a circle of speckle leafed bushes. Its early history and the date of when it was built were unrecorded but it was certainly older than the university, a single plain rectangular cell with a stone alter under the eastern window. There was no means of lighting except by candles and a wooden box of these was on a chair to the right of the door, together with an assortment of candlesticks, many wooden, which looked like discards from ancient kitchens. Since no matches were provided, the casual improvident visitor had to make his or her devotions, if any, without the benefit of their light. The cross on the alter was of carved oak, perhaps by a local carpenter either in obedience to orders or under some private compulsion of piety or religious affirmation. Except for the cross, the alter was bare. The chapel was a cold place. The polished limestone floors were buffed to an age old shine by decades of worship. The walls were of a simple white-washed plaster, the roof an elaborate show of exposed oak rafters and cross beams. Rows of pews that were steeped in antiquity and worn by the presence of praying worshippers, were arranged traditionally one behind another.

Outside the early morning sunshine spilled light through the stained-glass window directly behind the pulpit. A cool breeze drifted down the aisles, between the pews, between those worshippers who attended when they felt the need for the company of God. They were gathered in silent prayer in the small chapel, while the university's church was undergoing extensive restoration.

The Priest knelt by the alter, his hands clasped together in prayer. He was a tall man; some would say skinny, beneath thick curly ginger hair, wearing casual clothes and a tweed jacket that had leather patches on each elbow. His eyes were tightly closed in this act of prayer. His face calm, almost serene, bathed in the coloured light filtering in through the stained glass window. By his side, sat his Bible, the Priest's most prized possession, it was a small leather-bound edition with wafer-thin pages that were edged in gold. And, this man would willingly die for this little book.

The Priest was fully aware of the people around him and he

felt privileged to be a part of their faith and to worship alongside them. They were all there to commune with the Lord and to receive his blessing. The Priest sighed; this was as close to contentment as it could get.

Footsteps.

Something stirred inside him; something ate at the Priest's karma like carrion pulling-over a rotting carcass.

The footsteps approached slowly, calculated, with care. The sound struck a discordant note in the Priest's soul.

The Priest continued to pray, keeping his head bowed; he heard the sound of the other worshippers hurriedly leaving the small university chapel and he knew that this intruder was not friendly even before any words had been spoken or actions taken. He knew that this was the enemy.

"Lord, protect me against the dark forces of evil," said the Priest suddenly, his voice loud with the clarity of polished glass, booming around the near-empty chapel. "For I am your obedient servant, Lord. Amen."

The Priest climbed slowly to his feet. His hand reached down, closed over the small leather bound Bible, and placed the book in the pocket of his jacket. It was then, that he raised his eyes and looked straight at the intruder who now stood in front of him.

The man was tall, had a lean physique with a full beard and cropped black hair, wearing a black suit; his eyes were of the brightest blue that watched the priest warily, the stare drilling into his mind with pure hatred.

The Priest stood perfectly still, surveying the man.

"You are not welcome in God's house," he said, his words soft, steady. "This is a place of worship; peace and love."

"I am here to kill you, Priest." The man took a step backwards, his gloved hands making fists in anticipation. The blue eyes constantly fixed on the Priest and his moss green eyes slightly blood-shot noted the killer's stance and assortment of concealed weapons; the fluid flow of movement.

"What creature from hell are you, who dare to enter God's holy ground? I would liken you to vermin; I would say that you are infidel in God's house; I would say that you need to leave before the wrath of God strikes you down."

The Priest waited, arms folded across his chest.

The killer attacked.

* * *

The police patrol car drove through the roads of the University City. The officer at the wheel of the Ford Focus drove at speed, using his blue light at junctions and traffic lights; overtaking other motorists with only inches to spare as he raced towards his call.

He approached the university, went through the main gates; and could see a small group of people gathered outside the chapel. As the Ford neared they spread out, he parked the car and stepped out into the crowd.

A group of four older ladies stood huddled outside behind a man carrying a brown leather briefcase. They were all peering at the door of the chapel as the rotund older police officer came towards them.

"Come along now, people, stand back, let me through" barked sergeant Pat Crocker.

"There was gunfire!" said one frightened lady, her handbag clutched tightly to her coat. Her eyes held a haunted quality - she had been one of the worshippers, who had left hurriedly.

The man carrying the brown leather briefcase stepped forward, and immediately introduced himself as one off the university dons. "I didn't know if I should have gone in to check on the Priest?" He looked relieved that the Sergeant had arrived. "Lucky to get here so soon, Sergeant!"

"Definitely not a good idea, sir. Whoever fired those shots could still be in there."

The Sergeant cursed under his breath. Firearms! He spoke into his radio, asking the estimated time of arrival of the firearms unit. A moment later a BMW pulled-up and three SO19 officers climbed out of the Armed Response Vehicle. All three officers were heavily armed, carrying; Glock 17, 9mm automatics, Benelli M3 Super 90 12-guage shotguns, and Heckler & Koch MP5 sub-machine pistols.

"You are positive it was gunshots you heard?" The Sergeant asked the man, as the SO19 officers strode towards them.

"Oh yes. We all heard them. No mistaking, Sergeant."

The SO19 lead officer stepped forward towards the heavy oak door, knarled and stained with the passing of time. He reached, turning the rusting iron handle. The other two officers had gone around to the back door and were mirroring his actions.

The Sergeant stood back looking on with the small crowd. A

shiver ran through his body as a cold wind caressed him.

The lead SO19 officer knew; could feel that death was waiting for him inside the chapel. And then with a great act of courage, he stepped through the portal alone, his MP5 sub-machine gun clasped firmly in black gloved hands.

* * *

The Priest stood, hands in pockets, staring down at the dead Assassin. He had been tossed across the chapel; his head split open, like a melon, against unforgiving stone, tearing flesh and destroying bone. Blood seeping onto the aged flagstones, creating an interesting congealed crimson pool around the twisted broken corpse sprawled at the foot of the alter. The Assassin's unique custom-made, mini sub-machine pistol lay, black and evil, against the floor of the chapel. The stench of cordite hung heavy in the cool air, gun smoke drifting from the barrel. The Priest nudged the weapon with the toe of his shoe. Then, stepping carefully forward with a word or two of annoyance, he reached down and grabbed hold of the limp body. The head rolled slack, but incredibly, there was a groan of immense pain and the right eye that was still intact, opened. The Assassin's mouth moved wordlessly for a second or two and the Priest lifted the paralysed but miraculously living man up into a sitting position.

"Are you trying to repent for your heinous act of violence, my son?" He asked quietly.

"I... misjudged..." The Assassin's left eye hung by a thread, its socket disintegrated on impact. The dull right eye screamed hatred, and anger, and frustration. "I will not make the same mistake again."

"I fear you will not, my son." said the priest as kindly as he could. He suddenly slapped the Assassin hard across his face, and a grimaced sound of pain came forth with spittle and blood, erupting from the man's mouth. "Who sent you? And how did you know I was Ferran & Cardini?"

The Assassin's lips formed a firm line.

He remained silent - he was not going to speak.

"Come on, do yourself a favour and tell me. I can make that pain go away."

"I will tell you nothing, Priest." The voice was hoarse, laced with agony; the Priest sighed again, and holding the body upright with one hand he reached down and pulled out a custom-made flick-knife. The gleaming titanium handle had been made for the Priest's grip only, a sharp click, and the shining narrow six-inch blade appeared instantly. The razor sharp edge had been case-hardened to the highest standard - it was an evil weapon with only one obvious function: to kill.

"Are you absolutely sure, my son? Are you sure that you cannot share this information about these evil-doers for whom you work, with me? If not, then the Lord will deal with you through me, and as his loyal servant I must do his bidding to the best of my ability." The slender blade of the knife glinted in the last remnants of light filtering through the stained glass window.

"Fuck you."

The Priest raised the knife. Light gleamed from the blade; reflecting in the eye of the Assassin.

"Has God shown you the light yet, my son?"

The Assassin remained resolutely silent; instead he stared up with hatred.

"Then I must show you the error of your ways."

The blade came down and around with precision and practiced skill - a single swift cut to the throat. The Assassin gurgled one last time, blood sprayed in a long arc across one of the white-washed walls; and the priest cleaned his blade on the Assassin's clothing before allowing the dead body to topple and lie at his feet.

The Priest looked up, eyes narrowing. A figure moved into the chapel, cautiously; the priest retracted the blade and quietly replaced the flick-knife back into its hiding place. He smiled when he saw the black-clad figure of the SO19 senior officer moving towards him, HK MP5 steady in his gloved hands.

"Ah, the troops have arrived, just in time to save me."

The armed police officer removed his gas-mask and slung the MP5 over his shoulder. He stared down at the dead body, then up at the priest. "You killed him, Priest?"

"God works in mysterious ways, my son," said the Priest, with a kindly smile. "He was punished for his evil desecration of God's holy place of worship." The Priest gestured to the many bullet holes in the plaster and wood, across the stone, and the tiny holes in the stained glass window where fading light crept in.

"He certainly does. Shall I call in a clean-up team?" The stench of death and cordite was stinging his nostrils. The chapel - a place of love and worship - had become a charnel house.

"Best left to our people to deal with it," said the Priest calmly, and strode out into the fresh air.

* * *

The Kirill Government Research Establishment - Scottish Highlands. Steel and non-reflective glass interlocked within the very granite of this inhospitable part of the world, a massive complex that was not visible on the surface or from the air - but went ten levels *below*. A feat of engineering, and the Government's best kept secret.

Claudia Dax reclined back in the leather chair, and gazed out over the rugged mountain terrain on the monitor before her from within the depths of the underground complex; she watched the wind spin and whip the powder snow into a spiral of eddies, shifting and dancing, twisting as if possessed by demons. The Scottish Highlands. How Claudia loved and loathed this desolate region of Scotland; how it lived, a land of such diverse personalities, of such contrasts; a place of life and death; a place of beauty and a place of great ugliness, hardship and fear.

The Scottish Highlands - a *vast* rugged landscape of nature's hostility. A huge landscape of jagged rock, smashed into mercy by nature and her cold wet climate.

If Claudia tried, if she closed her eyes and *really* tried, she could imagine that she was somewhere tropical, smell the sun-tan cream, the surf breaking over the exotic coral reef. It had been too long since she had enjoyed the sea; far too long.

Claudia was considered the best in her field: she had passed her GCSEs at the age of ten; A-levels at the age of twelve. She had then been one of the youngest students to ever be accepted by Oxford University at the age of fourteen - by which time she had already achieved a degree with honours in computing through The Open University distance learning tutorials. By the time she arrived at Oxford, she was well on her way to graduating in advanced computer science and artificial intelligence. Artificial intelligence was just that - artificial. Scripted routines that were *scripted*...

Claudia Dax had pioneered a new school of thought: the concept of self-learn, self-teach, self-programme. The ability for the programme to *learn and actually adapt by altering its own core code*. To

111

possess *real* intelligence, instead of a being told by way of pre-written directional script.

Kirill had snapped Claudia up after the publication of her second paper. And now, aged twenty-six, Claudia was an incredibly wealthy young woman living a life of dreams in a secret location within the vast wilderness of the Scottish Highlands. Although, incredibly wealthy, it was nothing as vulgar as finance and money and *material possession* that kept her at Kirill's establishment - despite the desolation of the land: it was to do with her exceptionally competitive nature and her aspirations for the future. She could have chosen to work anywhere she wished: Berlin, the Bahamas, Washington - all had a particular lure for her sought-after programming genius. But Kirill was based in Scotland. And Kirill was at the very centre of all the important computing breakthroughs that were happening.

Claudia Dax *had* to be at the centre of that importance.

Otherwise, her rise to the pinnacle of her chosen field would have been for nothing.

She was sitting at the terminal, linked to seven servers and harnessing the processing power and speed of one hundred sub-processors. Her fingers blurred across the keyboard and then she paused, adjusting the settings of various programs and sub-routines that were running in the background. She was the creator of her current project - spotted the glitch even before the security scripts reported it; she adjusted the code and sat back as figures flickered across the screen. LED lights randomly flashed at her.

Claudia Dax rubbed her weary eyes, ran fingers through her auburn hair. She suddenly realised that she was incredibly hungry - and incredibly tired, although she accepted these were small discomforts in comparison to what had recently gone down at Scorpion HQ in London.

Scorpion HQ - vaporised.

She shivered, and closed down the external view on one of her monitors.

Claudia gazed through the tinted glass at the offices below her; most of the terminals were empty, she glanced up at the clock, surprised to see it was 8.30 p.m.

"Bloody hell," she said wearily. She had been working since 8 a.m. without a break, her concentration complete, and her focus intense and uninterruptible. Now her body and brain cried out for sustenance and she sighed to herself, climbing to her feet and stretching her perfectly formed athletic body. Her muscles ached and screamed for an intense gym workout.

Instead, she realised what she actually needed was a long cold beer. Very cold and very long.

She took the lift up to her private quarters - all the programmers employed at the highest level of security clearance were given the most luxurious living quarters two floors below ground level of the complex. This was one of the benefits, one of the perks, one of the *expectations* of working for Kirill's prestigious team. They were offered the best salaries, the most exotic holiday packages, numerous opportunities to work worldwide and the opportunity to work on the most exciting cutting edge projects with the most powerful computing hardware ever created.

And Claudia Dax was, quite literally, at the very top of the pile.

She stepped through the door into her apartment, stripped off her clothing and revelled in the feeling of the air-con on her skin. She walked barefoot and naked across the Italian Marble floor to the wet-room, as she stepped under the shower head, warm jets automatically started and she lightly soaped her tanned skin. She massaged shampoo into her dark auburn hair, washed it free and then stepping out, towelled herself dry.

Still naked, she crossed to the American fridge-freezer and pulled free a bottle of ice-cold beer. She flipped the cap, and took a long, well earned drink. Then she set about preparing a light salad... what with the recent worry and speculation surrounding the Scorpion network and the total destruction of its London Headquarters, satisfying her hunger had not been high on her list of priorities until just now.

She revelled in the uncomplicated task of preparing the salad; she enjoyed the simplicity of slicing the cucumber, the crunch of the lettuce as the blade cut through its heart, and the reward of arranging everything neatly on the plate after the brain draining mathematical calculations of an average day working on the Chimera Programme.

Claudia Dax was on her third beer when the comm. buzzed.

Picking up the wireless handset she hit the answer button.

"Yes, what do you want?"

"Sorry, Claudia. We have a problem with the Chimera Programme."

"What is the problem, this time?"

"The programme's chameleon mode has caught a cold. In turn, the self diagnostic script is showing signs of erratic behaviour."

"Damn. I'll be there in five."

The emotionless voice at the other end of the comm added:

"You don't have five minutes, Miss Dax. Get down here now, that's what you get paid such an exorbitant salary for. And, I would remind you that Professor Kirill is expecting Chimera to be glitch free in under seventy-six hours."

"Yeah, yeah, I understand and you don't need to fucking remind me of the countdown. I'll be down in five minutes."

She killed the comm. connection.

"Shit..." she muttered, forking a large amount of salad into her mouth and taking one more swig of beer. She tossed the empty bottle into the bin where it clashed against the other empties. She disappeared back into the bedroom, brain turning over possible reasons that could have caused such a catastrophic problem to occur... and all the time at the back of Claudia's mind was the nagging doubt about Scorpion, and what happened to their HQ - and about Ferran & Cardini International...

She did not see the flashing blue curser on her screen.

* * *

Claudia Dax loved the small hours.

The early hours of the morning when everything was quiet and still; when everyone else was sleeping; when the world appeared to be dead.

Claudia was often wide awake at this time; there were no distractions, she could think clearly...

And now: 3.30 a.m.

She lay on top of the duvet wearing her light cotton pyjamas, staring up at the ceiling. She rolled from the bed and stood for a moment. The air-conditioning whirring quietly in the background and she sighed, brain awash with binary codes, calculations and projections for the Chimera Programme. She smiled to herself, and then wandered, seemingly without purpose or direction, out of her apartment towards the lift.

Claudia gazed out through the three-sixty degree glass module as it descended silently. The doors opened.

Claudia Dax listened and with a sense of foreboding stepped, still in her pyjamas and bare feet, out onto the luxurious carpet, her whole body tingling with the audacity, the daring of her actions... to creep around on her own in a top security Government research establishment at night... naughty, very naughty...

She walked the corridors while virtually all of the other inhabitants of the complex slept, and after passing several security officers who merely nodded sedately at her presence, she moved stealthily to the unguarded air conditioning shaft leading up to ground level and the natural elements beyond. She raked her auburn hair back with both hands and slipped the elasticated band in place to make a pony-tail, stepped towards the ventilation grille, crouched down, and pulled it gently towards her. The grille came away easily, and as usual she was completely alone, as she made her way through the maze of tunnels...

She reached the exit at the rear of the ground-level complex. She produced a key and, without effort, overrode the electronic sentry software - after all, if her exceptional programming skill could not be used to her advantage sometimes...

Claudia stepped *outside*.

The cold highland night hit her as she took a few steps, revelling in the feel of the fresh air, the real world, the possible *danger* of being outside in her pyjamas in the Scottish Highlands. Knowing, that all around her, heavily armed guards were concealed at their posts. Part of her wondered if they could see her, and merely ignored her eccentricity, her need to be outside. Another part of her revelled in the feeling of breaking the rules. But, only so far... She couldn't go any further towards the perimeter or the guards would most certainly spot her and report the breach back to Kirill: personnel were only allowed out of the establishment with an armed escort. But she sometimes had to be completely alone, and to breathe the fresh mountain air, completely alone.

She gazed up at the star-filled sky for a long while, moonlight glinted across her slender figure, and she thought how lucky she was to have a body that many women would die for, and every man in the department fantasised over.

She patted her flat belly. "Still firm and strong," she sighed.

She stepped back into the artificial world, sliding the protective grille back into place and twisting the toggles to the locked position. She re-instated the security sentry programme and readjusted the log to how it was before her little jaunt outside. Digits flickered across the small screen and Claudia checked that she had not trodden in any debris from outside.

If only they knew, she thought.

A shiver ran up and down her spine; half in delight, half in fear.

Yes; she had been the best programmer and systems analyst - in her final year at Cambridge, possibly the best ever. But there had been something else; a chink deep inside her soul that led her to *hack*...

She found it easy, had honed her skills, and refined them to such a degree, that she had managed to computer rape some of the largest international computing organisations. She had cracked their supposedly unbreakable passwords, entered their databases and played with their files - just for a laugh... She always felt alive and turned-on by smashing their personnel files. The adrenalin rush she always got from fucking around with their finances was better than any drug induced high.

Claudia knew what drove her; knew that she had been born with a gift. But she hated - *loathed* - authority or anything which said, you will do it our way, and no other way... Her usual response to this was very simple... Well, you can all fuck off.

Claudia thought of herself as something of a cyber-freedom fighter - data protection? Nothing was safe in the twenty-first century. She wanted to open up the cans-of-worms that lurked beneath global organisations and governments. Find their dirtiest secrets and make them public on the Internet. She had the skill and knowledge to do this. To break the code of their digital locks and keys. She had the Chimera Programme at her fingertips...

Claudia smiled mischievously to herself.

Well, she had written the Chimera Programme script. Although no-one would ever know, because Kirill had already taken all of the credit for it himself. The British taxpayer had funded it, and Scorpion, under the watchful eye of GCHQ, had been conducting the field trials, which had looked promising to say the least. Chimera was capable of infiltrating any network - unseen. It could take control of any computer and override the system within seconds; hack world data banks; match the individual identities of every known major league organised crime criminal and global terrorist alike. Take control and utilise strategic military and spy satellites to coordinate ground, air and sea forces anywhere on the planet...

116

Chimera was the ultimate Artificial Intelligence - but it was more than that - it was constantly learning - constantly adapting - constantly changing...

Chimera gave the infected computer the ability to think, to possess the ability to know what was right, and what was wrong; feeding every piece of hidden data back to GCHQ. It would be the ultimate weapon against global terrorism, and the British would be at the forefront of this awesome new technology. Scorpion could conquer the ever growing terror of organised crime and drug cartels raising billions of dollars every year to fund the likes of al Qaeda, of gun runners and bomb makers, as well as Assassins...

Claudia shivered. She understood that the stakes were high; she had not really understood or taken on board the implications before the total wipe-out of Scorpion HQ in London. But now with the deaths of so many innocent people, she felt chilled to her core.

Claudia knew; this was no longer a game on a screen.

And that it had most likely never been.

Claudia walked back to the lift, and then, decided to drop by the central processor lab, snoop around, see what the automated machines were up to at this anti-social hour of the day. The machines were programmed to run routine operations during the small hours and so there was little fear of meeting anybody at this lonely time.

After descending to the lowest level, she trod silently through the carpeted corridors to the central lab. She stopped. She accessed the first Armourlite glass door and then as this closed, she was left standing in the airlock awaiting the second door to open - it was then that she saw her.

A tall figure...

Claudia Dax froze.

The young woman was motionless, standing near the machine that had the Chimera Programme loaded onto its hardrive.

Claudia stared for a long moment. No movement came from the woman and Claudia tried to meet her gaze, positive that she had been seen and yet aware that the woman gave no indication of having spotted her.

Claudia hadn't seen her before. Perhaps she was a new security officer, drafted in from London?

Or was she one of Kirill's own people? Sent to oversee the last few vital elements of the programme that would see it complete and fully operational...

Claudia sank slowly to the carpet and sat, hidden by the solid lower panels, wondering what she should now do. She crawled over to the door that had admitted her, and swiped her security pass. The door slid open silently and she crawled out into and along the corridor, turned the corner, then got to her feet and, with a smile and sigh of relief at her unbelievable luck, ran as fast as she could to the lift.

A few minutes later, she was back inside her apartment, pacing about her living space, a glass of Jack Daniels in her shaking hand, sipping it slowly and wondering what the tall athletic young woman had been up to; why had she been there?

Her heart was still pounding as she pondered the strange woman she had witnessed; black skin-tight cat suit, cut perfectly to every contour of her slender body, hair blond, cropped. The eyes of the palest blue. The woman had appeared relaxed yet, threatening... very, very threatening!

Claudia shivered, and sipped again at her drink.

Who was she?

Must have been drafted in as additional core security staff to watch over Chimera in the final stages of development. But what about all of the other security measures, weren't these good enough? Weren't the electrified razor wire fencing, the SAS trained guards, the bomb-proof concrete walls and armour plated sliding doors - enough to protect this planet changing programme?

The answer was of course - yes.

Claudia laughed softly, bitterly, to herself, as she stared out over the mountainous terrain through the wall-mounted fifty inch LCD flat-screen monitor.

Pondering her very strange and very near encounter, Claudia took another sip of the amber liquid, enjoying the smooth flavour. A word crept into the recesses of her mind; a word she had once heard spoken, when overhearing part of a conversation between Kirill and Ramus and one other, whom she did not know...

"*Assassin...*"

They had all stopped talking and turned to stare directly at her, when they had realised that she was working in the computer suite they had just walked in to. She apologised and had left the room immediately.

But now; the word seemed to come naturally to the fore-front of

118

Claudia's mind, from somewhere deep in the vaults of her remarkable memory. It seemed to fit into the scheme of personal bodyguards and enforcers...

Assassin. An Assassin. The Assassins? Was it just one, a dozen or many? No matter, because it always came down to one thing - killing.

A shiver ran through her body, realising that she had drunk a little too much, and then downed the rest of the whisky in one gulp.

She decided she would ask her friend and work colleague, Ed King in the morning. If anyone would know about new security measures being initiated, he would.

Yes, definitely a good idea; He was Kirill's assistant chief of security, and may even know about the Assassins.

Maybe.

Chapter 10

Dillon crashed down onto the frozen ground with his brain screaming anger-filled hatred, fuelling a re-renewed energy within him. His soul filled with cold detachment, like a giant's hand giving him a nasty squeeze... *"Fight,"* howled his sub-conscious alter-ego. But Dillon could not; for the briefest of seconds, he could not; it was as if he had an enormous flat slab of concrete pressing down on him. Without consciously knowing it, he reloaded the Glock with a fresh magazine by sense of touch in his jacket pocket as the footsteps came towards him, and his brain seized and the footsteps suddenly increased in pace and...

"Roll!" his brain screamed at him.

Dillon rolled, the Glock now in his hand and pumping bullets up into the air.

A kick sent the weapon spinning across the frozen ground.

Dillon curled his lip in a nasty smile. The promise of what was to come foremost in his mind...

A diesel engine started - the Landrover. The Assassin's head snapped right - Dillon leaped, arms latching on to the attacker's legs at thigh height, teeth sinking into soft flesh. The attacker screamed with intense pain, and instinctively fell backwards, dragging Dillon back down onto the frozen ground. Dillon twisted to the left, rolled once, and re-positioned himself to attack; he slammed both fists into the Assassin's face. One blow, two, three, four, and five. He felt, as well as heard, bone break under the balaclava.

The Landrover, pluming smoke, accelerated out through the archway from the courtyard.

Dillon staggered up.

The Assassin's foot lashed up into Dillon's groin and he stumbled back; the scene flashed red, there was a crunch of gravel as heavy off-road tyres skidded to a halt. Exhaust fumes spewing out like a dragon's breath.

Dillon looked up into the Assassin's face.

Black clad - unreadable...

But the eyes. The eyes were the bluest blue, and filled with hatred.

The figure stood, legs slightly spread, arms raised in classic karate style, waiting, to finish the job that it had been sent to carry out. Dillon scrambled to his feet and the eyes were solidly fixed on him, boring into his very being, and he grinned, a very nasty grin.

"You ready to die, ass-hole?"

"I have merely been toying with you, Mr Dillon. But no more."

Seemingly, from out of thin air; the Assassin produced a slender evil looking knife. The highly polished blade glinted menacingly in the early morning sunshine, and the Assassin lowered its head. Dillon managed to draw his own long bladed knife and spat blood into the snow.

"Well if that's the best you've got, then let the party begin. And you wanting to fight with knives... How fortunate."

The Land Rover's diesel engine revved, plumes of black smoke spewing out of the exhaust. Dillon could see Tatiana looking back over the seat; the white reverse light came on and Dillon understood...

The Assassin attacked.

Blades flashed and sparks flew as they engaged in this final clash.

Dillon drew back with blood weeping down his forearm. The smile fell from his lips, as he stared down at the sliced skin. They circled and Dillon edged the Assassin closer.

Dillon rushed forward - as Tatiana floored the Land Rover's accelerator and the engine roared loud. The Assassin came at Dillon, blade slashing left and right, and then turned - Dillon dived right.

The slab like back door of the Landrover hammered into the Assassin; the body was violently thrown backwards in a tangle of limbs to collide with a three hundred year old oak tree at the edge of the drive. The bloody knife fell to the frozen ground. The Assassin collapsed in a sprawling broken heap.

Dillon - breathing hard - looked slowly to the left at the knobbly off-road tyre merely four inches from his nose. He wearily dragged himself to his feet and glared at Tatiana's reflection in the side mirror.

"You almost killed me."

"But I didn't. Get in," she hissed, pain lining her face.

"Give me the Walther. I want to check our friend over there."

"Get *in!*" Tatiana screamed.

Dillon half turned and his jaw dropped in amazement and disbelief. The Assassin had survived, was leaning against the tree. Piercing blue eyes met Dillon's gaze, the balaclava hood had been discarded, and the bloodied face of a young blond haired woman confronted him. She sprinted forward at incredible speed over the frozen ground... Dillon dived, scooping up his Glock, and then dragged open the door and sprawled full length across the back seat of the Landrover as Tatiana hit the accelerator. Spitting snow, the 4x4 roared down the track, sliding left and right, bouncing over the potholes and shooting off down the lane.

Dillon stared out of the back window.

The Assassin was close behind, a gloved hand reached out, brushed against its right boot and Dillon couldn't believe what he was witnessing, the Land Rover's engine screamed and Tatiana's foot floored the accelerator pedal with an aggressive stab...

The Assassin slowed to a walk and then stopped, arms limp by her side, panting with the sudden explosive exertion, blue eyes holding Dillon's gaze.

"What is going on? How the fuck did she survive the impact, and how on earth did she manage to run like that?" said Dillon.

"Are you hurt?"

"Hurt, I'm way beyond hurting." He said. "How about you?"

"I'm bleeding again, and feeling just a little..."

Dillon felt the 4x4 swerve. He clambered over into the front seat, and helped Tatiana to bring the Landrover to a halt at the side of the road. Dillon swapped positions with Tatiana, and then handed her another sterile dressing, which she held against her re-opened shoulder wound as Dillon, hands sticky with his own blood, floored the powerful diesel engine and they sped off up the mountain road.

* * *

Dillon drove the Landrover hard and after twenty minutes left the relative safety of tarmac roads behind, off-road tyres kicking up loose powder snow once again, the Land Rover's diesel engine finding it easy in its natural environment. He found the narrow track, and drove into the wilderness. Finding a secluded gateway that was flanked on either side by dry-stone walling, he jumped out, leaving the engine running. He unlatched the heavy wooden five-bar field gate, and then stared into the distance at the brooding dark woods on the far side of the heather down. The howling of the wind made him shiver and, as he started back to the warmth of the Landrover's interior, large snowflakes began to fall heavily. He eased the 4x4 over woodland debris and killed the engine.

"Let's take a proper look at that wound."

Dillon helped Tatiana onto the rear seat and checked the reopened gunshot wound. Blood had clotted; the flow reduced to nothing more than a trickle now. Tatiana's face was ashen grey with pain.

"I'm sorry Tats. But we're all out of painkillers," said Dillon, stroking her hair.

"Don't worry about it," she said, smiling. She closed her eyes, and winced. Dillon eased himself out of his jacket with difficulty, his ribs clicking beneath his battered and bruised flesh with every movement. He checked the various knife wounds on both his arms; these had clotted and had almost stopped bleeding, but some required stitches.

"Some of those wounds need attention," said Tatiana.

"I'll be okay." Dillon delved into his holdall, and pulled out a small plastic bottle.

"What's that?"

"Cyanoacrylate." Dillon immediately saw her bewilderment, and added. "Superglue. Sticks skin together in seconds, and better than any other method when on the move."

"Oh. Are you sure?"

"Positive. It was the Americans who first found out the real benefits of superglue during the Vietnam conflict." Dillon said as he ran the nozzle along a two inch gash running down his forearm.

"Did you manage to pick up any provisions?"

"I always keep field rations hidden under this rear seat. I'd say we have enough for a couple of days, and then we'll have to head back to civilisation and re-stock. Have you any cash on you?"

"No. Only plastic. How about you?"

"Three hundred in twenties."

"We can top up at a cash machine."

"No good. It leaves a trail. The cash I've got will have to be enough."

"So why don't we leave a trail?" said Tatiana. "Only it'll be a false one! We'll draw out as much cash as possible at a number of cash-points - let them track the transactions, and then double back and head in the opposite direction?"

Dillon considered this for a moment. They were going to need

123

a lot more money, wherever they were going. He nodded, smiled, and, bending down, kissed Tatiana on the cheek.

"Thanks for saving my neck back there," he said. "Now we're even."

Tatiana's arm came up and pulled him back down to her. They kissed passionately, and for a couple of seconds, the world seemed to be at peace again.

Dillon pulled away, his gaze intensely locked to hers.

"Come on. We have to get going."

"Can't we stay here tonight?"

"If what you say about these Assassins is correct. Then she will be coming for us right now, and that means we need to put some serious miles between her and us. You understand?"

"Of course. I'll sleep - you drive."

"No problem." Dillon kissed her again, and pulled a heavy blanket from the back and wrapped her in it. He climbed over into the driver's seat, and started the powerful diesel engine. After a moment, he turned the heater dial to hot, checked the fuel gauge, then reversed slowly from the wood, tyres crunching over twigs, and out onto the heath land. Drove back to the gateway and out onto the lane.

"Where are you heading?" Said Tatiana sleepily, pulling the blanket up tight around her neck.

"You'll find out when we get there."

"Any flying involved?"

"A little. But nothing to worry about."

"Damn it Dillon, you know I hate flying."

"It's the only way, Tats. Sorry."

"Oh." Tatiana snuggled up against her makeshift pillow and closed her eyes. Dillon angled the rear-view mirror and watched her sleep as he drove through the countryside; the cool air from the partially open side window made him shiver occasionally as mile after mile of tarmac and the rare traveller sped by in a blur.

* * *

The Landrover drifted across the white line, a sitting duck for any oncoming vehicles. Dillon swerved violently back to the correct lane as horns blared and headlights flashed. He wasn't sure, but he must have dozed off, just for a split second, and cursed himself for doing so. Snow had turned to heavy persistent rain and sleet the further south they drove. The windscreen was awash. Thunder clapped overhead in the dark brooding sky; he re-adjusted his rear-view mirror and saw the Xenon headlights glowing white behind him. The driver of the car, horn blaring, impatient to overtake.

"Okay, Okay," Dillon said quietly. He increased the speed of the wipers to cope with the deluge of water falling out of the sky, eased up on the accelerator and then took the Landrover around the roundabout and out the other side towards the east and Edinburgh. The Highlands were now just a bad memory, left behind until this mess was sorted out...

He drove on bitterly through the inclement weather.

* * *

It was just before dusk when Dillon pulled the Landrover into the lay-by. Half an hour earlier had seen him in a Tesco-Express store buying supplies - everything from biscuits and crisps to tinned Tuna and Diet-Cola through to basic travel medical kits, T-shirts and hoodies that weren't covered in blood and a number of mysterious items which he kept hidden in one of his holdalls. Now they were both cleaned up and wearing a fresh change of clothing, they looked at one another and Tatiana ran a hand through her hair. She'd just taken some pain-killers - the maximum dose - but was still obviously in considerable pain...

"What now, Dillon?"

"We steal a plane. Or anything else that will get us airborne."

"Steal a plane... are you out of your mind?"

"Now there's the question. But, no, I am not, and the reason for stealing a plane, is that if we just strolled onto an airfield and asked to hire one; we would immediately give our location away, because it would be immediately logged with the authorities. And, for another, whoever it is attempting to track us would know exactly where we were the minute we log a flight plan. I do not intend to bring attention to our whereabouts. So it's lucky for us that privately owned small aircraft are stolen all the time, and that they only ever call in the local plod. Now, we need to get to the next village where there is a small private grass strip; they have a few single prop aircraft, but mostly gliders. However I do know that there will be a twin turbo-prop tow-plane in one of the Nissan hangers, which will do us nicely."

"Dillon," said Tatiana slowly, "Surely there will be security patrols and possibly dogs?"

"The only security they have is a padlocked gate at the entrance to the field, and every member has a key to let themselves in and out whenever they want. A lock pick should do the trick..."

"And assuming we get onto the airfield and manage to steal an aircraft. Do you know how to fly... whatever it is you're going to steal?"

"Cut my teeth on single and twin engine Cessnas. Admittedly, it's been a few years, since I last flew a fixed wing plane. But they're all the same. Joy-stick. Rudder. Flaps. Landing gear. Hey, come on, don't look so sceptical - after all said and done, it could be a lot worse. That weirdo Assassin could have murdered us both back at the castle. So why the grim smile?"

"You're barking mad," said Tatiana slowly. "And tell me you don't still plan to visit Ezra?"

"Yes, I'm sorry Tats - but I do need to see Ezra. He is the only one who can possibly help us."

"He will most likely try to kill us. Well you," she corrected.

"Your perception of him as a war-mongering butcher is completely exaggerated. The giant geek is a monumental softy, with a heart of gold..."

"Yes," said Tatiana slowly. "But don't forget you shot him in the ass and almost destroyed his right hip. He won't forget that in a hurry. Surely you haven't forgotten..."

Dillon shrugged nonchalantly. "I saved his life by shooting him in the ass. Remember why I shot him? Anyway, he'll understand," came the simple reply. "He's still alive, isn't he?"

Tatiana rolled her eyes. "Christ, Dillon. You've still got that bloody death-wish, haven't you?" She looked sternly at him, and rubbed at her tired pain-filled eyes. "Where is he living these days? Do you know if he's still playing havoc with his little computer games?"

"I'm not falling into your trap Tatiana. And I'm not going to divulge where he is," said Dillon with a boyish grin.

"You *are* completely off your trolley," Tatiana said with feeling.

"It helps in this business. That's why I've stayed alive for so long." He coughed. "But I'm a realist, Tats. And, it's one of the many reasons why I decided to opt for the quiet life for a while up in the Highlands."

"You like the thrill of danger to much. The possibility that the next assignment might be the one that takes you out. Permanently..."

"Perhaps. You know me better than most."

"No perhaps about it. And these Assassins are being used to take out Scorpion units and anybody who poses a threat to Ramus and Kirill's 'New World Order'. That means you, Dillon." She said the words without emotion.

"You said that these Assassins were originally a secret society that disappeared into obscurity. But Ramus and Kirill have somehow resurrected their modern day equivalent? Well, surely that means they had access to the Scorpion network, and that was how they managed to track each unit down and terminate them. But, it also means that they have access to the Ferran & Cardini secure network as well."

"So why not contact Vince Sharp. Get him to look into it?" said Tatiana simply.

"Definitely not." Dillon's words were spoken softly. "No contact. We do it my way; if Ferran & Cardini have been compromised, and the bastards are waiting to lock onto our signal. The moment we try to make contact the lights on their tracking screens will light up like a Christmas tree."

"Maybe you're right. But isn't it worth taking the risk? After all Ferran & Cardini could help us."

"I can do without their help," Dillon said without humour. "I'm better off on my own - and that's how it's always worked best."

Tatiana shook her head slowly and ran a hand through her blond hair.

"So, when are we going to break the law and embark on this mad scheme of theft from a private airfield?"

"Theft? No, I'm only going to borrow an aircraft from my old friend Lord Roth."

"Oh, you didn't mention that you knew the owner of the airfield. But what about the police? Won't they be notified, when the plane is found to be missing?"

"There you go again, thinking about the negatives of this little enterprise. I'll tell you what; I will leave him a note. How does that sound?"

"Cavalier, to say the least."

"Well, unless you hadn't noticed. We don't really have the time to sign the hire agreement in triplicate." Dillon said sarcastically. He pulled out the battered Glock from its shoulder holster, and stared at it lovingly. "I'm sure if we run into any bother, my old friend here... Well you know what I mean." His smile was without humour.

* * *

Night fell. With it came a bitterly cold wind and sleet.

Dillon slammed the Landrover's door shut. The Assassin would find the 4x4 soon enough, of that he was sure - but then, hopefully, the couple would be far away from this place. Far away from the violence and pain they had already suffered.

Dillon supported Tatiana as they moved carefully around the edge of the wood. Before long they came to a pair of heavy-duty high metal gates, a customary notice board nailed to one of the gate-posts, clearly stating that 'trespassers will be prosecuted'. Dillon produced a small leather pouch from his jacket pocket. "This is where we start breaking the law. But don't worry - this is such a small airfield that no-one will discover anything adrift until the weekend, when the gliders start turning up."

Tatiana stared at Dillon hard. "Can you please hurry up? I'm freezing my tits off standing out here in this bloody awful weather."

Dillon nodded. "Somebody is trying hard to bring down the UK and global economy with the most powerful ever computer software programme. And all you're worried about is your tits falling off."

Dillon continued to jiggle the lock picks around inside the padlock. "And, we find ourselves embroiled in a cat and mouse game to get to those bastards, before they're able to push the green button. Only one little problem. They've teamed up with these Assassin weirdos, who have eliminated the Scorpion network, possibly the only organisation that could have destroyed them, and are now trying to kill both of us..."

He stood up and shrugged, moved forward, and pushed open one of the gates. Then, when they were both on the other side, he closed it again and replaced the padlock.

The airstrip squatted mostly against the darkness. A long hanger with a rolling roof-line stood lonely at the side of the strip with another low timber building alongside, and a two storey building furthest from them, the control tower, Dillon thought. And, beside the hanger was a single damp and glistening aircraft.

"Is that the plane?" Tatiana asked quietly.

"Yes. And, I'm hoping that it'll be fully fuelled and ready to go. She's got excellent range. Fast. Come on."

They made their way slowly across the grass, and Dillon halted. He checked the area ahead of them with a night vision monocular, and once satisfied that there were no obvious security measures in place they moved towards the twin engine Cessna. They circled the hanger and finally scurried through the driving sleet to crouch under the shelter of a tin-roofed lean-to. Slush and ice-cold water poured around them from the non-existent guttering. Splattering incessantly onto the hardstand beneath their feet. Dillon pointed through the gloom. "You wait here. I'll go and see if it's unlocked." Tatiana nodded from under her faux-fur hood. He moved away from her, and was soon a ghost in the sleet. His senses were alive, and he felt incredibly awake: energy flowed through him and the pain from the beating he'd taken back at the castle had all but disappeared. He moved forward.

He halted beside the Cessna, slowed his breathing, and focused, the Glock in his left hand glistening in the gloom. Just behind the wing he reached up, tried the cabin door handle, and immediately discovered that it was locked. It was the fourth pick that gained him entry, forty-five seconds later. The door opened easily outwards, exposing the dark interior.

Dillon reached up and pulled down the steps, which thwacked against the hard-stand. Then he went back for Tatiana and helped her back to the aircraft, constantly aware that they were sitting targets out in the open...

Tatiana crept forward through the sleet, her outer clothing drenched through to the lining, and soon were both climbing the steps and into the dry interior of the cramped twin engine plane.

"Where are we going, Dillon?"

"Santorini!. Oh and possibly a stop off in Dorset!"

"A Greek Island. A stop off in Dorset? You're joking?" she said, and then; "So I was right?"

Dillon looked her in the eye. "Right about what?"

"Charlie Hart?"

"Don't know what you're talking about."

"Gold Bullion, Dillon. Gold Bullion..."

"Oh that. Yeah, there was a rumour of gold bullion. I'll admit, I did look when the dust had died down. Didn't find any though."

"Yeah, pull the other one. Like you said, I know you better than most, and I did think it ever so slightly odd, how you announced your retirement shortly after that assignment. How else could you have afforded to buy that bloody great big castle? It all clicks into place, Dillon, and I've never forgotten what you said about having transferable currency?"

"Can you just drop the bullshit about gold bullion, please?" Dillon said, as he quickly went through a pre-flight checklist. Then added, "It really was only a rumour, you know... Now let's get the fuck out of here, before that Assassin catches up with us."

Tatiana nodded, and wiped water from her face with the sleeve of her jacket. "You sure you know how to fly this thing, Dillon?"

"Yeah, just like riding a bike..." Dillon grinned, and engaged the starter. "Now lean back and chillax."

* * *

The silver Ducati motorcycle flashed through the night, tyres gripping the wet tarmac, groaning under pressure as the powerful bike hit speeds of over a hundred and seventy m.p.h. The sleet and rain smashed down from the blue-black clouds overhead, and the Ducati finally pulled to a halt behind the Landrover.

Light-weight boots splashed down in a large muddy puddle.

The black clad figure stood beside the bike, staring towards the heavy metal gates and across the apparently deserted airfield. A twin-engine Cessna taxied along the grass strip with engines roaring, climbing steeply up into the night sky and disappeared, navigation lights blinking through the gloom.

The Assassin stared into the darkness, her eyes alert, unblinking, unmoving. Then as dogs barked and their leads slipped free, the figure moved fluidly, swiftly, climbed back onto the Ducati. Within seconds the full face helmet was on and, the Bluetooth comm.-link was re-activated.

"He's escaped," came the soft feminine voice.

"How has this happened?"

"He was ready. He had sophisticated warning systems in place that..."

"Stop. These are merely excuses. Do you know where Dillon is now?"

"He escaped - he stole an aircraft. Heading due south and flying low."

"He will keep below radar, making it almost impossible to track him conventionally. But not so difficult for a satellite. Keep your comm. open and head towards London."

"Understood. Out."

The Ducati was fired up, tyres hissed, the silver motorcycle disappeared into the darkness with only the barking of dogs following the roar of sound emanating from the tailpipe - and nothing remained to provide evidence of the Assassin's recent passing.

GCHQ Transcript 4. INTERCEPT OF RECENT SOUTH AMERICAN NEWS REPORTS. NON-CLASSIFIED STATUS.

Extracts from daily newspapers, Sao Paulo, Rio de-Janeiro, Salvador and Brasilia, Brazil:

The business quarters of Brazil's largest cities were left in chaos yesterday when every credit card terminal linked to the country's largest banking institutions, re-routed every transaction made during normal trading hours to a number of holding accounts in Zurich, Switzerland. Panic ensued as stores eventually discovered that they had unknowingly been robbed of their entire day's takings. Early reports speculate that over two billion dollars have been misappropriated. A spokesperson from the Brazilian security service, stated. "This was not just the work of organised crime syndicates. The software and expertise required to carry out such a sophisticated, hack, was far beyond their capabilities. The security service is following up information received and investigating claims from the banks concerned that this crime is the work of a malicious employee with in-depth knowledge of the programming of credit clearing protocols. Our computer fraud department is also following up leads; to see something like this happening was a travesty. We have every resource and top people working on this case as we speak."

No official statement has so far been made by the Brazilian Government or by any bank official.

131

Chapter 11

Alix stood on the roof of the tall modern building, a look of frustration and anger on his face. Behind stood Lola, both shocked into silence. Below them the landscape of London that had been changed forever by the small but deadly nuclear device that had been detonated inside Scorpion HQ.

"I can't believe what happened here," said Alix softly. He reached into his jacket pocket, pulled free a cigar and lit up. Smoke plumed around his face, swirling in the cold air. He took a deep and heavy draw.

"Those bastards," said Lola, her expression malevolent.

"Yeah," drawled Alix. "But which bastards, exactly?"

They moved off the roof-top and used the service stairs all the way down to ground level. The bustle of activity following the immediate blast had subsided; no longer did emergency service vehicles line the area where Scorpion HQ used to occupy. At least seventy people wearing hard-hats and hi-visibility jackets picking slowly through the rubble and debris, machines lifting blasted concrete slabs and massive H sections of steel reinforcement had already been cleared from around the cavernous hole; all of the bodies had been recovered and taken to mortuaries all over the city. They walked across the park, away from the blast zone, away from the devastation and total destruction, away from the lost lives and smashed worlds. They got into the Mercedes van; driving away in silence.

* * *

The cliff top road was deserted; rain beat against the Mercedes windscreen, the black of night turning grey as dawn started to break over a tumultuous ocean. The battered van hissed its way through the deluge, headlights carving slices of yellow from the murky gloom. Lola leaned back in the passenger seat, looking out from somewhere inside of the fur-lined hood of her parka coat, at the coastal landscape unfolding before them.

"You sure it's at the end of this road, Alix?" Said Lola, miserably.

"Positive. I've only been here once before, but I remember where it is, and what a fucking desolate and lonely place it is."

Alix guided the van with care; along a narrow unmade lane as they drew nearer to their destination, through a tall gated entrance, and still the rain pounded down and Lola began to wonder if agreeing to this meeting had been the best decision she had ever made.

The Mercedes van slid to a muddy halt on the grass verge.

Rain and sleet danced in the beams of the headlights.

Alix stared at the Sat-Nav screen. "Well according to this, it should be just on the other side of that wood. On the right." He selected first gear, and they moved forward with a jerk and the back-end of the vehicle swung to the left and then the right as they picked up speed; Alix was right, they found the small granite stone chapel. He parked discreetly away from the chapel entrance. Steam hissed from the cracked radiator as Alix killed the engine.

"Do you think he's in there?" Asked Lola casually.

"I doubt it, but you never know with the Priest."

The rain had eased off and Alix stepped out of the van, an automatic pistol in his gloved hand. He stared around; scanning the countryside in all directions, then saw headlights and a car creeping up the lane towards him. Inside the van, Lola had slotted a fresh magazine into a Heckler & Koch MP5 carbine and she held the muzzle low, unseen; a precaution.

The car halted, steam immediately rising off of its muddy tyres. It was a silver Aston Martin DB5, identical to the one that a well-known big-screen secret agent of the 1960's used to drive.

"Everything okay?" Shouted Alix.

The Priest climbed out of the vintage sports car.

"Oh yes, my son," he said. He looked around, and, with his Bible clasped in his right hand, walked slowly towards Alix.

"I hate this place," said Alix miserably. The rain was falling again and soaking through his protective clothing to the skin; his face a sheen of water.

"God sends the rain to nourish the land, my son. So that seeds may be sown and life can flourish." The Priest beamed, moss green eyes shining.

Alix frowned.

"That might, or might not, be true Priest. I assume you got the secure email I sent to you?"

"I did. The infidels have been busy. They seek to destroy everything in their path."

"I thought - *think* - that I can trust you, because I know you are one of the main Tactical Planning Officers at Ferran & Cardini - one of the main men, the partners' ears and eyes, yeah?"

"By your trust, I assume you mean the MP5 rained on me from your van, by your very pretty friend Lola?"

Alix shrugged, grinning. "You can't blame us for taking precautions - you know how it is."

"Indeed I do," said the Priest calmly. "What is it you seek, my son?"

"As you know, things have gone from bad to worse; we've just driven up from London."

"Scorpion HQ?"

"Yes," said Alix sombrely.

"We must pray for their souls," said the Priest, great sadness in his voice. "And yet, before prayer, I cannot help but feel that this crime must not go unpunished."

"We need your help," said Alix softly. "You have the highest clearance level at Ferran & Cardini, and to be honest, you probably know more about what's going on at Scorpion than we do..."

The Priest's eyes glittered. "There is no Scorpion, well not in an operational sense, anyway. There have, shall we say, been... *complications.* What is it you have in mind?"

"Find out who is responsible - gather together all remaining Scorpion units and go after them. Terminate every single one of them."

"First you will need to find the source; then you will need to find the target."

"That's why we're here," said Alix. "There's nobody else we can trust - and believe me, it was hard deciding even to contact *you.*"

The Priest stood, both his hands deep in the pockets of the black overcoat he was wearing, rain dripping from the brim of the black fedora hat. He thought, long and hard, brow furrowed; finally, looking skywards, he smiled at Alix, then reached out and patted him gently on the shoulder. "I have been given guidance, my son."

"Really, so quickly?" Alix looked up, nervously, at the heavens.

The Priest nodded. He placed his hands together, as if he were going to prey. A frown appearing across his forehead as he concentrated. "The Lord works in mysterious ways, Alix. But he will lead us and protect us, and the Lord will guide us."

"You sure about that, Priest?"

"My faith in my Lord is unwavering, Alix. I am merely his physical medium on earth, and the one chosen to carry out his will. Yes I am sure. But I am going to need help on this journey. Under normal circumstances I would call my old friend, Jake Dillon. But, he had a visit from a unit of these Assassins, got them all except one. He used one of his pay-as-you-go mobile phones to contact me. Told me that he was shipping out with Tatiana."

"Bloody hell." said Alix, and immediately added. "Sorry, didn't mean to say that."

"No need to apologise, Alix. But... as you are now here, my friend. Sent, I think, by the Almighty. You can be of assistance to me."

"What kind of journey?" Alix's voice was suspicious.

"As TPO's at Ferran & Cardini, we have always worked closely with our equivalent rank at Scorpion. Between us we keep tabs on a variety of people and locations around the world; keep an eye on them, shall we say. There has been an increase in hostile activity at various locations and we sent Scorpion units to investigate and in some cases, baby-sit some of Scorpions key personnel - just before Scorpion HQ was destroyed in London. The partners had instructed me to look into a matter of grave importance concerning a Scorpion unit. I was on my way to the assignment when I received your transmission."

"So now we can all go together?"

"Your assistance would be greatly appreciated, my son. This increased activity would appear to be linked with various hot spots of trouble around the globe and at Scorpion HQ in London. The partners of Ferran & Cardini have a strong hunch of there being a connection."

Alix nodded.

The Priest smiled. "We will have to meet at the old Sarum private airfield in Wiltshire - I have a few jobs to take care of first along the way."

"No problem. Just name the time."

The Priest glanced at his wristwatch. "Twelve hours from now."

"We'll be there," said Alix softly.

* * *

135

The twin engines droned like bees gathering honey. Tatiana woke up, rubbed her eyes, and watched the sun dancing across the tops of cotton-wool clouds. She yawned, enjoying the view for a few moments; far below, the brilliant blue landscape of the Mediterranean, marked with the Islands of the Balearics, reminded her of long past holidays, and much better days - happier days before the imminent crisis that now loomed and would grip the world's economies and governments and cripple them beyond recognition...

She shifted on the uncomfortable seat. Winced as the stitches that Dillon had so expertly sown her together with, pulled tight.

She glanced across at Dillon. "You okay?"

"Never felt better." Although, Dillon's wane smile, told a different story.

"Where are we?"

"We've just flown over Mallorca."

"Mallorca. I had a few good holidays there in the past. My father owned a villa in Puerto Pollensa, up in the north of the island."

"How are you feeling?"

"Honestly? Battered, bruised, and sore, but I'll live. You hungry?"

"Starving."

"Which bag is the food in?"

The blue one has food and drink in, and I apologise in advance for the amount of junk food content. I swear, somebody should sue the manufacturers of that shit."

Tatiana rummaged. Found food - or a close approximation thereof. She ate, and so did Dillon, even though his hands were firmly gripping the Cessna's control column.

"You look tired, where are you refuelling?"

"We're heading for Sicily to refuel."

"I thought you were never going back to Sicily? Something to do with the Mafia wanting you real bad after you destroyed their very large shipment of cocaine. Wanted by men with machine pistols who want you very, very dead?"

"Well, yes. But when I say Sicily, it's a biggish island and what I mean is that I've arranged to rendezvous with an old friend, just outside of Ragusa. That's on the other side of the island and a long way from Palermo."

"So there'll be no time for sunbathing or sampling the exquisite local food?"

"Not this time, luv. I'm sorry. Anyway, the less time I spend on that island, the better."

They were still over the sea, and the sun glittered across waves and tiny crests of foam. Tatiana watched Dillon carefully; she could see his concern about landing on Sicily but he hid it well. The Mafia chased him all over Europe; he had killed every one of his pursuers one by one before returning to the UK. The Mafia have long memories... She had read it in his personnel file, and as he always said, it wasn't the Mafia that bothered him; it was the one million Euro contract that they had put out on him...

Hours had passed.

The 'rendezvous', much to Tatiana's horror, was a narrow dirt strip cut between lines of olive groves. Dillon brought the twin engine Cessna down in a swirl of dust, taxied to the far end, turned, and came to a halt, much to the bewilderment of a small group of olive pickers who were sitting in the shade eating their lunch. Tatiana watched Dillon go across to them from the Cessna's cockpit, decidedly on edge and alert for any signs of trouble.

She needn't have worried. Dillon, all smiles, nodded in her direction and she watched as one of the older women, dressed traditionally in black garb, lead him away to throw back tarpaulins concealing drums of what Tatiana assumed was aviation fuel. She did not understand how Dillon made contacts, nor how he had arranged this little meeting; so she decided that it was probably best not to ask.

An hour later, when Dillon climbed sweating and covered in dust into the cockpit, Tatiana had been sleeping again. She smiled wearily at him. "We fuelled up and ready to go?"

"We should have just about enough to get us to Santorini. That's assuming we don't meet with any problems along the way, we're going to be flying low altitude and under radar..."

They flew low with the sun high in a sky of brilliant blue...

Tatiana decided it was quite romantic or it would have been if she hadn't taken a bullet in the shoulder and they hadn't been running for their lives. What happened? She thought, what had happened to her near perfect world? It had been going so well, so smoothly.

* * *

Ezra walked slowly through the spectacular landscaped gardens of his hillside home, gazing around in appreciation of the vividly colourful scene; looking down he observed honey bees hovering and settling on the abundance of large blooms throughout the garden. He lifted his head slowly, hair whipping gently in the light breeze, and gazed out across the breathtaking view before him - a medley of browns and burnt orange merging into the dazzling blue of the ocean. The amber light of early evening flowed effortlessly across the island landscape like molten honey, breaking across white painted villas, moulding itself around the trees. Although, Ezra could not see them from where he was sitting, sheer cliffs rose up hundreds of feet from the ocean floor and he could feel the past violence of this ancient land within his soul.

The high voltage electric security fence, made the large man feel comforted, solid and real without any fear. Ezra sat in his private grounds knowing that he owned outright everything, and everyone around him was a part of him, belonged to him - and he belonged to them; a symbiotic relationship that made Ezra smile. His hand reached out and, lightly touched the shocking purple petals of the flower. He sighed.

The sun was sinking, glinting a deep burned red in his dark eyes.

He rose slowly to his feet, pulling himself to his full height and massaging the constant ache in his right hip and lower back. Moving away from his view-point, he was soon walking back through landscaped gardens, along wide sandy paths, winding back and forth, and leading uphill towards his luxury villa complex and the last glimpses of the sparkling dance of the sun's sinking rays. Ezra walked on, the limp in his left leg becoming more pronounced with each step he took, sweat rolling down over his temples, his long grey hair flowing behind him in the light breeze, his automatic Browning cumbersome, yet comforting, in its leather shoulder holster concealed under his robes.

As he walked, the Scorpion G8 link comm. pressed against his right thigh through the pocket sewn into the Bedouin style robes he was wearing. He hated the heavy device. It had been hacked of course, by his own programmers - just because they *could*. The small device had been dismantled and reassembled minus certain circuitry and software. Ezra kept the G8 close to him at all times; it was a constant reminder of distant, better days.

Ezra halted for a moment, turning, hands on hips, regaining his breath.

The landscape of Santorini spread out before him, the most awesome of panoramic views he had witnessed in his many years of travelling the miserable ball of rock called Earth.

Ezra loved the Greek Islands and in particular, Santorini; that is why he had chosen this place in which to set up and run a state-of-the-art listening and monitoring station for the Israeli Intelligence Agency - Mossad.

He pushed on up the last steps leading to one of the villa's many verandas overlooking the orange tree orchards filling the slopes all the way to the edge of the cliff tops. This vision of contrasting colour splashes against the brilliant blue of the ocean beyond, filled his complex mind with calm, soothed the raging bull that burned within his soul, found the soft spot in his heart and allowed him to coast through each day with ease.

The interior of the villa felt luxuriously cool after heat outside. Ezra touched the age-worn spine of the hard-back edition of the Bible, tilted it backwards and; immediately, a secret panel in his purpose built library opened to reveal a stairway leading down to the bunker and his centre of operations.

He moved to one of the many computer screens, logged in, and checked for anything new.

This cannot be correct, he thought.

The GCHQ intercepted communication between Ramus and Kirill, must be wrong.

A cold shiver ran up and down his spine.

Dillon would never dare come to Santorini... Ezra laughed out loud then, his laughter echoing out through the bunker. And if he *was* coming to the Greek Island - and by the level of encryption, it seemed that it was a top priority to find and intercept him - if the miserable excuse for a human being *was* coming to Santorini, then the chances were that he was coming to find Ezra.

"I swore that I would kill you the next time we met."

Ezra's voice was deep, incredibly deep and melodic - almost theatrical in its delivery, a rich voice, the voice of an actor, not the voice of a...

"What are you?" He thought.

"What have you become?"

He had been re-assigned by army intelligence. They had sent him to London to work on a very special new anti-terrorist project. Scorpion.

He sneered in contempt.

Ezra shut down the screen, got up, and started to pace the room, thinking, planning, fuming...

He went outside and continued to walk, leather sandals now kicking sand as he moved along the path, winding through the garden to the perimeter fence and a string of proximity sensors and anti-personnel mines.

Scorpion...

They had a lot to answer for. A *hell* of a lot to answer for...

He reached the perimeter fence, and immediately turned and started back the way he had come. The walk had relaxed him, as it always did. Ezra mounted the steps up to the southerly most veranda of his home and sitting on one of the wicker chairs, smiled to himself knowing that hiding below the simple white-washed walls was a hundred million pounds worth of technology under the ground in the form of extremely high-tech suites, weapons systems, and a large underground garage and workshop facilities and...

Ezra's eyes glinted.

And *something else.*

A breeze licked the dust on the timber floor, sending it in some sort of exotic dance across the veranda.

How the world had changed, he thought. How it has descended into a quagmire of terrorism, violence and world-wide fear.

He shivered.

How *I* have changed...

He caught sight of movement to his left, partially hidden by trees, but he was sure someone was there. Ezra moved cautiously to the far end of the veranda and down the steps out of sight, so as to outwit, Demitri, his personal bodyguard. A former Russian special forces Sergeant, who had fought in Afghanistan, Iraq and Iran, fighting the Taliban - and who liked nothing better than to play chess. He had been with Ezra for the past five years - and was never far away from him...

The big Russian had spotted him moving along the veranda, and had quickly moved around the villa, and was now standing behind Ezra, the Uzi across his chest, the safety catch switched off. Ezra grinned, stood up and turned around.

"You okay, Boss?" Growled Demitri, his broad face split into a smile.

"Damn you, Demitri. You've done it again. How do you move so fast and so quietly," said Ezra.

"Many years of dodging bullets, Boss."

Ezra shook his head, "Yeah, and I guess that's why I employ you, just to keep you safe."

Demitri smiled. They shook hands, and Ezra went back up the steps onto the veranda and into the cool interior of the villa.

Such a nondescript *façade*, he thought.

A simple disguise, concealing technology the world could not even begin to comprehend.

His sandals brushed silently against the polished marble floor as he made his way along the corridor to his library. He went to one of the shelves, and to his prized hard-back edition of the Holy Bible; tipping the spine back, the secret panel opened, and Ezra descended - down the steps and through the rough-hewn narrow corridors - to the operations bunker.

Welcome to Heaven, Ezra thought.

* * *

It was early evening when Dillon flew the twin engine Cessna across the shimmering Ionian Sea west of Greece. Sunlight glittered, accelerating over the horizon. Tatiana was sitting with her head resting on Dillon's shoulder when the whole aircraft shuddered.

Tatiana stirred. She turned, her gaze fixed on Dillon's.

"What was that?"

The aircraft shuddered again, and then moments later, a trail of thick black smoke came from behind the starboard engine. Dillon leaned forward, eyes scanning the digital read-outs, and cut the fuel supply to the engine. The prop hummed as it slowed and then it stopped altogether.

"Tell me we don't have a problem."

"We have a problem," said Dillon through gritted teeth. "Looks like we've sprung an oil leak. Damn-it."

The aircraft had to land, and soon. Tatiana's grip tightened on Dillon as fear flashed bright in her eyes. Breathing deeply, he turned the Cessna south. "We'll have to land as soon as possible."

141

Dillon knew the area well, and hugged the coast through the Gulf of Patra and chose a spot on the west coast of Peloponnesus, where he knew a certain landowner of disreputable character.

Dillon brought the Cessna in low over the sea. Sparkling waves of the brightest blue crashed to their end in a crescendo of white foam. They cleared a long stretch of beach-hugging trees and a wide sweep of unspoilt white sand. The Cessna approached a wide tree-lined grass strip with a grandiose country farmhouse located at the end of the cutting and touched down smoothly, then bumped along the short grass towards the dazzling white-walled house. Tatiana gazed up at the building as they rolled to a halt, bushes and trees whipping to either side, the drone of the one good engine invading this otherwise peaceful paradise. The house was large, built from stone, the lofty roof supported by huge oak beams rough cut and lashed together with thick ropes skilfully tied by local craftsmen.

Several men, dressed in black suites, ran forward towards the plane. They were all carrying guns.

"A welcoming party?" asked Tatiana.

Dillon smiled. "They know me here. Don't worry." He killed the engine, which died quickly, the propeller humming and clattering to a halt. Dillon helped Tatiana down from the cockpit, down the steps, and onto the grass where they were immediately aware of the heat.

"Warm, isn't it? Just what the doctor ordered." Tatiana said huskily. "How long will I have to endure this heat while you fix the motor?"

"As long as it takes."

"Oh, only it's quite a shock after sunny old Scotland," she said and smiled sardonically.

Dillon greeted the men and explained his dilemma in fluent Greek. He and Tatiana were escorted back up to the house at gunpoint by the obviously suspicious security guards.

As they reached the porch a man appeared, wearing a loose fitting white shirt over stone-washed denim jeans and retro sand suede desert boots. The man had a shabby-chic look about him, and the dark brooding eyes of someone who mistrusted everyone; and the mini-sub machine pistol in his hand looked very menacing.

"Sappho, I have a major fucking problem."

The older Greek man smiled, a broad smile, breaking the spell of impending doom, and bellowed, "Jake Dillon, you old mongrel!

How the devil are you big man? I thought you'd retired or died? Come up here and give old Sappho a hug."

* * *

Their stay was short, sweet and very much to the point. The starboard engine had blown an oil seal, and Sappho said that he would get his mechanic to take a look at the problem.

The aircraft was towed off to a large barn, and Tatiana's wounds were attended to by Sappho's personal physician. He re-stitched Dillon's handiwork, and applied fresh sterile dressings and gave both Tatiana and Dillon a shot of antibiotics. They were shown up to one of the many guest suites, where they showered quickly to remove the grime and staleness of travel and battle, sweat and blood.

When they'd freshened-up, they waited on the porch of Sappho's impressively large white-washed country house in the early hours of the morning. The sound of a powerful 4x4 broke the relative silence; a Mercedes G Wagon rumbled into view, the silver coachwork covered in baked-on mud and dust, the headlights carving up the night. The vehicle came to a halt, and Sappho jumped down. The big Greek man, bald and grinning widely, slapped Dillon on the back, making him groan in agony.

"She's all fuelled up and ready to go, Dillon. How about your woman, the doc take care of her?"

"His woman?" Tats hands went to her hips, her stance on the porch changing subtly from submissive to aggressive with barely a change of muscle tone.

Sappho glanced at Dillon, who had a wide grin across his face.

"I did not mean to offend, young lady. Please accept my apologies for assuming that such beauty would be with such a mongrel like Dillon."

"That," said Dillon dryly, "is a slur on my exceptionally good character. And I thought you were my friend?" A frown creasing his brow.

Sappho shrugged. "I am your friend, Dillon. And you also know that I only speak the truth." Sappho smiled. "Now, it's been a long day, I'm tired, and your plane is not going anywhere, the nearest oil seal is on the mainland and will take three days get here. But, if you are in a hurry; I have a forty-five foot power cruiser moored in the harbour,

143

and like I said, she's fully fuelled and ready to go. The weather reports are all favourable for the next two or three days. Or if you prefer, you are most welcome to stay until we can get your aircraft fixed."

Dillon looked at Tatiana, and sighed. "Staying is a lovely notion, Sappho. But we've really got to be on our way. So, I'll take up your offer of the boat."

"I'll have one of my men take you down to the harbour. Wherever it is you are going, look after yourselves, and don't destroy my boat. And Dillon, don't forget, you call Sappho if you need help."

"Don't worry, Sappho. I'll look after your boat," grinned Dillon. "I'm forever in your debt, old friend."

Sappho waved his arms around expansively, "No, Dillon. You are like family, and we Greeks always look after family." Sappho bellowed an order and one of the black suits stepped forward, and then disappeared into the white-walled country house, then returned with a large rucksack.

"A few supplies for your onward travels." The big Greek man smiled. He ran a hand over his bald head, where a sheen of sweat could be seen in the light of the porch. "Now you be careful out there, Dillon. This not a part of the world for a lily-livered Englishman!"

Dillon laughed, patting the man in return, his affection genuine. "You take care yourself, Sappho. And remember: we were never here. And we didn't steal that Cessna that's in your barn now. We merely borrowed it!"

"We are Greek, Dillon. We have the most dreadful of memories."

"They got into the Mercedes, and one of the black suits got behind the wheel of the big 4x4 and the next moment they were speeding over loose gravel towards Sappho's private harbour, and a forty-five foot power cruiser that would take them across to Santorini.

They stepped out onto the dock, unloaded Dillon's holdalls and the rucksack that Sappho had given them, and took them all to the boat. Dillon looked at what had fifty years previous been a luxury craft, but was now very much like the Mercedes. Covered in grime and years of neglect. The paint on the metal hull was flaking, and rust showed through, and parts of the starboard side gangway were worryingly riddled with rust peppered bullet-holes.

"This old tub has been in the wars," said Tatiana softly.

"Oh don't let first impressions fool you. This is very much a wolf in sheep's clothing," said Dillon, helping Tatiana across the gang plank and onto the rear deck of the boat. "What did you expect?"

He slung the holdalls and rucksack into the deck, then went aboard himself.

"A what?"

Dillon went through the sliding doors into the main day cabin and on towards the bridge, Tatiana followed. "A wolf in sheep's clothing. When you want to give the impression that something is innocent and harmless, but in fact it is quite the reverse." Dillon put the key that Sappho had given him into the ignition, and turned. The in-board diesel engines rumbled into life, belching thick black smoke out of the stern into the murky grey light of dawn.

With the powerful diesel engines idling in neutral, Dillon went outside and ordered Sappho's man to cast off the bow and stern lines, and then went back to the bridge. Within minutes they were heading out to open water at high speed, the metal hull slamming down onto each wave with a loud slap, and suddenly, suddenly the safety of the dockside had gone and a terrible mist had closed in around them.

"Don't worry, we'll soon pass through this murk" explained Dillon. "No ambient light... just water and fish, lots of fish."

Dillon knew that all around them stretched clear water. He switched on the spotlights which cut two slices of life ahead of them, but all around was the promise - the inherent threat - of a global meltdown...

"Remember what I said about the wolf in sheep's clothing?" Dillon reached underneath the main control console, feeling for the button he knew was there, and pushed it. A moment later secret panels slid back to reveal three flat screen monitors, Dillon already had the wireless keyboard in his hands and was typing in a series of access commands. The screens lit up and option menus immediately appeared, Dillon activated the night-vision option and the next moment they were looking out through, what appeared to be, green coloured glass. The sea landscape appeared surreal, but visible. He then selected radar jamming and then set the course for Santorini on the auto-pilot. Lastly, he activated the weapon's systems and placed them on standby.

"Relax, sleep" said Dillon. "The main stateroom is forward, and I think you're going to need all your energy when we meet Ezra. I'll rest up here on the bridge"

The dark water rushed past, and as the two Ferran & Cardini operatives rested, the ocean surrounded them completely.

It was over an hour past dawn. The sun had risen, a bright flash over the horizon. The ocean had turned from the murky half-light inkiness to the brilliant blue of a new day - and a blow-torch heat beating down upon them. Their heading was monitored and maintained by the auto-pilot. Clear blue water was all around them interspersed with small isolated islands...

The powerful inboard diesel's pushed the metal hulled cruiser forward at a steady twenty-nine knots. Schools of silver coloured fish scattered as the boat aggressively cut through the Sea of Crete.

Tatiana moaned tenderly, fingers coming up to touch the sensitive area of her shoulder that had so recently been punctured; Dillon had claimed that it was healing nicely, but to Tatiana it felt like it was on fire... a poker through the wound searing her flesh. The sun rose; so did the temperature. Dillon turned on the air-conditioning inside the bridge, and the cool air flowed into the cabin. Dillon settled into the seat and checked the gauges and data readouts on the three monitors.

They passed an island on the starboard side, where a small group of people swimming and sunbathing in a crescent shaped sandy cove, waved as they went by. The few houses that could be seen were built of stone, wood and white-washed rendered walls, which glowed in the strong sunlight. Dillon waved back as they rumbled by. Tatiana, smiling for the first time in many hours, also waved back at the people on the beach.

They left the idyllic island behind, on a heading for Santorini, the cruiser eating the sea with ease. They pressed on; mile after mile, hour after hour, under the singular piercing eye of the baking sun. It was incredibly hot outside, almost unbearable even with the breeze coming off the sea.

Another two hours saw them approaching the most southerly tip of Santorini. Dillon remained on course for another twenty minutes and then disengaged the auto-pilot. As they approached the west coast bay of Thira he took the helm, and brought the forty-five foot cruiser to a sudden stop, the boat gently rocking on the swell. Reddish-purple cliffs, created by a violent volcanic eruption around 1600BC, rose up hundreds of feet before them.

"Up there," he said simply.

"What?"

"One of Ferran & Cardini's monitoring stations... and Ezra."

Tatiana stared. "All I see is a lot of red rock, Dillon. I obviously knew that there was a facility somewhere in the Cyclades - after all, I *am* a Ferran & Cardini special operation's liaison officer - but I had no idea that it was located on Santorini!" Tatiana's voice was a little strained, her gaze looking skywards.

"We'll moor up alongside the old dock at the far end, away from the other boats. It's still too early for the cruise ships, but when they do start to arrive, there will be hundreds of tourists putting ashore here. And then we'll take the cable car up to the top. Someone will be waiting, of that you can be sure. They'll have watchers. We haven't got this far without being tagged, even with the radar jamming activated. Let's just hope that Ezra hasn't given his men the order to shoot us on sight. But then, that wouldn't be his code of conduct, would it now, Tats?" He gave Tatiana a sly sideways glance. And she knew; the mistrust was still there. He wasn't sure if she was real or... or what? A Government spy?

But then, in all the years she had known him, Dillon had never truly trusted anyone. It would have surprised her if he had changed now.

The silence of the early morning was fractured by the tinkling bells of the mules making their way down to the port for the cruise ship arrivals. Those adventurous enough, mount-up, and are taken up the 853 feet of ancient trail way, all the way to the top of the cliffs. Dillon and Tatiana, were not in the mood for a mule ride, and took the cable car all the way up the almost sheer cliff face to the town perched on top. As they stepped outside, they were greeted by four black-suited men. They were all sporting concealed weapons under their jackets; Dillon assumed that they would be carrying 9mm Glock automatics, standard issue and his favoured weapon. Dillon watched them warily, his own Glock in his hand with the safety off, inside his jacket pocket.

He smiled broadly.

"Hello boys. It's good of Ezra to send a welcoming party, but we don't want to cause a scene. Do we?"

"You're to leave Santorini at once," said a large man in Greek. He moved forward, patent leather shoes covered in dust. "You are not welcome here."

"But maybe I'd like to catch up with an old work colleague while

I'm visiting this magnificent island. Perhaps you know old Mr Happy Ezra?"

"There is no one on Santorini of that name," said the big man.

Tatiana leaned across Dillon and saw one of the other men grin, the big man looked sternly at his subordinate, dark eyes narrowing, his expression reprimanding.

"Tell him that his niece, Tatiana, is here."

The man stared. He did not blink. Then he nodded at one of the other men, who spoke briefly into his concealed microphone, and then went and whispered conspiratorially in the big man's ear. He spoke quickly to the others and then turned to Dillon and said. "We walk straight through to the far side of the town, and then to the white-washed villa on the hillside. Try nothing funny or Arte' here..." he patted the other man on the shoulder: "Well, his gun is silenced and he will gladly kill you both without a second thought."

The large man led them through the narrow streets of Thira, past cosy bars and restaurants, and chic fashionable shops and boutiques. Dillon walked with Tatiana at his side; Arte' was directly behind them all the way to the high electric gates of a large white-washed villa.

And then they were inside the grounds of Ezra's villa complex. Inside Ezra's lair.

The black suited men followed them, automatic weapons now on full view, bristling, safety catches switched to off. As they walked through the colourful landscaped gardens, men and women were busy tending the borders and harvesting oranges from the trees in the orchard, while men rode sit-on mowers cutting the acres of grass. They turned a corner and, Dillon licked his lips nervously, and decided that he did not like this place...

Ezra was waiting, hands on hips, eyes staring out across his domain, mind deep in thought. Dillon halted at the bottom of the veranda steps, and allowed one of Ezra's personal bodyguards to take his Glock from him. Tatiana stood at Dillon's side, one foot resting on the first step, gazing up at the blazing sun for a moment before fixing her eyes on her - uncle.

Ezra looked round and his gaze met Tatiana's. He smiled briefly, and then he looked at Dillon and glowered, the kindly expression of a moment before disappearing from his face.

"You either have the nerve of the devil by coming here, or a death wish, Dillon. And before you say anything, I still haven't forgiven you for shooting me in the ass with that hollow-point. It took out most of my hip, you know? And now I'm reminded of it every day with this infernal limp. So, Dillon. You'd better have a very good reason for daring to come here."

Dillon said nothing. He made no move. He merely allowed his gaze to remain fixed on Ezra, a silent connection - a linking of minds that Tatiana did not quite understand.

"I was told that you had retired to an eccentric hermit-like existence in the Highlands of Scotland, Dillon."

"I had," said Dillon softly.

"I don't understand," whispered Ezra, eyes intense.

"It was... interrupted. And when I shot you, Ezra, it was to keep you alive, not to kill you."

There came a long uncomfortable pause

"You are a legend within the Ferran & Cardini history files, you know."

"That is misplaced, and you know it, Ezra. But thanks for trying to boost my ego..." Dillon said softly.

"How so? One cannot become a legend without the actions to back it up. You were *revered* by your peers and the partners and *feared* by your quarry." The contempt in Ezra's voice could not be missed.

"You're only alive today because of the bullet I put in you, Ezra. I know we've never seen eye-to-eye - because of my relationship with Tatiana, and because of my reputation... And I know you will have read all of those emails sent out by MI5 when they embarked on the smear campaign against me... But you have it really, really wrong. I know you will find it hard to trust me on this... but you need to hear us out, Ezra, because we need your help..."

Ezra was silent. He lifted Dillon's 9mm Glock and played with it in his bear-like hands.

Dillon calmed his heart rate; he relaxed his muscles and readied himself - for Ezra's body language was all wrong, it was the body language of someone in preparation.

Dillon's eyes surveyed the available weaponry and he realised, realised too late that maybe he had overestimated Ezra's ability to forgive and forget.

And then it came to Dillon, an understanding that Ezra was the same. The same as Dillon, the same *breed*...

'This is dangerous,' Dillon's sub-conscious told him.

Dillon closed his eyes momentarily as pain seared through his exhausted mind, through his head, burning bright red with white hot edges; he dropped slowly to his knees, cold sweats gripping him, and Ezra no longer existed and nothing mattered and the adrenalin that had been keeping him going for so long was no more there. His head rolled from side to side as a cloak of darkness wrapped itself around his mind. A low moan growled through his lips and Tatiana was with him, holding Dillon in her arms. She stroked his brow free of sweat, rocked with him at the foot of the steps and looked up at Ezra.

"Get him inside. In the cool. Now!"

"What is wrong with him?" Came Ezra's deep voice.

"I don't know. He's most likely exhausted... Help him, uncle. Please help him."

Ezra gestured and the biggest bodyguard approached, lifting Dillon easily and carrying him up the steps and into the villa and depositing him in one of the guest bedrooms. Ezra stepped into the air-conditioned room behind Tatiana, "I will help him now, Tatiana. But I cannot guarantee what will come later."

"What? You really can't see it, can you?"

"See what?" Growled the big Greek.

"You can't see for the red mist of anger and hatred. Haven't you realised after all these years, that you and Dillon are the same. You call him an Assassin; a force to be reckoned with. And what the fuck were you when you were a Ferran & Cardini field officer? What the hell were you doing in Berlin, and Istanbul, and then later in South Africa, in the first place? You are kindred spirits... and you are a fucking *hypocrite.*"

Ezra stood for a moment, staring hard at Tatiana. She lowered her eyes then, a feeling of overstepping the line causing her face to redden with embarrassment. Ezra stepped forward and placed his large hands on her shoulders and then kissed her on the forehead. "I have missed you, young lady. And despite everything I said to you before, I wish you no harm. I'm over the moon that you've come back to your uncle Ezra."

"And what about Dillon. Do you wish him harm?"

"Dillon will come to no harm while he is a guest in my home. I promise."

Ezra lifted Tatiana's head. Wiped tears from her cheeks. "I'm sorry. Can you ever forgive me for what I said just now? I do know

150

that Dillon is fundamentally a good man, honest, and loyal to the end. But I also understand that you're pissed-off with him for putting a bullet in your ass, but he did save your life."

Ezra raised his hands in mock submission, "Let us not dwell on this now. I will hopefully see you both at dinner, which will be served at eight o'clock on the south veranda." The big Greek then turned and left the room as the afternoon sunlight drifted through the plantation blinds.

GCHQ Transcript 5. INTERCEPT OF RECENT NEWS INCIDENT LEVEL 5 CLASSIFICATIONS.

At 04.30 AM (GMT), a number of leading banking institutions from a number of EU countries including Italy, Austria, Belgium and Germany reported computer system failures, leading to an involuntary suspension of trading for a 30 second period.

When systems were re-booted, bank officials found that during this 30 second involuntary shut-down, certain government holding accounts had been accessed and an undisclosed amount taken from each of them. However, early speculation by some experts estimate up to seven hundred million Euros of tax-payers money had been snatched from each account that had been hacked into.

Prior to this, no bank had reported any technical failures or any suspicious factors.

A spokesperson for Interpol made this comment: Interpol is working closely with Intelligence Services from all of those countries who have suffered this computer hacking disaster. We are comparing data of organised crime syndicates including terrorist organisations and are also combining computer crime departments in order to maximise available resources.

Chapter 12

The small private Boeing jet flashed through the moonlight, engines whining in deceleration. Mountains reared all around, snow capped peaks soaring skywards. The sleek aircraft banked and came smoothly down to land amid and seemingly *within* the mountains, undercarriage dipping as tyres made contact with the tarmac runway. The plane taxied to a halt and a single emergency vehicle at the rough rocky perimeter of the runway sat watching in the extreme cold, headlights blazing through the light snow fall. A black Range Rover raced across the apron as the cabin door was opened and the on-board steps lowered.

The only passenger aboard the private jet stepped out, the fur collar of his coat pulled up around his face, shielding him from the biting north wind. He was a man of small build with sandy coloured hair that was softly greying at the temples and was neatly trimmed and combed. He wore an expensive Italian suit and the finest handcrafted Italian shoes. He carried a slim aluminium briefcase in one perfectly manicured hand, and descended the steps with measured care, apparently unaffected by the Arctic conditions of cold that contrasted so dramatically with the comfortable conditions of the recently pressurised aircraft cabin.

"Professor Kirill, welcome back, sir." The voice was heavily accented, and Kirill nodded at the man garbed in black military combat gear. Kirill seemed unconcerned that his bodyguard was now more heavily armed and carried a black Heckler & Koch MP6 carbine, and a webbing belt sporting half a dozen hand-grenades.

The driver of the black Range Rover opened the rear door and Kirill climbed into the warm air-conditioned interior. The door clicked solidly shut, protecting the occupant from the inclement weather outside. The military-clad man climbed into the front passenger seat, and a moment later the heavy off-road luxury vehicle was purring and driving off the tarmac runway and onto an un-made track carved between two mountain ranges.

They drove in silence. At first the track was pot-holed and rough and, then merged into a narrow country road, slushy and strewn with natural debris from recent storms. They drove around tight bends and along even narrower lanes until they were almost at their destination, the Range Rover's heavy off-road tyres humming and bumping, and eventually came to a crossroads. All the while Kirill sat, perfectly composed, eyes closed, mind-set calm.

They turned left, the track started as a gentle incline and after half a mile became steeper as it wound its way up the mountain side; and as the terrain became more hostile, the Range Rover demonstrated its ability to cope with even the worst off-road conditions. Kirill allowed himself to smile at this rough and, some might say inhospitable, God-forsaken place that was such a contrast to the luxuriant interior of the vehicle he was travelling in. The thought pleased him.

They had to stop once, while the track was cleared of fallen rocks. With a wave of apology, the bodyguard slowly - painfully slowly - removed the debris out of the vehicle's path and Kirill was on his way without emotion flickering even for an instant on his neatly barbered face. His bright eyes stared straight ahead.

The Range Rover rumbled and bumped up the mountain side, its destination the Kirill Government research establishment, somewhere in the middle of the Scottish Highlands - its purpose un-guessable.

Kirill required very little sleep; he considered it to be nothing more than an interruption in his busy non-stop schedule. Ordinary people slept, and Kirill was no ordinary person...

"Sir."

Kirill looked into the rear-view mirror and the eyes of the driver.

"Are we there?"

"Yes, sir."

The Range Rover halted at a sheer slab of impenetrable rock. The driver spoke into his radio-link, and a moment later the slab parted and they drove into the mountain. Inside Kirill's lair.

The interior was cool; controlled. Polished stone floors stretched away in the large reception area; it was almost like a hotel, with low leather couches and tall potted palms placed strategically. A long curved reception desk stretched along one wall and glass elevators in clear shafts went down to the carefully temperature and humidity-controlled depths where the main servers and the virus software research and development was carried out.

Kirill shook hands with Gregson, the head of the virus software R and D department.

"How are you, sir?"

"Well, Gregson. Considering I was shot and almost killed recently."

"I heard about that, sir. We were all sad to hear about your niece. She was a nice kid. Was it true that it was an assassination attempt?"

Kirill stared malevolently at the man, who had suddenly become very pale.

"I... I... meant..."

"You will never mention my niece again," the words were spoken softly.

"Yes, of course, Professor Kirill."

"Tell me what the overall status is with Scorpion communications?"

"Since the total wipe-out of Scorpion HQ in London nobody seems to know what is going on. All G8 communications have been suspended by GCHQ - we tried to find out who had been in the building at the time, but this information was withheld from us. And considering that their main Hub had been destroyed..."

Kirill merely nodded, then asked, "How successful has the Chimera accelerator programme been?"

"We have successfully hacked into 99% of all networks targeted."

"And what of the 1%?"

Gregson smiled smugly, "That was our own network, sir. We set up a trial hack using one of our most powerful stand-alone processors, which was loaded with an exact copy of Chimera, and then routed around the planet back to this establishment. The attack programme was analysed, located, and terminated within a millionth of a second by Chimera."

"How?"

"Since the last time you were here, professor, Chimera's chameleon script has further developed itself. By the time the attack programme had reached it, Chimera had completely re-written itself, and was no longer the hunted but rather the hunter."

"Excellent, Gregson. So Chimera is ready then?"

"Yes, sir."

"And what of the un-scheduled access into the registry files? The system must have lit up like a Christmas tree."

"Yes, sir. This is still a mystery to us. Ramus has called several times, and wants to speak to you upon your return."

Kirill left the group behind and stepped into the elevator and the calming silence as the glass door closed behind him. The tube hissed away and carried him down to his luxury living quarters on the lower level floor that he occupied alone. He kicked off his shoes, draped his jacket over the back of a low backed chair and walked past a variety of sculptures and carvings towards his study. He went straight to one of the fine cherry wood cabinets, which concealed a humidor, and from inside the temperature controlled cabinet he pulled a fine handmade Cuban cigar, then poured himself a brandy and sat back in his plush leather high-back chair. The comm. buzzed.

Kirill took a long draw from the cigar, enjoying the rich smooth flavour, which filled his senses with its fullness, then hit the button.

"Yes?"

"I have several things on my mind, Kirill. How much time will you need to apply the final elements to the Chimera Programme?"

"Two days, at most. The Gopher Protocol Code just needs a little fine tuning."

"And we will start to see the results, when?"

"Almost immediately. I am assured that Chimera will work at a 99% rate."

"And the Satan virus and worm release element has been installed and implemented?

"I am assured, by my top programmer, that if a computer is connected to the World Wide Web at the time of launching the Satan virus it *will* become infected. Irrespective of any anti-virus protection installed."

"Excellent. How are you feeling after your near-death encounter?"

"I have felt better." Kirill smiled nastily. He stubbed out the cigar, took a sip of brandy and swivelled round in his chair to stare at one of his many fine oil paintings. This one in particular was his favourite as it could hold his gaze and never cease to amaze him; he loved the way the artist had captured, forever in time, the serenity of the lake scene. He loved the way in which the early morning lighting and rising mist, created a surreal calm in a world of mayhem.

"I have a piece of good news for you. Jake Dillon - has been located. Tracked. He is presently on the Greek Island of Santorini. Despite Dillon's best attempts to evade us it would seem that our extensive network of satellites has worked well. We tracked him, but his destination is quite obvious - he seeks Ezra, at that infernal listening and monitoring station, I wish I could forget about."

"Ezra," said Kirill through an exhalation of smoke. "There is a name I have not heard for a very long time."

"I had hoped that he would have died by now," came the soft voice at the other end of the comm. "But then, Dillon is almost doing us a favour. They have discovered the covert location of the European collective Government's establishment for software research and development. Yes by an amazing coincidence, it would seem that Ezra is the man who seeks to create his own version of the Chimera Programme."

"The fool," snorted Kirill. "He would need years to develop anything like my Chimera Programme!"

"I agree," Said Ramus, "but the fact still remains that he has working knowledge, available technology, and copies of the basic Chimera blue-prints and cryptographic algorithms. We need to ensure the safety of this information - we must either retrieve or destroy them. We can kill two birds with one stone."

"How many Assassins will you send?"

"Have no fear, old friend. I will send enough," said the voice of Ramus softly. "There cannot be that much resistance; after all, we will have the element of surprise on our side." He laughed softly.

"The Assassins will erase them all."

"Good."

"Our time is coming, Kirill. Can you taste it? Our time is definitely coming and when we have complete control, we will not abuse our power, we will not fritter away our resources like so many political powers have done through the ages, and let evil corrupt men rule the world. We will be just and fair... not weak and pathetic... but to get that far, first there must be mayhem and suffering on a global scale..."

Dark eyes glittered and there came a pause. A long and thoughtful pause. "I have a request," said Kirill eventually. He was still facing the oil painting that dominated the wall, but something was changing within him, something strange, and something he could hardly bear. Somehow the colours were disappointing to him now; what he craved was reality.

"And what is that?" asked Ramus.

"Dillon: I want a guarantee. I want that bastard dead."

"I'll see what I can do." Said Ramus.

Night was turning to dawn across the Scottish Highlands. Outside, the temperature had plummeted and the sky was perfectly clear, stars fading into temporary oblivion as the sun embarks on its daily journey. Kirill still sat in his chair, the room now in total darkness, only the glow of a cigar in his hand evidence that he remained in the deep underground office, awake, alert, dark eyes glittering. He scratched at the scar on his belly self consciously.

He stared at images of the mountain range, just a blackened outline in the low cold light of dawn, stark and foreboding on the monitor screen. Nothing stirred; there were no lights, no movement, and no intrusions. This place was emptiness; this place was a void. The establishment was invisible; a non place; a deniable spectre in the maw of the Scottish wilderness.

Kirill smiled softly to himself.

All around him, in the silence, he could almost feel the hive of activity. A small army of workers: programmers, hardware engineers, hackers, the world's finest computing minds working together on some of the most excitingly advanced projects ever embarked upon.

The Chimera Programme. The first-ever self-learning chameleon virus programme.

The prototype of an artificial *mind*. That knows no boundaries.

The ultimate *virus*...

Kirill had created Chimera to be used against terrorists and organised crime syndicates. But had soon realised that with some fine tuning, it could be used to bring down, almost any network including; banks, military installations, police and other emergency services and government departments: it could infiltrate any type of computer, and, within the blink of and eye, access encrypted files and extract every scrap of information, before shutting the computer down. *Permanently*. It would be the perfect weapon. It would make him, and Ramus, and the *others*... it would make them rich, it would make them powerful but - more importantly...

It would make them God.

Kirill sighed, exhaling a spiral of white smoke into the darkness. Diffused light invaded the black. A figure stepped forward, and soft bare footsteps approached.

He gazed up at the figure, naked now, body perfectly toned, perfectly formed; muscular and tanned. Kirill licked his lips and met the blue-eyed gaze of the young blond-haired woman. To Kirill, this was his idea of the perfect female - athletic and nubile.

Kirill's gaze travelled down, and then back up again across the perfectly formed thighs, hips, stomach, breasts - and to the face. The tanned skin with her piercingly blue eyes.

The face was beautiful.

Cold and beautiful.

Kirill smiled a strange twisted smile.

He could feel desire and lust rise up through his body. "If only you were real," he said picking up the remote handset off of his desk, and ending the three dimensional hologram programme, the room was thrown back into total blackness.

Chapter 13

Dillon knew it was a dream, and yet somehow that made it worse. While awake he had some element of control; but in the dream he was merely a spectator and already knew the order of events and the outcome. Knew what happened, knew about the organised crime syndicates and drug cartels, and knew about the shocking after-effects when the *special* drugs were handed out freely to those addicted, to what had become known as Death Candy, in every major city around the globe... and yet, again and again he could relive those dark moments with dismay, anger and pure hatred - but without control or the ability to stop the potential death toll rising into the tens of millions...

He stood, his boots planted firmly on the wet slippery deck of the huge oil tanker that cruised through the dark black waters of the Barents Sea. Dillon's eyes were dark, deeply ringed, and the black uniform he was wearing smeared with grime and dried blood. The cold sea-breeze had turned his face numb, the tips of his ears tingled with the first signs of frost bite. His gloved hands clasped the Heckler & Koch machine pistol, the magazine fully loaded with mercury tipped rounds.

The British nuclear powered submarine had been on a hunter-kill mission to intercept and board a Colombian owned oil tanker carrying Death Candy that was destined for every European city. What Dillon, and the submarine's attack force, had found the mind could not comprehend. The entire hold of the tanker was full of drugs...

Death Candy.

It left a bad taste in Dillon's brain, like a poisonous line of cocaine.

A laboratory manufactured hallucinogenic drug, Death Candy was destined to be handed out like a plague across all of the European states.

The tanker was huge, had been stripped of anything unnecessary, so as to hold the maximum cargo. The drugs, man-made and devastating, would have done the job they had been designed to do, if the submarine had not found them in time.

Dillon was stood on the slippery deck, machine pistol cold. One

159

of the assault team's junior officers waved, moved towards him, and their bleak gazes met over the millions of tons of Death Candy.

"There's activity," said the Lieutenant coldly.

"So I heard over the comm."

On their way to intercept the tanker, the submarine had picked up radio chatter between the tanker's captain and what sounded like the owner of the lethal cargo. And just before the crew and captain were overthrown, a distress signal had been sent out by the tanker's wireless operator. Its message simple, under attack...

Dillon and the young navel officer sprang into action, along with all the other men from the submarine's attack force.

Helicopters roared overhead, forward machine guns blazing, spitting bullets across the decks of the tanker and into the sea, and Dillon and the young naval officer sprinted forward with Heckler's juddering in their grips, faces grim, giving covering arcs of fire for one another as they crouched, bullets ricocheting on the heavy metal deck beneath their boots. Terrorists dressed in military style combat uniforms abseiled from the helicopters, Kalashnikov mini machine-pistols blazing as they ascended to the deck of the tanker.

Dillon spun and put a bullet in the face of a terrorist... but, almost by reflex, the terrorist's gun was firing, pumping bullets.

One caught Dillon square in the chest, his bullet-proof body armour saving him. With a gasp he was lifted off of his feet, punched backwards with a fist of iron and thrown down heavily onto the oily deck...

He landed, the wind knocked out of him, momentarily dazed, as all around him, wildfire was let loose and the death toll started to rise. The attack force was overcome in minutes, so many terrorists, too much firepower. And then the heavy blow that sent him spiralling into blackness...

* * *

"Whoa!"

Night had fallen over Santorini. Dillon awoke with a sudden start, a terrible searing pain inside his head. He could smell wood burning outside and pushed himself up into a sitting position, the events of the dream flooding through his mind in waves.

Tatiana was there, sitting by the side of his bed. Her hands were

160

cool against the clamminess of his skin as she laid him back down and pulled the single sheet up over his naked body. Dillon's eyes focused and he realised that the room was dimly lit by a single candle. The noise of insects spiralled in through wooden shutters; *below them* was a hive of technological advancement - a state-of-the-art spy station disguised by a simplistic mask. Distantly he heard the crackling of a fire and the subdued voices of the armed guards.

Dillon rubbed his head. "Any painkillers?"

Tatiana handed him tablets and a glass of iced water. "You dreaming about terrorists and drugs again?"

He nodded. "Yeah, that and death."

"Death?"

"Don't worry about it." He took the painkillers and washed them down with the mineral water.

"They've given you a good look over and checked all minor cuts and gashes on your body, and given you the all-clear on all counts. You'll live, but the doctor who examined you couldn't say why you collapsed outside earlier."

"Just tired and a blinding headache, that's all." Dillon said lamely.

"Well, they gave you a thorough check-up; you are in the peak of health apparently." Tatiana smiled softly. "And, the doctor commended you on your handy stitch work on me. He confirmed what I already knew - that you saved my life." Suddenly, Tatiana stood and slipped out of her shorts and t-shirt. Moonlight glinted on her taut, athletic body; on her firm stomach, ample pert breasts, and smooth tanned skin. She climbed into bed beside Dillon and lay on her side, pressing herself against his warmth.

Suddenly, Dillon's headache had gone. And he felt himself panic for the briefest moment. A feeling he had not allowed himself, since he had split up with Issy, now consumed him. Lust...

"Tats..." he whispered.

Her fingertip touched his lips and stayed there. She leaned forward, her lips brushing against his cheek. He groaned, mouth opening, teeth gently biting Tatiana's finger. Her free hand came up and stroked his hair. He turned, rolling towards her - the feeling of her soft skin, soft breasts, firm shapely legs pressed against him and he was instantly enveloped in her womanliness. And he allowed himself to press against her as he gazed into her eyes and they were silent for long, long moments. They kissed nothing more than light touching.

Dillon's hand came up and rested on Tatiana's hip and she groaned, voice low and husky, scent invading Dillon's mind and consuming his brain; she parted her legs a little, allowing him to press further against her, further into her, further towards that feeling of euphoric pleasure beyond.

"You're feeling better, then?"

"I'm sure, given time, that I'll make a full recovery."

"Well, I'd say that you were already making progress, Mr Dillon." The words came a little breathlessly.

"Perhaps with a little more pressure applied to the right areas..." He said mischievously, eyes glowing in the gloom.

Tatiana pouted, "Well, I'll just have to double my efforts on those areas!"

"Now *that* sounds just what the doctor ordered."

They writhed around beneath the solitary sheet, holding one another. They kissed softly, enjoying each other's heat, each other's gentleness.

"You sure you're okay?"

Dillon grinned. He couldn't help himself, despite the aches and pains from his recent beatings, which had returned to haunt him.

"Yeah, I'm feeling fine now, thanks." Dillon lied easily.

"I try to please," she said softly and smiled, nibbling his chin.

"How did you stop Ezra from shooting me?"

Tatiana pouted, "Dillon, you can't just ask me that sort of question after..."

"Well, I need to know." He propped himself on one elbow and looked down at her. His free hand traced twirls over her breasts and reaching down, took an erect nipple between his teeth, and mischievously bit ever so lightly.

She gasped in mock pain.

"I didn't stop him. *You* stopped him. Your words, your actions."

"What actions?"

"Whatever is going on inside your head? It was on your face." Dillon ran his fingers through his hair. Then he sighed.

"I've never truly understood what goes on inside you," she said.

"It's complicated. Even I find it hard sometimes."

"Try me. *Trust* me Dillon. I'm an intelligent girl. Something has been tearing you apart for years; something has been burning you up and you were grappling with whatever it is when you were stood in front of Ezra." Tatiana searched for the appropriate words to describe what she had witnessed. "It sometimes appears as if you're two very different people. One side of you appeared calm, calculating and extremely dangerous, who wanted to go on the offensive with Ezra; one side of you wanted to back down and give in. I saw it, Dillon. I saw it on your face; I heard it in your voice."

"Do you understand the term; split-personality?" He said suddenly.

"Like *Schizophrenia* - voices inside your head, that sort of thing?"

"Sort of. You see," he paused, uncertain. Tatiana squeezed his arm reassuringly. "I've managed to control and hide this thing inside my head from *everyone* for virtually all of my life. As a child it was merely a voice talking to me. As a grew older, the voice became more aggressive, only coming to the surface when I was placed in situations extreme stress. Even the shrinks didn't spot it. It's what has kept me alive all these years." He said. "But since the Charlie Hart assignment in Sandbanks, I've been getting headaches which were one of the reasons I decided to take time off from active assignments."

"And that's why you always kicked up such a fuss at every six-monthly psychiatric assessment?"

"Partly. But that was mostly done for effect, and I used to find it funny - being able to deceive the experts. I never told anyone, because it would have complicated my life, and they'd have tried to say that I was barking mad. The thing is it only comes to the surface when I'm under extreme pressure, and then it takes over. I hardly ever remember what I've done afterwards."

Tatiana was silent for a long time. She hugged Dillon tight.

"It sounds like a guilt complex."

"I know exactly what it sounds like. I understand only to well, what it sounds like. A load of old bollocks. That's why I never speak about it; I live alone with a burning in my soul..."

"But this alter-ego has kept you alive all these years. You shouldn't beat yourself up because of something you have no control over?"

"I should be able to control the murderous thoughts I have when *it* starts to surface... and that's the bad thing. Take Kirill's mansion in Cornwall - I was as sure as fucking dead. Betrayed by those I thought I was there to protect. I no longer cared if I lived or died, right there in that kitchen, and simply gave myself up to my subconscious... That's when the real killing started and the body count continued until I was well clear of the house. Can you understand?"

"This is just too weird, Dillon." Tatiana said.

"You're in no danger. I'm in total control..."

"I'm not frightened, Dillon. And I do believe you," whispered Tatiana. She kissed Dillon's ear and held him for a long time until she felt his breathing become regular and he was sleeping. Her fingers traced gentle strokes along his spine - and after a while she fell into a deep sleep beside him.

* * *

Dillon awoke in the gloom. Tatiana slept in his arms, a warm embrace. Dillon disentangled himself with care, then, pulling on his trousers and taking his cigarettes and lighter, he crossed the room and stepped outside.

There was an armed guard stood outside of their room, a man called Christopher, sporting Adonis good looks, jet black tousled hair, and a Santorini tan. The big Greek man smiled the sort of sheepish knowledge-filled grin that said, "You sure know how to party loudly." Dillon returned the grin, padded down to the far end of the veranda, and sat down on one of the cane easy chairs.

A cool breeze whispered across his skin. He lit a cigarette, stretched out his legs and gazed out across the dark Santorini landscape towards the sea. The stars were bright against a dark canopy and Dillon tilted his head back to allow a soft spiral of smoke to escape his lips and rise into the vaulted ceiling of the veranda. The nicotine rush whizzing through his brain, the harsh French tobacco scorching his lungs, and he blinked as a man's voice called from somewhere on the other side of the olive grove.

"How are you feeling, Mr Dillon?"

Dillon turned and smiled up at Ezra who was standing with his hands on his hips, breathing in the night air and the rich scents deeply - a love affair with the ambiance. His eyes were unreadable, his appearance neat and his greying hair well groomed, neatly combed and oiled. Dillon caught the distant scent of coconut oil.

"Much better, thank you."

"Would you care to walk with me through the grove?"

"It's a fine night. A walk would be good."

The two men stepped down from the veranda of the white-washed villa and the sandy soil felt soft, comfortably cool under Dillon's bare feet. They moved between the olive trees, inhaling the earthy moist scent, moving through the gloom a little uncomfortable at first: untrusting. As they walked, Dillon offered Ezra a cigarette. They both lit up and stopped within a small clearing on the seaward side of the grove. Dillon lifted his face in an attempt to attract the slightest of breezes to evaporate the sweat covering his body.

"This is a very warm place to live, Ezra," said Dillon eventually.

"Yes it is," rumbled Ezra uneasily. The cigarette seemed tiny in his huge hands. "But we don't always have a choice in these matters. The Partners are hard task masters. They command, and we mere mortals obey." He smiled a smile without humour, bloodless in the moonlight.

There was a pause. The breeze whispered between the trees.

"I think I'm following in your footsteps," said Dillon.

"So it would appear. I have been reading up on your recent - ah, shall we say *adventures* in both Cornwall and Scotland. Tatiana has, of course, filled me in on some of the details. It would seem that wherever you are - death follows closely."

"Well, I admit someone appears to want me *dead*, if that's what you mean."

"Hmmm. That would be the most logical assumption; a thought that did leap to mind is that you were set-up. Used. A tracker with the sole function of leading somebody to me. After all, Scorpion has had units all over the planet systematically terminated - wiped out by teams of highly trained Assassins. And yet they only sent one after you. Strange, don't you think?"

"Yes."

"And further moves have been played across the global chessboard."

"Such as?"

"Computer hacks to all of the international banking institutions - billions of dollars stolen. The authorities all confirm the same thing. They haven't got any idea of how a hack of this magnitude was carried out; because there was no data evidence left behind. And the other thing is that no-one has claimed responsibility, which is odd, because geeks like their fellow geeks to know how smart they are."

There was a long, long silence. Ezra enjoyed his cigarette. Six hours ago the Thames House grid was hacked into and a total lock-down initiated. Remotely. The lock-down lasted for forty-five seconds; afterwards the geeks could not find any form of data footprint of the hack. In all of these attacks, all that is left - is a lot of red-faced and very confused people."

"Bloody hell, Ezra."

"My sentiments exactly," Ezra said softly.

"Do you think these hacks are linked to Scorpion being wiped out and the attempts to terminate me ..."

"Dillon, I *know* for a fact that no official agency wants you dead. We have much bigger problems... And the Assassins, the one that came for you, I fear these killers are not in the employ of any legitimate organisation. Whoever it is, has resurrected an ancient order of very dangerous killers."

"Who sent them?" Asked Dillon, voice hard, humour vaporised.

"I don't know," Ezra sighed, and scratched his chin. He ground his cigarette stub into the earth. "Although, I have my suspicions."

"I have a few suspicions of my own," snapped Dillon. "Now I know that you still want me dead Ezra - and I can't say I really blame you after what we went through: I thought I'd misjudged you when we arrived here."

"You had," said Ezra softly.

Ezra faced Dillon, who looked up at the big man. Ezra rubbed at the scar on his right ass cheek self-consciously and Dillon noted the movement, remembered in vivid Technicolor that it had been his own bullet that had wounded Ezra's flesh, and given him a permanent limp.

"You are Dillon, Ferran & Cardini's most resourceful man - or used to be. No longer do you seek adrenalin rush assignments; you have become withdrawn, hidden away in the midst of the Scottish Highlands with nothing more than your own company and a bank of computer screens as your window to the outside world. But let's not forget the knowledge you've amassed over the years, and the awesome ability in tracking people down - and in killing them... Now, I had thought of killing you," said Ezra. "Right here on Santorini... But I feel, Dillon, that would be wasting a valuable resource, and I have a far greater use for you."

Dillon lit another cigarette. And offered the opened packet, Ezra took one, and lit it with a slim gold lighter.

"And what might that be?"

"The anger I have harboured against you has gone. You love Tatiana. And because of your love for her, I forgive you for shooting me in the ass; we need to pull together during this time of great need... Tatiana needs you. Dillon, somebody is trying to de-stabilise governments and economies all over the planet - why? Scorpion was the defence and has been all but destroyed. Scorpion was the firewall against this sort of thing ever happening; Scorpion was certain death to those individuals and organisations who oppose all that stands for good in this world."

Dillon frowned. Ezra was one of the strongest, most honest men he had ever met. There was no streak of weakness - Ezra had shot sleeping men, wounded men, dying men. Dillon would not have been a problem... and this reinforced the notion that the world was full of shit.

"What the hell is going on here?" Dillon asked softly, turning his eyes away from Ezra, gazing through the olive grove towards the ocean, moonlight glinted off of the water in the distance. "Who is using highly skilled Assassins, to systematically take out Scorpion units and are now tracking me? Who do you *suspect* is behind all of this?"

Ezra shrugged, but looked away. Dillon caught a hint of something; something unsaid, something he almost grasped but missed in the darkness. Ezra was hiding something. Hiding something very bad.

"Only a handful of Scorpion operatives have survived," he rumbled, rubbing wearily at his eyes. "But more - the destruction of the Scorpion project took only forty-eight hours from start to finish." Ezra turned to look into Dillon's eyes. Dillon's face showed unconcealed shock.

"Forty-eight hours?" He whispered.

"Yes, forty-eight hours - two days. Our Assassin friends are looking for something - something retrieved by Tatiana many months ago, and passed on to me for safe keeping. A possibility arises, Dillon - the possibility that you were *chased* here. This facility is highly classified... Not even Tatiana knew, but you sure as fuck should not have done either. This is way outside the normal boundaries of Ferran & Cardini.

Dillon nodded, smoke pluming from his nostrils. He scratched the stubble on his chin with the tips of his fingers.

"You really think it's that black and white? I lead the bad guys

167

here, because they know you have, whatever it is they want back, and they think they know that I know where you are? Are you off your trolley?"

"Why did you come here, Dillon?"

"Answers, Ezra. Answers."

"And because you had no other options and nowhere else to take Tatiana. Since my brother killed himself, where else would you bring her, except to her uncle Ezra, despite your initial misgivings and our *differences*?"

Dillon dropped the cigarette. Grinding the remnants into the hard earth. He turned to meet an impenetrable gaze and their stares locked.

Dillon smiled resignedly, "So what is it you have, that they want back so badly?"

"The original blueprint for Chimera."

"Chimera?"

Ezra waved his hand dismissively. "I believe that we and the rest of the world are being given a taste of what exactly Chimera is. But for now my inquisitive friend, I advise you get some sleep, what is left of this beautiful night. In the morning, I have many things to show you."

"Now I'm completely confused. You obviously know who is behind all of this."

It was not a question.

"I know," said Ezra, smiling - again his smile held no humour. It was the smile of a shark cornering its prey. The sinister smile of a natural predator.

The wind blew up from the sea. The olive trees shivered in the breeze.

"This Assassin has followed me here, then. To Santorini?"

"I'm afraid that it won't just be one, but many. The blueprint I have in my possession is, shall we say, instrumental to the downfall of the world powers and the world-wide monetary system. They know that the information and calculations contained within it, becomes the chink in their armour: their *Achilles Heel*. They cannot let them go un-retrieved, and they therefore cannot let me live. I hold their secret in my hands, like a God holding the key to the birth of a new planet." Dillon shivered as Ezra's words enveloped him like the stench and smoke of a burning corpse.

"They *will* come. And they will come very soon."

Dillon frowned, lit another cigarette and blew a plume of smoke into the night air. He knew that Ezra was holding out on him, and it pissed him off badly.

"Well bring it on. Let's see what they're about..." He said quietly.

* * *

Ezra stood in the shadows of an olive tree, thankful that Dillon had gone. The man made him uneasy, put him on edge. Ezra did not trust him; his eyes held too much the look of a killer. He watched closely as one of his personal bodyguard detail exchanged duty. They disappeared into the gloom, moving like ghosts, and he took a long, deep breath, staring up at the vast vaults of the night sky. A cool breeze at last caressed his skin. He rubbed at his chin. He closed his tired eyes.

But the images haunted him.

From another time.

From a different world.

Water and slime glistened on the rough dark stone walls. Russian voices calling out in the darkness, men, women and children, all embedded with the deep emotion of terror. He moved down the steps, boots thudding dully on the ancient stone. He was deep underground; the weight of the castle above, pressing down upon him.

Kirill and Ramus were there. They were pawing over calculations, algorithms and he was with them. Rows of monitors lined the walls of the former KGB torture dungeon...

Ezra opened his eyes, stared again at the night sky.

"What did *you* do?" he murmured wearily. "What in God's name did *we* do?"

* * *

Alix stared at the Westland WAH-64 Apache Longbow attack helicopter, resplendent in Artic camouflage, with its narrow fuselage, chin mounted guns and disposable armament of rockets and missiles mounted on stub wings. The helicopter was also equipped with the Longbow millimetre wave radar system to enable it to find and identify its targets. Alix turned back to Lola, who was leaning against

169

the battered Mercedes van, smoking a cigarette.

"You say that you can actually fly this Apache?"

Alix nodded.

"You sure?"

Alix nodded again.

"It looks far more complicated close up."

"It is. But that shouldn't be a problem, as I could be considered an Apache veteran."

"Apache veteran?"

"Yeah, flown one of these babies many times. Albeit, as a computer flight simulation..."

"What. You've only ever flown this thing as a fucking computer game?"

"Well yes. But don't worry, computer simulation - real thing, there's no real difference between them."

"No difference. Only that we'll have about five-thousand feet of fresh air between us and the ground."

"Look, we have no choice. And we couldn't very well waltz onto a military base and requisition one of these things with an experienced combat pilot and a navigator? Now when I give you the order, I need you to climb in - you see the release for the cockpit there? Good. Climb in - insert this key, turn it clockwise and hit the green buttons on the dash. You got that?"

Lola frowned. "I thought you'd sorted this, Alix? And I thought we were waiting for the Priest?"

"I did, I sorted it with my old mate, Tiger Jones, whom I served with in Afghanistan. He flew the Apache here, and if he ever gets found out, they'll throw him in a cell and bury the key forever. Now, these are the keys, and I have the ignition sequence stored up here." He tapped his head. Blowing smoke through a cheeky boyish smile, Lola slapped Alix on the back. He didn't flinch or move. "And as for the Priest? Well, he's a little bit late and we can't hang around any longer for the insane fucker."

"Late?" Said Lola. "Don't you mean that *we* are early?"

"Depends on how you look at it," said Alix. "Look Lola, Scorpion is finished, we are being shafted left, right and centre by these Assassin dudes - we need to find out, and find out fast, what exactly is going on. Tiger's base was the nearest one to this private airfield with this sort of technology."

Lola looked around, her face carrying the full weight of guilt. Across the deserted airfield other aircraft sat unattended, mainly Cessna single and twin engine aircraft, a couple of Bell helicopters and an Air Caravan single propeller aircraft belonging to the local Sky-Dive centre. Behind them, large hangers, originally used during WW1 to house fighter planes but now owned by private companies involved in various aviation activities, stood dark and still.

Lola looked up into the night sky. Heavy clouds rolled, and wind whipped at her with the promise of rain.

"Can you really fly this helicopter?" Asked Lola suspiciously.

"Easy - like a walk in the park. Now, where the hell is the Priest, we need to get going. We've got those masked Assassin fuckers killing Scorpion units and Ferran & Cardini field agents all over the place, and I've got a sneaky suspicion they're not far behind us."

"Come on," said Lola, dropping the butt of her cigarette. Smoke trailed from her nostrils. She ground the remains of the cigarette under her boot and zipped up her combat jacket to the neck. "Let's get on with it then."

Alix and Lola moved swiftly to the helicopter, Alix opened the cockpit door and they climbed in. Lola moved around the hi-tech war machine, poking here and there; she kicked away the blocks from under the wheels and climbed up, squeezing in to the navigator's position. Alix started the ignition sequence, then the twin turbine. The engine whined, and then roared and Alix smiled like a small child opening a special present on Christmas morning.

Rain started to fall from the dark tempestuous skies.

"I hope you know what you're doing," Lola said, as the Apache engine noise increased.

"Have faith my lovely, have faith." Alix said grinning.

"Here we go! Let's see what this little baby can do. Scotland here we come..."

Out of the gloom, doing perhaps sixty, sixty-five across the grass airstrip hammered the Priest's Aston Martin DB5; the vintage car slewed around, wheels locked, skidding in a broad-side halt in front of the Apache in a scythe of water.

The door swung open and the Priest stepped out of the iconic sports car, he stood for the briefest moment, looking straight at the cockpit, and then crossed swiftly with his Bible in hand; long leather overcoat flapping, and climbed up into the helicopter to be greeted by two blank stares.

Well done, you two, for convening so early. It is good to see that God's work is going to be carried out with willingness and punctuality."

"Right," said Alix, casting a glance at Lola. "We were just warming up her engines."

"And *are* they warm?" Asked the Priest softly.

"They are now."

"So what are we waiting for? Onward, Christians! Let us find out the source of this scourge."

The Apache, engines roaring with power, lurched up from the grass airstrip, rotated through three-hundred and sixty degrees, then shot straight up a thousand feet; it halted, hovering, rotated ninety degrees, then with its short squat nose dipped, hammered forward into the heavy falling rain.

Alix grinned sheepishly. "Sorry! Just getting acquainted with her!"

The rotors thumped overhead as they raced through the downpour.

Lola found herself staring out and down at the bleak landscape below. They passed over towns and villages, vast open spaces of fields and forests; cars moved like ants through streets. In high-streets, shoppers cowered under large umbrellas and rushed between shop awnings for shelter from the heavy rainstorm. A feeling of melancholy came over Lola as she watched these tiny people in their tiny houses with their tiny lives.

"I know exactly what you're thinking," said Alix.

"And what might that be?"

"You're looking at the people - ordinary people going about their daily business, secure in their ignorance. Not aware of world events unfolding around them. They watch the news; believe the propaganda spewed out by the media - like sheep. They have no real concept of what is really going on, of what the stakes are."

"That's really quite profound for you, Alix."

Alix smiled broadly at her, showing remarkably white teeth.

"Lola, you're so philosophical, girl." Alix said, "It's not profound, it's a fact based on my observation of ordinary people."

"Are you ordinary, Alix?" Asked the Priest casually from the rear of the cabin.

"Hell no. Ordinary is definitely not something I've ever done, Priest."

Lola patted his arm. "Steady tiger. The Priest was only kidding with you, and we both know you're not ordinary. A little weird sometimes, but definitely not ordinary."

Alix nodded a big smile across his face.

The Apache banked, heading towards the north east coast of England; below, cliffs sailed into the distance and they were flying low over the cold hostile grey North Sea one hundred feet below them. There was tension between Alix and the priest.

"We're not going any lower," said the Priest through gritted teeth.

"The wave formations will mask us against radar," said Alix softly, eyes bright in the glow of the instrument panel.

"And what about the possibility of downdraft? It could drag us down at this low altitude and straight into Neptune's watery embrace." said the Priest looking down at the foaming cauldron below.

"You can get out any time you like, you insane religious bastard."

"God will protect us, Alix."

"God will not protect us, Priest. Because he doesn't really exist - does he?" Alix gave Lola a sideward glance, and they both knew that he was messing with fire and brimstone.

"You do not know God's will, as I do."

"Ok, Priest. Perhaps he does exist. But I've never heard or seen him, and I haven't seen the light, either."

The Apache dropped closer to the waves; sea spray covered the windscreen and Lola and the Priest stared out wearily, watching the effervescence water, the crests of the white foam against the rolling dark grey liquid.

"Do you know anything about this place we are going to?" asked Lola, after long moments of silence.

"A little," replied the Priest slowly, his eyes hooded. "It's a top secret Government research facility, exclusively used for military computer software development by professor Kirill and his team of nerds, because of its inhospitable location, it was built deep beneath a mountain. The Ministry of Defence is the governing department, but Kirill only answers to Downing Street. It's run as a military centre, an impregnable place from which the Government can securely develop weapon's systems and the like."

"So how did they discover that Kirill was using the facility for his own end?"

"A lowly level three programmer at the facility overheard

a conversation and had the presence of mind to report it back to London. From that point the Ministry had GCHQ monitor every single incoming and outgoing communication by land-line, fax, email and mobile phone."

"What's this facility like?"

"Impressive, my child, very impressive. It is built high up on a ridge of a mountain. There are only two ways to reach the place - by air, or by a single car width un-made track. Kirill's facility is a state of the art fortress; almost impregnable. An elaborate system of tunnels underground travel across and *down, deep down* - access and ventilation shafts, vast storage rooms, research labs, kitchens, and living modules - all carved from within the rock."

"Apart from the obvious defences. What's the security like?"

"Heavy! Special Forces trained security personnel patrol the interior of the facility as well as the surrounding terrain. Then there are the laser guided machine-guns, there are at least six of them strategically located, that are controlled by the central facility computer system. This might all seem like the impossible, but God will show us the way..."

Lola shivered.

"This could get messy with lots of bad death." Alix said matter of factly through his helmet microphone

"What's new." said Lola.

"We have no choice." The Priest said softly.

"They said that Kirill was a raving fanatical mad-man. But given his choice of location, I'm not so sure about that." Alix said.

"He might be mad and he might be a fanatic. But he is still considered the most eminent computer programmer in the world." Said the Priest.

Alix nodded.

They remained in silence for the rest of the journey.

GCHQ Transcript 6. Transcript of recent news article. NO FURTHER ACTION REQUIRED.

The Hoover Dam hydro power station was completely shutdown this morning. The shutdown lasted for five minutes, leaving many thousands of inhabitants and businesses without power.

The reactivation occurred as an automated sequence that left technicians and engineers without answers concerning the nature of this apparent security breach. When reactivation occurred, all passwords and security protocols were initiated without supervisor intervention. This would suggest either a highly complex virus in the facility's software. Although some early speculation suggests a sophisticated hacker/terrorist involvement.

The American Secretary for Technology, Bradley Glover, was unavailable for comment...

Chapter 14

Dillon and Tatiana had a simple breakfast of fruit, bread and cheese brought to their room by one of Ezra's personal assistants, Spiros, and washed down with strong black coffee. Dillon gestured for Spiros to stay, and the swarthy young Greek man sat on a chair by the window. He poured himself a coffee and grinned over at Dillon.

"They say you're a very dangerous man."

Dillon shrugged and grinning back, said. "You look quite dangerous yourself."

Spiros shook his head, long dark hair swaying. "No. Mr Dillon. I am here because of my expertise with computer based surveillance programmes. My primary role is to ensure that this facility runs smoothly." He smiled broadly, and sipped his coffee. "I'll let Ezra tell you about that; he may not want me talking like this."

"And there was I thinking that you were just the hired help. Tats, doesn't he look like the hired help?"

Tats nodded, taking a bite out of the peach she was eating.

"Sorry to stereo-type you, but it's your whole demeanour. Far too subservient."

"Hired help - subservient!" Spiros stood up and added. "I am no-one's hired help, and I am a serving field officer with Interpol, seconded to this facility to act as technical support."

Dillon held up his hands in mock surrender, "Whoa, hold on there, Spiros. I was only fooling with you, no offence man."

"No offence taken. Ezra simply asked me to bring your breakfast to you as I was passing your rooms. Now if you'll excuse me, I have much work to do. Thank you for the coffee, and should you require anything else, please speak to housekeeping." Spiros said, as he turned and left the room.

"An officer with Interpol, and a computer based surveillance programmer, eh? I wonder just what the hell my illustrious uncle is up to down here on Santorini under the British Government umbrella."

"Well I'm sure it's not legal," said Dillon.

"With Ezra, it never is."

They dressed and, stepping into the early morning sunshine, saw

Ezra sitting on the veranda steps. He turned, smiling up at the couple and said, "Looks like we've been lucky."

Dillon stood, stretching his back. He lit a cigarette and inhaled deeply, "Lucky?"

"Nothing has shown up in signals; we've scanned all of the usual channels using the hacked satellite links we have access to. There are reports of you - both, something about a stolen light aircraft, nothing about your heading, and no mention of Santorini. If your enemies - *our* enemies - are coming here for us, then they are remaining extremely quiet about."

Dillon snorted. "Don't get lazy, Ezra. Just because you can't see them, doesn't mean they are not there."

Ezra frowned, his face hardening. "I know that, sonny boy. And we have been making preparations. The operation is far bigger than you - or anybody - suspects. It would appear that we are safe from discovery, for now. You therefore, can help *us*."

"Help you? How?"

Tatiana smiled down at Ezra. "My uncle Ezra, Dillon, is as you know, a hacking genius; he was one of only a handful of hand-picked programmers who worked on the Chimera Programme at the very outset of the project. You hold the computer access codes for a number of secret Government departments."

Ezra cut-in, "Your assistance could solve a little problem we have with decoding information that could greatly help us..."

"Just what the hell is it that you are doing here?" Asked Dillon. He leaned against the balustrade, looking out over the Santorini landscape, olive trees rustled in the caress of the warm sea breeze.

"What we have here, is a covert listening and monitoring facility that is funded entirely by the British taxpayer," said Ezra. "In fact, we are the secret police of *all* secret government departments, including the Intelligence Services. If you like, the secret within the secret. Why Santorini, I hear you ask. It's off the radar - off the beaten track - it's my home and I was retired many years ago on a full pension. We are a mechanism to stop *bad* things happening."

"Hmm," Dillon rubbed at the back of his neck, easing the tension. "When I was a serving officer in army intelligence, I heard there was a secret police," he gave Tatiana a long sideways glance, "but I didn't know you were involved."

"Not many people do. Our cover is, and always has been, that of a simple olive grower. This serves us well with the locals who we employ at picking times, and saves any awkward questions being asked. And, as all of the facility is deep underground our work can be carried out here, unhindered. Ironically, we are the people who are supposed to have all the answers, and yet there are things happening and we're at a loss to discover the real reasons. The Chimera Programme - is the ultimate military weapon - but something is out of place, a discordant note, and I'm not sure how deep it goes. You want to know what we do here, Dillon? We solve problems. It's that simple. And then we go hunting."

"Hunting?"

"Oh yes," said Ezra, dark eyes gleaming. "We go hunting."

* * *

The sun had long since set, darkness came and with it the time to eat.

Ezra had spent the morning showing Dillon and Tatiana around his private world under the arid landscape of Santorini; the olive groves flourished with the loving care of a small group of village women who came on foot to tend the trees and harvest the olives.

Now they were seated outside, around the back of the villa, where a small fire was burning in a wrought iron fire basket. Dillon sat in a wicker easy chair facing the view of the olive groves. Tatiana beside him. Ezra was sitting across the fire, large chunks of mutton on a skewer before him sizzling fat that smoked and flared over the flames. Also present - some of them meeting Dillon for the first time - were a few other members of Ezra's team whom he slowly introduced.

"This is Spiros; I think you have already met."

Although Spiros looked surly, he reached over, and shook Dillon's hand; his eyes glinted in the firelight.

"No hard feelings." Dillon said softly.

"No problem, everything's cool, dude."

"This is Franky; our resident computer hacker and presently attempting a spot of breaking and entering into Kirill's mainframe located in the Scottish Highlands. She learned her craft at the University of Ontario Institute of Technology, Canada."

Franky smiled a wide beautiful smile; of French Canadian

descent, she wore her sun-kissed hair in a shoulder length pony-tail, a silken mane, her lips were a deep red, shining in the glow of the flames.

She reached over to shake Dillon's and Tatiana's hands; Dillon's gaze met the intelligent bright eyes of the woman and he had to avert his gaze for fear of gawping blatantly at her beauty.

When she spoke, her words were a soft purr, a luxurious sound, the husky French accent of a predatory female. "I have heard many things about you, Mr Dillon. Ezra speaks with - shall we say, passion - about your colourful career."

"I am sure he does."

"Are you everything he says you are?"

Dillon was captivated by that beautiful gaze and magical French accent. He realised that their hands were still touching, her skin warm against his; the fingers stroking his hand with ever so gentle pressure.

"I really couldn't say."

"Oh, come now, don't go all British and modest on me, Mr Dillon." Franky broke the handshake, and turned, winked at Ezra, then back to Dillon. "He says that although you're a murderous bastard, you really are extremely *talented.*"

The men laughed; Tatiana glared, first at Franky, then at the side of Dillon's head.

"And this is Karp; another professional hacker. At one time he was wanted by the F.B.I. Interpol - MI6 - and the KGB, no less. That is, until he was able to teach them a few things about protecting their supposedly secure mainframes from hacker attacks; bought his freedom and all of their respect."

"Hi, man," said Karp, grinning. He was a wiry young man of Northern European origin, his head was completely shaven tight to the scalp; his round face seemed to be one huge grin. He shook Dillon's hand enthusiastically.

"Nice to meet you," said Dillon.

"And you, dude, ignore Franky, she's a weird bitch. It's nice to have some new faces round here, we're stuck down there," he said pointing a finger down at the ground, "and we rarely get to meet any new blood to tell us what's going on in the real world and liven up our evenings..."

"Karp!" snapped Ezra frowning.

"Sorry!" he replied. "They don't know?"

"Not yet. I am saving it," said Ezra. He smiled warmly over the flames at Tatiana and Dillon; the heady scent of Jasmine was everywhere. "Our struggle - it is the struggle to keep the security services from becoming what they aim to fight against and destroy. Within any large firm or government department there is always an element of corruption; it comes from a myriad of different sources. You can never really be sure from where. We are here to try and stop that; we have been specifically vetted at the highest level; our integrity is unquestionable." Ezra laughed at that. "Inspiring isn't it? They've collected a group of reprobates who were brought together for a very special purpose. To ensure that the good are protected and the bad perish. To ensure the security services remain on the straight and narrow. We work external to the security service policy. We remain hidden on Santorini, away from prying eyes, courtesy of the Greek Government, connected to the outside world via the Internet, spy satellites, every public camera in every major city. We are the hidden camera behind the grille and we are many and it spreads much further than this little gathering you see here... I am merely a small fish in a huge pond swimming with much larger fish." Ezra held his arms wide and chuckled. When he spoke again, his voice was low, eyes glinting in the fire light.

"Intelligence agencies operate as cells so that no one person can, if placed in a compromising situation, ever divulge information of any worth about the organisation as a whole. But that system is breaking down as the world-wide information highway becomes more vulnerable to malicious attacks from hackers, and unfriendly foreign organisations. There has been a spate of these attacks against large financial organisations and the British Security Service itself. And they were powerful."

There was silence. The flames danced and crackled. Ezra stared into the fire, deep in thought, the cloak of melancholy wrapping itself around him.

"I never thought for one moment, that it could so easily, and with such menace, access some of the world's most secure mainframes. With the Scorpion network all but obliterated, we sent out the warning signals to London and Washington. But they sat on them too long, and did too little, too late. As a result it has put the financial stability of the western world at risk, and there are wider implications. Strange events have been happening all over the world. A brand new malicious programme that can enter any computer that is connected to the Internet. In the blink of an eye, the entire contents of a hardrive can either be stolen or erased, or both. There is not even the smallest trace of evidence that it was ever there. You may have seen on the news how banks all over the world were robbed simultaneously - electronically... All sorts of shit, being blamed on software bugs and human error - but this is not the case. We have linked virtually all of these incidents, chasing them back to their source, but the paths are not clear. However, there is one thing that we *are* sure about - all these world events, all these monumental fuck-ups - are not fuck-ups, they are a trial of some sort, an initiation - and they all come from the same source."

"Chimera," whispered Karp.

"Correct."

"Which means they are testing the final scripts and that the programme is complete and almost ready to go fully operational."

"Yes - but it is not complete." Ezra nodded. "Chimera is merely showing off."

"Showing off - Chimera?" Dillon said softly.

"Chimera is the most powerful programme ever written. It has the ability to change its own scripts, so as to remain unseen. Basically, it enters the hardrive and simply becomes invisible, and because it works so phenomenally quickly, exits before any human can spot anything wrong. Chimera will push its own boundaries, just to see how far it can go. But they must have loaded it into the mother of all mother processors, for it to be able to do what it has already done... When they unleash it for real, it will happen quickly, and with devastating results. Everything will happen at once, and this programme can do it."

"So why haven't they done it yet?"

"There's a couple of reasons," said Ezra smoothly. "One, is that we know about Ramus. And MI6, along with the S.A.S., are out looking for him as we speak. Two, the Chimera Programme isn't quite finished - it's working, and it's running at around ninety-five percent but it isn't quite complete. A premature move on his part would prove fool hardy and could even mean failure, if his plan is too succeed, he will need to be one-hundred percent certain. And finally, we have the blue-prints, which means that we understand what it is and how it works. And we know how to stop it."

Dillon looked from Tatiana to Ezra. "You have the blue-prints for the Chimera Programme? How the hell did you get them?"

Tatiana smiled bitterly. "It took a lot of time and effort, Dillon."

Dillon shook his head, rubbing at his tired eyes as Tatiana moved over to Ezra and placed her hand on his shoulder. "Are you okay, uncle?"

Ezra looked up at his niece, and smiled weakly. "Yes, but soon you must leave this place. One of our spy satellites has intercepted much chatter regarding both you and me. We estimate that they are sending Assassins, and that they will be here by the morning. It would seem that they want back what they think is rightly theirs."

"We are not leaving, Ezra."

"If it's okay with you, we'll fight with you, Ezra." Dillon growled. "You say that there are Assassins on the way? Well, they drove me out of my home and they've chased us both across Europe. But I'm damned if I'm running any more from these murdering scum - we may be few, but we can make a difference. Shouldn't we be doing something now?"

"I have many good people working on this thing - we can do no more than we are already doing," Ezra said softly. " But the *doing* is for later. Now is for relaxing, and for having a drink or three, and then - then we will prepare. We have no choice. We must stay and defend this facility and most importantly our work. It would take at least one week to evacuate the hardware we have down there, and to what end, there is nowhere to run and we would all, most likely, be dead. And anyway, our research cannot be moved at the drop of a hat. We must stay and defend ourselves against these infidels..." Ezra rubbed his tired eyes, and then stared at Dillon. "You say you are ready to fight with us, Mr Dillon... but I am troubled. Would you really?"

"What?"

"Would you really be ready to meet your maker?"

"Well, if not," growled Dillon, "then I'll see you in hell."

* * *

Dillon awoke with a start as the shrill sound of the alarm-clock invaded his semi-consciousness. His eyes opened slowly and he could just make out the stemmed glass of deep red liquid that he had enjoyed so thoroughly the night before. Images of flames crossed his mind; good food cooked on the open fire; good wine consumed in copious quantities; humorous bantering between the small group. The flushed cheeks of Franky...

He groaned with the pounding in both his temples, and as he sat up, realised that Ezra was standing in the doorway to his bedroom staring at him.

"Yes?"

"Get yourself up and then go and wake Tatiana. We meet outside in five minutes."

"Have you got any painkillers?"

"I have," said Ezra cheerfully. "Come on, move yourself. It's almost dawn, and we have much to do and little time to do it in. We have unwelcome visitors coming."

The sun was just rising, a weak grey pre-dawn light gently caressing the horizon. Tatiana followed Dillon, whinging about the lack of sleep they'd had and touching the healing wound to her shoulder. "Ezra's painkillers are working, but not quick enough."

"They've cleared my head. That shoulder of yours still throbbing?"

Tatiana gave a wan smile. "I'll survive, I'm sure."

She moved across the veranda, linked arms with her uncle. "Do you remember when we used to go sailing on days like these?"

"I do, and I wish those days were with us again." Ezra's voice was filled with fond memories, tainted with sadness of a world gone terribly wrong...

"Me too," smiled Tatiana. "You make me feel like I'm back there again."

"If only." said Ezra softly, glancing over at Dillon who was leaning over against the balustrade and smoking a cigarette. "Hey, Dillon, come on. I have something to show you."

"Does that something involve a bed?"

"No. But it does have something to do with the Assassins."

Ezra led them down the steps of the white-walled villa: a clever disguise, an effective cover for what it concealed. He led them through the olive grove, and then out the other side over arid scrubland and a random stand of olive trees until they came to a rusting iron hatchway concealed by small rocks and dirt, and fallen leaves and branches.

"This facility has always had a 'Top Secret - Highly Classified' status. And as you both know, the villa and olive groves are merely a cover for what lurks below." Ezra said standing directly over the rusting iron cover. "While I am impressed with your skills in running me to ground, you really, really have no idea what you are dealing with... You really do not understand what it is you are *fucking* with here..."

He spun the rusted iron wheel, which moved with surprising ease. There was a hiss as the iron hatch was released. Ezra heaved up the hatch to reveal a shallow flight of steps made of stainless steel. Ezra removed a key from a chain around his neck; he went down the steps to a control panel; inserted the key into a slot and turned it. Returning to the others, saying, "Step back."

Dillon and Tatiana did as they were instructed.

There came a distant sound of a mechanical mechanism grinding into life, followed by a hiss as the ground opened up and the steps turned into a riveted stainless steel ramp, flanked by metallic walls and leading down to another part of the facility.

From the darkness below the lights running down the middle of the ramp-way shone like diamonds. There came the sound of diesel generators and the gentle humming of the air-conditioning units.

"Come." Ezra stepped forward and onto the ramp. Dillon and Tatiana followed him down the ramp into the darkness of Ezra's secret world - below the hot ground of Santorini.

Dillon stood eyes gazing at the array of hi-tech weaponry stored in rows of metal racks down both sides of the spacious armoury.

"Hell, Ezra." he said." I didn't realise you had such... *resources*."

Ezra smiled wanly.

"If only it were enough."

"Enough? Ezra, you've got enough weaponry here to start a small war."

"That may be. But they are sending many Assassins this time."

"How many, exactly?"

Ezra's dark-eyed stare met Dillon's. "The blue-prints... They want them bad, Dillon."

"How many?"

"At least twenty," said Ezra softly. And these will have been selected from their elite forces...

Chapter 15

Dillon stood in awe at the entrance of the huge chamber hewn from the rock. Metal racks full with an impressive array of weapons; positioned in neat rows down the length of the chamber, were a contrast to the rough harshness of the environment.

Computer monitors flickered across the wall at the far end of the cavernous room. Ezra walked straight towards them, saying as he walked. "These monitors control a number of concealed anti-personnel weapons that are concealed throughout and around the entire perimeter of the olive groves and villa complex." Ezra gestured at the wall.

"Mines, missiles and machine guns?" Said Dillon softly. "Bloody hell, Ezra. You must have some mighty powerful government masters to have such remarkably unlimited resources?"

"Let me take you through to the kit-room. As you will soon see, we also have all of the latest lightweight body-armour, so fit yourselves out with anything you want and then we'll talk battle tactics."

"Ezra, fighting a battle is one thing. But with the weaponry you've got down here, you could start a full-scale fucking *war*, old son." Dillon said, as he inspected a bullet-proof body vest.

Once Dillon and Tatiana had chosen their combat kit, Ezra explained quickly as they walked through a network of tunnels, gesticulating passionately with his hands, his eyes wide and focused; they came to many turns in the underground passageways - sometimes they branched off in two or three directions. Ezra would take a tunnel - seemingly at random - his boots treading the dust as he led the couple through the correct sequence of the...

"Maze?" asked Dillon.

"It didn't start out like that, but over the years it has become so. We have been busy boys down here under the rock." He grinned a broad toothy grin.

"So I see," said Dillon, brushing his way through giant cobwebs.

"Of course you want answers? You sounded surprised when I mentioned anti-personnel weapons. Courtesy of MI6 and the SAS, who smoothed the way with the weapons? You see, we act as guardians for this large cache of killing power. Why? I hear you ask. Well, when a special operations team need a little extra hardware, they call in and we respond by ensuring they get what they want. The reason for this is - personal protection of VIPs. The British Government owns a number of exploration drilling rigs at a variety of locations around this part of the world. Together with this, and they would deny it if asked, they also own the rights to many ocean sites with oil, mineral and precious metals beneath the waves throughout the Mediterranean and Aegean. But it doesn't stop there, the British Government also owns millions of acres of forestland in Poland, Russia, and Finland, and thousands more miles of desert throughout Africa and in a variety of locations scattered across the Middle-East... secretly, and under the guise of corporate business concerns. The British Government also has major holdings in many major corporations around the globe, including; drilling and mining, computer hardware and software development, military computer research and development, banking, you name it... It's beyond my comprehension, and it is financed entirely from billions of pounds siphoned out of the Treasury and away from the public domain." He said with acidity. "They have a finger in every pie; if you can make money out of it, the British Government does. Gold, precious stones, oil, gas, construction, computers. Behind closed doors, they are one of the wealthiest organisations in the world, even though they tell a gullible general public that the country has an enormous monetary deficit. And this is probably best for everyone, but..."

"And there is always a but," said Dillon easily.

"We talked about Professor Kirill last night: He is, was, the bright star of British computer supremacy. But now he has joined forces with a rather unsavoury character by the name of Ramus - together they plan to use Chimera to destroy economies and even whole continents."

"I knew that the Chimera Programme was rumoured to be incredibly powerful, but..."

"But nothing. Tell him, Tatiana."

Tatiana, who had gone quite pale, said. "The Chimera Programme *is* the most powerful virus based programme in the world - without doubt. It is so advanced, that not even the most innovative anti-virus software can combat against it. Chimera is self-teaching, so it is infinitely adaptable and works at lightening speeds to change its appearance - and can even make itself invisible. But the biggest breakthrough is that it does not work to ordinary scripts. Kirill wrote the original script, and then discovered the breakthrough purely by accident. The clever part is that you tell Chimera what it has to achieve and then push send. That's it - from that moment on Chimera is thinking for itself. But more than that, it can enter even the most heavily guarded military computer mainframe, take the information it was asked to obtain and leave - without a trace of it ever having been there."

"Without a trace."

"To within a certain percentage rate. It's not perfect - but it has already started to prove itself as brilliantly astounding."

They came to the end of a corridor, blanked by an alloy door. Ezra placed his hand, palm down, on the biometric reader panel - the door slid back to reveal a large chamber, full of thirty or more men and woman all working at computer monitors, The bunker was hewn from the rock, the walls rough and course, grained and grooved by the tools used to create this underground network.

"Impressive isn't it! We can monitor everything from down here, and we only have about fifteen minutes." Ezra stood gazing at one of the monitors for a moment, and then said, "Arm the perimeter machine guns and also the stingers."

"Are they on the island yet?" Dillon's eyes were bright, alert.

"Soon, but they have split into three attack groups."

Dillon frowned. "And?"

Ezra rubbed his chin stubble. "The good news is that they have come by sea, as we expected. Had they come by air, they know that we would have shot them out of the sky with our stinger missiles, long before they were anywhere close to the island."

"And the bad news?"

"There are a few more of them than we first thought."

"How many?"

"At least fifty. And they are armed with the latest laser guided hardware."

"What sort?"

"Tank busters..."

"What the hell are we going to use against that sort of hardware?"

"Faith, Dillon. Faith. And of course an armoury full of state of the art weapons."

Dillon met Tatiana's gaze, both simultaneously picked-up the underlying nervousness in Ezra's booming voice. Dillon paced around the room, his senses starting to stir in the dark recesses of his mind - adrenalin beginning to rise - anticipation of what was to come, turning to excitement...

* * *

Sunlight rolled over the ocean, white tendrils, dancing over the blue water. It glanced over the cliff top and through the olive groves. Occasionally a dog barked in the distance.

The men and women of Ezra's secret facility waited.

They waited for the Assassins.

Dillon stood to one side of the doorway, a Heckler and Koch MP5 machine carbine in his hands. He held the lethal weapon loosely by his side, for it had been a long time since he had used such a heavy piece of hardware, always relying on his loyal Glock 9mm automatic. Dillon didn't like machine guns; they were noisy, bone shaking instruments of mass destruction, to his mind.

Ezra came out with a jug of iced tea, handing Tatiana a glass full of the refreshing amber liquid, and then Dillon the same. They drank, Tatiana keeping her eyes fixed on the small portable monitor screen that she held in the palm of her hand. It showed the cliff top beyond the olive groves, with the sparkling blue vista of the ocean beyond, and at a touch, the image on the screen changed to those relayed by one of the concealed perimeter cameras.

Tatiana sported standard issue desert combats and boots. She held her sub-machine gun like a baby cradled in her arms; Dillon's gaze swept the horizon for any unwelcome movement, and after a few moments they both went back inside the secret facility. As they walked into the monitor room, Dillon was immediately aware of the tense air of anticipation and the nervous realisation that their secure and secret world was about to be smashed.

"Will they come, Dillon?" Franky said softly.

Dillon was sitting on the edge of one of the workstations, watching the monitor intently. The scene was surreal. An ordinary looking white-washed villa, olive groves, an abundance of colourful flora, their hues radiant in the sunshine... and in contrast, an array of hi-tech laser guided weaponry, all concealed and controlled remotely from this underground facility.

"From what I saw in Scotland, they'll come," he said, passing her a cigarette.

She looked at the open packet. "I'm supposed to be giving up. But these are stressful times." She took a cigarette, and Dillon offered her a light from his slender gold lighter.

Tatiana came over and sat down beside Dillon. "How's your shoulder?"

"Okay, thanks." She smiled, but the smile was merely masking her nervousness. "It still feels like someone is sticking a red hot poker into my shoulder every time I move my arm. How are you feeling?"

"Like I've been hit by a train. But no problem, Ezra gave me some more painkillers. I just hope they kick in soon, as I have a feeling that I'm going to need a clear head and my wits about me soon enough..."

They waited in virtual silence.

"Do you think we can fight them from down here with the remote weapons?"

"Honestly. No chance. These Assassins are the elite, they will almost certainly be conversant with the majority of weapons that we have here - and how to disarm them."

Dillon scratched an imaginary itch on his chin while wishing the headache, that had once again made its presence known, gone. "I hate these blasted waiting games; I work much better on my own."

"We know," said Tatiana, glancing round. "But unfortunately we have little choice."

Dillon stood up and paced around the room, hands firmly placed behind his back. "Whatever happened to the world I knew?"

"Global computer terrorism. That's what happened." Franky said.

Spiros appeared from one of the passageways off of the main chamber; he carried a small circular optical disc in one hand, and was smiling broadly. He gave the disc to Ezra.

"There it is, Boss."

"Is this all the data?"

"Everything - it would surely make Kirill weep."

Dillon's head snapped around at the mention of his name, his eyes sharp. "Kirill? I shot that bastard in Cornwall - he should be dead."

"He most certainly is not dead, Dillon. Ferran & Cardini has been keeping an eye on professor Kirill for many months, on behalf of HM Government. He is believed to be inextricably involved with the systematic destruction of Scorpion, and he's not working alone. As you know, his facility is located in one of the most inhospitable areas of the Scottish Highlands - but as always with Kirill, he has shrouded himself in such a cloak of secrecy, that we are having trouble establishing how he is able to implement his game plan and still evade every attempt to monitor him. He is very good - he is extremely well-connected at the highest level, this bastard is almost untouchable. And since the Scorpion network and mainframe has been completely destroyed, it is pretty hard to check out certain facts now. To be honest with you - this situation can only get worse from here on in."

Dillon made a kind of snorting noise, and then said. "Kirill," he spoke softly. "He is definitely a major player in everything that's taking place; I can feel it in my gut. He was ready to kill me back in Cornwall. Which means that he has obviously become more adventurous - more reckless..."

"Your report came in to Vince Sharp, who went straight to the partners with it. But it was too late getting to Scorpion HQ." Said Tatiana.

Dillon nodded; his headache was now making him feel particularly tetchy.

Tatiana was sitting in front of one of the monitors.

"So what do you know about Kirill's facility in Scotland?" There was a glint in Dillon's eye; Kirill brought back the bad memory of the assignment in the South of England, and now he knew that one day - one day soon, he would meet the man again. Dillon would have a little chat with him, and then he would *kill* him...

Ezra frowned. "Every step of the Chimera Programme development process, has taken place at Kirill's facility in Scotland. Some of the basic scripts were leaked recently over the Net and there have been some pretty pissed-off people... especially since we also have the blue-prints containing a vital missing script for this extremely dangerous programme." Ezra laughed without humour.

"After we've shown these Assassin fellows some good old fashioned Greek hospitality, we could do with popping over to say hello to professor Kirill and his team of hackers. I'm sure they would be very interesting to talk to. But considering what they're planning for our world economy, that place must be locked down so tight that even a mouse wouldn't get inside."

Tatiana spun round in her seat, "Ezra, you'd better look at this."

Ezra went to Tatiana's monitor, resting his large hands on the back of her swivel chair and stared at the flickering screen in front of her. "Shit," hissed Ezra, "something is wrong - everything looks normal." His gaze flicked from Tatiana's monitor to the screen next to her - but there was nothing, nothing visible, no black clad Assassins clambering up from the cliff top or through the olive groves. Nothing.

"So what's happening, Ezra?" Tatiana's voice was a little shaky.

"Normal is not good." Ezra pulled a small black device from his pocket, which had a series of green and blue LED lights flashing. He looked up at Dillon. "This device has only one function, to let me know when there is a security perimeter breach... Those bastards have out-smarted our early-warning surveillance systems... But how did they do it? No matter now, we don't have the luxury of time to deliberate this problem. If the worst happens, we have one last surprise up our sleeve, and you don't want to be within a mile of this place when it goes off."

"What is it, Ezra?" Tatiana asked.

"An Electro Magnetic Impulse weapon. It's located directly under this chamber. When the device is detonated it will destroy everything organic within the immediate area and all electronic equipment within a one mile radius will be deactivated and the hardrives erased. However, once the device is armed this facility will go into a state of hibernation, every electrical appliance and all of the computer hardware that is here, is fitted with special shielding against the impulse blast."

"How do we leave?" Dillon said softly.

Ezra pointed to an alloy panel at the far end of the chamber. "If the situation looks hopeless, I want everyone to try and make their way back to this chamber." His expression was sombre, his voice low.

"It will be the only way of getting away in time, and the countdown is set for 60 seconds," he walked over to the panel, "behind this panel is another tunnel that leads straight down to the base of the cliffs. There are purpose built sleighs on the other side, which run on a mono-rail all the way to the bottom. The hidden exit will automatically open once I've pushed the countdown button." He looked around the room for a brief moment, and then said. "It's time to meet our enemy. May luck be with us all."

He turned and went out through the tunnel, followed by Dillon,

Tatiana, Franky and Spiros and a number of security guards; who were all wearing body armour and headsets within their helmets. The heavy metal door slid closed behind them. Moving to the mouth of the tunnel they remained deep within the shadows, Dillon pulled free his Glock and brought up the Heckler...

His mouth was suddenly dry, he felt the adrenalin pumping through his heart, and a slow burning sensation deep within his subconscious.

Bullets screamed, a short burst smashing into the rock an inch above Dillon's head, showering him in dust and debris. There was the *whack and splat* of a bullet entering flesh and a security guard, who was standing at the front of the line, smoking and resting his gun across his arm, had his head obliterated in a violent spray of blood, brains and bone. The entire side of his head and face disintegrated and now covered the rough-hewn wall of the tunnel entrance. His legs buckled from under him and he dropped, twitching and blood trailing crimson to the ground.

"Stay down!" Screamed Dillon as rapid automatic gunfire erupted all around - and he suddenly *knew*, remembered how the Assassin's had avoided his own sophisticated security system and early warning mechanisms back at his home in Scotland... and the bastards had done exactly the same here - they'd bypassed the security network and were now - inside the facility perimeter.

Why use such brash and head-on tactics, when stealth and cunning could have so easily carried their game off more smoothly.

And Dillon knew that this noisy full frontal attack was a diversion. To draw their attention. After all, who *wouldn't* hear the distinctive battle cry of a Heckler & Koch MP5 SMG firing at full throttle?

Dillon hit the dirt hard, pulling Tatiana down with him.

On the opposite side of the tunnel, Ezra crouched low, keeping his back tight to the rough wall as machine-gun bursts roared, screamed and echoed into the tunnel from outside. Dillon glanced left and was momentarily stunned by what he saw. A squad of ten or so Assassins were pinning them down in the tunnel entrance while another two were advancing towards them carrying, what appeared to be missile launchers. They moved with amazing agility and speed, their movements effortless as they sped across the olive grove - machine guns continued to thunder.

"Aim for their heads, it's the only area without armour!" Bellowed Ezra, and, keeping low, crept his way nearer to the mouth of the tunnel. Seeing Ezra, Dillon launched himself forward and as he landed, rolled and fired his Heckler on fully automatic to give covering fire. An Assassin was picked up and slammed backwards off of its feet and onto the arid earth with a series of holes where its face had once been. Dillon looked pensive as he took in the scene, no more than a few seconds had passed, before he was firing another short burst at four Assassins to his left, he rolled and, another rapid burst to his right, and three more went down into the dust - their heads almost severed from the vicious fusillade of bullets.

Ezra had managed to work his way to the far side of the olive trees, he saw Dillon rolling and heard the Heckler firing at the Assassins, who were dropping like stones all around him. And then all was quiet.

There was a *click*, followed by a concussive *boom*. One of the two Assassins carrying the missile launcher was picked up and tossed spinning into the air and slammed into the trunk of a tree. All that remained of the dead Assassin was its badly burnt body minus both legs and what was left of the upper arms, the grenade blast so fierce, that it had literally ripped the Assassin open as easily as shelling a pea from its pod. Smoke spiralled up into the air, and Dillon threw another grenade for good measure, taking out the second Assassin in the blink of an eye.

Dillon could hear the sound of death all around him.

And then chaos prevailed. Assassins came from all directions, black-clad, hooded and lethal; some carried small cross-bow, while others held mini-Uzi sub-machine guns firing on semi-automatic. Dillon and the security guards were responding with short bursts of return fire and grenades. Seconds later, detonations sounded and Dillon grabbed Tatiana's arm and led the way towards, what they had first thought, was simply Ezra's villa - Ezra's home.

Ezra was knelt down on one knee, the Heckler MP5 held firmly to his shoulder, firing short bursts at the Assassins nearest to him; talking rapidly into his headset. He was giving orders to his people inside the locked-down chamber who were monitoring the scene outside through the network of covert cameras and who were also operating fixed position machine guns to little or no effect due to the Assassin's stealth and turn of speed... His new instructions were implemented immediately. Commands were input and soon the computers took control of the machine guns, which started firing short bursts of ten-millimetre hollow-point rounds. Locked onto their targets; the bullets were like scythes, dropping Assassins like flies as each round slammed into their heads.

Those Assassins left standing diverted their attention towards Dillon and Tatiana and chips of stone and render were chewed from the wall behind them.

"Hell, where did they come from," he shouted above the noise of chaos and destruction, dropping low to the ground and changing the magazine in the Heckler. The Assassins charged - and were cut down by Ezra's Heckler, felling them like trees, their bodies thrown limp like rag dolls.

They hit the ground hard.

Three rolled and sprang back onto their feet. The advanced lightweight body armour that they were wearing, saving them from certain death.

Dillon wiped the sweat from his eyes, wiped his hands on his desert combats and fired another short burst of rounds at the remaining Assassins who were firing from the edge of the olive trees.

Dillon blinked.

Something dark and ominous crept like a black fog across his soul; superimposed across the beauty before him was a dark shroud like nothing he had ever seen before and his senses flowed, time slowed, everything became 3-Dimentional High-Definition.

"We have to get back, back inside the villa..." he hissed.

Tatiana nodded, gun clasped tight.

They moved forward using a low retaining wall as cover. Bullets were coming thick and fast at them, and the Assassins still standing, were firing on full automatic, the smell of cordite all around them.

"What is it?"

"There were seven Assassins, and now there are only four of those bastards firing at us. So where are the other three?"

Dillon's comms. earpiece crackled and Ezra was talking to him, "Dillon, place your hands over your ears and keep them there."

Dillon relayed Ezra's instruction to Tatiana. But, she'd also heard her uncle over her own comm-link, and both hands were already held tightly over her ears.

A moment later the first of five stun grenades went off, followed by the next and the next... Everything immediately became quiet. Only the breeze running through the trees could be heard.

The sun beat down. Dillon wiped sweat from his brow. His

mouth was dry - too dry. His body ached from the beatings he'd recently received at the hands of the Assassins. Worst of all was the pain in his lower back, the pain annoyed him and partially impaired his movement.

There was a distant *boom* of heavy-calibre.

The missile hit the villa with devastating effect. The entire west wing and immediate out-buildings had been disintegrated, flattened to the ground with brick, plaster, and timber blown everywhere. Fire was already ripping through the rest of the villa. Dillon shook his head, slung his Heckler over his shoulder and grabbed Tatiana's hand.

"This is madness - we have to leave."

"Where's Ezra?"

"It's too late for him. They're using ship to shore stinger missiles from a boat out there," Dillon gestured towards the ocean in the distance. "Come *on!*"

"Dillon, I don't want to die like this" said Tatiana.

"I don't want to die at all," said Dillon.

They sprinted up the path and around the corner of the villa. Dillon ducked as a number of bullets smacked into the render just above his head. There was a scream to his left as Spiros was knocked off his feet, the side of his head wiped away with a large calibre sniper's rifle. Death had been instantaneous. Tatiana screamed, and Dillon leaped up and emptied a full magazine in the general direction of the Assassin who had fired the lethally accurate shot.

Dillon spun round - was too late, a black clad figure was upon him... Tatiana's gun rattled in her hands and the sound of gunfire was all around him... He was slammed down hard against the dirt, and for a second thought he was actually dead. Dillon kicked out, rolled over and the dead body slithered off of him, he sprang up on to his haunches and started to move back towards the tunnel entrance, keeping Tats close to him every inch of the way.

Dillon motioned her to stay low, and as they rounded a corner, he pulled free, raised the Glock in his left hand and shot the Assassin standing in their path through the back of the head, watching blood and gore spray and the figure collapse in a tangle of limbs. Dillon grabbed Tatiana's hand, and as they stepped over the dead body, he said in a raised voice, "Where the hell is Ezra?" Tatiana said nothing.

Dillon glanced round at her to make sure she was okay, "You okay?" A figure ran at them head-on - Tatiana whimpered - the mini

Uzi machine pistol in the figures hand lifted a fraction and Dillon could see the finger on the trigger, sensed the applied pressure, pushed Tatiana away and squeezed the Heckler's trigger as the same time as he dived. Bullets lightly kissed Dillon's cheek, so close that he momentarily felt the heat of their passing; a line of bullets caught the figure and slammed it into the air, arms flaying around wildly, then it landed twisted and dead.

"Let's go." Dillon snatched Tatiana's hand and dragged her after him. To one side he could see some of Ezra's men fighting hand to hand with a small group of Assassins, in what looked like a bloody exchange of knives.

Dillon sprinted towards the entrance of the tunnel and stopped a short distance away. He checked behind him.

He wasn't sure how many Assassins were left, or how many of Ezra's security force were still standing - as he glanced down at Tatiana, who had been dragged along behind him in his mad flight for safety away from the furious gun battle. There were spots of blood on her face, and Dillon could feel her hands shaking. He looked into her eyes and said slowly, "Don't panic, Tats. I promise you, we are *not* going to die - and I *will* protect you. But I need you fully focused. Come on, we have to keep moving, and Ezra's escape route is at the end of that tunnel"

"But how..."

"Don't worry about it. I will look after you." Then he leaned forward and kissed her gently.

Dillon found himself remarkably calm, an insane sort of calmness which he had only rarely experienced in extremely dangerous situations.

He was thinking in black and white. Everything was suddenly very clear - logical.

He felt no panic, no fear.

It was what had set him apart from all of the other field officers during his time at Ferran & Cardini.

"Follow me."

Dillon led the way swiftly, Tatiana close behind him. They entered the mouth of the tunnel, bullet-chewed walls, and the rattle of gunfire left behind them as they moved into the underground facility. The noises of violence growing evermore distant, as they moved deeper towards their only hope of escape.

Dillon gripped the Glock tightly with his left hand and inched forward down the narrow corridor towards the security door that led to the control room. He wasn't even sure if they would be able to gain access, he patted his jacket breast pocket, and it was still there.

His hands were slippery with sweat. Dillon paused. His senses on high-alert, his sub-consciousness screamed at him, that there was imminent danger.

Two Assassins appeared from one of the smaller side service-tunnels in a flurry of movement that shattered the otherwise stillness. Their hooded heads lowered, as they saw Dillon and Tatiana standing in front of the access door. Dillon turned, to see them both lift their Uzi's, Dillon's Glock snapped up and he squeezed the trigger - bullets ripped across the short space.

Dillon sprang forward as the figures came at them. One was knocked off it's feet, as the hollow-point bullets, that Dillon favoured, smashed into its head. The other Assassin leaped at him as…

…the Glock clicked on empty.

The dead man's click - usually meant the kiss of death…

A fist was thrown forward, only just missing Dillon's nose as he swayed backwards, and then spun; his left elbow coming around with incredible speed against the back of the Assassin's head, which was hammered forward and down by the blow. Down onto Dillon's knee that was already travelling up, and which connected with bone-shattering force.

But the figure still managed to slam a fist into Dillon's kidneys.

He was knocked sideways, searing pain, through his torso, spittle spraying from his lips. He seemed to momentarily halt in mid air, then fell suddenly and hit the ground hard with a dull *thud*, groaning with the incredible pain. The Assassin stepped over him, moving towards Tatiana.

Dillon rolled over, temporarily unable to move.

Tatiana cowered in front of the masked figure, which was poised, ready to strike. The Assassin stopped, effortlessly bent down to retrieve its Uzi and then pointed the black emotionless muzzle at Tatiana's face.

Dillon, in his state of immobility, fumbled a fresh mag into his gun; then he brought the Glock up and rolling over fired the pistol one round at a time; all time had slowed and Tatiana was about to be executed in front of him. It would be his fault, and he had promised to keep her safe. Promised to protect her. Promised to keep her alive!

The first three hollow-point bullets hissed past the Assassin's head.

The black-clad figure spun round - but Dillon wasn't fazed, he kept on firing and bullet number seven found its mark. The figure was suddenly jerked and kicked back, holed and smashed and bleeding profusely, to twist and land in a heap in the dirt next to Tatiana. She recoiled away from the body, her face contorted with the absolute horror of the scene, and then she started to weep with the trauma of what had just taken place. And just how close she had come to being executed. Dillon felt the Glock click - the magazine empty, and he reloaded with a fresh mag and pushed himself up onto his knees.

"*Behind...*" came a voice from deep within his sub-conscious.

Dillon rolled, faster than any middle-aged man had a right to move. A line of bullets peppered the rough-hewn walls to his side in a shower of rocks and thick dust. Dillon's eyes fixed on the swaying figure of the Assassin, the side of its head partially torn open, a sticky thick trail of blood and gore covering the hood and soaking the black outfit. The Assassin's cheek hung as a loose flap of skin.

Dillon sprang to his feet on a surge of adrenalin, and leapt.

The Uzi spat once - and was silenced.

Dillon took the bullet; a lucky shot, that had sliced across his side just below his ribs and the body-armour he was wearing. Searing heat erupted as the bullet carved a neat line of fresh blood to soak into Dillon's clothing. The force of the blow spun him around and sent him crashing to the ground.

There was no pain.

That's really bad, he thought.

No pain is really bad.

He rolled over, his blood covered hand in front of his face, and the sticky red liquid looked dangerous. It looked bad, the colour of something that shouldn't see the light of day.

Fuck, mused his subconscious, suddenly calm.

The Assassin should have been dead, but Dillon had seen this drug induced trance once before and, to his mind, this was the only explanation for the Assassin to still be standing. Dillon watched as it swayed around, in slow motion, in its own pain, as it fitted a fresh magazine to the Uzi. Dillon could do nothing. The Assassin stepped lightly forward, intense stare boring down into him and he recognised that gaze, those insanely blue eyes, from back in Scotland, from back at his home when it had been violated.

"Nice to see you again," he croaked.

"Mr Dillon. It has been a pleasure."

The soft female voice held no pain, no emotion? Thought Dillon. And there was that voice again, were these Assassins all female, or was his mind playing tricks on him?

Dillon could see the finger start to gently squeeze the Uzi's trigger. And the Assassin's hooded face exploded.

Dillon watched, dumbstruck, as a rain of blood, brains and fragments of skull showered him. The black-clad figure crumpled slowly to the ground and was then completely still.

Dillon's focus switched: from the corpse in the foreground to *behind* the corpse where Tatiana stood, Uzi in her hands, a faint almost hysterical smile on her lips.

"You owe me a big one, Dillon," she whispered weakly.

Dillon coughed, and said. "I need something to cover this wound," his voice was soft, he pushed himself into a sitting position. Warmth had spread across his torso and down to his crotch.

Tatiana knelt by his side, inspecting the long bullet wound running down Dillon's side. Her gaze met his. She swiftly tore the arms off of her shirt and made a thick pad, which she applied, and Dillon's world of pain exploded to a new height of searing heat, that made him gasp and expel a string of expletives...

And the headache inside his head started to burn.

Returned to burn deep inside his brain.

"Tats, this is turning out to be a shit day," he croaked.

Dillon struggled to his feet, the pad of cloth pressed firmly to his side by his trouser belt. Tatiana bent, retrieved his Glock and helped him reload the blood spattered weapon with a fresh mag. They both took the Uzi's off of the dead Assassins' bodies, slinging the weapons over their shoulders and then they took a deep breath.

"What now?" Tatiana's voice was barely a whisper.

"We get the hell out of here, that's what." Dillon patted his jacket pocket, the small digital device wasn't there, panic immediately gripped him and a bitter bile rose up into his throat. It must have fallen out during the fight. He started frantically looking around the tunnel for the device, and moments later, Tatiana picked it up from out of the dirt; covered in congealing blood and grime.

"What do I do with this, Dillon?" Asked Tatiana softly, her

shaking hands holding the device up for Dillon to see.

"It's a digital lock reader. Hold it over the DigiPad on the door and push the button in the left-hand corner. The numbers will all change from red to blue when it has the combination sequence." Dillon said, holding a hand to his head that felt like it was going to split open at any second.

Tatiana followed Dillon's instructions, one by one, each of the red lights turned to blue, and a moment later the access door to the control chamber slid silently open.

"Come on," she said, finding a new level of strength, feeling the adrenalin surge through her battered body once more. She entered the chamber with the Uzi held tightly, her finger on the trigger. Looking around the empty room, everything was as she had seen it earlier, but now it was only the monitor screens that emitted any form of life. "Dillon, you'd better take a look at this."

Dillon stood by her side, the screens were linked to cameras and what he was watching made a shiver run up his spine, and then all the way down again. Outside of the tunnel entrance a close combat fight was taking place between at least a dozen of Ezra's security guards and Assassins, who out-numbered them by two to one. "Shit. We have to get out of here - fast..." Tatiana and Dillon both heard Ezra's voice in their earpiece and the message was simple - it was time to leave the party.

They had exactly sixty seconds, before the Electro Magnetic Impulse went off.

All of the computers started to shut down and the stark white lighting turned to red. Dillon led the way to the escape panel, and into the escape chute.

They stopped just behind the doorway, Dillon listening intently for any sounds outside in the main tunnel. And then the devil himself started banging on the metal door. They were using a large calibre Gatlin gun in the tunnel outside, to smash through the door. He pushed the button that Ezra had shown him to initiate a full lock-down, then jumped into the brake seat of the sled, and motioned Tatiana to also get in. "No time to lose, Tats - they're knocking at the door."

I hope this thing works," she muttered, getting into the forward seat of the sled.

Dillon released the brake and the sled started to ease forward. A moment later; and they were hurtling down through the tiny tunnel towards the exit at the base of the cliffs.

The sled ran noisily on its mono-rail track, all the time picking up speed as it descended the one thousand two hundred feet to sea level. Dillon fought with the brake around the bends, and let the bullet shaped toboggan run free on the straights, moments later they shot out of the tunnel in a shower of sparks; Dillon applied full brakes, slowing to a halt into a cavernous area where two other escape sleds had already been abandoned.

They stopped just behind the other sleds and wasted no time in finding cover behind a stack of heavy looking wooden crates near to the entrance. Dillon leaned against the rough-hewn wall, bathed in sunlight. The salt air from the sea smelled good, Tatiana found it hard to believe that they had just left a place where a raging battle was taking place, and that her life hung in the balance, suspended by a delicate thread of fate.

Her gaze searched the cavern and the entrance that appeared to lead out to a small cove, all the time she was searching for Assassins.

Searching for the deadly killers... How many of them were left? And did they know about Ezra's escape chute?

They both felt the tremor as the Electro-Magnetic pulse was set-off. And then calm...

Dillon tapped Tatiana on the shoulder, "You ready to move out?"

"We don't know if they're out there." Tats pointed out through the entrance.

"Well, there's only one way to find out," Dillon said, the Glock firmly gripped in his left hand.

They moved forward, keeping low, and edging their way slowly until they had a clear view of the cove. Dillon's gaze snapped round to the left and came to settle on a twenty-three foot inflatable rib. Fast, with a shallow keel, making it the ideal craft for shallow water. But the best part was that it was deliciously close with its nose pulled partly up onto the shingle beach.

The worst part was that between them and the boat - there was absolutely no cover...

"Come on," said Dillon. "You see the rib?"

Tatiana looked along the beach. "Yes," she said softly.

"I need you to run. Do you think you can do that?"

"Yes."

She took a final look up and down the beach. The cliffs above were totally blind to their angle of view, they could only hope that there were no Assassins waiting for them...

Dillon and Tatiana stepped out and away from the sanctuary. They ran.

It took an eternity...

With each step their bodies screamed at them - protesting for all the relentless punishment meted out to them over the last few days.

Half way across the beach, Tatiana looked back inside the cavern and spotted two Assassins' jumping off one of the escape sleds. They moved so quick, effortlessly. She turned and threw herself down onto the shingle, flattened belly down, held the Uzi tight into her shoulder; looked down the sights, and fired a continuous burst. Bullets slammed into the cliff-side, spraying small chunks of rock and debris everywhere. The two Assassins split up; running like Gazelles, changing direction in the blink of an eye to evade the rain of bullets being directed at them, Uzi's firing on automatic. Bullets kicked up shingle at Tatiana's heels as she ran towards the shoreline.

Dillon was stood in the prow of the rib, the Glock held in both hands and pointing straight at Tatiana as she ran towards him. She knew exactly what he expected of her, and she reacted accordingly, lunging forward and rolling over on the shingle. It only took two bullets, each finding their target with lethal effect, and stopping the Assassins - dead.

Tatiana stood up, and straightening her clothing, let her gaze drift around the immediate beach area and then up towards the cliff top high above them in search of more Assassins.

Dillon shouted across to Tatiana to get into the rib. Once she was on-board, Dillon opened up the throttle and powered at full speed out of the cove, towards open water.

"You okay, Dillon?"

Dillon looked round, smiled weakly at Tatiana, and then increased the speed - the twin Volvo Penta outboards at the stern of the craft roared and the props bit harder into the water. They headed straight out to the deep water of the Caldera, Dillon looked behind and spotted two fast moving power craft heading directly for them. He looked at Tatiana, and said over the noise of the engines, "I'm afraid we're not out of the woods yet. We've got company." Tatiana's head snapped round, the two power racers were gaining on them, fast - too fast for her liking...

The rib raced forward at full throttle. Every now and then, Dillon looked over his shoulder at his pursuers, who were still gaining on them. He turned to Tatiana and shouted, "Take a look in that locker. See if there's a flare gun inside." Tatiana knelt down and pulled open the locker door, reaching in she rummaged around and finally pulled out the flare gun and a box of cartridges. Dillon swapped positions and let Tatiana take over control, telling her to head straight for the islands of Palea Kameni and Nea Kameni, and then make a course for the sound between them.

Dillon found four one-gallon fuel cans stowed under the starboard passenger seat, lifted two of them out onto the deck, and went to work on them. He looked up over the rib's rail and saw that they were still there - hammering along, keeping pace... "Hell, don't they ever give up?"

Tatiana urged the rib on; the pursuing crafts - whatever they were - they were incredibly powerful. They didn't gain, but they were not going away, either. They sped along in the sunlight, a foaming white wake trailing behind them, and deep blue water all around them.

"Talk to me, Dillon. What have you got in mind?" Tatiana shouted, adding, "They're still behind us and closing in, you know."

"Just keep the throttles open and the pointy-end aiming straight for the water between those two islands."

Moments later they were racing through the sound between the islands, sheer volcanic cliffs flashing by on both sides, rising up to meet the cloudless blue sky high above them.

At the narrowest point, Dillon randomly threw two of the fuel cans overboard, keeping the other two. He instructed Tatiana to kill the speed; stood in the stern and fired a flare at each of the cans - igniting them one at a time in a spectacular series of explosions, and within seconds the surface of the water was ablaze.

"Tats, I want you to lay flat on the deck, and whatever happens - stay there." He manoeuvred the rib around so that they were partially hidden under the overhang of the cliff, and he had a clear view of the channel.

They waited...

Time stood still, as they waited to see the two powerful boats that had been following them, come bursting through the wall of flames, as Dillon knew they surely would. A second later they came through at high speed - there were three Assassins in each craft and they all wanted Dillon - dead.

The raced past Dillon, who wasted no time opening up the throttles and surging the rib forward, now as the pursuer. Dillon fired the first flare at the trailing boat, veered to the left, accelerating, and opened fire with his Glock set to automatic at the lead craft. The flare hit the cockpit with a devastating effect, within seconds the entire craft was being consumed by intense flames. Two of the Assassins were killed instantaneously as the interior became their own personal crematorium, the third jumped overboard, only to be fatally struck by the bow of the rib, as Dillon came racing back up the channel.

Three down and three to go, he thought...

The remaining craft spun round and chased Dillon back up the channel. Bullets slammed into the rib from the machine pistols of two of the Assassins behind, shredding the inflatable pockets running around the edge of the deck.

Dillon swerved the rib to the right and headed for the cover of a rocky islet jutting up out of the water. He dropped the power to an idle, just long enough to allow himself to reload the flare gun with another cartridge and then immediately broke cover, surging forward from behind the islet and through the wake of the Assassin's power boat as it raced by.

Bullets scythed across the rock face of the Islet, sending chunks of debris splashing into the water. Dillon pushed the throttles wide open, spun the rib round in a ninety degree turn, just as one of the Assassins turned, brought its Uzi up, and fired a continuous burst straight at the windshield of the rib. Dillon ducked as the glass shattered into a million tiny pieces all over him and the deck, and also showering Tatiana who remained sprawled face down on the deck, hands clasped tightly together over the back of her head.

"For fuck's sake," she hissed. "Will they never stop?"

"Not until we are dead - or they are..." Dillon shouted over his shoulder, and urged the rib on; made a series of evasive manoeuvres, all the time trying to get a clear shot in with the flare gun. Then he got his chance... He knew that it would be his only opportunity and he made it count. The flare hit the Assassin at the controls in the centre of its chest. The black-clad figure slumped over the side rail and fell, dead, over the side, the other two Assassins responded, one taking over the control of the power boat, the other moving forward.

As the dead Assassin went over the rail, Dillon was already spinning the rib round and as he raced past his pursuers, tossed a hand-grenade onto the deck of their boat...

By the time the grenade exploded, Dillon was racing through to the other end of the sound and had just enough time to look over his shoulder and see the explosion wipe-out the boat in the blink of an eye.

With a foaming wake trailing behind the rib and no Assassins pursuing them, Dillon pulled back on the throttles and eased himself onto the seat. Tatiana came and stood next to him, her arm went round his neck, and she kissed him on his cheek.

He looked up at her. "What's that for?"

"For keeping your word. You looked after me and kept us both alive. Thanks."

"You're welcome. Now it's time to get the hell out of this place, and take Ezra with us. I only hope we can find him in time..."

"So do I," Tatiana said soberly. "So do I."

* * *

Franky froze. A figure was crouched in the tunnel, an Uzi SMG levelled at her.

After fighting alongside Ezra and his group, Franky had been told to keep well back, but as the battle raged on, everyone had either been killed by the Assassins or had fled the bullets to find safety. She had retreated back into the tunnel and along the passageways towards the control room deep underground...

That had been the plan. To meet; to regroup if the situation became hopeless.

And the situation had become totally hopeless...

Franky stared at the shadowed figure. It had to be an Assassin; it had to be. She cursed the dim lighting down in the depths of the tunnel...

Slowly Franky raised her hands in the air.

The Uzi SMG was beside her, digging into her ribs.

She did not dare look down at it.

"What do you want me to do?" She asked gently, not wishing to antagonise the black hooded, armed and extremely dangerous assailant.

The muzzle remained pressed firmly against her clothing. The masked face expressionless, the brilliant blue eyes scanning the tunnel. The figure remained perfectly still.

There was a slight tilt of the head and a word whispered, almost inaudible - *die*; the Uzi spat, and Franky was slammed backwards against the rough hewn wall of the tunnel, blood splashing up the rock, the bullets cutting a line straight up through her chest, throat, and ending their journey slamming into her skull. She slumped down the wall into a sitting position on the tunnel floor, limp and dead, the top of her skull split open, her brain exposed and bloody, glistening in the surreal emergency lighting of the tunnel.

Suddenly, silence reigned.

The Assassin's head snapped right; the Uzi moved in an arc to cover the tunnel opening.

Karp sprinted into view, his handsome face changing from a happy smiling visage into a snarl of rage as his eyes fell across Franky's still corpse and he staggered backwards. His mind racing, confused, as he regained his footing and then felt the damp wall of the tunnel against his back.

"Franky?" He shouted, stumbling towards her. His hand reached out, fingers stroking her bloodied face, sliding in the congealing gore soaking her smooth skin.

"Franky!"

Tears rolled down over his cheeks.

The bullets cut into his back and Karp didn't even know what had hit him.

* * *

Spiros wiped his bloodied lips with the back of his hand and closed his eyes, listening. He stood in the tunnel corridor, the Heckler MP5 sweat slippery in his hands and he knew; knew that death had come and whoever was the executioner had killed both Franky and Karp. They were good; they may not have been military trained, but they were fast and they were efficient.

Get a grip, screamed his brain.

He took several deep breaths, feeling sweat soak him under his shirt, cold and clammy.

He moved forward; not towards the gunfire, but away. He had heard the shots; perhaps forty or fifty rounds in all had been fired.

This wasn't assassination, this was butchery. He had heard Karp's raised voice calling out Franky's name; understood the intensity in his tone; knew the man - his friend, his comrade - was dead.

Spiros halted, the Heckler swinging from his shoulder.

He was at a junction with three tunnels before him.

"Spiros!" came the distant voice.

Spiros frowned; Ezra?

There came another cry, this time of pain.

Ezra is injured?

Spiros moved forward, still cautious, staying low and close to the wall of the dimly lit tunnel, every sense in his body on high alert, even the sigh of the breeze through the tunnel seemed to be amplified. He came to a small circular chamber with four smaller tunnels leading from it.

He halted.

He turned, turned again.

And then the figure stepped out from the shadows. His eyes widened. The barrel of the Uzi swung around but it was too late and the SMG was already pointing at him and he saw the gentle flex of muscle beneath the black skin-tight clothing and could read the figure; could read its amorality.

Spiros closed his eyes.

Using the tips of his fingers he signified a cross in front of him, opened his eyes and looked straight into the eyes of the figure stood in front of him.

And then the game was over.

* * *

The Russian built A-25M flying boat swayed rhythmically on its mooring, in Gialos Bay on the southernmost tip of Santorini. Dillon had spotted the three seater amphibian aircraft when they had first arrived on the island. It was still moored just off the shore in exactly the same spot where it had been then, and now this was there way of getting off the island and their route to safety - quickly...

Vince Sharp was seated on the pebble beach, gaze locked on the open water between Nea Kameni Island and Gialos Bay. He watched the wake of the small craft cutting a direct line towards him; away from a billowing thick black plume of smoke rising up into the brilliant blue sky. He frowned, deep furrows appearing across his forehead, as he listened to the sound of the powerful outboard of the craft getting closer.

Dillon went round the aircraft once to take a look at it, and then skilfully beached the rib about six feet away from where the Australian was standing.

Dillon jumped down from the rib and went across to Vince Sharp. "You made it. Thank the heavens, you're a sight for sore eyes, and I can honestly say that I've never been so glad to see an overweight Australian in all my life. How are you my old friend?" Dillon said, genuinely pleased to see his friend.

"Ditto - but to be honest, chap. When I got your email, I went straight to the partners who put me on a private jet and a priority clearance all the way from the UK. Thought I wouldn't make it in time, to be honest with you. The chatter I was intercepting between Ezra and GCHQ did not make good listening. I'm very surprised to see you both still alive." Vince sat back down onto the beach.

"Got the seaplane, I see. Did you manage the modifications that I asked for?"

"Yes, and a few more for good measure. Now listen up, people. The 6-cylinder engine has been tweaked, increasing the cruising speed of 150MPH to 200MPH, but with this, came the need to double the capacity of the fuel-tanks. The bonus there is that we've also increased the range that it will now achieve, which originally was around a thousand miles and is now up to around eighteen hundred miles." Vince stood up and pointed at the aircraft. "Under each wing you have forward and rear firing machine guns, and at the tip of each wing you have a single stinger missile launcher. Inside the cabin you have all of the standard kit, with the addition of a monitor screen and a HIDSS helmet linked to all of the weapons, as well as three cameras, one mounted forward in the nose-cone of the fuselage, there's another above just forward of the engine mount, and a third mounted at the rear in the tip of the fuselage. All three cameras are equipped with night-vision and heat seeking modes. And that's about it really. Oh, I mustn't forget the last modification you asked for - and I can tell you, Jake. Adding a forth seat in an already cramped cockpit was a feat in itself. But why the extra seat?"

"Because there will be four of us leaving this island."

"Four?"

"Ezra is the forth. That is if we can find him..."

"Surely, if he's still alive he will have gone to ground, wouldn't he?" Vince said gently.

"Maybe he is dead. But, I don't think so, he's as wily as a fox, knows this island like the back of his hand, and could lose himself for days underground within that network of tunnels under his facility" Tatiana said walking down to the water's edge.

"What about the enemy?" Vince said.

"We've lost them for the moment, but I've no doubt that we'll be seeing them again. So, I think it's time to get the hell out of here." Dillon said, and walked off down the beach to join Tats. "You okay?"

"Yeah, fine thanks. Although, this shoulder is killing me and my head aches like it's going to explode. But otherwise, I'm fine."

They all waded out to the aircraft with Vince getting aboard first, followed by Tatiana and then Dillon climbed the ladder and settled himself into the pilot's seat.

Dillon wasted no time in bringing the A-25M on-line, the single prop spun-up, soon reaching idling speed. Dillon flicked a switch; his HIDSS helmet sprang to life and he went through a quick familiarisation routine, before releasing the mooring line and powering the amphibian craft out into deep water. He turned the nose around into the light breeze, pushed the throttle forward; and a moment later they were skimming over the water at one-hundred miles per hour. The engine roared as the aircraft leaped up into the air and sped across the clear blue sky, sun glinting off of the single variable pitch propeller. The virtual screen on Dillon's visor lit-up with proximity missile warnings, as they circled Ezra's villa and the secret facility one-thousand feet below. The engine howled with power as the A-25M skirted the villa and olive groves where Dillon could clearly see the damage caused by the Assassins' attack.

Dillon told Tatiana to watch the camera monitor screen for any unwelcome guests.

"Doesn't appear to be much going on down there now," said Dillon. "The defence systems are still armed; even though it looks quiet enough; I'm not getting any closer, just in case there are Assassins inside the control room and they've re-booted the mainframe."

"What if they are *in* the control room?" Vince said, dabbing the sweat from his brow with a dubious looking handkerchief.

"Ground-to-air missiles. Ezra had them all over the place, and they're all showing a status of being armed and dangerous."

He took the aircraft lower; they swept wide around the olive groves. A lone Assassin glanced up as they flew over. A stream of bullets from its Uzi SMG followed but the A-25M was moving far too swiftly. The aircraft banked over hard to the right, and levelled out at three hundred feet as it raced towards the cliffs, disappearing over the brow towards the water below. Dillon headed out towards the Sea of Crete, before lifting his visor and turning to Tatiana, said. "So what do you want to do?"

"Make another pass, but come in from the north side of the island; Ezra must be down there somewhere. If anyone can get out alive, it's Ezra." They flew over the deep blue water of the Aegean Sea, keeping low and close to the island's eastern coast-line. Returning low over the arid land from the north, sweeping as low as Dillon dared with ground-to-air missiles in the vicinity. The A-25M circled the villa grounds and olive groves several more times. There was no sign of Ezra, nor any other members of his staff for that matter. "I'm switching the cameras to heat seeking mode. Keep a close eye on your monitor screen."

"What am I looking for?"

"If there's anything alive down there, it will show up red on the screen."

The next moment, Tatiana shouted from the rear of the cramped cabin. "Dillon, you'd better drop your visor and take a look this."

Dillon gazed at his virtual screen inside the HIDSS helmet. "Hell streuth. Why do they not give up."

"I think we can assume that Assassins are in control down there." Vince said, and then added. "If they are, then those missiles could be extremely hazardous to our health."

"I agree. So what do we do now?" Said Tatiana. "I know Ezra is my uncle, but he's very adept at looking after himself."

"I've got something on the forward camera." Dillon swept round in a wide arc once more.

"What is it?"

"Three figures. Running away from one of the olive groves..."

"Try and get closer next time, Dillon. Let's see who it is."

The A-25M banked, flying straight towards the glinting sunlight. Like a bullet it hurtled across the sky and then suddenly dropped, gliding in a descending arc towards a dirt track ran parallel to the cliff

210

top, the deep red colour of the volcanic rock stood out against the deep blue of the sea far below.

Tatiana could see distant figures, sprinting over the parched dirt. And then she recognised Ezra.

"He's on his own," said Dillon.

"Can you shoot his pursuers?"

"At this altitude and height? I'll cut all three of them in half! Ezra's far too close to them... It's impossible to distinguish the targets with these type of machine guns anyway..."

The amphibian aircraft roared over the cliff top and banked at distance, single propeller flashing silver against the sun; and then they returned for another pass. Ezra, surprisingly for his bulk, was sprinting ahead of his two pursuing Assassins. He was unarmed... and carrying something in his clenched fist that glinted a multitude of candy colours and then, in a flash they were over and gone.

Dillon banked the aircraft once more - a distant droning insect to those on the ground.

"If I land, we'd be sitting ducks," shouted Dillon. "Vince, what do you think?"

Vince was sat in the rear of the cockpit with his net-book on his lap. "They're armed, both carrying SMGs and they're closing on Ezra fast. They obviously want him alive, or they would have shot him by now. But he hasn't got much longer."

"Dillon, we've got to help him!" screamed Tatiana. "We've got to help him now!"

* * *

Ezra, sweat pouring down his body, glanced up as the A-25M roared low overhead. He was as good as dead, he knew, but the small circular optical disc he was carrying in his right hand could not fall into the wrong hands...

Under any circumstances - could not.

The missing blueprints were now hindering the progress of the Chimera Programme - availing Ferran & Cardini and the Government valuable time. And as Ezra had said before, those individuals involved were enemies of every Western democracy, and Ezra was their Achilles Heel. Their weakness.

How could Kirill and Ramus hope to hold every government

around the planet to ransom with the Chimera virus programme if there was an identical programme to counter all the commands? There to throw a spanner in their plans for a worldwide computer meltdown? There to *piss on their fire* before the fire is even lit? No, they needed the blueprints.

Ezra did not dare to glance over his shoulder. But he could hear them, hear their rubber soled running shoes on the dirt of the track. Ezra considered himself a fit man, but these two bastards had chased him for miles; virtually all of it across uneven cross-country terrain. The Assassins had known the exact layout of his facility, and from the very start, had played out the entire attack with the sole intention of drawing him out and to send him fleeing across the countryside with bullets at his tail. It hadn't taken them long to separate him from his group. They had known. Known what he carried.

A grim smile twisted his lips. He kept going, finding that extra reserve of energy, stored for such occasions. Ezra's endurance had been pushed to its limit and he could feel his body using every last drop of adrenalin, using reserves that he never dreamed he had - the large man did not know how he still managed to put one foot in front of the other.

For the past half a mile the two Assassins had slowly wound him in, like a big fish on the end of a line. Now they were just thirty paces behind him and panic settled like a dark demon across his soul. With his heart pounding, all that he could think of - was what to do? What in God's name was he going to do?

Why hadn't they just simply gunned him down as soon as he'd started to run?

They knew; knew that he held the key to the final piece of encryption that would fully complete the Chimera Programme - the key to unlocking everything stored on the small disc. With him dead, it would take them a lifetime to crack - but with him alive, and drugged to do whatever they wanted?

Mere minutes. He'd seen, first hand, what they could do.

He shivered. He did not want to be caught.

Better to *die*, he thought.

He strode on keeping up the pace with every ounce of strength left in his body.

And then he was there...

There was a shout from behind him as one of the Assassins

realised what was about to happen.

Ezra pounded up to the ridge and in silence, without looking down, leaped with all his might. Hands lightly brushed against his back. An Assassin had followed him, not from choice but from momentum and speed.

Ezra had launched himself over the cliff and into - nothing...

He kept the disc tightly gripped in his hand.

There were no final words. No shouts of *Geronimo*. Ezra merely kept his mouth shut, even though the world had opened up before him... So large... So colourful...

And he knew; this was the first time he had truly *seen*.

The first time he had *felt*.

And the first time he had felt so *light and carefree*.

Fresh Santorian air raced past his tear-blurred vision.

Ezra fell.

* * *

"No!" screamed Tatiana from the cockpit of the aircraft.

The A-25M banked once more; the forward machine guns rattled off hundreds of rounds and the Assassin on the cliff top was cut to pieces - it all happened so quickly that it didn't even know anything about it.

"Get down there, down to the base of the cliffs," she commanded.

"What good will it do? Ezra's gone, Tats." Dillon said softly.

"Just do it, Dillon."

Dillon stared at her for a moment, but altered course and flew along the cliff top and then dropped down towards the sea far below. He flew a wide circle and came in low over the water, waves rolled onto the shore, but showed no signs of life. For a while Dillon cruised up and down the stretch where Ezra would have dropped, searching; but Ezra had gone.

"Tatiana, we can't search forever," Vince said gently.

"I know. Just a few more minutes."

Propeller whining, the A-25M circled and searched. Finally, it veered off, climbing steeply, and then headed north, away from the shoreline, away from the cliffs, away from the island of Santorini.

To the west the sun was starting its journey over the horizon, and behind them in the distance the red cliffs of Thira. Dillon was drained and exhausted, had levelled out at five thousand feet and the A-25M had reached its cruising speed on a northerly heading.

"Take me away from this place," whispered Tatiana.

* * *

The two Assassins walked slowly into the control room, stopped just inside the doorway, looking down at the congealing blood they were standing in. Then looked around at the blood soaked prostrate figures sprawled over workstations and on the floor, their blood sprayed up the walls and across the ceiling of the chamber.

"Ezra is not here," came the soft female voice. "And now they are all dead." The Assassin pulled off its black hood, and in the process revealed feminine blond hair, soft blemish free skin and, the most piercingly blue eyes. She went to one of the security camera monitors, typed in the start run time, and watched the footage for a few moments. "He ran towards the cliff top. Ezra jumped - is dead, his body lost to the ocean, and the disc with him."

"What shall we do now?" The second Assassin looked searchingly at the first.

The soft voice was calm, she shook her head and turned away, stepping towards the escape tunnel hewn through the stone and the welcoming calming coolness beyond.

The Assassin abhorred the heat. She hated this place.

Her words echoed back, hollow and empty.

"We bury our dead and then we leave this place."

* * *

It was night.

Small waves slapped rhythmically against the steps of the Venetian boat house.

The A-25M amphibian aircraft swayed gently on its mooring ropes with the swell of the lagoon, clicking, its metal cooling slowly.

The fire was a small one, the dry wood burning without smoke. Vince brewed tea in a little tin pot and Tatiana sat, chin on her knees, arms around herself, staring into the flickering flames, lost; lost in a world of her own creation. Dillon was sprawled out asleep on a pile of old tarpaulins in the corner of the boat house, this was the first time he'd actually been out for the count, allowing his brain to re-charge. He was grey with exhaustion, but had kept them going, and safe, until they were securely inside the enormous boat-house belonging to an old friend of Dillons. They'd landed on the lagoon, heading straight for one of the private islands and relative safety.

"You any closer to knowing what the hell is going on?" Vince asked, over the rim of his mug.

Tatiana nodded. "I think so. Things are starting to become clearer."

"You still want me tagging along?"

"We're going to need your hacking skills, mate," Dillon stretched his arms above his head as he walked over to where Vince and Tatiana were sitting around the fire.

Tatiana looked up. "We will?"

"We will." Dillon nodded, sipping at the sweet hot tea as one hand probed tenderly at his various wounds. "We're heading back to Scotland, back to the Highlands," said Dillon. "I think it's time we paid Professor Kirill a visit regarding this Chimera project of his."

Chapter 16

The A-25M amphibious aircraft, piloted by Dillon with Vince snoring loudly in the back and Tatiana dozing next to him, soared through the pouring rain, refuelling at a small provincial airfield in southern France before heading north to the borders of Belgium, the Netherlands and beyond. Dillon cruised the A-25M, its single prop engine humming behind the cockpit, their heading due north into the howling wind and rain that was rapidly turning to sleet.

They cruised over large areas of open French countryside, small towns and large cities. Dillon glanced down at the fuel gauge, he had pre-determined that they would have to re-fuel again by the time they reached the Netherlands, and touched down at a private airstrip just south of Amsterdam. Dillon flew the aircraft in silence, with only the engine noise for company, and half an hour later was leaving the Dutch coastline behind them and only the North Sea ahead. All the way to their destination - Scotland...

* * *

Alix had altered his course to avoid the severe weather coming off of the North Sea, and was now heading for the Scottish Highlands up the west coast. The Westland WAH-64 Apache Longbow attack helicopter cut effortlessly through the rain, its rotors thumping overhead as they cruised over the Isle of Man, and across the Mull of Galloway. Twenty minutes later they were flying over the Grampian mountain range, rising to an incredible altitude until the mountains snaked away like giant dragon's teeth behind them. Alix dropped back down to a few hundred feet above the ground and changed course again. This time the Apache headed straight for the Sea of the Hebrides, passed over the Isle of Skye, and ten minutes later as they entered the Northwest Highland mountain range.

"Down there." Said the Priest softly, peering forward a little and looking out of the side window and pointing at the bleak, rugged and snowbound, yet beautiful, landscape below.

The Longbow helicopter cruised for a few minutes until Lola,

Alix and the Priest saw it; it was a giant of a mountain rising up from the earth, jagged and fearsome, capped with white sparkling crystal ice.

"Eagle Point," said Alix, his voice filled with awe, as it had been the very first time he had arrived at this place. "Awesome, isn't it?"

"And the Stage School," whispered the Priest. The Stage School. The nickname for an old disused SAS training complex built into the north side of the mountain, well above the timber line and far away from roads of all description. One could only reach the facility by two routes - one was by air, the other by an electrical winch, that most likely had not been in commission for well over four or five years, used to haul up a huge wicker basket large enough to hold up to eight men wearing full kit. The winch worked on a steel line from the wheelhouse located half way up the mountain side, at about seven hundred feet above the valley floor.

Alix brought the helicopter in high, then swooped steeply towards the opposite mountain slope, hugging the ground before climbing past snow covered black runs, and higher still, speed decreasing with the changing pitch of the rotors.

"You see anything down there?"

"It's too distant and the light is failing," said the Priest. "Head for that clearing down in the valley, there in amongst the trees. We can reach the base of the mountain on foot. That will be the only sure way to avoid detection. They won't expect anyone to be stupid enough to attempt to climb the north face."

Alix brought the Apache helicopter to a hover twenty feet above the clearing, did a quick visual scan of the area, and then landed gently. The rotors slowed, engines dying and clicking, and the three travellers stepped out from the warmth of the cabin onto a forest bed of pine needles and dead branches that crackled softly under foot. Melting ice dripped from the trees around the clearing and Alix and Lola found themselves looking around, deeply concerned.

"Which way now?" Alix said looking around at the cold wet landscape, adding a moment later. "This place has the smell of trouble about it."

"That's because ultimately, Alix. This is a *horrifying* place." The Priest's words were true and both Alix and Lola knew it...

Lola approached the Priest, who was kneeling, one hand holding his Bible, the other touching the frozen earth, head tilted up and eyes closed as he prayed. "We heading for the basket?" she asked.

"Yes. I have been given divine guidance. We must go now, darkness will soon be upon us and it would be helpful if we could get to the base of the mountain before then." He stood up. Shouldering their back-packs the small group moved off between the trees, heading out along the valley made slippery by mud and fern.

Before long they were all sweating and covered with smears of dirt. The going was tough. There were no natural paths and lots of heather and bracken to hinder their progress.

The Priest led the way, and Alix dropped back to walk with Lola as they fought their way over the rough terrain.

"Do you know what that mad bastard has in mind when we get to the base of that mountain?" Alix said quietly.

"Well, he's not the most talkative. But I'm sure he will let us know soon enough. I think we need to wait until we've had a good look around; see exactly what's going on up that mountain."

"What's up that mountain is certain death, if we're not extremely careful. The last time I was here, I was part of an SAS squad, wet-nursing Kirill and his nerds. I didn't like this place then, and I like it even less now." Alix said matter-of-factly.

Lola said nothing.

Eventually they came across a pathway; heavily overgrown, a man made trail just wide enough for two people side by side. They were able to walk more easily now, aware of their destination as darkness started to creep up through the valley and an eerie ambient blackness fell across the earth. As total night fell like a shroud, they emerged into a small clearing at the base of the sheer jagged rock that appeared to go all the way to heaven. The Priest motioned them to stop and they all dropped to a sudden crouch. A silenced Beretta appeared in his hand and Alix crept up to kneel beside him. "What is it?"

"I heard something."

Alix palmed his Glock 9mm, complete with silencer, and squinted into the gloom.

They waited for an indefinable amount of time, kneeling there in the gently falling snow. Up ahead there was a slight bend in the trail, sparsely wooded; beyond the turn squatted the old wicker basket landing platform.

Alix closed his eyes, focusing on the sounds and smells all around him, the fresh ozone heightened by the clean crisp mountain air. After five minutes of concentration, he was just about to give up. The Priest and Lola just behind him. They moved forward cautiously, halting, constantly checking their surroundings in the gloom - eyes fixed, ears alert.

As they rounded the bend they came across the snow covered landing platform with the large eight man wicker basket, similar to those used for hot-air ballooning, resting alongside a small run-down building. Its timber structure, decaying from years of neglect and non-use. A thick steel wire connecting the basket to the winch-house far above. The door to the building was firmly closed against the ten-below temperature outside.

The wind howled mournfully through the valley, a light glowed within the timber building, glimpsed through shrouded windows.

Sentries, signalled Alix. *Two*.

The Priest and Lola both nodded.

You both wait here, Alix signalled, and again the Priest and Lola nodded.

Alix moved towards the door, keeping low and being careful not to make any sound. He stood up, back against the damp wood. From inside, he could hear low voices, the accents Far Eastern, possibly North Korean by the sound of it, complaining about the drafty old building being colder inside than it was out. Where were the SAS, then? He thought to himself with a grim smile. And what were communist soldiers from a closed state, doing in the Highlands of Scotland?

He moved cautiously around to the side of the building and from this new vantage point, he could see the two soldiers sitting opposite each other in front of a small two-bar electric fire. Alix heard the whine of heavy rotors, and glimpsed up to see the flashing red landing lights of a military Chinook helicopter.

He remained perfectly still, his eyes now fully adjusted to the gloom. The religious man's source had been right. There was definitely something strange going on here.

There was a noise from inside, the sound of boots on timber, Alix turned, facing the door - which suddenly burst open to reveal one of the uniformed men, stocky build and heavily muscled like a Rottweiler. He was smoking a cigarette that dangled from between his lips and a lethal looking Daewoo K7 9mm silenced SMG slung from his shoulder. He was squinting - and his eyes opened wide as he saw Alix's smiling face.

Alix's fist connected with a *crack*, and the Korean guard was punched backwards to land heavily on the frozen earth in front of the timber building, knocking him unconscious as his head grazed the smooth surface of the concealed rock. As the second guard appeared in the doorway, Alix instantly brought up the silenced barrel of the Glock, so that it was level with the man's face. He stood perfectly still, Daewoo K7 9mm SMG in his hand at his side, not sure what to do next, all the time thinking to himself - can I kill this son-of-a-bitch, before he kills me...

"Don't even think about it, sonny," growled Alix as the young man looked at him, then down at the K7. The guard made his choice went to bring the K7's barrel up, and the Glock *spat* in Alix's grip; the guard was flung back inside the building, sprawling out on his back in the middle of the small room. Blood spattered up across the walls, and from the obliterated skull, blood and brain matter oozed out to mix with the grime and dust on the wooden floor, pooling around the man's head. Alix cursed.

The Priest stood up, Lola followed, and they both walked over to Alix, who was now standing over the unconscious first guard. Alix kicked him sharply in the kidneys, making him gasp with the pain, as he moved past to the guard lying on the floor inside. Alix checked the dead guard and then stepped back outside; Lola had grabbed hold of the living guard and had dragged him up into a sitting position, and was shaking him by the shoulders.

"How many of you are there?" Lola spoke to the semi-conscious man in fluent Korean.

The man shook his head, a mouth as narrow as a pencil line.

"What are North Korean soldiers doing here," said Lola. "And what the hell are they really guarding?"

"What do you think about the cable, I suppose it's likely to be shot to hell; not many people know about this access to the facility, and less reason to guard it. I think though, that these two Herberts were down here *because you never know...*

"Why not use Assassins?" Lola said looking around.

"Be thankful they're not," said the Priest, adding. "But these two intrigue me. Why are there North Korean soldiers in Scotland? And how many more of them are there, because they didn't walk here on their own."

"These fuckers are packing Daewoo K7 9mm silenced

submachine guns. The thing about this particular SMG; is that it fires a subsonic 9mm cartridge, and utilizes a simple blow-back system, has three firing modes, single shot - a 3-round burst and fully automatic. In the auto mode it has a cyclic rate of fire of 1150 rounds per minute. And that scrawny bugger was definitely going to cut me in half with his. Good thing he didn't get the chance. Stupid young man."

The Priest was standing between the basket and the building, looking up at the very distant winch-house above. "Kill the light inside," he said softly, and dropped his rucksack onto the timber floor. He pulled free night-vision binoculars and peered up through the snow filled expanse.

"There's movement up there, helicopters coming and going."

"What are they up to?"

"Can't tell from down here, angle's all wrong and this snow isn't helping either," said the Priest. "Even as we speak two more Chinooks have landed and taken off again. So it must be something important to risk manoeuvring large helicopters around these mountains in such bad weather. The top of this mountain is very busy for a Government research and development facility, I'd say."

"So what now?"

"We need to get closer."

"This basket hasn't moved for quite some time," said Alix slowly.

"I doubt it would be safe, even if there was power still piped into the winch-house, which is highly unlikely. What are you thinking?"

"I need to get closer," said the Priest. "I will go up the wire."

"That would make you more insane than me." said Alix softly.

"You forget, Alix. The Lord will protect me."

"Really..."

"He has done okay so far, as I'm still alive."

Alix ran his hand through his wet hair, and then peered up at the swaying cable running straight up the side of the mountain and into - nothing - total darkness. "I will, of course, have to come with you," he said without enthusiasm.

"That will not be necessary, Alix." Said the Priest.

"Excuse me, Priest." growled Alix softly. "We haven't come to this God forsaken place to sit on the side-line. We're here to find out who and what has totally obliterated Scorpion, and is fucking around with a potentially devastating global computer virus; I can't let *you* go alone."

Alix smiled, and then walked back to Lola. Spoke to her for a moment, before walking back to the basket and stared upwards. Alix knew from his time here that this area of the facility was virtually invisible to the prying eye.

"That's an awfully long way to climb," said Lola, coming to stand beside him.

"Yeah, so I see. Grab your pack, if you're coming."

The Priest stepped forward. From his own pack he took out a small metallic device; he checked it over and inspected the clamping mechanism.

"You brought one of those new climb assist gizmos with you?" The Priest nodded, and pulled out two more of the tiny devices, handing one each to Alix and Lola. He then picked up one of the Daewoo K7 sub-machine gun, unclipped the magazine and checked that it was fully loaded, and then slung the lethal weapon across his shoulder. Alix did the same and then went over to stand beside Lola who was checking over her Heckler & Koch MP5. A moment later and the Priest was attaching the small climb-assist device to the base of the thick cable just above the wicker basket.

"How convinced are you, that these are the bad guys?" Lola asked the Priest.

He gave her a sideways glance and nodded "On a scale of one to ten, I would say ten and a half. If it transpires, as I think it will; then this facility is now under the control of those other than professor Kirill, and that they are planning, according to intelligence reports, what will almost certainly be a global computer Armageddon. This place makes an ideal base for that sort of operation - mostly because it is so easily defended. Anyone who knew about the SAS Stage School facility would know that much of the equipment that was left behind could easily be utilised, even with a modicum of military expertise."

"Well, we'll soon be finding out," said Alix. He pulled a black balaclava over his wet face, and the others did likewise; now, all in black and carrying the K7 silenced SMGs and regulation issue Glock pistols, the three of them looked truly terrifying.

"Lola, you stay down here. Keep your comm. open at all times, and yourself out of sight. We'll be banking on you to make *sure* that we don't get any nasty surprises at the back door." The Priest said. Lola nodded and immediately moved off to her position inside the timber building.

The Priest was checking the mountain for any activity through his night-vision binoculars. He was agitated, annoyed at what he was viewing. "There's far too much activity up there, two more helicopters have just left, and one more has just landed. It would appear that we've chosen a busy time to visit, but it would account for our approach run not being questioned. They obviously assumed that we were just another in-bound."

"Good," said Alix. "This means that they'll be too busy to see us coming."

"Maybe," the Priest said looking through the binoculars again. "We'll just have to go see, won't we?"

Alix smiled grimly from behind the black mask. "Now you're talking my language. Let's go do the Lord's work."

"Alix, you're now talking my language. The Lord will surely show us the way."

The Priest slipped the looped strap of the climb-assist unit around his wrist. Made a last minute adjustment and ensured that the device was tightly locked around the winch cable. He looked briefly at Alix, and then pushed the tiny button to activate the servos, motors whirred, and the next moment he was lifted up into the air, as the device pulled itself up the thick winch cable.

The wind howled, snow had turned to sleet, lashing down in torrential proportions. Alix stepped up to the basket, attached his own device to the winch wire with a *click*. Its servos whirred as it settled into place around the thick cable and a tiny red light flashed, then went out. Alix slipped the looped strap around his wrist and looked up into the darkness and the storm. The cable was slapping around in the gusting wind, he swallowed hard, braced himself, and a moment later he was on his way up the wire towards the winch-house. The Priest was gone, swallowed up by the total blackness. As he neared his destination, he looked down. Deep below, falling away into nothingness, was a valley of snow covered rocks, a place where nothing lived, nothing survived. Ever...

It would be a long, long fall... followed by a gravity induced death.

Alix breathed deeply. He spotted the Priest up above him, he was just below the winch-house, about to go inside through the trap door. He nodded back at Alix, had his Glock 9mm pistol in his hand as he disappeared up through and into the timber building.

Alix waited a moment before moving again, waited for the sound of gun shots but only the howling wind was there with him, buffeting his watering eyes as he soared up into the winch-house.

* * *

Kirill came awake suddenly, cursing the wounds that he had received during his recent visit to his home in Cornwall. Dillon would pay for not dying, as planned. His time would come, as sure as there was fire in hell. He scowled as he ran a hand through his hair and sighed softly. He got out of bed, stood up, stretched his arms up above his head, and then headed for the wet-room. He could smell himself, his own body stink from a restless, sweaty, sleep.

Kirill hated feeling dirty. Hated the thought that his body had produced such a sour odour. The comm buzzed. Kirill halted, caught between the need to wash the stink from his skin and the need to answer the internal comm; he knew that it would be important. It had to be important, for someone to invade his personal time. A lot of bad stuff was currently going down. "Damn." He walked back to his office space, reached his desk, and pushed the comm button. "Yes?"

Outside, beyond the false environment of his apartment and the cam-link images of the highland landscape, the extreme weather from the previous evening had blown itself out, and the sun was rising over the mountain range. Golden light danced across the distant snow-capped peaks, wind lifted fresh powder snow in waves, rolling down the sheer slopes to fade away through the cloud base. But on this sour-tasting morning the incredible and magical sight of dawn delivered via high-definition optics did little to calm Kirill's sense of foreboding.

"Ezra is dead."

"Good. What about Dillon and the girl?"

"Dillon and the girl are another problem."

"So the Assassins failed to terminate them?"

"I'm afraid it is much worse than that; Dillon is now much more informed, has now experienced the Assassins on two separate occasions - and survived. Most disturbing of all, is that I think he has discovered what the missing link is. That it is required to complete the Chimera Programme."

"Does he know that I am still alive?"

"It is a possibility," said Ramus softly.

"I want that bastard dead," said Kirill. "And I want him dead right now!" Kirill's voice had suddenly risen to become almost hysterical. He stood, sweating profusely, his heart pounding in his chest, hands

224

slippery against the polished quartz top of his desk.

"Calm yourself," said Ramus, his voice low.

"I'll calm myself when Dillon is well and truly dead," hissed Kirill.

"Now, now you are forgetting yourself," whispered Ramus, his voice easy, like a razor sharp blade cutting through soft skin tissue. Kirill paused then; he caught the sinister undercurrent of danger in Ramus' voice. You did not fuck with Ramus.

He curbed his tongue. He closed his eyes for a brief moment, and then said, forcing his voice back into its more usual urbane tone which completely contradicted his present lack of civility. "What I mean to point out, is that Dillon has proved himself to be an extremely capable adversary - an extremely dangerous and well trained individual. He has outsmarted and out-paced both the Assassins and ourselves all the way to Santorini and beyond. If he knows that I am alive then he may come to find me. You didn't see him in Cornwall, Ramus; I have never seen a man move so fast - kill so many. It was like being in a bad dream with no way out. It was *terrifying.*"

"Kirill, your priority now is to move quickly towards the completion of Chimera. Nothing else is important. We have twenty-four hours, and then we start the process. Mr Dillon is my problem and I can assure you that I do not intend to fuck about with this man. *Terrifying* or not." The heavy sarcasm could not be missed.

Kirill paused. Some of his earlier composure had returned and he cursed himself; he had displayed weakness. And to Ramus of all people... But Kirill could still remember Dillon's white hot bullet drilling into his body, a manoeuvre so fast he had seen nothing: merely wondered why the hell he was lying on his back with blackness quickly descending upon him...

"Twenty-four hours? When Ezra jumped over that cliff to his certain death on Santorini. He took with him the last piece to the Chimera jigsaw puzzle. The programme is ninety-five percent ready. And that is where it is likely to remain - short of a miracle. Operative but not fully effective..."

"Your people will just have to work harder, then. Won't they?" There it was again, that razor edge to Ramus' words; the implicit challenge to Kirill's authority was there. "The majority of your people are with us; but there is a hard-core element who do not know when they are being offered a once in a life-time opportunity. The days of an orderly and calm world are numbered - if they will not join us, they will die. Along with anyone one else who dare to oppose us."

"Ramus, may I ask why there is such urgency? We are simply not ready yet..."

"You may. Ezra is dead; but the Chimera blueprint has not been recovered. And as we speak, Ezra's body has also not been recovered. If Scorpion or Ferran & Cardini have copies of those blueprints, they could write an identical Chimera Programme to challenge us - the difference being, that their virus will be smarter than ours because it will be able to run at one-hundred percent efficiency. Our plans would not stand any chance of success, Kirill, not a damned hope in hell. We need to be strong! Assertive! And we can't do that until every last remnant of Scorpion and Ferran & Cardini has been erased." Ramus sighed through the microphone of the comm. "Just get on with the task, Kirill: twenty-four hours. You know what the alternative is... All of your equipment is to be transferred to my stealth ship; even as we speak, everything except what you and your team will need to work with, is being transported by my fleet of helicopters and moved to a temporary secure facility awaiting my arrival."

Kirill ground his teeth hard. Ramus had no right to talk to him in this way, after all, they were supposed to be equals, and after a moment of awkward silence, he said, simply. "I'll start right away." He cut the connection and stood, stunned, gazing at the large wall mounted monitor, which showed the snow-capped mountain range of the Scottish Highlands.

He could sense them; sense the programmers, from basic right up to level one - the highest, the analysts, the coders, the hackers - sense them all around, below and above him. All of them going about their duties, some of *them* will see another Highland dawn break - some of *them* would not...

We know who you are and where you are, he thought.

And those bureaucratic buffoons in Whitehall, who had placed Scorpion on such a high pedestal, only for it to be knocked off so easily, was to be their ultimate weapon against global terrorism.

Your time has come.

Oh, how I have waited for this moment, he thought, his mind rethreading the path of time, retracing years and decades. Visions resurrected in his mind; resurrected, re-visited, and buried again. Kirill remembered the time he had defected to the west, and the many murders that were carried out because of his actions.

You are all finished. Almost finished, he thought.

And yes. We will *take* control.

But first? First we must ensure that those who oppose us are taken out of the equation.

* * *

The A-25M flying boat banked gently, gaining altitude as it approached the mountainous regions of the Scottish Highlands. Vast and wild, and still an adventure.

Tatiana gazed down at the mountains, the narrow crevasses and rocky gullies, the deep depressions, some filled with the freshest crystal clear water of the mountain streams, the occasional herd of deer on the lower slopes casting their gaze upwards and scattering as the small aircraft droned low overhead, below the prying radar. Tatiana spotted lone shepherd huts and the occasional village; as they made their way through valleys and over snow-capped peaks and the further north they went, the colder it became and the harsher the landscape appeared.

Dillon shifted in his seat, groaning with the effort of the movement.

"How are you feeling?" Asked Tatiana.

"Like a piece of tenderised meat. Beaten black and blue to within an inch of its life."

"Much pain?"

"I've had worse," said Dillon.

"Well, I'll give you a shot of painkiller when we touch down, just to take the edge off. I think you'll probably be stiff for a few weeks."

"What's new. It's an occupational hazard." Dillon gazed out of his side window, down at the mountains, the thought of his home being not far away, a tempting proposition as a stop-off. He rubbed the back of his head, mind spinning, confused after recent events. He glanced across at Tatiana - who was staring down at the landscape flowing like a river below them.

"How about you, Tats? Are you okay?"

Tatiana did not turn, her gaze fixed on some distant non-existent point.

"I'm fine." Her voice was cold.

He reached over and took her hand and squeezed her warm flesh.

227

"I'm sorry about Ezra - what he did was brave and selfless. He did it to protect his people, his facility. But most of all, he did it because he knew what would happen if the content of that optical disc fell into the hands of the enemy. He was the key to their success - and their failure. He also knew that by sacrificing himself, he would be giving us more time and slow down their progress finishing the Chimera scripts... If this terrorist Ramus is in league with professor Kirill, he obviously wants that programme running perfectly, and obviously has big plans for it. And *if* it really can take down the mainframes and networks of every major banking and finance institution around the globe, as Ezra said, then..."

"If?"

Dillon shrugged. "Sounds too far-fetched to me. But *if* it can - then whoever controls such a weapon, for that is what it is - will become extremely powerful and, in the process, wealthy beyond comprehension."

"There's more to it than that, Dillon."

"Dillon frowned."

"This programme - the blueprints that I saw when it was in its infancy of inception: they were mind-blowing. If it became fully operational in the wrong hands - it could completely re-map and take over the banking world. It would fuck-up every stock market around the planet. But more than that, it would worm its way into every computer in every government computer system, and it would not discriminate. It learns on the run, intuitively adapting itself, making itself invisible. But remains there, inside, waiting for the command. The command to terminate. Chimera is the ultimate weapon that will be in control of every weapon's system in existence..." Tatiana rubbed taut muscles in the back of her neck, in an attempt to ease the tension.

"Don't you see, Jake. Everything is computerised and connected to the biggest highway in the universe. The Internet. Everything..."

"A sobering thought, wouldn't you say?" Dillon said with a brief sideways glance.

"Oh yes, it's sobering alright, Dillon."

She glanced back at him, her eyes red-rimmed. "I was really quite fond of Ezra, you know. Even though we didn't always see eye-to-eye. He was an impressive man, who made the ultimate sacrifice because he knew it would give us more time. He knew that it would give *you* more time but..."

"…but?"

"I can't help thinking there is something out of place."

"Like the Assassins?"

"Yes."

Dillon smiled grimly. "If we find who has resurrected this age old society of killers, we find out who is manipulating Kirill, and the Chimera Programme. And we know that the same person is the one who's been systematically destroying the Scorpion network and killing the assault teams."

Tatiana merely nodded, and Dillon reached over and stroked her cheek, wiping away the tears. "We've got to stay focused, Tats. This conversation has got to keep for later," he said. "Ezra was a master of deception, How do we know, he might have even faked his own death." His words just slipped out, even Dillon knew that only a miracle would have saved Ezra from a messy death. But it had to be said, silence was not a good option, and Tatiana had to be looked after. Talking made it easier for her hurt to feel better…

Tatiana remained silent. She simply gazed back out of the window but her fingers took Dillon's hand and squeezed gently. He said no more but she knew that he was there. There for her…

Dillon smiled inwardly.

I wonder just how lethal this Chimera Programme really is. He thought, as he banked to the right and the A-25M responded to his touch.

And more importantly, who is it wanting to unleash its power to gain world-wide computer dominance? It could be this terrorist, Ramus - or it wouldn't be beyond the realm of possibility if a government were involved or behind him…

The face of Kirill floated into his mind; he remembered that chilling smile, and the ice cold look in the man's dark eyes. He had believed; believed in his actions, without a hint of insanity. He would have killed Dillon there and then in Cornwall, and not thought twice about it…

You bastard, Dillon thought.

But then - that was far too easy. Kirill was not in charge; he was merely one of the monkeys, dancing to the tune of the organ grinder. Someone much bigger, more powerful and altogether much more intimidating. Somebody who wanted Scorpion out of the way - destroyed… But Scorpion had been almost invisible, only those seconded to Scorpion, a hand full of Ferran & Cardini personnel, and the Prime Minister's office knew about the special anti-terrorist task force. It's terrorist clean-up operations had been so successful that the world-wide press had started to ask questions as to *who* it was behind the termination of some of the worst terrorists of modern times. But security had held and secrecy had remained in place.

Realisation came like a bolt out of the blue.

It had to be somebody on the inside.

It had to be somebody at the top of Scorpion - Ferran & Cardini - the Prime Minister's office.

Betrayal...

Treason...

Words that went completely against everything Dillon believed in.

Every now and then, he looked over at Tatiana, who was now sleeping, snuggled inside her parka hood, which was pulled up around her face for added warmth. Vince was still snoring loudly in the back of the cabin, and Dillon had never felt so alone in all his life; as he flew the small amphibious aircraft through picturesque vallies. He gazed out of his side window at a clear blue sky, the sun glinting off of the fast moving white water rapids a hundred feet below them. After another mile, Dillon spotted what he had been looking for. A loch, remote enough not to have hoards of sight-seeing tourists, and just long enough to allow him to land safely. He brought the A-25M in at the far end of the loch, skimming over the surface of the water, the aircraft becoming heavier and heavier, until it was able to power through the still water and up onto a small sandy beach.

The others awoke, coming round from their slumber as he touched down. Once he had scuffed the skids up onto the beach, he didn't waste any time releasing the cabin door and struggling with stiff aching joints and muscles, to descend the ladder. Tatiana and Vince followed. All of them stretching away the tension as they stepped down onto the wet sand, enjoying the fresh mountain air after the staleness of the cabin.

Vince plundered his rucksack, bringing out a small Primus stove and set about boiling a pan of water for a brew of tea. Tatiana sat down on a large rock nearby, gazing out across the expanse of the loch, and Dillon walked up the beach and back again, looking around warily.

"If that tea takes any longer to brew, I'll die of thirst here mate."

"You always were an impatient man, Jake Dillon. These aren't teabags full of floor dust, you know. What I'm brewing here, is the finest Indian leaves that money can buy. And the proof will be in the tasting, mate." He looked up at Dillon, handing him a steaming hot tin mug of the fresh brew.

Dillon took a sip, and looking over the rim of his mug, "Not bad for an Australian." The big man smiled good humouredly and handed Dillon another cup, which he took across to where Tatiana was sitting.

"I don't like it. Why have we put-down here? We could be spotted from any one of those mountains, sitting ducks for the taking." Her words were spoken with little emotion, or even a glance up at Dillon.

"To be honest, Tats. I needed a break, I'm not a fucking robot, you know. Have you ever seen what happens to a light aircraft when the pilot nods off. And anyway, anyone could have heard the sound of an aircraft engine for miles around, that's why I chose this particular loch to land it on. This area is uninhabited. No villages, no crofters, nobody for miles around."

"How long do we stay here?"

"About an hour and a few more cups of tea. And maybe then I'll be ready to take on the mountains and valleys again. I only hope that we can make Kirill's facility in time to meet up with the others."

"The Priest is with them. They'll be there, okay." Tatiana got up off of the rock that she had been sitting on and stood staring directly at Dillon for a moment, and then said, "Coming up here will not have been for nothing, you know, Dillon?"

"I'm glad to hear it, Tats. Because since you arrived back in my life, I've been shot at, stabbed, almost blown-up, my home has been trashed, and I've never flown so far in such an uncomfortable aircraft. All because of this bastard, Kirill..."

"Kirill is the key to everything that has happened, and he is at the end of all this."

"Is he really going to have *all* of the answers?" Asked Vince.

"Only if I ask the right questions and apply just the correct level of pain," said Dillon. He paced up and down the beach for a while. All the time thoughts about his present situation running freely through his tired mind.

Tatiana went over to where Vince was now watching over his pan of boiling water. "You okay, Tatiana?"

"I'm fine, Vince. Thank you for asking. But it's Dillon, he's changed so much. Do you think he's okay?"

"I could say that there's absolutely nothing wrong with him. But like you, I'm seeing a Jake Dillon that I've not seen for a while. Of course, it could be that this whole affair is moving along at such a fast pace, and the killing is so prolific, that he's having to think on his feet - on the run, so to speak. Or, it might be his *old* problem showing itself once again!"

"Old problem?"

"You of all people must know?"

"Haven't got a clue what you're talking about. Talk to me, Vince."

"How do you think he's stayed alive all these years? Skill, instinct, experience. Well, I suppose you could call it all of those rolled in together. But something changes inside his brain when he's under extreme pressure."

"Such as?"

"He kills people. Usually with exceptional ease." Vince said, as he poured more boiling hot water into the small teapot.

"But, that's what he has been trained to do."

"Yes that's true. But part of the reason why he came up here to Scotland, was to get away from all the killing. That last assignment he was given for instance; remember the one? The stolen Vermeer painting, Charlie Hart on Sandbanks. We should all remember it, because that assignment turned out to be one of the biggest smuggling operation busts - ever. Afterwards, Jake told me that it had turned into a blood-bath at the house near Lyme Regis. But, that as he was killing each and every one of those men sent to *kill* him. He felt nothing, actually found himself enjoying the killing so much, that it eventually felt like he was watching from afar. Affected him really badly, and then that Issy went and left him. Well, that was the last straw, it had all took its toll, to the point, where he had to get off the Ferran & Cardini International merry-go-round for a while. Or, in his own words, go completely mad. Personally, I still feel that he made the right decision, and I'm glad he got out. It saved him, Tatiana. Saved him from himself... We've kept in touch over the last year or so, and that's why I've been able to keep an eye on him. Make sure that he didn't become a candidate for a stay at a secure unit."

"I had no idea, Vince."

"Well, it's not something that you shout about from the rooftops, is it. You and I are the only people who know about this. So let's make sure it stays that way. Okay?"

"Absolutely okay, Vince."

"He might also be a bit twitchy about flying illegally the entire route from Santorini. If we had been caught flying through airspace where we'd not got clearance... We could have got into some major trouble.

"It's a good thing that Dillon stayed below five-hundred feet, then."

"What's that about staying below five-hundred feet?" Dillon said gruffly.

"Oh, nothing. I was just saying to Vince, that we're going to have to stay covert."

"Easy to say. I'm the idiot who has to weave that aircraft between those mountains. Vince, how are we doing for fuel?"

"With the extra fuel tanks that we installed, we've got plenty to get to Kirill's facility, and then enough to get us out again."

Dillon nodded, and sat down on a near-by rock beside Tatiana. He said, rubbing his eyes, "I suggest we get going soon. How far away from Kirill's facility are we?"

Tatiana, picked up the e-map reader beside her and tapped a point on the map. "We're presently about a hundred miles south of the facility. As long as we stay low - and lucky for us there's not that many inhabitants in this area - then we can carry on skirting up through the valleys, to the northern most mountain range, and our final destination. We'll be able to head for the co-ordinates Ezra gave to me on Santorini, just before the Assassins attacked..." Tatiana's voice trailed off. She glanced at Dillon whose eyes were closed, his face stony. "How long will it take us to get there, Jake?"

Dillon opened his eyes, "I can have us there within an hour, but from here on in it's going to be a much harder ride; there's definitely a military stealth presence, although I'm not entirely sure why, probably a legacy from the old SAS training centre that is now part of Kirill's complex. We'll stick out like a sore thumb, of course, and the area around the complex will be a no fly zone, especially as we're not exactly flying any official colours or markings. This A-25M is Russian built and will be quite happy flying low over land as well as water, but everything will have to be done more cautiously. And here's the real peach, I'm not used to flying in such unfamiliar and treacherous terrain."

"I wish I hadn't asked."

"We are taking a great risk going into that area by air - over land would be much safer, but would take too long to get there." Vince said.

"He's right, of course." Dillon's words were casual.

"But you both agree. It's a risk we must take?"

Dillon stood up and looked back at both of them, saying. "Of course. If we don't do this thing. Well, the alternative doesn't bare thinking about, does it?"

Vince poured out more tea, which they all drank sweet and without milk. Steam swirled off the open pan and Dillon felt suddenly at peace. The aches and pains - which he had grown accustomed to - had lessened and he felt almost comfortable, almost his old self...

He could not put his finger on the reason for this sudden surge of good feeling, but the beauty of the Scottish Highlands had something to do with it, and the feeling that he was about to do something life changing - boded well with him. They were no longer the *hunted*, but the hunter... He had already changed the way he was thinking in his mind, was now thinking like a predator, the one who was now in control.

It might only be limited control, but now he was calling the shots.

Use these Assassins to do your dirty work, he thought. I'll kill everyone of them.

Let's see what explanations and answers you have, Professor Kirill.

Let's see what song you sing.

* * *

An hour later and Dillon and the others had restored the beach, as if they had never been there, and climbed back into the cramped cabin of the A-25M.

Dillon warmed up the engine, then eased the amphibious aircraft out into the deeper water and used the entire length of the loch to take-off. Pushing the throttle forward he increased the speed, and was soon skimming over the surface of the water. As the aircraft neared the far end of the loch, Dillon pulled back on the control column and they lifted smoothly up into the air. As they were gaining height he had to bank hard over the left to miss the sheer cliffs of the mountain range looming up before them. The aircraft's fuselage shuddered under the extreme pressure of the manoeuvre, and as the A-25M levelled out, the valley landscape was there just two hundred feet below them.

Dillon eased back the airspeed, Tatiana looked out of her window, Vince had his laptop open, hacking into the mainframe at Kirill's facility. As they droned over the rugged terrain, Dillon - now fully awake, alert and seeming more like his old self after an hour or so of rest, only occasionally winced at the stabs of pain within his battered body. He slid down his helmet's visor, at the same time activating the flight-information display. The terrain ahead of the small amphibious aircraft sprang to life and Dillon gasped at the digital image.

"I'm impressed, Vince."

"So you should be, the amount of favours I had to call in to get it."

Data started to roll down both sides of the visor; images fed from the fuselage mounted camera's appeared in separate boxes that Dillon could enlarge with the slightest movement of his eye. Symbols appeared and potential hazardous terrain highlighted with different colours. Dillon noted the weapons-system tracker in the top left corner and he licked his lips nervously.

"How much control do I have here, Vince?"

"None. Not until I log you into the flight-programme from my laptop."

"And if you don't log me into it?"

"Well, then I control all of the weapons-systems from back here."

"Good. Let's leave it like that, then."

"Okay. If you say so, Jake. But is there any particular reason why?"

"Because I say so. Trust me on this, I'll fly, you keep your eyes glued to that screen of yours."

"What's the flashing red light on the left-hand side of my visor?"

"That, is definitely not good. In fact, way bad news. Air-defence warning signal - Stinger missiles, machine guns - the full monty, mate."

"How far from the facility, are we?"

"Twelve miles at most. We need to re-think our approach strategy, and fast, Jake."

"I'll drop down to ninety feet and look for somewhere to put

235

down. They might just send out choppers and this amphibian is no match for what they'll send up." After some distance, Dillon brought the A-25M down on a small loch between two mountain ranges. Gentle, tree covered slopes rose up to meet the sheer cliffs flanking the expanse of deep water. Dillon taxied the amphibian aircraft up onto a secluded beach - the propeller wound down.

Dillon and Tatiana climbed down from the cockpit, while Vince flicked a few switches and armed the aircraft's anti-tamper defence system, then eased himself down. He carried his laptop in one hand as he walked towards them. "You're not going to like what I have to tell you."

Dillon looked at the big Australian, knowingly. "Surprise me."

Vince opened the laptop and set it down on a large smooth rock. "The route that we need to take is crawling with early warning sensors, most likely set-up by the SAS when they established the training centre up here. These early warning sensors will be linked via Kirill's mainframe to any number of patrol squads - maybe two or three heavily armed and well trained soldiers in each squad. Now, we might get lucky and just manage to sneak past them, might. But I can't guarantee that we would get past them - *undetected*. There is also the strong possibility that if we don't get through - Kirill and his merry band of computer nerds, might just, not be there. Your main man could vanish."

"What do you suggest?" Tatiana said.

"Well. It's something I stumbled upon, just before I left London to come and meet you on Santorini."

"So what is it?" Dillon mumbled impatiently.

"A special forces weapons and vehicle stash." Vince looked at both of their uncomprehending expressions for a brief moment; "Don't look at me as if I'm barking mad, you two. I'm not joking, they have them all over the planet. Ezra was a caretaker of one. They are extensively equipped with all manner of goodies, including; all-terrain stealth vehicles. It just depends what your priority is - speed or stealth? Now, I've been thinking. I could get us there in the A-25M but we might trigger some of their more sophisticated sensors - just depends what they've got!"

Dillon paced up and down the small beach. "Show me on the map."

Vince brought up a map on the screen - tapped in a command

and the screen updated itself; the overlay that covered the original map with modified information. Dillon and Tatiana knelt down on the sand in front of the screen, and Dillon traced his finger over the highlighted terrain.

"Where is the Kirill facility?"

Vince pointed. "Somewhere within this mountain range here," making a small circular motion with the tip of his finger. "It can't be that easy to hide, although they do try. By all accounts it's a labyrinthine complex hewn out of the mountain rock."

"Couldn't we take a less direct route, say, by way of no sensors or anything that is likely to blow us clean out of the sky?"

"It's possible, but something is already taking place up there. GCHQ has intercepted some chatter taking place between chopper pilots and the facility. In fact, there's been quite a lot of air movement taking place over the last twenty-four hours. It looks like they're already shipping out. We could try - but to be honest, Jake, I think we're going to have to run the gauntlet, or dear old Professor Kirill is going to do a vanishing act. The software I've loaded into the aircraft's processor should keep us partially safe, but don't go blaming good old Vince, if we run into a little heat."

"Great. Any other good news?"

"I can re-map the co-ordinates to take us to the special forces' weapons and vehicle stash; or as near to it as possible. Lucky for us, it's quite close to a loch."

"Hmmm." Dillon scratched at the stubble on his chin, and decided that he needed a shower and a shave. He felt the cold air of the Highlands, touch the back of his neck.

"Okay, let's head for the stash, and then I'll go in by vehicle alone, and you can wait at the aircraft with Tatiana -"

"I'm coming with you, Dillon," Tatiana said.

"No way, Tats. You're in no fit state."

"Who the fuck do you think you are, Dillon. You - do not order me around."

Their glares locked. Dillon shook his head. "I work better alone."

"Well, I'm not asking you to wet-nurse me, either. I can do that quite adequately myself. But I've not come this far, just to sit on the sideline and simply watch these bastards from afar. I'm going in, Jake, and I'll either go with you or without you. *You* can accompany *me* if you feel up to it - after all, the beating you've suffered over the last few days must have slowed down your reflexes a little bit. And remember who got you out of Ezra's bunker alive... Without me you'd have been just another kill for that Assassin..."

"Whoa, point taken." Dillon held up his hands. "If you really want to come..." "You should know better than to mess with a fiery woman, Jake." said Vince.

"Show me on the map exactly where we would have to land; and how far it would be to this special forces depot." Tatiana pointed at the screen.

"Okay," Vince enlarged the image on the screen, "The only place for us to land, is this small loch, here." He indicated a point on the map, "It's only just long enough for us to land on, but it is doable. From here, it's only about half a mile to the depot, and another mile to the facility itself."

Dillon glanced up at a foreboding sky, low thunderous clouds rolled over them, the promise of foul weather to follow. He looked at Tatiana, and then at Vince. "Let's get on with it, then."

* * *

The A-25M rocked gently on the water at the edge of the loch, hot metal cooling in the light breeze even as they were camouflaging the fuselage with anything they could lay their hands on. Thirty minutes later and they'd covered the half a mile distance to the depot.

They stood, staring up at the wall of rock before them.

"Where is it?" asked Tatiana.

"You're looking at it."

Tatiana gazed up at the jagged vertical surface of the mountain that now barred their way. The rock was a dark granite grey, scarred, part of a landscape scoured by the severest weather that nature had thrown at it since the beginning of time. It was a sanctuary from the bitterly cold north wind. It was a mountain with a sense of history.

"It's a wall of solid rock, Vince."

"No, you've got to look harder."

Special forces depots were dotted all over the globe, and carried equipment specific to the sort of territory in which they were located. Periodically they would be checked and re-stocked by Government officials. On numerous occasions they had made a difference between life and death.

All of these depots were located under the ground or behind rock and even inside disused mine shafts. Monitored via live web cams and linked via a military satellite to a secure server, images end up at an automated monitoring station located in a bunker beneath Whitehall. Any undue change in temperature, or unauthorised movement inside any depot, is instantly relayed back and the nearest military unit dispatched to investigate.

Dillon pulled out his Ferran & Cardini smart-phone and held it in the palm of his hand.

"This little beauty has the pre-loaded software to open doors. But if I switch it on again, our position will be immediately given away?"

"That's true. But if they're that good, they know where we are, or where we're going. We just have to concentrate on staying one step ahead. Act, don't react, yeah?"

Dillon switched on the handset and accessed the application. It *blipped*. There came a release of compressed air from somewhere behind the rock and, raining debris from above, a huge circular section of the mountain side suddenly shifted - sliding back into the rock, allowing access to a deep dark interior.

Dillon and Tatiana moved forward; Vince watched them walk into the gloom from the entrance; after a moment he also moved inside, went forward and found the nearest bench, where he placed his burner and proceeded with the ritual of getting a brew on.

They stooped, peering into the gloom lit by triggered emergency lighting set into the side walls on both sides of the wide access tunnel.

"Let's see what little goodies are stashed here."

They descended the ramp; against one wall was an array of weapons, from mini machine pistols to sniper rifles and even a couple of Stinger missile launchers. All weapons were neatly lined up in racks and protected behind glass screens. Ammunition sat in wooden crates in one corner, and there were several large metal containers, the type used on freight ships. Dillon moved forward and pulled open the doors of the first container.

Tatiana frowned.

"A quad bike?"

"It's more than that," said Dillon, a hidden sense of joy in his voice. "It's modified for these conditions - this machine has a much more powerful motor, more torque, and an array of extra special modifications and upgrades. It's a dream machine, Tats."

"I would have preferred a four-wheel-drive with a nice warm cabin."

"Sounds cosy, but these things are best for running over this rough terrain - as long as you know how to handle one. This quad will eat whatever is thrown at it; look at the tyres! Just wait till we get this baby out there."

He walked into the container and sat on the quad bike, hand tracing the contours of the fuel tank. His gaze roving around the machine as he got off and stood back. The engine was much more powerful than the standard one fitted, with its curious design and powerful output. He tapped the enlarged fuel tank. "Full and raring to go; all we have to do is turn the key and fire her up."

"What modifications does it have?"

Dillon pointed to a place just below the twin headlights; four, small bore barrels poked forward. "Mounted sub-machine guns with ammunition on four drums stored either side of the fuel tank up front. Mounted on the handlebars is a GPS sat-nav, sat-phone, and data panel for all of the gizmos. It has a stealth exhaust system, and this baby will run silent - silent and deadly. And special mudguards which stop all the shit from flying everywhere and over us."

Dillon moved around the large machine, before getting back on and firing it up, true to his word, there was nothing more than a gentle purr. "If anything can get us to Kirill's facility over land, then this is it."

Tatiana shook her head. "The mental scars are still there from the last time I rode on the back of a bike with you."

Dillon grinned boyishly at her. "Don't worry, luv - this ride will be much, much worse."

* * *

The quad bike climbed the ramp with ease, its engine note nothing more than a whisper; tyres bit into the dirt and Dillon pulled a perfect wheelie towards Vince.

"Very nice, chap," remarked Vince, nodding as he held out a steaming hot mug of tea.

Dillon jumped off the quad and walked over to the big Australian, accepting the offered mug. "There's only packs of field rations down there, which is better than nothing and they'll keep us going for the time being."

Vince delved into his rucksack and pulled out a large red apple and tossed it across to Dillon, who deftly caught it in his left hand. "I'll regret giving you that, when all I've got to eat is a dried meal in a bag."

"Thanks mate. There's another thing."

"What's that?" Vince sipped his brew, his eyes suspicious.

"Back down there, I saw an AMSD OM 50 Nemesis 12.7mm sniper rifle. With a telescopic night sight."

"What of it."

"It's got some sort of fingerprint recognition trigger instead of a conventional one. "I was wondering if you'd set it up for *me?*"

"A Nemesis, eh. Not an easy rifle to set up, but I'll give it a go. Why that particular weapon? There must be hundreds of weapons to choose from in that armoury."

"It's not just a rifle, Vince. It's the ultimate long range sniper rifle."

"Possibly, and I'll agree it's most likely the best weapon here." The two men walked back down the ramp to the weapons store and Vince proceeded to personalise the Nemesis trigger grip to Dillon's hand print, using the software on his laptop. "Now that this grip is associated with you - no one else can use this weapon, even if they wanted to. Just remember that you cannot just pick this up and fire it. You must let the reader inside the grip recognise your hand print, first. Although, this only takes a fraction of a second to complete."

"Yeah, Yeah. I know all of that stuff, and I won't forget."

"I've seen you in action, remember! Waiting is not something you do so well, along with treating your equipment with respect..."

"I'll take extra care of all my equipment, I promise." Dillon said soberly, but the grin across his face gave him away.

"Yeah, right, I've seen the condition of that Glock you carry around with you."

"Used but never abused," said Dillon. "The fact is that it's so worn and yet still functions perfectly, is a testament to my love for it. And it wouldn't have lasted this long if I'd casually tossed it aside, now would it?"

Vince muttered something incomprehensible.

"Now, now, Vincent. Leave Dillon alone," said Tatiana softly, moving out of the gloom. She carried a Glock, several spare magazines and some boxes of ammunition. She handed Dillon some of the magazines and ammo boxes and stashed the rest in the pockets of her jacket, saying, "I also grabbed a few of the field ration packs, they're under the quad's front seat."

"I'm hoping that we won't be gone long enough to need them," Dillon said, smiling grimly.

* * *

The special forces depot also contained clothing necessary for the locality, in case they were separated from the quad bike: thermal base layers and traditional Arctic camouflage fatigues were chosen.

"Wrap up, Tats - we'll blend in and at least we won't die of hypothermia."

"Are there any helmets in there?"

Dillon shook his head. "Balaclavas only. Don't worry, we're not going to crash."

They spent a few minutes getting into their clothing, Dillon fooling around despite the seriousness of their predicament. When both were fully dressed, they stood staring at each other and Dillon's hand reached out and stroked Tatiana's cheek.

"You look stunning, as always."

"What are you after?"

"Absolutely nothing. I merely wanted to tell you, that's all."

"You old charmer, Dillon. You're so full of crap."

"So a man can't even be romantic, even if the timings off and the situation, so wrong on so many levels?"

Dillon smiled, tension easing from him. "Come on, best we get going. thanks to this unscheduled diversion, we're already running late. You got the co-ordinates for the facility?"

Tatiana punched the numeric codes into the quad's sat-nav to guide them to Kirill's mountain.

They both sat on the quad bike and Dillon fired up the machine. Tatiana settled herself on the back seat of the huge machine and they both turned, gazes fixing on Vince Sharp. "You know the procedures, Vince," said Dillon.

Vince nodded. "Be careful, mates."

Dillon laughed, pulling on his goggles. "Oh, we'll be careful, mate. But we'll also be lethal."

All four wheels spun, gripped and the next instant the quad bike shot away...

* * *

Dillon had warned Tatiana of the perils of riding pillion on the quad, how she should watch his every move, and not to throw herself around on the machine. "We'll be travelling over some extreme terrain, and it'll get rough at times, but all you've got to do is hang onto me with everything you've got."

Now, as the quad bike surged forward, Tatiana's heart was in her mouth; the rain had returned and was now beating down, mud and water sprayed up under the splashguards on both sides, and they left Vince behind as they powered on up through the first valley. A torque-filled engine throbbing beneath them like an athlete's heart beating at full rate. The quad sailed over the waterlogged ground, cutting out any need for tracks or roads, and as they crested a ridge, Dillon still piling on the power, the quad's front wheels lifted from the ground in a shower of debris and water spray.

Another world opened up, a world of rolling heather, a great mauve carpet caressed by the wind, stretching off to the horizon. Nothing else moved, nothing stirred in this bleak harsh environment: no trees, no inhabitants - just the occasional covey of grouse taking flight. Two words sprang into Tatiana's mind to describe this place.

Total isolation.

They powered forward, down the lower slopes of the mountain, and even though it was still raining and the wind bitterly cold, sweat was trickling down the riders' backs. Dillon wrestled with the huge quad bike, he could feel the ground soften under the knobbly off-road tyres, trying to pull the powerful machine one way and then the other; he fought back, increasing the power, building the speed, rising from the seat a little to stand on the pegs with Tatiana clinging on tightly behind as they crested another rise and sailed down the next slope. Dillon kept the power on and the speed kept creeping up; past 50 m.p.h., the low carpet of heather sped by in a blur all around the charging quad bike. Occasionally they hit a buried rock, the bike's suspension dipping, absorbing, but Dillon kept true to the line they were taking, kept the quad racing over the open wilderness of the Scottish Highlands.

They charged along under dark clouds and heavy rain.

Dillon wiped the moisture from his face with the back of his gloved hand, wincing as the rough material ran over his wind-burnt lips. The rain beat down, making him blink behind the goggles as he read the GPS coordinates, his face feeling as if it had been whipped with stinging nettles.

They rode on, merging with the landscape around them; valleys blending with mountainous slopes, an undulating landscape that they navigated with great effort. The quad bike carried them forward, until finally the mountains became bigger and their way seemingly became barred.

They arrived at a vast loch, the expanse of water appeared to go on forever, sandy beaches and huge rocky outcroppings of stone rearing up out of the water in the distance. Sheer cliffs rose up to meet the dark brooding sky on both sides, and Dillon powered down the quad as they descended from the foothills towards the water's edge.

Dillon picked his way around the shoreline heading towards the far end of the loch.

They rode on, the quad's powerful motor running silent.

"Thank God for that!" Tatiana spoke over the sound of the wind and rain. She was clinging on tightly and Dillon, who had sat down in the saddle once more, could feel her hands around his waist gripping on for dear life.

"Mental ride, eh?"

"Oh it's mental, alright," Tatiana agreed.

They picked their way around the edge of the loch, thick cloud overhead and the rain still beating down, Dillon's eyes focused on the Sat-Nav. He swung the quad left, then unleashed the powerful machine up the slope towards a pocket of ancient Caledonian pine trees, slowed as he looked for a cutting through to the other side. He glanced to his right and found what he was looking for, a man made cutting big enough to allow them access and passage all the way to the other side of the forest. Accelerating, Dillon gritted his teeth and negotiated the ruts and rotting debris, all four wheels spun as they shot into the darkness of the forest's interior. With a wail from Tatiana, they powered forward, lights blazing, shadows dancing on either side as they sped on. As they shot out of the forest, the quad slewed to the left. Dillon had to brake hard and the powerful machine slowed as an old ravine loomed - Dillon circled in a wide arc, blipped the throttle and then opened up the power, the quad powered up quickly and they leaped from the lower slopes of the huge mountain, dropping a good ten feet to land on the other side. Suspension dipped, Tatiana's shriek was cut short with a grunt, and the quad sped on as if nothing more than feather had interrupted its trajectory.

Dillon brought the quad to a halt, looking over his shoulder at the leap they'd just made. "You okay, back there, Tats?"

"You could have warned me!"

"No time, luv. Just had to go for it."

"No time, you rotten son of a bitch!"

"That's the fun of quad biking," shouted Dillon. "Everything happens in the blink of an eye."

They cruised on over the carpet of heather that covered the terrain, picking their way between rocks and fallen debris. To their left stood a mammoth of a cliff, and as they wound their way further north, Dillon realised that it would have to be negotiated to reach the next stage of their journey.

For the next half an hour they followed the shoreline of the loch. Then, slowing his speed, Dillon dropped a few gears. Finding a narrow track that led up an insanely steep slope of rock, he slowed to a halt for a moment, his eyes focused intently.

Tatiana was exhausted and extremely tetchy, "This is fucking awful, Dillon. I'm being bounced around all over the place back here."

"You do not have to steer this beast. Why do you think that the guys that usually ride these things are such physically fit sons of bitches?"

"Why have we stopped here?"

Dillon lifted his goggles for a moment, rubbed at his eyes, and then wiped the rain from the goggles' surface with the cloth he pulled from his jacket pocket. "If we carry on following the shoreline of the loch, we'll simply swing around and be heading in the wrong direction - we need to follow this track, we need to climb up and out."

"Climb up and out? We'll never be able to..."

Tatiana had spotted the narrow track leading up the mountain slope until it reached the sheer cliff face, and then apparently disappear into the rock.

"Wait a minute."

Dillon's goggles were already back in place, he twisted the throttle; the quad bike lurched forward, needing little encouragement - they hammered up the slope, tyres chewing up the ground beneath them as they accelerated towards the rock face. Dillon twisted the throttle, getting every last ounce of power from the machine, the engine roared and could be heard even through its stealth shielding...

The quad bike covered the ground quickly, the gap between the rock only becoming apparent as they were almost on it. They shot through the gap, sheer rock rising up as far as the eye could see, both riders clenching their teeth and all four tyres biting into the lichen covered rock... The pass had widened and Dillon had increased their speed, until he saw what he had been looking for - the other end.

They came out of the pass into another valley, Dillon bringing the quad to an abrupt halt, so that he could scan the area before moving on.

"You really are a crazy bastard, Dillon," Tatiana shouted at the back of Dillon's head.

"I try my best," Dillon said with a broad smile. "But if you think that was bad..."

He turned and pointed to the other end of the valley, and the mountain range waiting, quietly waiting for them.

"So it's another bloody mountain, so what?"

"It's in our way."

"Dillon, even this quad won't go up that."

"It will if you find the right trails and paths."

They sped along for another hour. Tatiana was exhausted, and she knew that Dillon was tiring - and becoming increasingly frustrated because of these natural obstacles that were hindering their progress to get to Kirill's facility and Kirill himself.

As the daylight started to dissolve into darkness, Dillon halted, wiping away the rain from his goggles again. The steep lower slopes of the mountain looked daunting as the others had before - but this time it looked huge, made more formidable by the smooth lichen covered rock turning into giant steps nearer the summit that were weathered with time. They formed a steep and treacherous series of ramps, rising up in to the darkening sky.

"Dillon, please don't tell me that you're thinking of..."

"It's our only option, Tats. And this baby will eat that rock."

"No Dillon. I value my life."

"And I value your life, Tats. But I value Kirill's death more," Growled Dillon. He blipped the engine. "Hold on, we're going to do a spot of extreme hill climbing."

The quad moved forward - gently this time and with care as Dillon's gaze swept across the slope and at the rock ahead and above of them like some crazy game of snakes and ladders. He eased forward along the foot of the cliff, back and forth a couple of times to get the measure of the narrow trail way that wound its way up the mountain, all the way to the summit. Then, only when he was happy, did he gingerly start to move forward, opening up the throttle a little and turned the nose of the quad towards the steep climb.

With precision and control, Dillon eased the quad up a series of gentle slopes, blipping the power around the tight bends in the trail. Rubber gripped, the huge quad bike surged a little and Dillon had to slam on the brakes to regain control. They climbed up the mountain slopes into the low cloud base, Dillon kept the pace up, the quad consuming the ground with ease.

Now halfway up, Tatiana gazed down. If it had looked unreasonably steep from the bottom, now it looked insane; she felt suddenly vulnerable, gazing down at the valley far below, bordered by more mountain peaks stretching or as far as the eye could see.

Low clouds tumbled over the rugged landscape, impatient to reach their never ending destination, the mountain slopes foreboding in the failing light of day. Tatiana put her head against Dillon's back, closed her rain drenched eyes and prayed.

The quad jolted, and then bucked as it went over an area strewn with small rocks, its tyres scrambled and kicked up debris as the powerful machine fought its way up the slope, bumping and rocking, as Dillon, sweat rolling down his forehead, grappled to keep the quad moving forward and upright. His gaze focused intently on the ground in front of them as they neared the summit, and then finally, they were over the top and Dillon had dropped down through the gears as they started down the other side. Loose rocks made the quad slip as tyres struggled to grip the loose ground, and they started to pick up speed.

Tatiana patted his shoulder.

"Yeah?"

"I think we need a break."

"Sounds like a good idea. I am truly done-in."

They continued down the mountain for a while longer until Tatiana's sharp eyes spotted a small copse of trees, outlined by eerie half-light. Dillon altered course, and before long the trees came closer and two weary riders were able to dismount and stretch tired muscles and aching joints, the canopy of the trees protecting them from the persistent rain.

They were hidden from view in amongst the trees. Dillon had strung up a camouflaged waterproof sheet between the lower limbs to protect them from the weather that did not look as if it was going to improve, the quad's engine clicked as it started to cool.

"We'll grab a few hours' sleep, and then set off at first light." Dillon said, as he spread a ground sheet on the ground.

"Jesus, it's cold. Whatever processed you to come and live up here Dillon?"

"You really don't know anything about me, do you?"

"I know that you're one mad son-of-a-bitch. So that must have something to do with it."

"Yeah, yeah... Now let's get some sleep."

Dillon slumped down onto the ground sheet exhausted, and ran his hand over the soft earth. "This place is *old*," he said softly, his voice carrying a tone of awe. "I mean, really old."

Tatiana nodded, retreating into the hood of her parka. Moaning in mock ecstasy, at the thought of sleep even though it would only be for a few hours. Her thoughts turned to a far off holiday in the Bahamas. "I never believed I could be so cold," she complained, closing her eyes.

Dillon smiled. "Unbelievable - we're on our way to a meeting with almost certain destruction and all you can complain about is the cold. Lady, this is nothing; you should try this place in the middle of winter... Now then you would have something to complain about."

Tatiana emerged from somewhere inside her fur lined hood and propped herself up on her elbows and glowered at Dillon for a while, thought about replying with a caustic retort, decided it wasn't worth it and laid back down on her back, closed her eyes and tried to sleep.

Dillon checked the map using the light from his torch and discovered that they were only about two hours away from Kirill's facility. As long as they still had the element of surprise on their side, they would arrive at the coordinates that the Priest had sent him in his last encrypted email, without incident.

And then... ...what?

Dillon knew: he would interrogate Kirill. And then he would kill him. There was nothing Kirill could say that would excuse him of the crime of betrayal.

The Government might have brushed Kirill under the carpet.

But not Dillon. It just wasn't in him, and besides - Kirill had it coming to him for setting Dillon up, and attempting to kill him in Cornwall...

Dillon lay there in the dark, reliving that day, that night at Kirill's country retreat in the heart of Cornwall, reliving that dreadful moment when Kirill and Zhenya Tarasova had turned against him, forcing Dillon to awaken his dark side. And then for a few black and white moments, Dillon did what he did best - kill and survive...

Dillon blinked, wiped sweat out of his eyes.

That's right, he thought. When he was under pressure, he saw everything in black and white.

Why?

Dillon felt himself shiver and he opened his eyes - back in the real world - and his gaze settled on Tatiana sleeping.

His mind was running over the many events since she had re-entered his life. And then it dawned on him - perhaps she was not only working for Ferran & Cardini International, but also for Kirill; *he* didn't lead the Assassins to Ezra. *She* did!

Dillon remembered what Tatiana had said about the work role she now held. Her job title was tagged, Government Liaison Officer, but her real function was acting as the eyes and ears of the partners of Ferran & Cardini within the corridors of power. Tatiana had been involved with the Kirill project team - had been involved with the Chimera Programme, from inception... She has always known what Chimera is capable of, and what it could do in the right or wrong hands. So, maybe she works for - Mr Big, whoever he was.

She had pleaded with him to take on the bodyguard assignment in Cornwall. What a naive fool he had been, not to have seen that as a set-up. The bullet from the Assassin was only meant to wound - otherwise she would be dead. She had willingly jumped back into bed with him during their visit to Ezra's place on Santorini. How convenient that was, fuck him, and fuck up his mind - soften him up, make him more susceptible to suggestion and direction.

Dillon became aware that Tatiana was staring at him strangely. She was speaking to him, but everything seemed surreal; he felt light headed, his mind spinning, running wild with doubt and mistrust.

Tatiana reached out to touch him, her mouth open, and her words unheard.

Then the scene swung back into focus, and Dillon re-took control of his mind. He looked into Tatiana's concerned eyes.

"Dillon, are you okay? You look awfully grey, you need to get some sleep."

"I..." began Dillon, then halted. He realised, then, that he had been having a dream, and was most likely mumbling in his sleep, which had woken Tatiana up.

Dillon shivered. "I think I'm suffering from exhaustion or something and didn't realise just how weak I must be. I'll be okay, let me get some sleep."

"Good," soothed Tatiana. And as she lay back down, she suddenly felt lonely - and incredibly vulnerable.

She shivered as a gust of wind and rain whipped up leaves around where they lay.

What would she do if Dillon died out here?

What would she do if she was left alone?

Tatiana shivered again, deep down to her bones.

When she looked around at Dillon, he was asleep. She reached over and pulled the blanket up around his shoulders; she did not see the 9mm Glock in his hand as he nestled in the darkness. She did not see that the safety catch was slipped into the *off* position. And, of course, she could not see the bullet already loaded into the firing chamber.

* * *

A white mist hung lazily in the valley; the wind and rain from the previous night had completely blown itself out, leaving only the cold and an eerie stillness. They had decided against building a small fire, despite the chill of the mountains; this part of the Scottish Highlands was not as desolate as it first appeared, and all they needed was for a spy satellite to pass overhead and pick up their heat signature, or Kirill's security force stumbling across them as they cooked their breakfast.

Tatiana, weirdly, felt very alive; as if she'd never been tired, never been asleep, as she sat huddled in her parka and wrapped up in a thick blanket, only her face visible from within the furry hood, eyes staring up at the hazy sky.

Around her, ancient Caledonian pine trees added colour and texture to the wild glens - and the mountains beyond - everything was still. Occasionally noises would interrupt the silence; the cries of stags, and the unmistakable sound of antlers locking in combat.

After a while, Tatiana gazed across to watch Dillon's face in sleep. She studied the lines, the broken line of his nose, the profile of his strong chin, the unruly hair that she knew he would claim required a thorough washing. His shape was obscured by the fur lined parka coat and thick blanket covering him... and her mind wandered off to better, happier times that they had had together...

She killed the fantasy.

Dillon had been cold since Santorini. Cold and strange...

He had killed so many times on behalf of the realm, that he carried a demon in his soul that took possession of his mind during times of extreme stress. Who would have believed that a man who appeared calm and calculated on the outside - could be so tormented and damaged on the inside.

Tatiana smiled to herself, lifted her hands and rubbed at her eyes. Pain stabbed at her shoulder like a hot poker; the bullet wound nagged her, it still hurt every time she moved her arm - and to top it all she was starting to wish for a shower...

Paid Assassins.

She smiled again, although the taut grin held little humour.

She had met numerous men - and a few women - while working as a liaison officer for Ferran & Cardini International; many killers, murderers, Assassins, members of the security services... their names were various, their objectives usually one and the same. To locate, and to terminate. And she had found one connection that linked them all like a gold skein - as they tiptoed on eggshells, skirted around the edge of insanity. After all what sane person could kill in cold blood? Kill in the cold light of day... No matter what the cause or justification.

And, sooner or later, something had to give.

With all the security service people that she knew, no matter how professional, how adept at killing, how granite-like they appeared - it was still all bullshit. They were just flesh and blood, like every other human being. And they might be able to block out the self-loathing for a while, but it always came back to haunt and torment them. Their lives as trained killers was finite; only as long as they could hold on to their nerve and *their* sanity.

Scorpion, Ferran & Cardini, and the security services, were just like the Armed Forces, Tatiana understood this now. They all absorbed people; used people; destroyed people - and then they pissed them away. Field operatives were expendable; they *had* to be expendable

251

because there was no such thing as a killer without a conscience, no such thing as a person without a soul. There was always a spark there... somewhere.

Tatiana sighed, and felt for her mobile phone in her pocket. She pulled it free and stared at the black touch-screen. When in GPS Sat-Nav mode it could navigate somebody to anywhere on the planet, but of course, Dillon had forbidden her to switch the thing on, which made her feel insecure. And that wasn't a nice feeling... She caressed the slender device between her thumb and forefinger, then, settling back, pulled a small knife from her pocket, slipped back the rear casing to expose the battery, and removed it. She took the blade and levered out the printed circuit board. The phone gave a warning buzz that Tatiana ignored; she examined the inside of the phone without its innards, and smiled.

She pulled out a slender LCD Screen - about the size of a credit card - and using an extendable cable, plugged it into the phone' battery. It immediately came to life, brightly glowing blue, and Tatiana couldn't help feeling very strange about using such a high-tech piece of equipment in the middle of such a natural place. And yet here she was, using the latest cutting-edge agent technology.

She started to scroll through a series of scripted instructions.

She tapped in a short message.

With a pursing of her lips, pale and dry from the harsh cold environment, Tatiana clicked on *send* .

And then it was done...

    GCHQ Transcript 7. REUTERS NEWS ARTICLE OF RECENT INTERNATIONAL INCIDENT.

    One of the world's largest financial clearing houses was left stunned and in chaos after the mainframes serving their worldwide network crashed this morning.

    Despite having multi-tier cryptographic security authentication and digital laser back-up systems, it left the company without facilities to carry on their business. Executives and traders were left staring at blank screens as system technicians desperately attempted to resurrect the mainframes staged at the company's main locations around the globe. The shutdown started in London, and within seconds had spread to: Paris, Berlin, Rome,

Hong Kong, New York, and Rio de Janeiro and after only ten seconds ended up in Sydney.

Sir Julian Rochford-Yarlington, C.E.O of Schwarz & Schwarz, claimed: "This is quite clearly an act of cyber terrorism! We have been attacked by some kind of super-virus, a new type of hack intent on causing total disruption of the world's largest and most powerful computers."

The effects of this crash will be felt by all; as even the most simple of tasks such as the everyday trading of currencies, have become, at least for the immediate future, impossible...

Chapter 17

Claudia Dax rolled over and opened her eyes, and stared at the ceiling. Darkness was all around her. Everything was silent - deadly silent. And yet, She knew. Knew that she was almost there, that it was almost finished. Knew that it was almost complete... A few tweaks here and there, some re-writing of certain codes and Chimera would be 100% ready; the world would not be the same again once Chimera was launched.

That could only mean that the programme was...

...*alive*.

She whispered softly.

Why then, Claudia mused, did she feel so pissed off?

And it came to her, a feeling of frustration, and anger: to create something so brilliant, to be involved in a project of such magnitude, ground-breaking, and then to have it snatched away and taken to some secret Government depository. To be placed in a strong box and hidden for all eternity! It was like creating a work of art and then hanging it in a damp cellar, never to be seen by anybody.

The Chimera Programme could be the ultimate weapon in the fight against terrorism... Chimera was self-learning, intuitive, could find out multiple encrypted computer trails, simultaneously, even the most heavily fortified mainframes could not hide from Chimera. Terrorists worldwide could not hide their computer activities as Chimera could; scan, decode, extract, and then send every scrap of data back to the relevant government agencies, in whatever country the tracked computer was located without anyone knowing that it was there, and all within seconds... But no. The British Government had other ideas for this breakthrough in virus programming, and that was to hide it away, because the politicians and bureaucrats were afraid of it. Were terrified of it falling into the hands of the very people being hunted. Terrorists...

And she could still remember Ezra's words, when he had contacted her. Claudia shivered.

She had complied with his wishes...

Copying the entire blueprint had been the easy part; getting them to Ezra had been where the real difficulty lay.

Don't ever call me un-resourceful, she mused.

Claudia smiled, emotions on her face conflicting, and she rubbed at her tired eyes. She knew that the Chimera Programme was a tip-top secret, and the top brass at the facility had the security so tight, not even a mouse could fart without them knowing about it. But what the hell, Chimera was almost ready, and she would be able to have a long, long, well-earned-rest.

Her duty to humanity, and Ferran & Cardini, and Ezra, was nearly complete.

Claudia Dax thought all these thoughts as she stared at the ceiling. Her hand came up, ran through her long auburn hair, and then she heard something; not so much a *noise* as a single high-pitched note on the very edge of her hearing...

Claudia frowned, and then sat up.

The sound was coming from the living quarters of her apartment. She leaned over the edge of the bed and peered through the connecting doorway to the other room; she saw a glow from one of her terminals. She didn't remember leaving it on. In fact, she *knew* she had not left it on.

And the terminal was protected. Electronically. Her own code. Her own sophisticated firewalls to intercept hackers, which she had tested by attempting to hack her own system; she had found it impossible. That meant that someone had hacked it, but that was highly unlikely. It must have been accessed; either remotely from somewhere else in the huge facility, or someone had entered her apartment. Claudia Dax shivered.

She jumped off the edge of the bed, looked quickly around, and picked up a heavy looking bronze sculpture from her dressing table. She had purchased it, after much deliberation, from a rare weekend break to Edinburgh, and was now thankful that she had.

She hefted the makeshift weapon.

It would make a very good weapon...

Claudia crept towards the open doorway. The light from the terminal grew brighter. Her grip grew tighter around the slender piece of sculpted bronze; her gaze flickered from the doorway to the head of the bronze. She made a concerted effort to control her breathing and her racing heartbeat.

Why would somebody be inside her private apartment?

Why would somebody from the facility be spying on her?

Unless they *knew*.

Suddenly she went cold.

And then something hit her - with the force of a sledge hammer in the face. If they had discovered that *she* had been the one to copy the blueprints and pass them on to Ezra... Then they would want to know why?

They would be extremely harsh with her, and would certainly not thank her.

Claudia reached the doorway. Peered cautiously around the frame. And saw - nothing.

The terminal screen was blank; a bright blue with only a flashing red triangle. Claudia's eyes fixed on this because it was a symbol that she had never seen on the terminal before - and it was *her* private terminal; she was the only person who could give it commands. It was her own from the ground up; including all of the software.

Claudia stepped across the threshold, moved towards the terminal, her gaze sweeping left and right, hand still gripping the bronze sculpture tightly. Fear had dried her mouth, she had difficulty swallowing; the thought of Kirill's *Big Boys* possibly suspecting her of the Chimera blueprints' leak was there, a foreboding of a *reality* of particularly nasty proportions just waiting to surprise her.

The red triangle sprang to life, a black cursor started to flash in the middle of it;

\# **Hello Claudia Dax.**

Claudia stood motionless, staring at the screen, a frown on her face. She shook her head and sat down, placing the bronze sculpture down on the top of the workstation, and typed her fingers a blur across the keyboard.

\# **Who are you? How did you get past my firewalls?**

\# **It's not important who I am. The important thing is that I know who you are. I would like to thank you Miss Dax - you have done a remarkable job in creating Chimera; I must congratulate you on a superb piece of programming and I give you full credit. Your scripts stand out from all the other gibberish I've seen. Tell me - where did you learn such a skill?**

\# **Why should I tell you anything? What's to stop me from shutting this terminal down and informing this facility's cyber security team?**

Claudia sat back, staring at the blank screen, and reached for the comm. But something was strangely wrong, and the IP address from where the message was coming from *was* being blocked; somebody had to be re-routing the message around the globe to mask its place of origin. She felt annoyed, and started to punch in the code for security as the following text appeared on her terminal.

I suggest you don't do that if you want to live.

Claudia's fingers halted, her stare moving from the screen to the comm. in her hand and back again. Were they watching her? Were they watching her *now*?

Damn - was there somebody in her apartment?

She picked up the sculpture and spun around.

But there was nobody there. She was completely alone.

She lightly bit her bottom lip.

Sweat tickled the small of her back under her pyjamas.

I am giving you this information because you are the one who created Chimera; I am giving you this information because you are the only one who can possibly stop it...

Your programming skills are world class, but you will need every ounce of this skill to stop a catastrophic act of terrorism being carried out by the programme you created...

Claudia stared. Her jaw dropped.

Holy shit, she thought, this can't be real. Chimera - terrorism?

She typed:

What do you want? And why is my life in danger?

Listen carefully - Professor Kirill knows that you leaked the blueprints. Because of the leaks and several other factors concerning the re-location of the facility where the final countdown and implementation of the Chimera Programme will take place, the complex you are now located in will be destroyed. At least half of all the employees involved within your unit are to be terminated - you have no idea how high the stakes, being played by people who employ you, are - it would appear though, that Kirill's agenda is at odds with the very highest echelons of Government.

The killing has already begun; check your personal gov-link to verify this.

You have perhaps five minutes before Assassins arrive in your private apartment.

Claudia smiled. It had to be a joke, right? A wind-up of monumental proportions by one or any numbers of her nerdy colleagues downstairs in the programme suite. The bastards! She had almost believed them!

The grin still beaming across her attractive face, she typed:

Who is winding me up?
Not a wind up - check your Gov-link NOW...

The word NOW continuously scrolled down the screen. The grin fell from Claudia's face. She moved back into the bedroom and went quickly to the side of her bed, felt for and located what she was looking for, and withdrew it. She had pulled free a tablet computer. Hit the power switch and watched its screen come to life. The 10" screen split into six smaller screens, each with a live feed from the facilities own security surveillance cams. She punched in the digits for one of her co-workers apartment, and her mouth dropped open. Then closed again. Quickly.

There was lone black-clad figure; black balaclava; it was standing outside the bedroom door. It held a silenced machine pistol. It did not turn as another figure - another Assassin - dragged the man from the bedroom. A tiny neat hole in the centre of his forehead. His head twisted towards the camera, eyes staring blankly straight ahead. Blood was running down over his left eye and cheek, and dripped as he was being dragged across the tiled floor and dumped by the door.

Claudia switched channels.

Bateman - hands held high above his head, a look of disbelief and horror on his face.

The knife flashed across his throat, severing major arteries cleanly, spraying blood up the wall and ceiling, spattering the large watercolour that he had loved so much. As he slumped down onto the hard floor in a heap, a red pool instantaneously gathered around his head.

Claudia flicked through the other channels.

More rooms were empty.

Some of them contained mutilated bodies.

She punched in another series of commands and a moment later the upper cargo level appeared on the screen. There were three Chinook transport helicopters, rotors idling, their cargo doors fully lowered and open, two of the three interiors revealing a plethora of dead bodies. Men and women, with whom Claudia had worked, bantered and talked with only a few short hours ago.

Claudia hastily moved back to her terminal.

The screen was blank.

Why? Screamed her brain.

Why are they doing this?

Why are they *killing* them? Because they know too much? Because of the blueprint leak?

She was sweating, suddenly panicked now. She ran back into her bedroom, opened the wardrobe, and pulled out a small pre-packed travelling rucksack. She threw her laptop inside and zipped it back up. She paused for a moment, thinking, what the hell was her next move going to be. Claudia ran to the door and halted abruptly, hesitating before opening it. They could be in the corridor outside. They could be in the lifts. They could be watching her right now on the security system, ready to terminate her contract of employment - permanently...

She inhaled slowly, trying to calm her breathing.

Keep your wits about you: think how you are going to survive this nightmare.

She looked up, as the air-con cut in. Hissing quietly.

Claudia Dax went over to her desk and dragged a chair back to the shaft and, reaching up, used the bronze sculpture to dislodge the stainless steel grille. It was going to be a tight squeeze but - but then; did she really have a choice?

She ran back into her bedroom randomly pulled out clothes from her wardrobe, and scattered them across the floor and bed. Then she went to the kitchen and picked out a long handle floor brush from the utility cupboard. From the chair she could just about reach the rim of the shaft, which bit into the soft skin of her fingers, and hauled herself up into the narrow tight confines of the metallic shaft. With trembling fingers she manoeuvred the chair away from below with the brush handle, and then replaced the grille cover back into place, shifted her position just to the right of the grille and waited, her heart thumping in her ears.

Three minutes passed.

Claudia heard it; a tiny *click*. The front door to her apartment eased open. Two Assassins slid through the opening like ghosts; they moved silently from room to room. They were very thorough as they moved around her apartment, communicating only with hand signals.

As quickly as they had arrived, they were gone again out into the corridor.

"She is not here." The voice was soft and feminine.

"We will find her."

"Report back to the control room; we'll come back in ten minutes and check again then."

They left the corridor.

Claudia pushed herself backwards along the narrow shaft, deeper in, the cool draught making her shiver, her *proximity* to death made her shiver even more. I don't believe it, she kept telling herself. I just don't believe it.

She moved on through the shaft, her mind pondering her current precarious situation. She had actually been lulled into believing that she was building Chimera to help in the fight against terrorism. Ezra had been the only one telling her the truth all along...

And now?

Now *she* was in the firing line.

Claudia Dax shivered again, and started to weep into her hands.

* * *

It was nearing dawn.

Kirill stood behind the parapet, watching the sun come up over some of the highest mountain peaks in Scotland, smoking a black Russian cigarette and enjoying the experience immensely. The freshly ground Columbian coffee, only adding to his pleasure.

A breeze stirred, and powder snow blew over his shoes.

He watched idly as black uniformed soldiers of Ramus's personal security detail, supervised the loading of the facility's hi-tech computer equipment into the cavernous belly of one of the Chinooks. The other helicopter was preparing to take-off, large rotors spinning, waiting to disappear to a secret location...

The comm. buzzed.

"Yes?"

"Are you ready? Have you ensured that everything has been removed, the last two helicopters are waiting to leave?"

"All technical items and Chimera related equipment have already been shipped to the mobile stealth facility. There is just the nuclear device to arm - I will send two Assassins to carry this out." Tobacco stained teeth smiled in the glare of artificial lighting.

"Good. After all, we don't want to leave your former masters in Whitehall with anything to allow replication of our unique toy, eh, Kirill? I assume that the individuals, who did not wish to join us, have now been liquidated?"

"All, except one employee; but I've got two of our best Assassins out tracking her down. But if they don't find her, the explosion will."

"Okay, Kirill - but you *make sure* she is found and dealt with."

"I think the Scottish Government might be somewhat pissed off when we set off this nuclear device. It was considered a great compliment when the SAS chose to build their Arctic training centre here."

"Save your sentiment, Kirill. I could not care less about governments and what they think. They can all go to hell, as far as I'm concerned."

"Has there been any word of Dillon's whereabouts?

"Yes. You were quite right; he is heading straight for you. He really must be stopped, although we have no idea of his exact location. Maybe he's come to find *you*, Kirill? Maybe he is still pissed off with you for pulling that gun on him in Cornwall? Maybe he wants to find out why you *didn't die*? That would make for a very interesting conversation, don't you think?" There was a twisted mocking humour in Ramus's voice.

"I thought you said you would take care of him?"

"Oh, have no fear, Kirill. I'm working on it."

The comm. cut. Kirill stubbed his cigarette out in the ashtray with measured aggression. All of a sudden it tasted like the, foul, dog-end that it was.

Kirill spoke quickly into the Bluetooth headset attached to his right ear, his voice carried an edge as sharp a Samurai's sword. His words direct and to the point, instructing the security guard at the other end. "Go and get the device." The guard disconnected, and Kirill looked dispassionately around the room, gaze tracing the contours of the furniture. Something was troubling him, a nervousness that made him feel uneasy, even with trained Assassins and his personal security guards surrounding him. Dillon wouldn't get within a hundred metres of him. Kirill laughed out loud, a deep hollow mocking laughter.

Two guards appeared outside Kirill's apartment. "Take the device down to level 8. Let me know when you are there, and I will join you to arm it. If you value your life - you will ensure that the maximum security is maintained at all times, do I make myself clear?" Both guards nodded their understanding.

He pushed the button on the comm. A feminine voice at the other end answered.

"Have you found her yet?"

"No, sir," came the smooth purring voice.

"Well, put more people on it and damn well find her!" He failed to hide his irritation and the tinge of urgency that had crept in to his tone. He took a deep breath. The tension and acid re-flux, he was experiencing, was making him feel nauseous. "I was given to believe that Assassins were supposed to be the very best at seek and destroy?"

"That is correct, sir."

Kirill cut the connection. He left his apartment, entering the cool depths of the facility, heart pounding, and perspiration rolling down his temples. Damn you to hell, Dillon, he thought.

Damn you.

* * *

Claudia Dax lay flat on her back inside the air-conditioning shaft, a mass of multi-coloured wiring directly above her, a slender tablet computer in her hand. The tears had gone; her mind working at full throttle.

She knew the facility's surveillance systems like the back of her hand; after all, she had made it her business to familiarise herself with every aspect of their programming. And, like all hackers, she had found all of the weak spots, and had then written in her own private backdoor - coding that had escaped the close scrutiny of the fail-safe programmers and had allowed her access to... *everything*.

On the tablet's screen, she looked out at the Chinooks, their rotors idling, pilots awaiting their orders. She saw Kirill stub out his cigarette, and she watched with tired and strained eyes as he spoke on the comm and then leave his apartment to disappear back into the facility. The tension was consuming her. And she knew: Knew that she was waiting to die and there was no way that she would be able to escape them - after all, where would she go? What would she do?

She was in the middle of nowhere.

Tears rolled down over her cheeks, flowing freely, and Claudia despised herself for being weak, and her self-loathing turned to self-pity and she cried and cried, and then everything was suddenly looking out of control. And why was this happening to her?

She stopped crying. Wiping away the moisture from her eyes with the sleeve of her pyjamas.

How long did she have?

Even if they were to realise that she had entered the air-con system, it would take them hours to search all the vents and shafts. After all, the facility was *huge*. And looking on the bright side, as she had watched on the monitor, the majority of the Assassins had already left on the earlier Chinooks.

"Maybe they would give up and all leave?"

Although she knew that was not an option.

She also knew that they would hunt her to the end...

Claudia closed her eyes for a moment, her mind in overdrive. How was she going to turn this situation on its head? From being a victim and the hunted, to being the predator and the hunter. But how the hell was she going to do that?

And then it struck her.

Claudia started to crawl carefully along the ventilation shaft.

She suddenly had a purpose - a goal to attain...

She needed an edge, something to negotiate with.

And if she had copied the Chimera blueprints once, she could surely do it again.

* * *

Kirill moved with the agility of a man half his age, his hands working quickly and precisely, as he placed each explosive package around the core of the facility. He moved with care, alert, the automatic pistol he was carrying in his jacket pocket had the safety catch slid to off. A reassurance against any unwelcome visitors, such as, Jake Dillon...

Where was that annoying bastard? He mused.

He pushed the thought from his mind. Ten, one kilo packs of hi-explosive, each with a detonator linked wirelessly to the mother of all bombs. A small nuclear device - capable of vaporising the entire facility and everything in it. The ten much smaller charges were there merely for good measure.

Claudia Dax would wish the day that she had taken a bullet to the head in preference to what was to come...

Kirill stood in the corridor and glanced down at the tablet computer in his hand and the plan of the facility on the bright screen. The complex had been dug out of the mountain and designed to be impenetrable from attack by air or from the valley far below. He attached one of the hi-explosive packages to an overhead beam, and then moved on to the next location.

Finally, Kirill found himself in the main programming suites. The power had been cut and all defence systems inoperable. The mainframes and all systems were silent, cold and dead.

Kirill sighed.

The thought of Dillon niggled away at the back of his mind. Ramus had underestimated the former army intelligence officer. He had thought it an easy task to kill him, even with his Assassins doing the dirty work. How wrong he had got that...

Moving to the main console, Kirill flicked a few switches. A panel moved back silently on the side of the mainframe case; there were no markings to show that the Chimera Programme was stored on the now exposed hardrive. The slender black box slid free, was presented to him, dull, totally unimpressive. He lifted it carefully, noting how it made the tiny hairs on the back of his neck stand up and bristle. He placed it gently into the inside breast pocket of his jacket...

Then, Kirill placed the smallest and final hi-explosive inside the mainframe. It locked in place and then blinked blue at him. He pulled the tablet computer from the bottom of the case he was carrying. He tapped in a series of digits on the screen; the menu opened up immediately as Kirill tapped one of the icons. The screen turned into a continuous waterfall of binary code, a never ending script, the final detonation command sequence. Once delivered up to the mainframe, the nuclear device would automatically count-down and no one could stop it...

"Have you checked that everything is in place?"

"Yes, Professor Kirill. Everything is now ready, sir."

He tapped the enter button, and synchronised all of the hi-explosive packs with the nuke. Confirmation was instantaneous.

Kirill nodded, placing the tablet computer back into his bag and turning his back on the Chimera project suite. Turning his back on the place he had worked and virtually lived and called home for the last four years.

He patted his jacket pocket, saying out loud. "You will soon be released from your black hole to roam free through every computer on the planet. Soon, you will create a new *world*. A world where politicians, the military, and even bankers will have no choice than to answer to us." Kirill's top lip curled into a viscous condescending snarl.

He met the two Assassins outside. Only one small six-seater helicopter remained, that would be used to transport him and the Assassins. He looked around nervously; checking that every last thing was in place.

Soon.

Soon the sun would rise.

And with it, the top of the mountain.

"Any sign of her?"

"No. We think she is in the air-conditioning shafts. Should we go and search them?"

"One of you go - take another look. But we don't have much time left. If you can't locate her, we'll have to let the explosion do the job for us."

Kirill swore, scratching the side of his unshaven face. His gaze scanned the horizon and he calmed himself, slowed his heart-beat. That Dax woman, was now holding him up; he should have been gone by now, enjoying a glass of his favourite Champagne, served at just the right temperature as the helicopter powered him away from danger to Ramus's stealth command ship.

The Assassin chosen to go and find Claudia Dax disappeared back into the facility.

The rotors began to spin above his head as the helicopter fired up. He climbed inside the cabin and nodded to the pilot.

"We will leave..." He checked his gold Rolex watch; "...in exactly seven minutes, unless that woman is found sooner."

The pilot nodded, and then went back to carrying out his pre-flight checks.

Chapter 18

Dillon opened his eyes and lay staring at the canopy of vivid green above him. Even though he had only had a few hours of much needed sleep. He felt refreshed and rejuvenated.

Checking his watch, it was about half an hour to full sunrise. Tatiana, who was just stirring, opened her eyes and saw Dillon looking at her. "What?"

"Time to leave. That's what."

* * *

They had been cruising on the quad-bike for fifteen minutes, heavy tyres thumping over rough tracks and twisting winding trails like the hardiest off-roader. They had passed small herds of deer and seen vistas of heather carpeting vast areas of land.

Dillon's gaze, behind his goggles, fixed on the horizon ahead; they were approaching the location of Kirill's facility as indicated on the map that the Priest had sent to him. He slowed his speed, the stealth engine dying to just above a whisper.

Dillon rubbed thoughtfully at the stubble on his chin.

"What I want to find out is where the hell do the Assassins fit into this puzzle? Where did they come from originally? What is it, which makes them the way they are? And is it Kirill, or someone else, controlling them?"

Tatiana shrugged. "They are highly trained killers, that's certain. And I have no doubt whatsoever, that the security services know far more than they're letting on."

"There's something very wrong here. They just don't fit into the picture, at all."

Tatiana had taken off the black balaclava, was running her hands through her hair, she nodded and said. "Perhaps they were part of the plan; maybe the Assassins - and whoever gives the orders to them - were simply trying to manipulate, *you* only. Not kill you, as we've been thinking. Perhaps they knew that by pushing the right buttons, you would respond and lead them to Ezra?"

"Perhaps," said Dillon bitterly. Then he saw the tears in her eyes. He twisted round on the quad-bikes saddle and gently wiped away a tear from her cheek. "You know, Tats. He could still be alive you know. Nothing is for certain."

"I think we're just kidding ourselves, don't you?"

Dillon shrugged, and then said. "Come on, we're nearly there. We have to focus and I need you one hundred percent with me."

"I wish we could have approached this place from the air," she sighed, glancing up through a seemingly endless valley that stretched out in front of them.

"Well, it would have been a damn sight quicker to get here, that's for sure," grumbled Dillon, kicking the quad into gear and spinning all four tyres on the powerful machine away up the track.

Five minutes later and as they came to a halt on a high ridge, they had their first sight of Kirill's facility, or what was exposed of it, from across the valley they had a clear view of the mountain opposite.

* * *

"It's up there." Dillon pointed.

The sun was starting its morning climb up into a foreboding sky, through clouds the colour of coal, heavy and turbulent, with the promise of much rain.

There was no hint of breeze at ground level, just the cold; but at least is was partly bearable during the day. Dillon ignored the tingling in his finger tips and concentrated on putting the sniper rifle together. The scope clicked into place and Dillon went through the relatively straightforward procedure of sighting it, making a few minor adjustments to the setting dials.

Tatiana squinted through the gloom. Behind them, hidden under an overhang of rock, sat the quad bike, engine clicking softly.

"What do you see, Dillon?"

"From here, I have a clear shot into the helicopter landing areas." The AMSD OM 50 Nemesis 12.7mm sniper rifle was located on its steadying tripod. Dillon's hands worked smoothly and efficiently, slotting the large caliber bullets into the magazine. "But, the facility is huge. That much is evident. There's three Chinooks up there all with their rotors spinning, and I'd say that they were just about to leave. I'm just sweeping the area for any external guards."

"You think we'll be able to get up there?"

"What I'm thinking Tats, is that I very much doubt if the Chimera Programme is still up there. And, that fortress has been specifically designed to repel all marauders - without exception. That's what I'm thinking!"

Dillon slotted the magazine into the weapon and returned his attention to the telescopic sight. Tatiana handed him a small square box that he attached to the side of the scope, which he then checked carefully with the practiced eye of someone who has been around weapons for a long time. "This little gizmo enhances the long range image by cleaning it up and sharpening before it reaches my eye. A bit like a photo-editing programme."

"So, what are you hoping to see now?"

"In an ideal world, Kirill. But I'm not getting my hopes up. I'll settle for a few of those Assassins; that will give us time and a window to get to the basket and up into the facility. After that... the hunt begins. We want answers to questions, like who are the Assassins and where did they all of a sudden spring from, and what was the reason for taking out Scorpion and a number of its crack squads?"

There was silence, except for the occasional movement of deer on the lower slopes. Dillon scanned the mountain side carefully, moving the scope backwards and forwards with extreme precision so that he did not miss anything. After a moment he flicked a switch, and the scope went to heat seeking mode.

"Well, look at this," he said eventually.

"What is it?"

"Lots of movement going on inside that helicopter bay," said Dillon quietly. "Listen, can you hear the Chinooks, their engine pitch has changed and they're getting ready for take-off. Now, I wonder where they are heading to." Dillon said, mostly to himself.

Tatiana peered through powerful binoculars at Kirill's facility. The outer screen of bullet-proof glass shimmered, blending with the ancient landscape.

She gazed up from their position, keeping the Chinook helicopters in clear view as the first one lifted off from its landing pad, then the second, and lastly the third one.

Dillon's voice was calm and calculated, as he said. "Well, that's a surprise. Look who's just crawled out from under a rock."

"Who?"

"Professor, bloody, Kirill. That's who. What a most satisfyingly pleasant surprise." Dillon adjusted his position behind the rifle sight, and Tatiana read the body language, understood it from the firing ranges she had been sent to while training for her current role at Ferran & Cardini International. He was getting comfy. Getting ready, ready to shoot, he wanted no mistakes...

Dillon placed his hand around the grip. Red lights turned to blue, and then to green. The Nemesis had synchronised with Dillon's grip and finger-prints - and was now ready to shoot.

Dillon flicked the rifle's safety to the off position. Rolled his head a couple of times to loosen the tension.

"What are you going to do?" Asked Tatiana softly.

"Do? I'm going to shoot that bastard, right between the eyes. Damn-it, he's gone and disappeared again. He must have gone back inside the building."

Dillon watched as the only helicopter left on the landing pad, a much smaller six-man Robinson, started its engine and the rotors started to spin. He wondered why they were leaving such a secure facility, and where they were going to.

"What I'd give for a cold pint of lager, right now."

"That's about the hundredth time you've said that, Dillon."

Dillon looked round at her, and said nothing. But she was sure that he had made some sort of snorting sound, before returning his eye to the telescopic sight.

They continued to wait in the cold and the damp. A northerly breeze was now blowing in and Dillon repositioned and adjusted the Nemesis to take this into account.

Tatiana went back to the quad and returned with a bottle of water and two nutritional breakfast bars.

"We've only two more water bottles left, after this one. So we'll have to be careful with it."

"Really. You city girls haven't got a fucking clue have you?"

"I'm only pointing out that our water ration is getting low, that's all."

"Bloody hell, luv. We're in the Scottish Highlands, not the Sahara Desert. Every stream is a watering hole. The water up here is cleaner than the shit they pour into those bottles, believe me."

Dillon grinned, flashing her a dark look.

He returned to the scope, scanning the surrounding countryside, before panning up in a wide arc to the landing area again. His eye caught a dark clad figure jumping down from the lone helicopter and moving around it, presumably carrying out its final pre-flight checks.

Dillon calmed his breathing.

The sight locked on.

The Nemesis fired.

The bullet took the pilot through the side of the neck; the slender figure slumped to the ground with blood pumping in a high arc across the fuselage of the Robinson helicopter. Then it was still. Dillon immediately swept the scope back and forth, looking for more targets to take down...

Kirill emerged and moved towards the helicopter.

"At last," murmured Dillon.

Tatiana had been lying on a rock, her weary eyes closed, and the fur-lined parka hood pulled up tight around her face. After hearing the *crack* of the rifle, she had scrambled over to Dillon and now peered through binoculars up at the helicopter. The engine pitch increased, the rotor blades became a spinning blur as it lifted up into the air.

Again, there was a *crack*.

Dillon released the electronic grip, and sighed.

The helicopter rotated ninety degrees, pitched forward slightly, and then came gently back down onto the landing pad with a bump.

The rotor blades stopped spinning and the only noise came from the wind. Calm...

Dillon looked through the scope, and the sensation was sweet; Kirill's panic in the cockpit. What to do? Where to run?

The cockpit door opened slowly - but no one stepped out.

Kirill's head then peered fleetingly out, then immediately disappeared back inside.

He was gauging the distance he had to run - no cover between the helicopter and the facility entrance that he had come through just minutes earlier.

Where was the shooter? Dillon knew that would frustrate the hell out of Kirill. And he was also sure that Kirill was cursing.

The man's hand-made Italian shoes hit the ground and Kirill began to run, head low, as he sprinted at a speed that surprised Dillon greatly.

"You're fast for an old man! Running as if your life depended on it," Dillon said calmly, a man relaxed, focused. He gently squeezed the grip. The Nemesis kicked, ever so slightly, and there was the *crack* as the round was discharged. "And of course, it does." He smiled.

Tatiana watched Kirill tumble forward onto the hard surface of the landing bay to remain there stunned. Or dead...

"Tatiana. It's at times such as these, I really love the work I do," said Dillon, smiling. He pressed his eye into the rubber cup of the scope. Watched Kirill, his face contorted in pain, gather himself up to his feet and then stumble forward, blood flowing freely, towards the inner sanctum of the facility and safety.

"Where did you get him?"

"Right where it hurts, in the left cheek of his ass. And boy, will that hurt."

Dillon squeezed the grip once more. Kirill was knocked off his feet, crashed to the ground, and lay there.

"Right thigh. That'll stop that bastard from running away."

Dillon remained still for a while, watching, checking for any stray security guards. "Let's go up and have a little chat to the man. He might be amiable to that now. What do you reckon, Tats?"

Tatiana remained silent.

* * *

Kirill lay on the wet surface of the landing bay near to the entrance of the facility, wondering what the hell had hit him.

And then he remembered the sound of the single heavy *thwack*, and an immediate loss of oil pressure as the large caliber round had smashed into the side of the Robinson's engine casing.

And then panic...

Blind panic.

He made a dash for the entrance. A searing pain, white hot, in the soft flesh of his buttock, pain like he'd never experienced before.

And then the second round - right thigh.

And tears of pain running down over his cheeks.

He rolled over into a sort of semi foetal position and tried to examine the bullet wounds. The cloth of his expensive hand tailored trousers had turned crimson and clung to his brutalised flesh. Blood pooled on the ground around him, spreading viscously from the two wounds.

Lots of blood...

Kirill's head snapped first to the left and then right, eyes searching the surrounding terrain in panic. Where was that damned sniper?

And then the association...*Could it be possible?*

Was it Dillon out there?

He shook his head, almost in disbelief. This is becoming a nightmare, he thought. After *everything* that I've been through! And he also understood why he had been shot in the legs and not in the head. Whoever had sniped him wanted him alive and was most likely on their way up...

Kirill rolled onto his belly and gritting his teeth, started to crawl. His clothing was ripped in several places and got covered in grime. His neatly groomed greying hair became flat against his scalp with the rain falling. His usually calm and composed face became a picture of panic, of comprehension, of *time running out...*

Exhausted and in immeasurable pain, Kirill lay sprawled on the wet ground, his line of sight had the winch-house clearly in view. He listened to the powerful electric motor pulling the basket up. Kirill pushed himself on, dragging his smashed legs behind him, fingers clawing with broken nails at the hard granite surface...

The winch motor suddenly stopped. Kirill heard the *clank* of the locking mechanism engage, and then the sound of boots on the timber floor inside the small building, and he willed himself to move forward; he did not look back, felt no curiosity whatsoever, just the basic raw animal instinct to survive... to stay alive... to stay ahead. There came a metallic *click*: the sound of a bullet slipping neatly in a firing chamber. Kirill let his muscles relax, exhausted, his adrenalin spent. He could taste the bitterness of failure. He didn't even have the strength to roll over onto his back...

The sound of boots grew nearer. They stopped.

The tip of the Heckler & Koch barrel prodded Kirill in the back.

"Haven't you bled to death yet, you son-of-a-bitch?"

"I'm still alive," said Kirill softly. "I knew you'd come here, Dillon. I knew it from the look in your eye in the kitchen at my house in Cornwall..."

"I don't like being set-up," snapped Dillon.

"It was a necessity."

Kirill felt strong hands grab him roughly and roll him over. He looked up into Dillon's face - much more battered than the last time they had met, the nose more twisted, cuts and grazes marking the skin. Dillon's eyes were dark, brooding, unforgiving... Beyond Dillon's palpable hatred stood Tatiana, a Glock in one hand, and an Uzi mini-sub machine pistol in the other. She appeared through Kirill's haze of pain, to be jumpy, on the edge, twitchy as she looked around to see if there was anyone else about that might have spotted them... Whereas Dillon was totally focused, dark eyes boring into Kirill's sole, like a tungsten drill.

"How many are still here?" He demanded.

Kirill smiled.

"You nervous, Dillon?"

"Nervous? Hell no, but you should be. We want answers, and you're going to give them to us."

"Or what? You're going to kill me? I'm already a dead man, Dillon. Chimera works, but not one-hundred percent. This makes me a condemned man awaiting execution... But now, now you are too late." He started to laugh.

Dillon shook his head. "I worked for a while with this guy, in Northern Ireland. He was ex SAS; worked as a freelance interrogator for British Intelligence and the CIA. He had a reputation for making the toughest men squeal like pigs at a trough. His preferred method of torture was the ancient art of Chakra. I learned a lot from him, about keeping a man alive whilst inflicting insurmountable pain. The trick is in keeping the person conscious at all times, that was the point." Dillon glanced over at Tatiana, then at the vast vista of mountains beyond the perimeter of the facility. There was no sign of activity near or far...

"You keep an eye out for any movement whatsoever, Tats. While I get this old man inside. Make him ready for our little chat."

"Chat?"

"You ever seen the look on a man's face when his internal organs have been messed with a little. And that's only for starters. The best is kept for the very last minute, but let's keep that as a surprise. But you'll find out soon enough, Professor..." Dillon started to drag Kirill across the landing bay towards the doors of the facility - which automatically slid back as he approached it. Dillon peered carefully into the brightly lit interior, the Heckler MP5 held aggressively, then dragged Kirill into the warmth of the temperature controlled environment of the Government establishment.

He dumped Kirill on the dark granite slab floor, then immediately took a look around. He moved warily, checking every corner until he was completely satisfied that they were alone. He spun round as the outer door opened with a hiss, and Tatiana came into sight, each hand held an automatic pistol gripped firmly. He smiled over at her and she responded with a wan smile, her face showing pain and fatigue.

"Anything moving out there?"

"No. There's nobody else in the helicopter, and only a couple of dead Assassins on the far side of the landing bay."

"Okay, any sign of the Priest and the others?"

"Nothing. If they are here, then they're remaining a little shy, aren't they?"

"Which is unlike the Priest? I think it's time to go get some answers."

"Dillon." She placed a hand on his arm. "You're not really going to torture him, are you?"

Their gazes met. He saw that she was in pain; saw the look of humanity in her eye. "No," he lied easily. "I'm bluffing him. But he doesn't know that." Dillon winked and smiled. He then walked over to where Kirill was half sitting, half laying, his hand pressed against his trouser leg, over one of the bullet wounds inflicted by Dillon.

"So Professor. Time is running out, and I'm still none the wiser why I was set-up. Why did you try to kill me in Cornwall, eh?" Dillon slowly unrolled a soft leather roll, and removed a long slender knife; the highly polished blade glinted under the artificial lighting.

Silence.

Kirill simply stared up at Dillon, a blank emotionless glower.

Dillon knelt down, roughly ripping open Kirill's trouser leg, and then gently pressing the cold stainless steel against the flesh just behind the knee cap. "Now listen up, old son. You start talking, or I'm going to slice off your knee cap." Blood started to flow freely as Dillon pressed just a little into the soft tissue.

Kirill grinned, showing his aging tobacco stained teeth, and then sat up slowly.

"You could never understand, *never* understand."

"Try me."

"There's not enough time."

"We've got as much time as it takes."

"Wrong answer," said Kirill. "You have precisely twelve minutes and -" he checked the cracked face of his gold watch; "- and thirty -three seconds. At which time the hi-explosive charges that have been placed strategically throughout this facility will detonate. That is to say, they will detonate simultaneously, along with the small nuclear device that I have positioned deep within the facility. The top of this mountain will be one massive firework, and you'll be sitting right on top of it."

"You're bluffing, Kirill."

"Why should I? After all, it's not as if you can't go and check."

"Dillon," said Tatiana. "If it's true, we'd better get the hell off this mountain."

"I came here for answers and I'm *not* leaving until I have them," said Dillon. "And if there really is a mini nuke up here, then the Priest will be able to disable it. You see, Kirill. There isn't a device worldwide that the Priest hasn't been able to deactivate." Dillon said arrogantly.

"He can try," said Kirill softly. "But this particular device has been designed without the off button." Kirill's condescension was met with Dillon pulling the Glock from his pocket, and pressing the muzzle under his chin. Kirill's eyes widened, and he hissed. "You cut the power, everything blows. This was a one-off, Dillon. There was never a soft option. Ever..."

"Where's the master switch?"

Kirill did not reply.

Dillon slipped the safety catch off, and adjusted the angle of the muzzle. "Ever seen a man with half his face blown off. You won't die, but hell would be a happy release. You're just going to have to take my word for that, Kirill."

Kirill met Dillon's dark gaze. He swallowed dryly.

"Over there, behind a maintenance access panel in the central pillar." Kirill's words were weary, filled with pain - and a touch of fear. But there was triumph there as well: an ultimate triumph. Kirill believed that he had won - no matter what Dillon did to him, no matter what pain was inflicted upon him.

Both Dillon and Tatiana sensed this.

Dillon led Tatiana towards the pillar, keeping his voice low.

"Where the hell is the Priest when you want him?"

"I've sent three messages to his phone since we arrived here. None of them have been acknowledged."

"Damn. Well we'd better take a look at this master control, then..."

Dillon knelt, and released the cover to the maintenance panel.

The multiple LED's flickered at him. There was no visible countdown - but then, why should there be? Whoever set such a device working already knew the risk they were taking and the time they had to vacate the area.

Dillon analysed the master control keyboard. It wasn't the usual, QWERTY layout; instead each letter had been substituted with a symbol. And the detonation of the nuclear device was handled by this processor. He scratched at his stubble.

"Shit."

"What is it? And what are those strange symbols on the keyboard?"

"I've only ever seen symbols like these, once before. This is a Masonic Cipher. Also known as a Pigpen Cipher, because when the symbols are arranged in a coded message, they often look like the layout of a pigpen."

"Masonic Ciphers - pigpens?"

Dillon studied the keyboard, and then looked up at Tatiana.

"A quick crash course in the Masonic Cipher, then. Firstly, you see these grids on the screen, looks like a game of Naughts and Crosses, doesn't it. Well, everything revolves around the grids. It's a variety of a substitution cipher - in each of the nine boxes is a symbol, which is a substitution for a letter. The trick is knowing what association a symbol has with a letter. You can create the code symbols in a way that makes it very easy to remember how to construct and re-create the key. Understand so far?" Tatiana nodded.

"But there's one other major headache with this type of cipher. You can also use keywords within it, to further complicate matters. In this format, pairs of letters are typed or written into each location of the grid."

"Whoever set this box of tricks up would have almost certainly had a keyword, followed by the remainder of the alphabet into the grids in letter pairs. He or she also knew that because of the rarity of this type of coded encryption - that it would be virtually impossible to de-cipher it in time."

"How do you know about things like this, Dillon? I've always had my suspicion about you being a closet nerd."

"Really?" Dillon continued to study the master control keyboard, consumed by the puzzle. The deepest recess of his mind stirring as he subconsciously rummaged around for answers. This cipher was incredibly complex. And Dillon knew it - maybe if he had three or four hours and a laptop with the latest code breaking software loaded, then he might have a slender chance.

But with the minutes counting down...

And worst of all...

Kirill knew it. Knew that they were completely shafted.

"Can the code be broken?"

"Every code can be broken, Tats. Given time... Unfortunately, time is not a luxury we have. What we need now is the Priest; he's the only one who could remotely have any chance of cracking a Masonic Cipher."

Dillon returned slowly, followed by Tatiana, to where Kirill was still crumpled on the floor. Standing over him, he glanced over at Tatiana. Both Tats and Kirill saw the look on his face: it was not a *kindly* look; it did not convey what could be termed as 'friendly'.

He paced slowly up and down in front of Kirill.

Dillon lowered the muzzle of the Glock; pointing it straight at Kirill's genitals.

"Dillon, this will gain you nothing."

"Keep your sentiments to yourself. Firstly, think twice before speaking, just answer my questions and your little package down there will remain intact."

Kirill met Dillon's gaze.

"Why did you try to kill me?"

Kirill remained silent, and then said. "It's extremely complicated."

The Glock kicked in Dillon's hand as the round was released, the bullet ripping through Kirill's trouser material, missing flesh by a hairs width. Kirill grabbed at his genitals, a look of both disbelief and relief on his face. "Are you crazy?" Said Kirill hoarsely, his voice having risen an octave.

Dillon circled Kirill and stood behind him. Placing the barrel of the Glock just behind his left ear. "Wrong answer asshole. I repeat, why did you try to kill me?"

"You were in the wrong place at the wrong time; things moved too quickly and we needed to take out the opposition before they realised they *were* the opposition." He slowly turned his head, meeting Dillon's gaze. "You see Dillon, in the scheme of things. You were considered to be the most dangerous of all. This is why you were placed at the very top of the hit-list."

"Considered dangerous by who?"

"By anyone who has ever come into contact with you." Kirill tried to shift his weight, groaning with the severe pain as he did so. He continued, "But most of all, by myself and my new associates."

"So you are no longer working for the British Government? Why would you do this?"

"The *British Government*?" Kirill laughed, a laugh laced with pain. "The *British Government*? You dumb bastard, the only thing this has to do with that particular institution is how pathetically weak the honourable members have become... Sycophantic, general-public ass-licking-weaklings, each time a new lot get in, they have the power to make good on all of those broken promises ever made by their predecessors. And yet they choose not to - ever wondered why?" He laughed again, grimacing.

Dillon's face had gone pale. He ran his free hand through his hair, cast a quick glance at Tatiana, and then prodded Kirill with the muzzle of the Glock.

"Who are you working for?"

"For the greater good. And myself, of course."

"And the virus programme? Chimera? Where does that fit into all of this?"

"The virus programme," said Kirill thickly. His head was tilted to one side, his eyes no longer meeting Dillon's piercing gaze. "Chimera. It is the ultimate seek-retrieve-destroy programme. Incredibly powerful - it can invade any computer, without a trace. It uses broadband connections, Wi-Fi connections and moves from one computer to another with lightning speed. It extracts information within a nanosecond and then on exit, leaves the hardrive with a little present that I call, a sleeper. A little sting in the tail, so to speak. The sleeper can be activated at any time and remains under our total control, one stroke of the keyboard and we shut down every computer that Chimera has invaded. Permanently."

"You're not working alone, Kirill," said Dillon softly. "Who else is involved?"

"Ramus. Whom, MI6, the CIA and, the KGB, have in the past attempted to assassinate, without success." The name sprang to Kirill's lips and he smiled, smiled inside; he remembered. Ramus was supposed to have *sorted Dillon out*.

So sort *this* out, you fucker, he thought.

"Ramus is the one ordering the killing and total destruction of the Scorpion network. He's the one who controls the Assassins and sent them after you..." Kirill met Dillon's gaze. "Surely you can see, Mr Dillon, I am just an innocent party to all of this."

He smiled, and his teeth were stained with tobacco and blood.

"Where do we find this Ramus?"

"You could try and find Ramus, but you'll not succeed. He remains constantly *mobile.*" Kirill laughed a nasty laugh.

"How?"

"Stealth-ship. And before you ask. I don't know where he is."

Dillon scratched an imaginary itch on his cheek. He glanced again at Tatiana; she had moved closer to the main entrance, both guns held low. It was obvious that she wanted out of this place, immediately. But equally as urgent, was her need to hear the answers as much as Dillon did.

"Is Ezra dead?"

"I would say so."

"You would say so, would you?"

"He fell over a hundred feet off of a cliff top. It would have taken a miracle to survive that, wouldn't you agree?"

"So you're high enough in the chain of command to be told about his demise?"

"I worked with Ezra on numerous projects for your masters, Ferran & Cardini International. He was also involved in the Chimera project at the beginning."

Dillon stared hard into Kirill's eyes, and the man looked up and met his gaze, his crumpled figure covered in blood.

"What is the significance of the Assassins, Professor Kirill?"

"The Assassins..." Kirill's eyes widened a little. Then he smiled strangely, revealing once again tobacco stained teeth, tainted with blood. "Ah... Assassins... They're - *something altogether different from you or I...*"

Kirill's gaze suddenly altered, lifted to something beyond Dillon, something outside on the heli-pad, and Dillon knew that there was the strong possibility that they were out there.

"Tats -" he started to shout a warning as he launched himself onto the floor, but everything was drowned out by the sudden roar of automatic gunfire. Glass exploded into the reception area; bullets slamming into the granite walls and pillars; they t ore into the oak furniture at the far end of the open-plan room, ending their journey as the wood splintered and yielded under the impact.

Everything was thrown into sudden madness.

Everything suddenly switched to black and white - in Dillon's mind...

And then... silence. The smell of cordite filled the mountain air, dust drifted through the gaps where the glass had been. He saw Tatiana, crouched behind a large metal container filled with an assortment of large exotic plants, wedged between the wall and a marble-faced pillar. She glanced up. Dillon gave a quick succession of hand signals...

Stay.

Wait.

Check Weapon.

Dillon glanced right; he could not see Kirill from his new position but he could hear him. At first he thought he was crying... But then he realised with rising anger that he was *laughing*. The bastard was actually laughing.

"So you want to know about the Assassins?" called Kirill. "Ask one of them yourself, Dillon - go on, ask the question yourself!" He laughed again, almost a cackle came from somewhere in the back of his throat. Dillon sighted the Nemesis scope, adjusting and shortening the focus. And at this short range, the next person to step through the doorway would be literally cut in half by the 12.7mm caliber rounds...

Everything happened at once - and it happened fast.

The Assassins made their move; there were four of them. Dillon squeezed the Nemesis trigger once, adjusted angle, and squeezed again and saw two of the black-clad figures drop almost simultaneously. The first took a bullet in the face and spun up into the air before being tossed violently, down onto the ground. The second caught a bullet in the throat, virtually severing the head from the torso, blood spraying in a wide arc across the walls.

The other two came through the doorway like circus acrobats, tumbling over the polished floor at speed - Uzi mini-machine pistols set to semi-automatic, firing at Dillon...

Dillon left the Nemesis on its tripod and dashed low across the reception area, using anything he could get behind for cover. Bullets ripped through the leather couches and ate the exotic plants, Dillon dived, rolling behind a pillar and then skidding, arms flaying around as he fought to get some sort of grip on the highly polished surface to face Tatiana.

The automatic pistol slid over the floor.

Dillon scooped up the familiar heavy bulk of the battered gun, placed his back against the pillar and a split-second later, spun out into the open.

Dillon dropped to a crouch, head snapping round to the left, and his gaze roaming the room in search of the other Assassins. The first Assassin lay, its skull broken, a sticky gluten matter pooling around it. The second lay a few feet away, its hooded head twisted at a bazaar angle to the body. *Where the hell is the Priest and the others, and why didn't I hear these bastards coming? Screamed his brain.*

"They must have come back for Kirill," whispered his subconscious softly.

There was a movement - a soft sound as soft rubber soled boots moved lightly over the highly polished floor, deep in the shadows at the far end of the room by the glass doors of the lift.

And then it saw Dillon.

Dillon was already firing: bullets tearing across the space, ripping through the gloom and punching the Assassin back against the glass door of the lift. A crimson smear appeared as it slid silently to the floor.

Dillon stayed low, eyes quickly scanning around the room for any other movement. The Assassin he'd just shot was in a sitting position against the glass door of the lift, its head slumped to the left, arms inert, both hands still holding the vicious Uzi mini sub-machine pistols, each forefinger still on the triggers, a red pool covering the highly polished floor around it. He moved cautiously, checked Tatiana. She had scrambled even further back behind the large metallic plant container by the entrance. *That's it, you stay just where you are,* he thought to himself. *Don't do anything heroic.*

The gun touched the back of his head, cold metal pressing gently against his skull.

There was a long pause.

"Do not make any sudden movement, Mr Dillon. It could be your last..." Came the soft female voice.

Dillon grinned, a nasty malicious grin. *"You damned idiot,"* he thought. *"There were four of them!"*

"Gun on the floor. Do it, or I will blow your face clean off. Now."

Dillon - moving very slowly - lowering his gun, he placed it carefully on the floor, and then stood up again.

"Very slowly, Mr Dillon."

Dillon stood, gaze roaming, searching for a way out.

"Move over towards Professor Kirill."

Dillon began a slow walk; he did not glance towards Tatiana's position but he knew that she could hear the exchange. He moved gradually into the view of Kirill.

Despite the fact that he had gaping bullet wounds and the pain that he must have been in. The man was smiling as if he didn't have a care in the world. He had struggled up and was now sitting on one of the couches, his back leaning against the soft black leather, and then he glanced casually at his watch.

"Four minutes and - twenty-five seconds, Dillon. The clock's ticking and then it's - big boom time." Kirill laughed, the laugh of a man resigned to certain death.

Dillon's brain was churning over in search of a solution to his immediate predicament, the voice deep within his sub-conscious saying over and over. *"Ask him straight out what it is he wants."*

"What is it you want, Kirill?"

"Want. I want nothing, Dillon. I have already resigned myself to death; in fact, it never ceases to amaze me how I've survived this long. My only pleasure now is to watch you go to *your* death, not knowing any of the answers. To know you died wondering where Chimera - where Scorpion - where Ferran & Cardini - and where the Assassins all fit into this rather interesting puzzle... You really have such low expectations of your enemies."

"You can at least do one good thing, Kirill."

"And what might that be?"

"You can let Tatiana go. She has nothing to do with this - nothing at all. Let her walk away from here."

"Oh, I'm afraid I dispute that, my friend!" Said Kirill dryly, his intelligent eyes glinting in the overhead lighting. "She is not an innocent, at all, Mr Dillon. Tatiana is not only the niece of Ezra, but she is one of *us*. Has been from the very start..."

Chapter 19

Wind and rain kicked up from the Scottish valley below, whipping Alix like a cat-of-nine-tails, the ledge that he was standing on, no more than six inches wide. A tiny figure looking out over an infinite void, down into a wide maw that would willingly devour him should he fall! Alix moved sideways, shuffling his boots, remaining fully focused, ensuring his foot-hold remained firmly on the ledge.

Clouds the colour of coal rushed past in a flurry of wind and rain.

Cold drops stung his eyes, and he blinked them free.

His heart was thundering in his chest.

After leaving the winch-house, they were confronted by a detail of six security guards, who were cut down with surgical precision. Heavy army issue boots could be heard running towards them; they split up, the Priest seeking sanctuary within the network of service tunnels that formed part of the original SAS training complex; and Alix heading for the elements outside.

Alix glanced right and could see the Priest, who had appeared out of the ventilation shaft network, and was now crouched by a large stack of fifty gallon drums. He caught sight of Alix and gave him a signal to; wait!

He then felt, more than saw, the Priest start to move out of his hiding place; thinking something was dreadfully wrong, Alix remained perfectly still, boots firmly rooted to the narrow ledge.

Alix then saw the activity inside the landing bay. The Priest pulled from inside his three-quarter length leather coat, a sawn-off multi-shot shotgun. The cartridges loaded with a heavier gauge lead and capable of bringing down an elephant at thirty paces.

Alix licked his lips, tasting sweat beneath his sodden balaclava. His arms were starting to feel the real weight of the MP5 carbine he was cradling, and his legs were beginning to go numb with the cold and tension. He glanced down, past the narrow ledge. A tiny demon in his mind mocked him: what if he lost his concentration, even for a split second and - slipped? What if the Assassins spot him? What if they start shooting at him?

Alix smiled. The wind buffeted him. Rain stung his eyes.

I wouldn't give any of this up for *anything*, he thought.

The Priest signalled him, and then started to move slowly forward. There were perhaps eight Assassins positioned at strategic points around the landing area, some were concentrated around the entrance to the facility. Black-clad figures biding their time, he assumed they were deciding what course of action to take next, to obtain access to the main reception area.

With muscles screaming, Alix drew round the Heckler & Koch MP5, flicking off the safety. With his right hand he signalled to the Priest that he was ready. The Priest acknowledged, replacing his small leather bound Bible to the inside breast pocket of his coat.

They both moved together, Alix slipped over the rampart and landed next to a pile of crates at the edge of the landing bay. He kept to a low crouch, moving forward, all the time watching the Priest for instructions.

Alix's brain began calculating; eight Assassins and three security guards...

The Priest had also spotted the security guards, motioning for Alix to deal with them...

Machine-gun fire rattled, to the left. And then, all hell was let loose, the large glass panels fronting the facility's main reception area exploded, Alix immediately reacted by cutting down the three security guards with one sweep of the MP5. The Priest was doing God's work on the other side of the landing bay, killing four out of the eight Assassins in the blink-of-an-eye. The four surviving Assassins all charged through the now open doorway into the facility's reception area.

Alix dived, hitting the ground heavily on his front as bullets whizzed past his head, and he rolled, his own weapon kicking in his grip, rain pounding him. From somewhere to his right, he could hear the *thwack* of heavy calibre rounds being fired; not daring to look up for fear of having his head shot off. The Priest appeared at Alix's side, "Are you hit?"

"No man, just felt like a lay down for five minutes."

Bullets continued to ricochet off of the stone rampart just above their heads, the shooter positioned above them on the far side of the landing bay.

The Priest lifted his MP5 above his head and emptied a full magazine in a wide arc. Alix shuffled forward to get himself into a better firing position, but the shooter had anticipated his move and was taking single pot-shots at him. He cursed this sudden turn of luck, and then returned the fire, exactly as the Priest had by emptying a full magazine directly at him or her...

How the hell had they missed this one?

All of the other Assassins and security guards had left with the Chinooks. This one must have been stationed at one of the observation points on the mountain.

It didn't matter now - all that mattered were the bullets! They snapped past him. Alix emptied another magazine and allowed it to fall free; it clattered onto the ground, bouncing once on the wet surface. The Priest was at Alix's side, the two men stayed low as they sprinted across the open space of the landing bay. More bullets howled past them, Alix wrestled a fresh mag into his weapon, flicking it around so that his arm snapped out, holding the sub-machine gun like a pistol.

"You want to fuck with me?" He screamed; sighting on the position of the shooter, as the fusillade of bullets tried to snuff out its lights.

Alix unleashed the awesome power of the Heckler & Koch MP5 and bullets streamed across the landing bay and ate a line across the fifty-gallon drums. Av-Gas immediately started to leak out and creep across the ground, heading straight towards - the Priest and Alix.

Alix met the Priest's gaze for the briefest instant; there was madness there, and anger, and strength. And then both men jumped over the rampart, bullets chasing their heels, igniting the lake of aviation fuel that had spread around the landing bay. An explosion, and then another, and another, as the fifty-gallon drums started to explode and flames billowed and shards of hot metal hurtled through the thick black smoke that was consuming the entire landing area.

Even before the two men had gone over the rampart, Alix had the pistol in his right hand, was firing a piton attached to a fine reinforced line into the solid rock of the landing bay roof and the karabiner attached to Alix's bullet proof vest was now supporting both of them from a certain death far below.

The entire landing bay was ablaze with flames licking every granite surface.

And then the fire died as quickly as it had been born.

Alix engaged the pistol's motor-drive and the line started to reel itself in, and they started to ascend back up to the ledge. As the two men were almost there a black clad figure peered over the rampart in search of them - Alix fired three bullets into the Assassin's face, and the killer dropped without a sound. Alix flicked his gaze left, and the Priest had gone.

He sidled over the rampart and then halted, dropping to a crouch, noxious smelling smoke swirling around him. And then he heard the sound of machine guns, with an immediate stream of return fire. There were two thuds as bodies slapped to the hard stone ground. Alix ran to crouch beside the wall, eyes scanning; the shadows and the drifting smoke his new-found friends. Before him the open entrance of the facility, a gaping gash where the armour plated glass wall had once been, everything bathed in a gloom and murkiness.

Silence followed...

From behind came a strange creaking noise. Alix focused his senses; the landing area was vast, and littered with burnt out debris. It was a sniper's heaven. But the problem was; Alix wasn't a sniper!

How many killers and guards had really been left behind?

There had been three guards, all were now dead. Four Assassins had entered the facility. Leaving only the shooter who had gone over the rampart, that left, he saw them out of the corner of his eye, two Assassins - they were operating as a unit. As he watched, they moved fluidly in and out of the shadows beside the burnt out stack of fifty-gallon drums - Alix watched them climb smoothly up and over any obstacle that stood in their way, as they disappeared from view. His eyes flickered on the burnt-out remains of the Bell Robinson helicopter in the middle of the landing bay.

Alix remained in a crouch. Remained perfectly still, only his eyes moved, scanning for any movement through the smoke filled area.

Imminent danger... And not from the obvious quarter. No, this was a premonition from deep within him.

Alix saw the Priest; he moved warily from the shadows and Alix realised, too late, that the Assassins had out maneuvered the big man and were positioned above him now. Alix raised his gun and started firing.

Bullets struck sparks from the metal fifty-gallon drums, and ploughed furrows in the stone walls. The Priest spun - and with surgical precision fired one long burst of the MP5 on automatic at one of the thick overhead cargo carrying cables. With a shearing of tortured metal it snapped, sending deafening echoes reverberating across the vast area and out into the mountain range. As the cable snapped, one half snaked its way out of the pulley assembly and slinked over the rampart, to fall away into the valley below - the second half whipped around the landing bay, a wrist snapping garrotte that slashed through the drifting smoke, slicing through anything that got in its path and snaked across the ground.

The Priest leaped, moving fast in the long black leather coat. The two Assassins opened fire from their vantage point, bullets whining from Uzi mini sub-machine guns as the cable was drawn back to connect with the other pulley assembly - it tossed fifty-gallon drums aside as the thick steel cable was heaved upwards, tearing through everything that stood in its way; it struck a stack of fire charred cargo crates with deafening booms, and then with a final *swish* and a final *thwack* as it struck the roof of the landing area and its momentum expired...

Off balance, the two Assassins leaped to be free of the danger. Alix's MP5 cut them both in half.

Finally everything became settled into stillness; through the drifting smoke and out across the mountain range, the rain was still falling heavily, and Alix still crouched as if to spring, uncoiled and nodded towards the Priest. They both moved warily towards the entrance to the facility, and gazed back at the destruction - the snapped, blackened cable, the fifty-gallon drums split open like sardine cans, the bodies of the dead guards and Assassins, and the flaming remains of the Bell Robinson six-man helicopter.

"Nice and quietly, does it then!" Alix said, rolling up his balaclava. He wiped a sheen of sweat from his face, and lit up a cigarette.

"It might have gone smoother, I'll grant you. But God moves in mysterious ways, my son." Acknowledged the Priest slowly.

"Wait, listen up. Do you hear what I hear?"

"Yes."

"I'd know that voice anywhere."

"Jake Dillon!" They both said it at the same time.

"Maybe God was smiling down on us after all. Perhaps he's found Kirill?"

"We'd better go in carefully, just in case there are any more of those nasty little buggers in there with him."

"Quite so," said the Priest with pious sobriety, and moved forward towards the entrance of Kirill's facility.

Alix took one long last pull on his cigarette, and then flicked the stub high into the air.

"Okay then, Kirill. Let's see what secrets you're hiding in there," he muttered, calming his fluttering heart. He followed the Priest and both men were soon concealed on either side of the open doorway, hidden by grey granite walls of mountain rock.

* * *

Claudia Dax paused; stared around guiltily, like a child caught stealing a toy, sweat pouring down her forehead as she moved closer to the large wall panel.

Her flattened palm pressed against the cold black glass of the bio-metric reader. She held her breath.

The panel slid open; a soft-touch keypad was exposed - she keyed in a complex series of digits.

Then the inner sanctum opened, to reveal the core processor, the nucleus of the mountain facility. The core processor that not only controlled the facility's environment but also, because she had been the one who had hidden it there, it held the final codes to complete the Chimera Programme which could allow it to operate at 100%! Kirill's very own core processor held the key to Chimera...

...and Claudia was the only one who knew that the key had been under his nose all this time!

She tapped in a few digits; there was a hiss, a disk slid into place and within ten seconds it was done. She pulled free the tiny silver optical disk and stared thoughtfully at its mirror-like surface.

To hold the most damaging data in the world in your hands, she thought: every scrap of information about the Chimera Programme. How it worked - its entire design - its heart...

The blueprints for Chimera's *soul*.

She smiled nastily to herself. Fuck you, you murderers, she thought; I have something you not only want, but you need! The final scripts had been there all the time, you just didn't know where to look, and now I have the data I need to create a Chimera that will operate at one-hundred percent.

And what's more, I can now build as many Chimera Programmes as I like...

Claudia thought back to all the blueprints, the designs. Chimera was a programme that, once loaded onto even the most basic PC, could launch itself onto the world-wide-web and leech data, constantly self learning, and taking whatever it wanted, when it wanted. Carry Chimera loaded onto a WiFi enabled laptop into any public building; within five seconds it would, without alerting even the most sophisticated spyware, have entered the network and taken control of every machine within the building. At twenty seconds it would have replicated a billion times across the globe, taking control of satellite links, weapons systems, government mainframes, and the world's stock markets. In effect, whoever launches a Chimera running at one-hundred percent - has total control!

It was a malicious parasite.

It could go anywhere, control anything.

It would make whoever controlled the source of the programme, the *most* powerful person on Earth.

Chimera undeniably worked at its optimum in amongst the most sophisticated of processors and programs. Designed to learn and adapt with stealth at lightning speed, and without leaving a spec of evidence that it had ever been on the host hard drive. Chimera was one of a kind. The most advanced mal-ware programme on the planet - and Claudia Dax had not only created it, but she now had the completed programme in the palm of her hand...

Claudia Dax reached forward, and then stopped. She glanced over her shoulder, half expecting to see an Assassin with the muzzle of its Uzi pointing at her.

But she was alone.

Claudia had found a black satchel type bag; she dropped the disk into a zipped pocket inside and turned... Only then did she see the red flashing LED light on the side of the black box like device attached to the side of one of the main server units.

As she stared at the device, the red flashing light changed, to amber...

Her mind worked quickly; the Assassins had all left, and those left behind, had been systematically killing those members of staff deemed 'expendable', apparently this barbarism was being overseen by Kirill himself, her boss. A flashing light on a device. This had to be a bomb. *Had to be.* It wasn't unreasonable of her to assume that they wanted to totally destroy the facility. Claudia had a gold-plated security clearance. She had access to most of the information that flew around the facility; and she knew, knew that Chimera was developed to be one of a kind - in total control...

Claudia took a deep breath.

Shit, she thought.

She wiped the sweat from her forehead with the back of her hand, turned, and then sprinted across the lab. Her footsteps light on the tiled floor; she bypassed several security doors and returned to the corridor and the ventilation shaft.

She hauled herself up into its confines.

And it was then that she heard the gunshots.

Claudia crawled as fast as the restricted space would allow. The shots continued to echo through the ventilation system and she wondered just what the hell was going on. She went through the shafts faster than she thought possible, knees and elbows sore from friction against the aluminium walls, sweat soaking her clothing. Finally, she reached the spot and, spinning around on her bottom, kicked free the vent grille.

She dropped down into one of the reception level female rest rooms that she used as part of her route during her frequent midnight jaunts outside. She moved to the entrance, looking cautiously around the doorframe, ever fearful that she might be spotted by a guard or worse, an Assassin. She ran, keeping low, her breathing heavy with fatigue, past conference rooms and security offices. She passed one of the facility's many guard stations, huge banks of monitors stood looking out at her, blank and lifeless. And even now, she felt their accusatory gazes against her sweat drenched face as she went by.

She reached the emergency exit. The solid round metal doorway looked as if it were stuck fast. She pulled out her security pass card, swiped it through the reader, there was a hiss and the door released outwardly... And she stepped out onto the mountain-side.

The strong cold northerly breeze hit her with its full force, sleet and rain washed across her body.

The cold sweat running down her back made her shiver involuntarily.

Claudia ran, fuelled by fear, fuelled by the guilt of her theft, pushed on by the concept of a bomb not that far from her. She left deep footprints in the snow; indelible, as in fast drying concrete.

Reaching the corner of the gangway, some primeval part of her soul forced her to halt, to peer around the reinforced concrete column. She saw the winch-house. She crept, as low as possible; peering inside, and then around the general area. Looking down, her gaze went instantly to the bloodied twisted corpses of the dead guards, not more than two feet away from where she was now standing. She gagged at the sight of so much blood, raising her hand up to her mouth to stop herself from throwing up. Glancing quickly around, she moved to the entrance and opened the door.

She went inside.

Closed the door gently.

In the gloom of the interior, she could make out the large wicker basket hanging over the trap-door that would take her away from the danger to the safety of the valley far below.

Claudia pushed the start button, and then climbed into the basket as the winch motor cut in and the two wooden trap doors started to open. Then, as if for the sole purpose of reassuring herself, she said aloud, "Please God, don't let anyone with a machine pistol in their hand, look through that trap-door now..."

* * *

"...She really is one of us, Mr Dillon. Tatiana has always been on *our side*."

Several things all happened at once.

Outside, the noise of the winch motor cutting in could be heard; and then the cable running out as the basket was being lowered.

Dillon turned back to Kirill and saw the look of shock on his face.

The *crack* of the Glock 9mm echoed across the reception area. The Assassin crumpled to the ground, relieving Dillon's head from the pressure of the gun's barrel.

Dillon's eyes flicked around the immediate area. He looked up and around. Into Tatiana's tired eyes.

"That was close. Felt the heat off that one." He said softly.

"If she had wanted to kill you, Mr Dillon. You would now be dead." Said Kirill, his voice was low and a little shaky. "When I said that Tatiana was one of us, what I should have said is that she is one of them."

"Don't listen to him," said Tatiana, her stare fixed on Dillon.

"Damn it, Dillon. I've just saved your life."

Dillon turned fully towards her. "So who are you going to kill now? Me or him? Tats - your gun is still pointing at *me*..."

"Drop your weapon, Tatiana."

They both turned. The Assassin had tossed Kirill a Black Beretta pistol that nestled evilly in the Professor's hand.

The Priest squeezed the trigger and the *crack* reverberated around the reception area. He was standing in the ideal position by the entrance to have a clear shot. The Assassin dropped to the ground, the side of its head obliterated. The second *crack* followed immediately, the bullet grazing the side of the Beretta's grip in Kirill's hand with bone shaking ferocity.

At the same time, Tatiana kicked the Glock across the floor.

The Priest and Alix stepped over the bodies of the other dead Assassins towards Dillon.

"Took your time, didn't you?"

"We made it didn't we?"

"And, lady and gentlemen. In just under two minutes you're all going to have to say your goodbyes to each other. Truly, a suitably fitting end to this act! So perfectly written! So beautifully performed!"

Dillon's alter persona stirred deep within his subconscious.

Kirill checked his watch and smiled. Dillon looked sideways at Tatiana whose face was unreadable; he swallowed as time seemed to slow, turn to infinity and he felt the familiar heightening of awareness at the back of his mind; waiting, watching, timing, listening and then, surging forward.

* * *

Dillon's other self took control...

He dropped to his knees and rolled - the Glock slipped like a glove into the palm of his hand.

He rolled rapidly, he came up fast to see Kirill, the small black Beretta wavering, pointing in the wrong direction because Dillon had moved so fast and snapped the Glock up - Kirill just had time to register surprise and absolute fear as Dillon pulled the trigger hard and four bullets slammed into Kirill's chest, ripping holes through his clothing, skin tissue and muscle, blood splattering like a crimson waterfall across the stone floor.

Kirill's head was slumped forward, sightless eyes staring down at his gaping chest. Very slowly, he toppled sideways onto the ground and lay still.

"That was way overdue," said Dillon quietly, his voice laced with satisfaction. He rounded on Tatiana, the Glock trained on her face.

"You make one false move and I will kill you. You say the wrong thing, you will die, Tatiana. Do I make myself clear?"

Tatiana nodded solemnly.

Then let's get the hell off this mountain top before we're all fried. Tatiana, the Priest, and Alix all moved towards the main entrance at a run.

Dillon, exhilarated, put another bullet into Kirill's slumped body. Then another. He stared into the lifeless eyes. Then he ran across the room, collected the Nemesis sniper rifle, muttering, "Can't let such a beauty go to waste," and sprinted for the open entrance.

Tatiana and the others had reached the winch house, a look of despair across her face.

"The basket is down in the valley," said Alix, "And we don't have the time to bring it back up, Jake."

Dillon was about to speak, but the Priest cut-in. "Forget the basket, we'll go down the same way that Alix and I came up." He beckoned everyone to follow him inside the winch house.

"We'll go down the wire two at a time," He extracted the climb-assist unit from his rucksack, and attached it to the thick wire cable.

"The motor mechanism will act as a brake on the way down."

"Is there a back-up system?" Asked Dillon.

"If it fails - say goodbye to this world for good. There is no back-up, Dillon. But I will say a prayer and hope that the great man up above is looking kindly down upon us."

"Oh, that's reassuring then." Dillon said sarcastically.

The Priest placed his wrist through the webbing strap, and then instructed Tatiana to hold on tight, for a quick decent. They went through the open trap door.

Alix and Dillon positioned themselves over the trap door, and then after a second or two disappeared down towards the valley far below.

Neither saw the figure crawling out of the shattered entrance to the facility.

There came a single metallic *click*...

An obscenely loud *boom* rumbled deep within the facility, followed by an intense rush of hot air up through every air-shaft and corridor.

And then came a huge ball of raging fire and gases; fire roared and screamed upwards and outwards; large chunks of concrete and stone and glass were spat up high into the air; an insane release of energies rushed screaming and burning out across the mountain range.

"Hold on tight, Dillon." Said Alix excitedly.

The cable quivered violently with the sudden bursts of explosive...

And then the fire came, slithering like a white hot snake out of the open trap door, bearing down on the two men.

As Alix adjusted the climb-assist braking mechanism to quicken their descent, they were buffeted from above by the fist of the explosion. The two men were thrown around like rag-dolls as the cable flayed around in the turmoil, anger and total madness...

The ground came rushing towards them, Alix shouted to Dillon.

"Get ready to jump clear of the basket and don't forget to roll or, you'll snap both your ankles."

Dillon landed roughly, rolling out of the force of momentum; followed by Alix who performed a near perfect parachute roll landing. Even though the tongue of the fire had expelled itself high up the mountain face, the heat pursued them and could still be felt at ground level.

And then - the mountain top exploded...

Everything was in chaos.

Tatiana gazed up through tears at a vision of hell raging high above them.

Then from a dull grey sky, large chunks of rock started to rain down upon them.

All four sprinted for the cover of the nearest overhang, as moments later the guard's station was turned into match-wood, and rocks fell out of the sky to pound the damp earth all around the immediate area.

Everything became calm.

"Whoa!" Alix looked around at the devastation, and then called, "You out there Lola?"

"Perhaps she got the hell out of here when the fireworks had started? Dillon said casually.

"How did you get here, Dillon? " Asked the Priest.

"Army issue quad-bike. Why?"

"Because we need to leave - and fast. If that really was a small nuclear device that has just been detonated, we need to get as far away from here, as possible. We're already running a risk of radiation exposure as it is."

Dillon stood with his hands on his hips, staring out at the scatter of burning debris littering the valley floor.

Tatiana approached him from behind.

"You feeling okay, Dillon?"

Dillon whirled, so fast that Tatiana blinked, taking an involuntary step back. Only then did she see the Glock pointed at her.

Dillon smiled. A wide grin.

"You fancy going back up there, Tats. See your old pal, Kirill, eh?"

"Dillon, you're acting very strange."

"Stop talking!" He spat the words out vehemently. "Don't you dare judge me, you little bitch. Do I have to remind you of the damning words Kirill spoke. You traitor."

"Dillon, he was lying." She whispered softly.

The Glock snapped up - pressed against the soft flesh of her slender neck, just below her left ear.

"The only reason that you're still alive, luv. Is that I want to put you in front of Edward Levenson-Jones and The Partners of Ferran & Cardini International. Now, get moving."

Tatiana turned and strode off down the valley towards the hidden quad-bike. Dillon smiled suddenly, his gaze upwards towards the flames and the smoke at the summit of the mountain. "Not so smug now, are you Professor..." He said quietly to himself, then turned dark brooding eyes to watch Tatiana walk away, fine swaying hips and long slender legs, temporarily mesmerising him.

He looked up once more admiring the devastation that had once been Kirill's top-secret facility. His gaze took in the huge torn blocks of stone and the sea of broken glass that had rained down from the mountain.

He nodded his approval, eyes sparkling triumphantly.

"Dillon, you said there would be fireworks. But hell man, that was one of the coolest pyrotechnic displays I've ever attended."

"Yeah, cool Alix." Dillon said wearily, as he walked away down the valley.

* * *

The rain had stopped and the night cold descended. Flames burned low, crackling softly, the only sound against the bleakness of the highland night. Against scarred and blackened chunks of rock, twisted metal and fused glass, something moved in the semi-darkness.

It lay amongst the debris, reaching, clawing the smoke-filled air blindly with blackened stumps, crimson glistening in blood-filled shallow cavities. Then it slumped, rolling on its back and cold eyes stared up at the black star-filled sky.

And, with every last ounce of life left in his charred husk of a body, Professor Kirill screamed.

GCHQ Transcript 8. <u>Transcript of recent international news incident</u>.

Chaos ensued amidst an entire shutdown of the British military satellite network earlier today. Contact was lost with ground, air and naval forces around the planet as UK computer and military experts battled to bring the system back on-line.

Disruption was also caused to UK domestic, satellite TV, internet services and many other digital communication systems.

There was an immediate cry from Government ministers, as to why this happened - and how. Ministry of Defence experts are blaming severe electrical conditions in space, possibly causing a malfunction of the satellite's advance warning system to temporarily shut-down...

Chapter 20

Dillon opened his eyes.

Tatiana was smiling down at him. He looked up into her eyes and saw understanding there.

"I am sorry..." he whispered.

"Shh." She placed a finger against his lips. "Don't speak."

"I don't know why it happens, or what I'm saying. It's as if I'm someone else."

"I know, Dillon, I've known for a long time..."

Dillon smiled weakly. Then he flinched as pain flashed through his entire body, through all of the wounds he'd incurred over the last few days.

He gasped. And his brain felt like it was going to explode from the wound to the side of his head that pulsated with even the slightest movement he made.

Tatiana looked suddenly worried. "Dillon?" She shook him.

"Dillon, what's wrong?"

He opened his eyes.

He smiled up at her, squinting.

"Nothing, it's just a headache, nothing to worry about, Tats." The Priest and Alix were standing close by, a look of concern written across their faces.

Dillon coughed, writhing in agony for a moment. "Hell that hurts. Have you any painkillers?"

"We're completely out, sorry, Dillon."

"That's okay. We need to get going anyway. We'll get Alix and the Priest back to their Apache, and hopefully Lola will be there already. We'll then make our way back to Vince at the SAS depot."

"That sounds good to me." Alix said nodding. The Priest looked up at the dark brooding sky and then back at Dillon. "Yes, we should make haste."

Tatiana helped Dillon to his feet, and he stood panting for a moment in the early dawn half-light.

Then, with great effort of will, he grunted, and climbed on board the quad bike. Tatiana jumped on behind him and the Priest and Alix jumped onto the wide mud-guards either side of her, and he fired up the powerful engine. Dillon closed his eyes for a moment as he composed himself - not just for the journey ahead, but for the realisation that Kirill was actually dead: and that the *quest*, as it was the fucked-up journey, he had to make.

It was not over.

It was far from over.

The quad bike moved off, bumping along the dirt track and then racing out down the valley towards the loch...

"Ramus," muttered Dillon. And, grimacing, he screwed the throttle round viciously.

* * *

Claudia Dax rode the off-road trails bike hard and fast. The 750cc machine was powerful and sped through the darkness, the suspension absorbing the bumps with ease, the headlight scything the pre-dawn light.

I've done it, she thought triumphantly.

I've got away.

I've bloody well got away with the Chimera blue-prints. The ability to create the most powerful programme of all time, the most vicious piece of malicious software the world has ever seen. And she had the only script that would be able to run at one-hundred per cent efficiency.

Claudia Dax smiled; and then decided that there might be someone following her and the smile fell from her face as she checked her mirrors. But only blackness swept across the highland valley behind her, deep and impenetrable. Before her, blood smears on the front faring of the powerful Yamaha trials bike did nothing to calm her racing heart-beat.

Claudia wiped rain from her face with a gloved hand; and then remembered the blood. She glanced down at the crimson streaks and her stomach turned. And then she remembered her friends and colleagues who she'd worked with, and got to know over the last two years who had been murdered in their beds, and her stomach did a double flip. She swallowed hard, suppressing her fear and the sourness of bile rising in her throat.

She was free.

She could now make a difference...

She could flood the world with the Chimera code; only her version would have the anti-virus element to the programme. She could stop a global computer melt-down.

The British Government would be implicated as the source of Chimera. Implicated, blamed and, damned by everyone... She could blow the whistle on the other bad stuff that Kirill had been working on.

Claudia needed to get to a powerful computer, and she realised the danger of her predicament. She was going to ruin their plans; they would want her dead... But then they wanted her dead anyway. Did they know that she had the only copy of Chimera that could run at one-hundred per cent efficiency? She doubted it - after all, they had been about to blow the top of the mountain - and surely that had been the purpose of the bomb-to stop any possibility of anyone pirating the programme. But then she could not rely on that, she could not rely on *anything*... She had to assume that they knew she had the copy of Chimera.

But something confused Claudia Dax. Why should the British Government and Scorpion - who she had always thought of as a brilliant organisation to work for - so why would they kill a large group of their own employees? And why would they destroy their own secret facility that had cost hundreds of millions of pounds of tax-payers money to construct and maintain? Why would they blow-up the Chimera project?

Something in the reasoning was flawed. Something was not quite right - like Kirill and the bombs, like the appearance of the black-clad and hooded Assassins roaming freely through the corridors of the mountain complex.

She could not understand why Kirill would do such a terrible thing.

Unless the Government and Scorpion had been betrayed!

Claudia opened the throttle wider, and the powerful trials bike surged forward, off-road tyres biting into the tarmac of the Highland road. She focused on the winding road ahead, but in the back of her mind, she was thinking about just how serious these people were - whoever they were. They knew that she was alive; they would have airports and seaports covered for sure... So how the hell was she going to get away with her life intact? She knew that whoever it was involved, would have limitless resources if they really *wanted* to find her.

She racked her brains. What to do?

Focus. She had to stay focused, she thought.

Get out of Scotland. Get as far away from the facility, as quickly as possible.

Get rid of the trials-bike as soon as possible.

Find a suitable disguise.

The four-stroke engine stuttered, just briefly. Claudia felt the slightest vibration travel through the bikes frame. She looked down at the gauges and the orange light that indicated that she was out of fuel...

"What? You pile of junk," she muttered, tapping the fuel dial with a gloved finger. "How is that possible?"

The engine stuttered again, and then stalled. She coasted to a halt, pulling over to the edge of the road, tyres squelching on the water-logged grass verge. She sprang off the machine, letting go of the handle bar as her boots hit the soft ground, the bike falling heavily into the ditch.

"Shit. Shit!"

She looked around at - wilderness. She reached into her rucksack and retrieved a metal canister, taking a swig of the refreshingly cold water inside.

"At least I won't die of dehydration," Claudia muttered sourly. She picked up her small rucksack, and pausing for a moment to take several deep breaths and to brush a few specks of mud from her jacket, she bit the bullet of panic and set off down the road. The tarmac road surface made the going easy, and as she walked, she cursed herself for not checking the fuel level before she had roared off down the valley. She also cursed for such bad luck and, most of all; she cursed herself for ever working for Kirill in the first place.

* * *

The Priest returned from the outcropping of rock, the Heckler in one hand, a canteen of water in the other. He yawned.

"How are you feeling now, Dillon?"

Dillon smiled, wincing at pain emanating from various locations around his body. He glanced up at the Priest; the last few days had taken its toll on him, lines around the eyes appeared much deeper and the bruises seemed to have darkened.

"I feel like I've been run over by that quad bike a few times. What about you? You look wasted."

"I'm fine, thank you, Dillon." He smiled. "I need to return to my flock, I've a sermon to give this Sunday coming."

"Yeah, I could do with getting back home. I've got a small castle to repair when I get back." Dillon said with heavy sarcasm.

"Yes, I heard they messed up your place pretty bad. But look on the bright side, Dillon. You're still alive, to fight the good work, another day..."

After a brief break, and making sure that they were not being pursued, they all climbed wearily back onto the quad bike and once again set off. Forty minutes later and they found the Apache helicopter, and Lola, who appeared from her hiding place, once she was certain of who it was.

"What took you so long? I'd almost given up on you all."

"Sorry. We had to take care of some unfinished business, back there. Took longer than we anticipated." Alix said, smiling.

"You okay, Dillon? You look like crap."

"It's good to see you too, Lola. And, thanks for asking, but I'll live."

After arranging to meet up as soon as possible, they all said their goodbyes, and Dillon and Tatiana set off again. This time to pick up Vince and then head back to the sea-plane that they'd arrived in. They travelled for an hour, until Tatiana spotted something and tapped Dillon on the arm, pointing.

"You see it?"

Dillon glanced up. "The bike in the ditch over there," she said.

"There might be someone injured. Let's go take a look."

"Wonder what happened?" Said Tatiana.

Dillon coasted down the road; and as they approached the ditched bike, Dillon reached for his gun, tyres crunched on gravel as he pulled up twenty feet back from where it was laying on its side.

Dillon climbed warily from the quad bike, eyes scanning the deserted Highland landscape. He moved around the trials bike and saw that the key was still in the ignition. There was no one around; he checked the ditch in both directions, but found no bodies...

"Ran out of fuel by the look of it."

Tatiana was holding a long-range scope to her eye. "In that case, whoever was riding it, is now on foot. That bike came from the facility, the security patrols used them."

Dillon glanced around. Tatiana immediately sensed that now - in a potential conflict situation - he gave no sign that he was injured: all pain had been pushed out of the way, as the adrenalin started to flow freely around his body for the moment.

"Could be a stray guard or an Assassin then, wandering around the countryside." Dillon slipped the Glock's safety to the off position for a little more reassurance. "But it could also be a biker who simply ran out of fuel."

"So let's keep going. We're still too far away from Vince."

Dillon jumped back on the quad bike and they charged off up the road with all four tyres gripping the tarmac and the stealth engine running at full throttle. Dillon kept the Glock in his hand and stayed vigilant as they raced forward.

They rode with a heightened awareness for the next hour as the sun broke through the cloud and sent welcome rays down upon them. They passed no traffic in that time, and saw no other living being. It was as if everyone had hibernated...

It was Dillon who spotted her.

"Look. Over there to the left, that track running parallel to the road." Dillon said, pointing.

The young woman squatted down behind the remnants of a low stone wall when she spotted the quad bike. But by then it was too late - Dillon's sharp eyes had spotted *her*.

They came to a halt and climbed off the quad.

Dillon moved off of the road and up the track, stopping just short of the dilapidated low wall. "Stand-up and show yourself!" He called.

Nothing moved...

Dillon pointed the gun at the pile of rocks. "Either you come out and show yourself or, I'll come make sure you endure a slow and painful death. You have to the count of three. One, two, three..."

The woman stood up slowly, hands held high in the air. She wore tight fitting stone-washed denim jeans and a brown leather sheep-skin flying jacket, and carried a small rucksack. Dillon gestured with the Glock. Out onto the road, where I can see you clearly."

Dillon moved closer, checking to see if she was alone. The woman was strikingly beautiful, her eyes bright. She looked frightened, terrified even. "Please don't shoot me, please," she said as Dillon came closer.

He stopped a few feet away, looking her up and down.

"What the hell are you doing out here in the middle of nowhere?"

"It's a long story," she said, smiling weakly. Slowly she lowered her arms, but Dillon waved them up again. He stepped in close and checked her for weapons, a cold sweat beading on his forehead as he fought with his inner turmoil of pain.

He stepped back. "What's in the bag?"

"Nothing much. Just a few personal items."

Show me."

Claudia Dax opened the rucksack; she slowly pulled out the few personal items from inside and then showed Dillon the inside which was now empty.

"What about the side pocket?"

Claudia unfastened the Velcro flap. Slowly she withdrew a small silver disk and instantly Dillon aimed the 9mm Glock at her head and her eyes widened, like a deer caught in headlights. Tears started to roll down over her high cheekbones.

"What is it?" Dillon asked.

"That's a relief. You're obviously not from the facility?"

Dillon raised his eyes, and smiled grimly. "Well, we did have a brief acquaintance with a man called Kirill."

Claudia looked into Dillon's eyes at the mention of the name.

"Where is he now?"

"Very dead. Are you going to answer my question?"

"It's the entire blueprint of the Chimera virus programme. So you've not been sent to kill me?"

"I don't even know who you are, luv. Come on, walk over to the quad bike; you look like you're suffering from the cold."

Claudia walked, with Dillon a few paces behind her, checking warily all around. When she reached the quad Tatiana smiled, and Claudia was allowed to lower her hands.

"And who do we have here, Dillon?"

"Haven't got a clue, Tats." Dillon took a long swig of water from the metal canteen.

"But, she has got the blueprints for the Chimera virus programme," said Dillon.

Tatiana's eyes widened. "Are you serious?"

"Very serious." Turning to Claudia, he said, "I'm assuming that you worked for Kirill?"

Claudia nodded. "Kirill had the majority of his staff murdered by those freaky Assassins. I hid in the air-conditioning shafts, and as all hell let loose, I'm assuming that was you and your friends? I managed to escape off the mountain in the basket and then steal a trials bike from outside of the guard-room. But before I left, I made a master copy of Chimera. So you're really not here to kill me?"

"If I was going to kill you," said Dillon softly, "we wouldn't be talking now. Come on, jump up on the quad. I assume you need a ride out of here?"

Claudia nodded, and climbed up behind Tatiana, squeezing onto the tail-end of the saddle, just above the two stealth pipes.

Dillon fired up the engine.

"Where are you heading? Or alternatively, you can have this quad in about three hours..."

"I'll go wherever you're going. I just need to get as far away from this place as possible," Claudia said wearily.

"Well, we'll see what we can do," said Tatiana, smiling warmly.

* * *

After a couple of hours they stopped for a break, and a little respite from the rain that was falling heavily again. They stood at the base of the cliff face under a craggy overhang that jutted out like a witch's brow. Dillon looked up, allowing a cold trickle of water to run down over his face.

"We'll be with Vince in about an hour and a half."

"Text him. Let him know we're on our way, and to get some hot food on the go - I'm absolutely starving." Tatiana said softly.

Claudia Dax had wandered off a little way, stretching her legs. Her clothes were stained, and her leather jacket had a long tear in one of the arms, she looked in a sorrowful state, as they all did. Dillon caught her attention and she moved over to him, accepting his canteen with a radiant smile of thanks.

How is it you know about the Chimera Programme? It's a top secret project," she said, lips glistening with water.

Dillon shrugged. "It's a very long story, luv, and believe me, we don't really want to burden you with our problems. Kirill was the man with the answers and now he's dead. Very dead."

"So the explosives detonated?"

"Yes," said Dillon, smiling a nasty malevolent smile. "Tell me; is this Chimera Programme really as powerful as they say?"

"Chimera? Oh yes. It works all right. And because it is completely self-learning, there is no limit to what it can do. As a virus it is lethal. As a programme that can; seek - search - retrieve, it is capable of stealing; not only documents and files, but the entire contents of even the largest network. State-of-the-art security software doesn't even know that Chimera has entered the system."

Kirill's words came back to Dillon.

This programme is so powerful; it will bring governments and global companies to their knees in a matter of seconds. It will throw up information about anyone or anything that could jeopardise its very existence. Chimera was able to enter the Government's most secure Ministry of Defence server, and extract information relating to certain elements of the Scorpion network. It then advised that the Special Operation Units should be eliminated to safeguard the project in the future. You see, these were considered the most dangerous. Along with yourself, Mr Dillon."

Dillon was starting to get a crystal-clear picture of conspiracy: Kirill and this other man Ramus were in league and planning a global cyber-terrorist attack on a scale never seen before. The Assassins were obviously the private army of Ramus and had eliminated the Scorpion squads and had very nearly succeeded in killing him. They had tried to take out Ezra and had destroyed his facility on Santorini, because they wanted the final piece of code that would allow Chimera to run at one-hundred percent and not be copied as an anti-virus. These were cold blooded killers who would stop at nothing to safeguard their objective. The ultimate control of every military satellite orbiting the planet in their quest for global power...

But what next? Where would they go next?

What would be their next move?

Bastards, he thought sourly.

"What do you know about the Assassins," he asked quietly, rubbing his tired eyes.

"The Assassins? You mean those people in the black skin-tight lycra?"

Dillon focused on Claudia. "When did you first notice them?"

She shook her head, "They arrived about a month ago. It was the Assassins who killed most of Kirill's research and development staff."

"Really…" Dillon scratched at his heavy stubble; it was making his neck and face itch bad and he needed a bath... Ye Gods, for even the most basic toilet! And a bath! And a cold beer! Or a glass of Champagne or two...

"My God," Tatiana said excitedly, rummaging in her pocket and pacing around. She pulled free her Ferran & Cardini smartphone.

They all turned to stare at the slender black device.

"Hell Tats. Did it bite you or something?" Dillon snapped. "You made me jump, and I almost choked on my water!"

"It's vibrating," said Tatiana.

"So what, it's most likely the partners checking up on you!"

"Dillon, as you know, it's not just a smartphone but also a secure line receiver and it's receiving now."

"Shit," agreed Dillon. He peered warily into the distance, and checked overhead in the skies. "So whoever is sending knows exactly where we are?"

"I suppose so."

"I thought the Government mainframes that served that phone of yours had been brought down?"

"They had, but someone must be routing through another smartphone. They're configured in such a way that allows them to work independently of the main servers in London, should the impossible happen and they fail - which they have."

Dillon slowly looked down, and then gazing out beyond the confines of their shelter, looked warily around the vast open space before them. He couldn't see anything suspicious but that didn't mean it wasn't there. "So then, are you going to answer it?" He said as Tatiana continued to stare at the sleek black device.

Tatiana touched the screen lightly. It immediately lit up with a soft blue background to a series of digits. Tats squinted at the data rolling down the page. It ended - reading:

CLASSIFIED TRANSMISSION - Level 1/ ENCRYPTED
SEND TO: T-0918273645   REC: E-1920384756

"Oh my God," said Tatiana softly. "It's from Ezra."

"That's impossible," said Dillon wearily. "We saw what happened on the cliff top on Santorini."

"But think about it, Dillon. If this was coming from Ramus, or whoever, then surely we would be fighting those Assassins for our lives?" There was hope in her voice, and her eyes had a sparkle in them. The tiredness and lethargy he had witnessed earlier had all but gone.

Dillon looked at the smartphone suspiciously, then at Tatiana.

"I don't like it. I don't like it at all," he said.

"And you think I do?"

Dillon remained silent, merely gestured with the Glock for Tatiana to open the file and read the message. She read:

> My dearest Tatiana, you saw me fall to my death on Santorini: But I survived, saved by the SAS at the last moment; but the copy of the Chimera Programme that I made was lost when I went over that cliff.
>
> I am now in Nassau in The Bahamas, meet me there in 24 hours - use coordinates 25.066667, - 77.333333. Time is running out, and Chimera will soon be launched globally. Our meeting is of the utmost importance...
>
> I know you will think this is a trap. If Dillon is still alive, tell him that the very clever device that his Australian friend Vince Sharp designed for the British Special Services; saved my life. Tell him that if it weren't for this incredible invention, I would almost certainly be dead.
>
> If you make it to the meet in Nassau, go to the Crystal Palace Casino and hotel; ask for a message for Jake Dillon at the main reception desk.

"He said that it was Vince Sharp's device that saved his life. He said you'd know what had saved him when he fell of the cliff on Santorini?"

Dillon nodded. He walked back to the quad bike, staring out across the windswept landscape. What he'd give for a cigarette right now...

Tatiana moved up behind him. She gently placed a hand on Dillon's arm.

"You okay?"

"Hmm. Maybe."

"It's a trap, right? Ezra is dead. We saw him jump, with our own eyes. We saw him die on Santorini."

Dillon nodded, turned around to face her, and looked into her eyes; and he saw it again, the desperation, the need to believe that her only next-of-kin was still alive. And yet... *Could* Ezra be alive? Could he have really been rescued by the SAS? Could he have been wearing a Chameleon Para-vest, something Vince had come up with in his lunch break, and could he have pulled the cord at just the right moment to brake that terrible fall into the water? The cliff top must have been at least three-hundred feet above sea-level. And if he did *survive* - is he now on the trail of those traitors who stole Chimera from the British Government?

Ezra had been a *very* resourceful man. Maybe, he had always had a contingency plan? But, it still left the question as to why he had not let the SAS take-out the Assassins. If he knew there was a squad on the island, why not let them fight the ferocious attackers of his facility on Santorini? And Tatiana, Dillon thought sombrely. If Kirill was telling the truth; if you really do work for the enemies of the British Realm - "traitors" - then you're a bloody good actress.

"We will go. We have to go."

Tatiana gently touched the side of his unshaven face with the palm of her hand. "Really?"

"Yes, but don't get your hopes up - and we'll do it my way. Understand?"

"Dillon, I know you think I..."

"Don't say it." He placed a finger against her lips. "Kirill was lying, I know. But I've got a really bad feeling about this - and yet, if Ezra is still alive, if the mad bastard did survive that fall, and managed to escape those two Assassins, and get off the island unseen... Well, he's just about the only ally we've got. It's not as if Kirill was any great enlightenment... All we got out of him was a name - Ramus - a name we already knew."

Claudia had come up behind the two and Dillon spun his gun in her face. He smiled weakly. "Sorry, force of habit."

Claudia waved his apology away. "You said a name just then, didn't you?"

"Yes I did, Ramus. An international terrorist; originally a Russian mafia hit-man, based in Moscow. Graduated from Cambridge with a First in applied mathematics, with distinctions. His link with Kirill is most likely kept deliberately fluid, which is why there's only the sketchiest details about him or his whereabouts. Have you heard of him?"

Claudia nodded. "Heard of him, met him, turned down an offer of sex with the creep. Thought I was going to get fired." She laughed softly. "Wish I had now."

"What do you know about him?"

"Very little. He visited the facility on a number of occasions. He was a pent-up tough looking guy. One of those stereotypical ruffians - but he had a certain refinement about him, that made him very different from others."

"Sounds like a really nice bloke," said Dillon, staring into the distance.

"You want to know an amazing coincidence?"

Dillon met Claudia's gaze. She smiled gently. "Sorry, I've been eaves-dropping. But I think you'd like to know this... Ramus, well, on the occasions when he visited the facility, I overheard conversations with Kirill - said he'd come straight from The Bahamas."

"New Providence, by any chance?" Said Tatiana, frowning.

"Nassau," said Claudia.

"Well, there's a coincidence," said Dillon grimly.

"So what now?" asked Tatiana; Dillon could see it in her face. She knew the dangers, knew that there was the strong possibility of the whole thing being a set-up, a plot to ensnare them. But she wanted - needed - had to know if Ezra was still alive.

Dillon looked into her eyes for a moment, thinking. Was she the bait to lure him into a trap?

They're either extremely clever and manipulative, thought Dillon. Or Ezra is onto Ramus... he's still alive, and on the trail of those dedicated to creating global chaos...

Decision time.

He scratched at the stubble on his face. He placed a hand on Tatiana's shoulder. "We'll go," he said softly. And smiled. "I have a lot of friends in the Bahamas."

* * *

Night was falling as the quad bike reached the SAS depot. Vince was there and was sitting at a small fire he had lit; his almost trademark metal tea pot brewing over the flames.

"Dillon, it's good to see you back in one piece, mate. What took you so long?"

"It's a long story," Dillon said, with a quick glance at Tatiana. "Is there any of that tea on offer? I think we could all do with a hot drink." Vince nodded, and poured out three mugs.

He raised his gaze in Claudia's direction, and then looked at Dillon quizzically. "You been picking up waifs and strays again, Dillon?"

"This, Vince, is Claudia Dax. She escaped from the facility shortly after the Assassin's started killing all of her work colleagues."

"Streuth. You're one lucky lady, then."

"Claudia has a master copy of the Chimera Programme!"

"Well, aren't we the lucky ones, then. I suppose you know that Ezra is still alive?"

"How do you know this?" Tatiana snapped.

"He emailed the partners at Ferran & Cardini, telling them to thank me for his Chameleon Para-vest. Said it saved his life when he jumped off that cliff on Santorini."

"Well I'll be, so it's true." Dillon said softly. "Tats also got an email from Ezra. He's in Nassau in the Bahamas. And wants us to meet him there within 24 hours."

"We going?" Vince said excitedly.

"Yes. But the problem is how do we get there?"

"You leave that to me, mate. I know just the man who can fix that for us."

"Who?"

"Edward Levenson-Jones."

Dillon felt his head ache at the mere mention of LJ's name. "Does he know that I'm back on the payroll, so to speak?"

Vince looked up at Dillon sheepishly, "We'll cross that bridge when we get to it." He resumed tapping furiously at the laptop's keyboard, and a moment later he punched the *enter* key, and said.

"There..."

"*There?*" Dillon mimicked.

"Dillon. Don't you know that, *there*, is a highly technical computer nerd's term?" Tatiana said laughing. Claudia joined in as well.

Vince looked up at them, unimpressed with the joke. The laptop made a strange pinging sound, announcing an incoming email. "Ah ha, LJ has sent back an encrypted response."

"That was bloody quick. It's good to see that he still works all hours, what does it say?"

"Well, I asked him for an aircraft to be made available and ready to take us all to Nassau."

"And..." Dillon said impatiently.

"And there's a Navy helicopter on its way to pick us up, with instructions to take us to the nearest military airfield. From there a Ferran & Cardini Learjet will fly us to the Bahamas."

"Estimated time of the chopper's arrival?"

"ETA is twenty-five minutes, give or take."

"Good. I think that we can safely assume, then, that LJ and the Partners are treating this whole Kirill affair seriously."

"Oh, they started to take this threat seriously, when the Scorpion squads started being assassinated, and Scorpion HQ was destroyed..."

"Great," said Dillon. He sipped the tea, and then held out the mug for a refill.

"What do you think, Claudia? Are we walking into a trap?"

Tatiana shot Dillon a sharp glance. "Dillon?"

"Hmm?"

"What's with asking the opinion of the girl we've just picked up and know nothing about?"

"I wouldn't say that, Tatiana. We know that Claudia worked at the facility, and that she has a full working copy of the Chimera Programme. What more do we need to know?"

Claudia hesitated before saying," Well, if you look at it logically, it is highly probable that you'll be walking straight into an elaborate trap. But, my gut instinct is that it's not, and that tells me that Ezra is still alive and on a mission - to stop Ramus."

"Thanks, Claudia. That's settled, then. We go - even if only to get away from the infernal cold of the Scottish Highlands." Dillon said finishing the last of his tea.

They could hear the distinctive sound of rotor blades beating the air long before the Sea-King came into view. They all looked skywards as the Royal Navy helicopter approached, creating an enormous downwash as it hovered into land.

* * *

The Westland Sea-King was noisy and relatively uncomfortable. But Dillon couldn't help feeling at home in this British made anti-submarine helicopter with its fully computerised warfare control systems, and Rolls-Royce Gnome engines. Dillon was sitting opposite Claudia, he'd decided that she could be of use; after all, she was at the centre of the Chimera Programme, and she happened to have a master copy of the full programme in her rucksack - something which Dillon acknowledged could probably be useful.

As the Sea-King buzzed low over the lush green landscape, the pilot worked hard to maintain their speed at an altitude of only two-hundred feet. Dillon looked out of the small porthole, watching the terrain race by below them, and it occurred to him that *maybe* Ezra was alive and had been captured by the Assassins. If he had been tortured, blackmailed, whatever, then maybe the Chimera master copy could be used in an exchange situation.

"Claudia?"

"Yes, Dillon?"

Sitting directly opposite her, their knees were almost touching, Claudia was an attractive woman, and Dillon glanced admiringly at her.

"You know Chimera intimately, don't you?"

"I helped create the programme; so you could say that I know it a little more than intimately..."

"Flippancy is something I can do without. So if you don't want to be left at whatever airfield we're heading for..."

"Okay. I concede - you are doing me an immense service, by letting me tag along with you all. Although, I'm a little concerned as to how I ended up sitting opposite a lecherous old pervert who keeps looking at my tits. Not that I mind, at all..."

"Lecherous old pervert?"

Claudia smiled, crossed her legs and slowly ran the toe of her shoe up the back of Dillon's calf.

Tatiana had heard, looked round the edge of her seat laughing. It was not a laugh of support.

Dillon flushed red. "Old?"

"Well, middle-aged, then." Her eyes sparkled mischievously.

"Middle-aged?" Dillon sounded aghast. "Do you really think I look that old? Jesus, I knew we should have left you up that mountain..."

"Dillon, do you have a question for the poor girl or what?"

"Okay. If we could load your programme onto a computer - would it conflict with the copy that Ramus is planning to launch?

Claudia shook her head, her main of red hair tousling around her face. "It's a virus, Dillon, not something you can simply load up onto any old processor, and then let loose globally. But change the little bitch's script slightly, and bingo, I can create the ultimate anti-virus. This would be more powerful than the Kirill version and would hack and crack anything..." Tatiana's eyes lit up at that. Claudia continued: "Point it at the global computer highway and it'll worm its way through the original code in under a second. The Kirill version won't be able to detect its presence because it will have the same Chameleon cloaking ability, but with one subtle difference. My version will have only one objective - to destroy the original code... Nothing is untouchable; nothing is hidden from it."

"Will your code be left inside the processors, mainframes, and servers that it cleans up?"

Claudia shrugged. "Any machine that it comes into contact with will benefit from a full hardrive scan. It will also be tweaked-up, and yes my version of Chimera will remain hidden on the hardrive. But, only as protection, nothing else..."

"What would be the reason for it to remain hidden on the hardrive?" Tatiana asked bluntly.

"Like many pieces of software, Tatiana, certain elements are always there, left behind on the hardrive even if the programme is deleted."

"I get the picture," said Tatiana softly.

"But do you? Chimera was originally developed to assist the Government in their fight against organised crime and terrorism. The main brief was to come up with the most powerful programme ever developed to retrieve encrypted information on targeted hardrives, and then destroy the hardrive. But what Kirill actually came up with, was a viral programme that could self replicate itself a trillion times in the blink of an eye, and be controlled to do whatever was asked of it by the main source."

"Main source?" Dillon asked.

"The server that the programme is initially loaded onto. Well, find that and we're in business to stop a global computer catastrophe..."

"Really? You mean you can actually *stop* this thing?"

"Oh yes. I can stop it, alright. The Chimera Programme that Ramus stole was running at around 94% perfect, but it was getting better by the day when..." Claudia trailed off. She coughed, gazing out at the passing countryside below the helicopter. "We had almost finished our work at the facility, the glitches in Chimera were being worked out, and the programme was almost ready to go operational. We were about to run a series of trials in the lab."

"So it was feasible to destroy the mountain facility? Because it had served its purpose?"

"I suppose," nodded Claudia. "But I don't understand *why*. There was no reason to destroy the facility. What a waste of a valuable resource!"

"Unless you didn't want anyone to get at the state-of-the-art hardware located in the main lab. You were *lucky*, that you weren't blown from here to kingdom come."

"Lucky?"

"Yeah, lucky. But, I'll give this to you - you've got balls, missy. And brains, you had the foresight to make a second master copy... Although, that begs the question of *why* did you make it? No matter. Hiding it right under their noses was pure genius."

"What are you insinuating, Dillon?"

"I'm not insinuating anything, Claudia. You made a copy, because as a former hacker, you know that with it, you're in a position of domination, if that tickles your fancy. But re-write certain elements of the script to create the anti-virus, and bingo, every major power on the planet would pay a king's ransom to get their hands on it. In fact, you would have the world at your fingertips!"

"You would need to know which scripts to alter... Which means you would need to *understand* the programme intimately, really *intimately*." Said Claudia.

"And of course, Ezra would have the right codes, Kirill would have *had* them, and this character Ramus no doubt *has* them. Seeing as they all had something to do with designing it." Dillon snapped.

"Ramus," said Tatiana softly.

Their gazes met; it all sounded too fantastic, but then, sometimes *fantastic* could happen. Take a terrorist; who makes it his business to acquaint himself with a government scientist who is working on a top-secret ground breaking project. The terrorist then sets about persuading him to join his cause, or whatever it is. He realises that he could make a mountain of money; blackmail the world's richest super-powers; cause a global cyber war; whatever. And he wants his five minutes of fame, to establish his own immortality; to further his own ends. To play at being *God*...

314

"This is beginning to sound like a megalomaniac's fantasy playground," said Tatiana coldly. "I don't think the world is ready for it."

"You're probably right," said Dillon.

"Perhaps that was why they destroyed the facility?" said Claudia.

"No. The effort required in planting such an explosive device and the unnecessary risk that Kirill appeared to undertake in overseeing it himself, indicates to me that he was ordered to stay behind, because someone knew that he would not survive. I'd say that our friend Ramus wanted him dead," said Dillon. "But I'm sure that when we come face to face with Ezra once more - then he'll no doubt have some answers for us."

The Sea-King banked round to the left and then levelled out over the glistening mountain peaks, rotors thrashing the air, its two Rolls Royce Gnome engines humming with reined-in torque and power; it banked to the south-west, heading for the coast and the airfield just north of Edinburgh...

And as they moved at speed over small villages, towns and open countryside. Dillon mused about their imminent meeting with Ezra...

Chapter 21

The Learjet 85 cruised at an altitude of thirty-three thousand feet across a cloudless sky of brilliant blue; flying in the black and gold corporate livery of Ferran & Cardini International, at an average speed of 500 mph over the Atlantic Ocean far below.

The aircraft came in low over Grand Bahamas and touched down on the tarmac runway with a squeal of brakes and rubber. The co-pilot's voice came over the intercom, "Ladies and gentlemen, welcome to Grand Bahama."

"I thought we were heading for Nassau." Snapped Tatiana.

Dillon held her gaze and nodded, "We are - eventually. But I'm still not convinced that we're only dealing with Ezra. If it was Ezra who sent that message?"

Dillon went forward and spoke in a quiet voice to the captain.

"Fly the Lear under five hundred feet until you reach the Florida coast, and then make sure you're on the radar from there into Tampa. The authorities will assume you've come through the Bermuda Triangle. Then file a new flight plan from Tampa direct to Nassau." The captain nodded, and Dillon continued. "One thing, though. Make sure you're only on the tarmac at Tampa for as long as it takes to fully re-fuel."

"Nassau?"

"Assuming we're not all murdered there? Make the jet ready for a quick getaway. If I remember rightly, the partners of Ferran & Cardini have a private hanger at the edge of the airfield apron. Use it. I'll message you when we're in need of flight. Understood?"

"Understood, Mr Dillon."

Dillon grinned, "It's always a pleasure flying with you captain."

"And life is always interesting when we fly you, Jake."

Dillon and the others watched as the Learjet disappeared from sight within seconds, its vapour trail streaking an otherwise clear blue Bahamian sky.

* * *

The night was hot and humid. Distant sounds of a boat party echoed across the bay, followed by the splash of revellers diving into the water in high-jinx.

A quarter of a mile away, the forty-six power cruiser probed the surrounding darkness. Dillon opened the throttles as they rounded Pinders Point and entered the Northwest Providence Channel.

The calm water parted easily under the force of the cruisers bow. A deep rumble emanated from the inboard V8 engine, the sound penetrating the early hours of the morning as the small group headed towards their destination - Nassau. Dillon sat at the helm, his gaze flitting from the green lit dials of the control console to the glittering black water ahead of them. Tatiana stood beside him in the opulent gloom of the luxury cruiser's bridge; she leaned forward, peering out through the windscreen over the lapping dark water.

"I always dreamed I would visit the Bahamas."

"Sorry luv, but this isn't going to be a holiday visit," said Dillon softly.

* * *

Dawn was breaking as the power cruiser entered the Northeast Providence Channel, heading in a south-westerly direction towards Nassau, the Berry Islands clearly visible on the starboard side as they raced by. Half an hour later Dillon eased back on the throttles and the hull of the forty-six foot craft eased back down into the water, half a mile off New Providence Island. He allowed the cruiser to drift with the tide, as he gazed through binoculars towards the busy port of Nassau. After a few moments he opened the throttles again and headed straight for the port entrance.

Dillon berthed the cruiser, shut down the engine, and went down to the day saloon to join the others. Vince was busy at his laptop, Claudia and Tatiana both looked up as he came down the steps.

"Anyone for breakfast?"

Vince looked up and said, "What are we talking here, chap? Eggs, Bacon, all the trimmings?"

"I think that can be arranged, big-man. I'll get right on it." Dillon went up on deck and made a call from his unregistered pay-as-you-go mobile phone. If anyone was trying to track him, they'd have no luck if he only used this handset. Most of all, Tatiana did not know about this phone...

Dillon re-joined the others, and twenty minutes later a beautiful Bahamian woman in her early forties was standing on the pontoon alongside the power cruiser with a very large rush basket in her hand. Dillon went out onto the stern sun-deck and greeted her with a wave.

"Margarita." He went down the gang-plank and hugged her affectionately.

"Well, I'll be damned, Jake Dillon." She held him at arm's length. Man, you're looking older and you've acquired more of those nasty little scars on your handsome face, since the last you were here."

"Been through a bit since my last visit to Nassau. But, it's really good to see you, Margarita. And girl, you're looking more beautiful with each passing year."

"Flattery will get you everywhere, you charmer."

"Did you manage to get what I asked for?"

"Of course, Dillon. Eggs, bacon, fresh bread and, tomatoes. Oh, and I also got the other special items you asked for. At the bottom of the basket; you'll find two Glock 20s with additional clips, along with the two-way radios you asked for, and a dozen small stun grenades. Happy?"

"Very. Thank you, Margarita."

"Good luck, Dillon. You know where to find me if you need anything else."

"Sure, and thanks once again. I owe you one, Margarita."

The attractive woman walked away, disappearing up the pontoon towards the Harbour Club, got in an old battered 4x4, and then drove off in an easterly direction along E Bay Street, disappearing almost immediately in the early morning traffic. Dillon went back inside to the others, made his way straight down to the galley, and immediately extracted the weapons and grenades. He placed one of the Glocks in the waistband of his trousers, the weapon reassuringly snug in the small of his back. He then concealed a spare clip in each of his pockets, and then hid the other weapon and grenades in his rucksack, which he slung over his shoulder.

"Dillon, you going somewhere?" Vince asked.

"I'm just popping out," said Dillon suddenly, moving towards the door.

"I thought you said you wanted breakfast first?" Tatiana said.

"Time for that later. I have people to see, errands to run; like I said, I have friends here in Nassau."

"Dillon?"

"Yes, Claudia?"

"Be careful."

Tatiana's head snapped round as if on a tensioned spring. A cold glint in her eyes.

Dillon paused for the briefest of moments, "I'll see what I can do." He stepped out on to the stern sun-deck, got in the inflatable dinghy tied up to the dive platform rail, and a few seconds later was powering out into the harbour in a cloud of two-stroke fumes.

* * *

Claudia lay relaxed on one of the day loungers on the sun-deck, weariness overcoming her. She pulled the courier bag close to her, her gaze falling on her hands, the grime under her usually manicured nails. She smiled gently. Once, that would never have happened: dirt would have been impossibility. But something had changed. She was lucky to be alive; and, it could have been so different.

Claudia removed the clear case protecting the small metallic optical disc from deep inside the bag. She held it up to the daylight, gazing at the master copy of the Chimera Programme.

"I hope you're worth all the trouble," she muttered, resting her head back against the pillows. They felt luxuriously soft - a complete antithesis to the last couple of days...

God, had it only been that long?

Since the facility had been destroyed.

Since Kirill had ordered everyone murdered.

Since Dillon had shot Kirill.

She shuddered, then closed her eyes and was able - for the first time in days - to relax.

Her breathing deepened and she licked her dry lips. The lounger was so comfortable that it made her want to stretch out and wallow all day long. Oh, to curl up and sleep for a lifetime; to curl up in a ball and *forget*...

Images flashed through her mind, the Assassins.

The Assassins clothed in black - black hoods - piercing blue eyes - feminine voice - able to kill - effortlessly...

319

Kirill, looking on as the people who had loyally worked for him, were gunned down and murdered.

Someone anonymous, talking to her on her private terminal; warning her.

There were a number of possibilities, as to who it had been. It could have been, Ezra? Or perhaps it had been Kirill himself? Maybe it had been someone else at the facility? Or was she going slowly and certifiably insane?

Claudia rubbed at her weary eyes as she mused over the possibilities...

He could have warned her. Edward Levenson-Jones could have warned her - it *was* feasible... Unlikely but feasible... But then, why her? Why *just* her? Why not the others?

She closed her eyes again, picturing Kirill and finding a little gratification in the fact that he had perished in the explosion. By the time Tatiana emerged from the galley carrying a plate full of delicious looking eggs and bacon for them all to eat, Claudia was snoring softly in the embrace of a deep, deep welcome sleep.

* * *

Dillon returned shortly after lunch, as Tatiana and Claudia were sitting down to hamburgers and fries. He carried several bags, and was looking tired but his demeanour was happy.

"Where've you been, Dillon?"

"Shopping."

"With what?"

Dillon winked. "Very generous friends. Now, I have a few presents for you two and I really must get something to eat. Can one of you, go get me whatever you've got there. Looks too good to miss." The sarcasm in his voice was painful.

"You seem upbeat, Dillon," said Tatiana softly.

Dillon smiled. "I've got a few surprises up my sleeve."

* * *

Dillon went below and stood under a cool shower, the water cleansing him of sweat and grime. He placed his hands against the tiles and allowed the water to run over the back of his head for a few long luxurious minutes revelling in the feeling of cleanliness that was creeping over him and through him...

And to complete the experience, his mind was now feeling refreshed and clear.

Perfectly clear.

Not marred by the cold-blooded murderous thoughts that occasionally crept up from the deepest recesses of his subconscious...

He towelled himself dry, his gaze catching the six polished metal spheres arranged neatly on a glass shelf above the sink. Each grenade containing a lethal amount of high explosive, designed to make a lot of noise and create maximum devastation.

As he left the shower room, rubbing at his smooth freshly shaved face, it was to see Tatiana walking back down the pontoon with a brown paper bag in her hand.

"I hope you're hungry, Dillon?"

"Let me at the food." He said, grabbing the bag off of her and emptying the contents onto the table. He unwrapped a cheeseburger and took a large satisfying bite out of it, split open another bag with French fries in, and ate some with his fingers.

"Manners, Dillon." Said Tatiana sternly.

Dillon carried on eating, and when he'd finished, he went below to get dressed. Five minutes later, he reappeared with a canvas bag, which he emptied on to the table. Ammunition magazines and bullets clattered free in a large pile.

"Holy-moly," said Tatiana.

"Get busy, ladies, if you please."

"Where'd you get all this?"

"You haven't been paying attention, Tatiana." Dillon said softly. "I used to be a Ferran & Cardini field officer; I worked in the Bahamas for three years; I worked with the C.I.A. on numerous occasions; I also know where they keep their weapon stashes. And, I've got a few contacts who are still 'working the lot' over here."

"I don't think I can go through with this," said Claudia, her face having paled at the sight of the bullets and the weapon magazines. Her eyes lifted, met Dillon's dark stare. "I'm not a fighter, I'm a computer programmer, and I haven't tagged along to kill anyone. I'm in this shit way over my head..."

Dillon smiled at the attractive young woman, nodding. "You are right, of course - and so far you've played your part well," he said. "So

I think that while I'm gone. The best thing for you to do is to hand over the optical disc to Vince and let him help you start to convert the Chimera scripts to Anti-Virus."

"Do you think Ezra is really alive? And if he is, do you think he can really help?"

"If the meet is genuine, then yes. If it is a set-up..." Dillon shrugged. "I'll go to the rendezvous with Tatiana, but go in alone to meet Ezra, and then bring him back here to meet you if this thing isn't a trap? That way you're not in the firing line - you just play the waiting game."

Tatiana shook her head. "I can't let you go in alone, Dillon. I must be there..."

"You have to, Tats." said Dillon. "This situation screams of very bad things; you can't expect me to put Claudia in such a dangerous situation - and as for yourself? Well, you know - and I know - that I work better on my own. If it really is Ezra, if he is alive, then so be it, we're on our way to stopping Ramus launching Kirill's version of the Chimera Programme; but if he has been captured, then I will do everything in my power to rescue him and I'll get him out of there alive... And then we can move on to finding Ramus..."

Tatiana sighed. "Okay. You're right. When is the meet arranged for?"

"Two hours. I have just a few more things to take care of."

"Where is it?"

Dillon met Tatiana's eyes and their gazes locked; he fell headlong into those beautiful, bright blue depths. He paused. And the question at the front of his mind was...

Can I trust her?

Kirill's words returned to him.

She's one of us... But she had helped him get this far still alive. Without her he would surely be dead... And since the Highlands Dillon had been playing his cards much more closely to his chest - revealing nothing... The perfect poker player... The perfect gamesman.

Tatiana smiled slowly.

"Don't tell me," she said, sniffing, her eyes unreadable. "I don't need to know the details and I fully understand that it could compromise you, yeah? You go alone and I'll stay here with the others, we'll be here when you return afterwards."

Dillon nodded at Tatiana and turned, gathering up all the fully loaded magazines into his canvas holdall along with the second Glock. The grenades he kept separate in another bag. He glanced at Claudia. "You'll find that you and Vince have quite a lot in common, you know. Hacking is *your* thing, gives you that adrenalin rush. And, if this gig is a trap, then I'm hoping that one or both of you can tap into one of the CIA's little spy satellites overhead and be my advance eyes." Dillon handed her one of the two-way radios that Margarita had obtained for him. "Here, take this. It's preset to a secure channel, just push the red button at the side when you talk and release to listen, yeah?"

"Push the red button to talk, right." Claudia Dax smiled, her eyes glinting in the sunlight.

Dillon took the jewel-case containing the Chimera Programme optical disc from Claudia. He brought it up to his face and stared hard.

"Hope you're worth it, hope those fuckers need you more than they need me dead," he said softly. Then he dropped the disk back into Claudia's hand and headed for the door.

* * *

The 4x4 SUV came to a halt in a small parking lot, deserted apart from three dusty old cars. Large metal waste bins lined one side of the area at the rear of the luxury hotel, the faint reek of kitchen waste emanating from them, mixing with the balmy humid air. Dillon opened the driver's door, scanning his temporary surroundings. Papers blew across his path as his boots touched the hot concrete under a bleached sun. He stood, stretched his back, and looked warily about: a predator, assimilating the various markers, alert and ready for action. Dillon reached back into the SUV, slipping various things into his trouser pockets and the many pockets of his khaki safari style gilet.

Dillon zipped up the jacket, checked his now clean shaven features in the SUV's wing mirror, then smiled into the eyes of his own reflection. It was a strong smile. A convincing smile. It would have to be to get him past the reception desk of the hotel where the meet was going to take place: the Ocean Club Hotel, an opulent 5-star playground for the rich and famous. Once a private estate, the hotel rests between miles of pristine beach and exquisite gardens inspired by the romantic grandeur of Versailles.

Dillon walked, hands in his pockets, clearing his mind for the meeting to come. He would have to be razor sharp; but then if Ezra wasn't there and it was nothing more than a set-up, Ezra would be conspicuous by his absence and the bad gig would be pretty easy to spot - and pretty quick to go down.

Moving out onto a wide path, Dillon walked swiftly. His gaze alert, watching, gauging the few people he passed on foot, searching for anyone who appeared out of place with bad intent. His eager scrutiny checked every car that purred down the sun-drenched drive to the hotel, checked interiors, looking for anything suspicious, out of place, no matter how small or insignificant. Dillon halted again, looking around. He turned left and began to walk once more, again scanning the surrounding area. As he closed on the grand entrance to the Ocean Club Hotel he slowed to a casual amble, searching for anyone suspicious lurking inside.

If they're here, he thought, if they're watching, then I won't see them. They will see me; but they will be like ghosts.

Invisible.

He halted, leaning against a low wall and pulling free a packet of American cigarettes. He lit one and inhaled, enjoying the sensation and buzz of the nicotine. Yeah, he thought, it's been a long time, my little friend. Far too long.

Ahh, the joys of a wealthy civilisation.

Smoking the cigarette allowed him time to think and scrutinise in his mind, his next move. There were several hazardous factors to take into account, the possibility of snipers was high on his list.

Dillon thought back to Santorini.

Ezra, running, the long jump out over the cliff...

The silent scream, legs treading nothing but air...

The long dive towards the ocean far below...

Despite his own pain and exhaustion at the time, he still remembered the one word that had leaped unbidden to his mind...

Dead.

There was no way that Ezra could have survived that three hundred foot fall. But perhaps there might have been the slim chance that he *was* wearing a Chameleon Para-vest... After all, Ezra had survived many attempts on his life. Escaped and survived.

Dillon breathed out a plume of smoke. The sound of laughter echoed from somewhere to his right and Dillon's head snapped in that direction. He relaxed. Took another drag. Breathed deeply, calming his suddenly racing heart.

Steady, he thought. Take stock of the situation.

He closed his eyes for a moment; the frequent headaches he had been experiencing were thankfully absent; the pain throughout his battered body was also subsiding and was nothing more than a dull throb thanks to an injection of a strong painkiller. The cracked ribs were nothing more than an inconvenience now, strapped up tightly under his clothing. The pain was, for now, a part of his life. A part of his very existence...

He finished the cigarette and flicked the butt into the bushes behind him.

Let's do it, he thought, checking his Omega watch.

He walked up the few steps to the impressive entrance of the hotel, trying hard not to focus exclusively on the lavishly appointed building, all the time scanning for anything or anyone suspicious. The fragrant scent of hibiscus and bougainvillea blossoms filling his nostrils.

Dillon's plan was simple. Ask for information at the Ocean Club reception desk. Make sure they knew his name and who he was meeting. He was sure events would unfold from there.

He nodded to the bellboy as he entered the hotel, the polished white marble floor feeling good beneath his feet as he crossed the plush, plant littered, foyer with catlike wariness. His gaze shifted to the left and then to the right. Men reading newspapers, a few couples milling around, a small group of women wandering through the foyer, one talking animatedly on her mobile phone. Dillon pressed the back of his left hand against the reassuring bulk of the Glock tucked in his trouser waist-band in the small of his back, and then he was standing in front of the reception desk and the beautiful brunette with her sparkling eyes.

"Good afternoon, sir. Welcome to the Ocean Club, how may I help?"

Dillon smiled his winning smile as his eyes used every reflective surface to check what was going on behind him. Then he said, "Hello. I have a friend staying here by the name of Mr Ezra Zimmerman. He said he would leave a message for me at reception about a meeting we have? My name is Dillon."

"One moment, sir. I'll check for you."

The brunette turned to the pigeon-holes behind the desk. Dillon rested his elbows on the elegantly designed highly polished cherry wood surface, gaze continuing to scan the people in the foyer. He watched a man with a goatee beard and shoulder length hair, carrying a black canvas holdall. Dillon felt the tiny hair on the back of his neck bristle, and partly unzipped his waist-jacket as the man with the holdall greeted a tall man of Middle-Eastern origin reading a newspaper. They left the foyer together.

"Yes, here we are, there is an envelope for a Mr Jake Dillon."

Dillon took the white envelope. He tore open the flap with his thumb; there was a single slip of paper inside. It read: Villa No-2. Come immediately - I'll be waiting. It was signed, Ezra. The handwriting was Ezra's and so was the signature. Dillon glanced around once more, then put the slip into his pocket.

"Thank you," he said. "Can you direct me to villa No-2?"

"Go through the gardens towards the beach. The villas are all clearly signposted, you can't miss them."

"Thank you again." He smiled warmly at her and walked out through the glass doors and Dillon soon found himself in the exquisite gardens. His hand curled round one of the tiny metallic explosive spheres.

Once again, the fragrant scent of hibiscus and bougainvillea was everywhere, as he walked along hand-laid rock paths and up stone steps. He ascended the terrace garden gazing at the bronze and marble statues from Europe as he went by, and at its apex stood at the arches of a 12th-century Augustinian cloister boasting a view over Nassau harbour. "This was one seriously cool crib." He said out loud. He blinked, and ignored the urge to light another cigarette.

He stood alone, looking out over the harbour. Thinking...

Just the way I like it.

He pulled free the round metallic sphere and stared at the small reflective device. He held the small globe, testing the weight. The grenade was hidden inside his loosely clenched palm.

Dillon carefully put the grenade back in his pocket and removed the Glock. Checked that there was a full magazine and one round in the chamber, and slipped it back into his waist-band. He gazed around one more time, and then moved off towards villa No-2...

"All very cosy," he said as he walked through the grounds of the hotel complex, it seemed to be quiet. Dillon approached villa No-2 and halted to one side of the gated entrance. He eyed the stainless steel number suspiciously as something inside him screamed: "This is wrong, this is all very wrong, Ezra is dead, and this is definitely a trap..."

Who wanted him dead?

Ramus?

There were easier and much cheaper ways to kill him than this. But then, now he had the Chimera Programme master copy, with which to do a little bargaining...

He glanced left and right, pressed the intercom, and took a step back.

"Come in," came a clear, feminine voice.

Dillon blinked. He realised that his hand was slippery around the metallic bulk of the Glock. He slipped the automatic into his waistband and wiped his hand on his trousers. He smiled nastily. Waited for the electromagnetic lock to release; before nudging open the gate as he drew the Glock once more.

Gentle laughter came from inside the villa. "Don't be shy, Dillon. Come on in and join us." There's no Assassin waiting with a silenced gun to blow your head off. No elaborate plan of entrapment to ensnare you."

Dillon moved cautiously forward, hesitating before stepping up onto the deck. He kept to the shadows, peering around the large plants. Ezra was sitting in a chair by the open window of the living area, a large glass of red wine by one hand, a cigarette in the other, and two beautiful women stood either side of him. Dillon glanced around one more time, then stepped up onto the deck and went inside. He still gripped the Glock 9mm automatic in his left hand...

"Nice to see you again, Ezra. And with such lovely companions. But I had this notion in my mind that you would be rather *dead*."

Ezra turned then, got up out of the chair, and stood. Dismissing the two women with the wave of a hand; he beamed warmly at Dillon, and raised his glass, sipping the richly deep burgundy wine, his eyes fixated on Dillon's left hand and the Glock held within it. "Always the cautious man, eh, my friend? I *do* quite understand your concern... If our situations had been reversed, and then I too would think it a trap…"

Dillon moved forward suspiciously, all senses alert, the Glock's safety set to *off*. Only when he was satisfied that they were alone in the room, did he fix his stare back on Ezra, who had turned, his dark-eyed gaze settling on Dillon.

Ezra smiled warmly. He motioned for Dillon to sit in a chair opposite his own.

Dillon remained standing. Ezra said, "I know you will find this hard to believe, but I was wearing one of Vince Sharp's prototype Chameleon Para-vests. As I went over the cliff-top, I pulled the rip-cord in plenty of time. When I hit the water seconds later, there were four Special Boat Service scuba divers waiting to make sure I didn't surface and to take me to a Royal Navy submarine that was stationed half a mile off the coast in deep water. You see, the British desperately wanted the optical disc I was carrying but the irony was in rescuing me, they bundled me onto one of those underwater jet-sled things, and in the process I dropped that bloody disc - and it became lost, leaving Kirill, yet again, with the only working programme in existence. MI6 was very precise - they had tracked me via my cell-phone, which I had been instructed to leave switched on, that's how they knew where I would make a splash when I took that fucking leap of faith. They pulled me through the water so fast, I felt like a fishing lure, I was the bait."

Dillon looked him up and down. The man stood before him had lost at least a couple of stone in weight, since Santorini; everything else about Ezra was exactly how Dillon remembered him. Dillon grinned wryly.

"You *do* look pretty good, Ezra. For a dead man." He lowered the Glock. "Tatiana will be thrilled that her uncle is alive."

"Ahh, my beautiful niece, Tatiana! I thought you might bring her along, but then - you thought this was an elaborate trap. A trap, as you thought me dead. Hah! Had you no faith in my cunning - even though it appeared that I'd plunged to my certain death..." Ezra's eyes sparkled as he took a step closer. "But then I have Vince Sharp to thank. His extraordinary parachute works incredibly well and makes the user completely invisible from a distance."

Dillon smiled, holding Ezra's dark gaze. "How about a drink? You're there enjoying that large glass of wine without offering me any? And after all the crap I've been taking from Tatiana these past days..."

"Yes I've been hearing about your exploits. MI6 has been following your progress with interest - although, it must be said, always a few steps behind you. I hear the Priest was with you in Scotland. Did that religious rogue behave himself?"

"He was just fine." Dillon slipped the Glock back under his

waist-band again but kept hold of the small grenade, hidden in his palm. He accepted the wine and took a sip.

Ezra's gaze remained transfixed on the glass and Dillon forced himself not to tip the wine into the nearest plant-pot as the other man turned to stare out of the open patio window once more. Something is wrong, screamed Dillon's brain. He sniffed the wine but didn't drink any of the deep red liquid...

Ezra turned to face Dillon again, a swift movement, a small black gun now in his large hand. "You should have trusted your instincts, Dillon. And, I truly am very sorry," he said. "Really sorry."

Chapter 22

Alix, Lola and the Priest stood beside the deserted hulk of the Chinook Ch-47 on the Norfolk beach. The cold northerly wind whipped up tiny whirlwinds of sand around their feet as they gazed inside the hold of the giant cargo carrying helicopter.

"Well, this is definitely one of the Chinooks that flew out of Kirill's facility," said Alix quietly.

"But the question is, what is it doing here in Norfolk," said the Priest, as he climbed up into the back and pulled free a large aluminium case. Using a small fire axe he smashed off the heavy padlock and lifted the lid. Inside were three metallic flasks, secured in the profile laser-cut foam lining. The Priest photographed the contents and in particular the identification number, and sent the image through a secure line to the main-frame at Ferran & Cardini International. Within seconds a response came back. He carefully closed the lid again and jumped down to join the others.

"What's in the big metal box?" Lola asked her voice nervous.

"It's yours, mine and every other sane person's worse nightmare, Lola."

"What, it's a case full of some sort of lethal weapon?"

"Something like that. London believes it to be a variant of *Bacillus anthracis...*"

"Anthrax? What the fuck is *Anthrax* doing on this Chinook?"

"Well, if I had to guess, I'd say that our late friend Kirill *was* and now Ramus, on his own, *is* planning mass murder. Now, this helicopter if I'm not mistaken came down pretty hard and was unloaded in haste."

The Priest went back up into the cargo hold of the Chinook and pulled the aluminium case out through to the open doorway. Lifting the lid, he said. "These three flasks not only contain one of the deadliest bacteria known to man, but according to F&C's intelligence, this modified variant is a hundred times nastier." He stared hard at Alix and Lola. They both looked from his eyes, that were the colour of coal, to the flasks then back to his eyes.

Alix shrugged. "You're going to have to enlighten us, Godlyman."

"This is a terrorist's dream weapon; they'd crawl over hot embers to get their hands on this stuff. This Anthrax would make governments everywhere sit up and pay attention. In the wrong hands these three flasks could wipe out many hundreds of millions of human lives, as well as wild and domesticated herbivorous and carnivorous mammals in the most devastatingly painful way. This is truly a fearsome weapon."

"So why have these three flasks been left behind?" Lola asked.

"Most likely because the case was up the front behind a bulkhead."

"Strange though, isn't it? Why leave it behind, even if the aircraft had been evacuated in haste? Lola said softly.

"Obviously, whoever left this case behind, will be coming back for it?" Alix said.

"I don't think so, Alix. Firstly, *Anthrax* - simply doesn't fit in with anything that's occurred so far, and secondly you can't just sell three flasks of Anthrax on the open market without the right contacts. But, that still doesn't explain what this Chinook is doing here on a cold and windy beach in Norfolk? And, it doesn't explain where all the other helicopters, that left that mountain in Scotland, are now? This is all wrong. This is all very wrong..." Said the Priest, as he rapidly tapped out a message on his smart-phone, and then pushed send.

"Suppose the Chinooks were all carrying a case like this one. Wouldn't they surely have all had a different final destination?" Lola said.

"That's a possibility, but still doesn't explain what this one is doing here. They abandoned their base in Scotland." Said the Priest calmly, adding. "We know that Kirill was left behind to set the explosives, and paid for that with his life. So what if he had become expendable and his Chimera virus programme is merely a side-show. Which leaves the Anthrax as the main performance?"

The Priest's smart-phone pinged once. He glanced at the screen and then looked up at the others. "This message is from the duty-officer at Ferran & Cardini. Intelligence reports from MI5 indicate that eight Chinooks, have now been located, abandoned, by the RAF at a disused military airfield not more than ten miles from here, which including this one, leaves only one out of the ten that took off from Scotland unaccounted for."

"Abandoned? Is there anything of interest on-board?" Alix asked.

"Automatic weapons, small and large calibre, and each Chinook was full to capacity with everything from 9mm to 12.5mm. Disturbingly, these larger calibre rounds are for a type of gun that delivers an awesome punch, have to be tripod mounted and can kill at a range of up to three miles. And before you ask, the security services found nothing else on board. They even had trained dogs over them and found nothing."

"Which surely means that the Anthrax had already been taken off of the aircraft before the security services got to them, or that it possibly was never there in the first place?" Alix said.

The Priest's smart-phone pinged again, as another message appeared.

"What does it say?" Lola asked impatiently.

The Priest held his hand up, palm forward, to hush her. He read the detailed message, looked up at them both and said. "The security service has found maps and charts; most were of the North Sea and the Baltic Sea."

"That's a lot of fucking sea," said Alix.

The Priest nodded. "Yes, I agree, but there is a glimmer of hope. Did you notice those large drums of fuel in the landing bay at Kirill's facility? Well, there were markings down the side of them. They were inscribed with the supplier's trademark: Tallin Oil & Chemical Co."

"Russian?"

"Estonian actually. The Tallin Oil & Chemical Co. operates out of its name-sake, Tallin. It's licensed to carry out exploration in the Baltic Sea and northwards, right up to the Arctic Ocean. The British Government has had them under surveillance for the past year using spy satellites as and when they're over that region, together with field agents on the ground. "

"Well, at least it gives us a lead to start with," said Alix.

"The MI6 field officers already on the ground in Estonia have indicated that this is definitely the strongest lead to date. I'll message the partners to have our own field officers on standby."

Alix nodded, enjoying his cigarette. "I have an idea. If you are right about the Anthrax being the main threat, then we will need to bring together some pretty elaborate technology. Very impressive technology. That we can coordinate from the cockpit of the Apache.

It has the capability and the on-board technology, from which to launch an offensive. And it'll only take the smallest of modifications. You can locate the enemy and pinpoint their exact position; and I..."

"And you Alix. What have you dreamed up for yourself this time?"

Alix grinned.

"...and I need to go see a friend of mine who lives close by. He's the only person I know who can hack into the computer systems of some people I want to take a closer look at."

* * *

"I'm really very sorry, Dillon," said Ezra. "Really sorry."

Dillon grinned nastily, the large wine glass in his hand, the Glock reassuringly pressing into the small of his back under the waistband.

Foolish, foolish man, he thought. Lowering his guard was amateurish and naive...

Foolish.

"So this Ramus character got to you, Ezra?"

Ezra shook his head sadly. "It's a lot more complicated than that, Mr Dillon. More complicated than you could ever comprehend, believe me. Now, I understand that you are carrying the optical disc with the Chimera blueprints on. I want it, please. It does belong to us, and should have been destroyed along with Kirill when he blew-up that mountain in Scotland. Had the imbecile done the job properly, you would have gone up with it."

Dillon allowed himself to frown.

"Answer me this one thing. You know when you were standing on the cliff top in Santorini, having been chased half way across the island by those *four* Assassins. They had you trapped with your back against nothing more than fresh air. What went through you mind?"

Ezra nodded; but it was there. A momentary flash across his face. A moment of...

Perplexity.

"You mean... Which one of the four should I have taken out first?"

Dillon nodded. "Ezra, tell me this. If all four Assassins were armed, why didn't they simply shoot you? Why the elaborate escape, eh?"

"I have no time for this, Dillon. Now give me that damned disc."

"Very sloppy, because there were only two Assassins. Which means that you're not Ezra?"

Ezra smiled then, a calm and collected smile. "Damn, Dillon. You are good and *you* are right. So what?" He carefully peeled off the latex face mask and then the prosthetic nose and ears. "Ezra's death was extremely inconvenient, his heart had stopped before he hit the rocks, his head being split open like a fat, ripe melon, just to make doubly certain of it. Of course, he wasn't meant to die, but his weight was too much for that Chameleon Para-vest. It simply collapsed as he pulled the cord. But I wouldn't expect you to understand, Dillon."

"Well, you're right there. But what does it matter, you're going to kill me anyway."

"My instructions are not to kill you, or even harm a hair on your head; there are certain people who would like a little... shall we say *chat*. But first you must hand over the optical disc that you are holding in your hand."

Dillon saw the man's finger tighten a little on the trigger. Impatience and anger starting to show on his face as he looked intensely at Dillon...

Dillon smiled.

He uncurled his right hand to reveal the small metallic sphere.

"Surprise, surprise," said Dillon dryly.

Dillon threw the sphere and saw the man's eyes suddenly widen, his mouth open in a silent curse!

Reflexes kicked in; there was no thought process required. The large man reached out in an attempt to catch the sphere.

His gun muzzle twitched.

Dillon's Glock was in his left hand and he was firing even as he dived for the bedroom. He rolled across the polished marble floor as the Glock's bullets tore into the wall and then the large picture window, with a crash of exploding glass...

Ezra's impostor was running.

Dillon took careful aim from the bedroom.

Just as the sphere hit the ground and automatically detonated.

The villa seemed to change suddenly from luxury hotel accommodation into a maelstrom of chaos. The furniture was picked up and tossed about and smashed to kindling wood in a fury of explosive obliteration. The floor shook and trembled; glass shattered; there came the splintering of timbers and the wrenching of metal.

Dillon remained on the floor under the bed, his senses running at full throttle as dust and debris spat through the doorway. He suddenly realised with horror that if the roof caved in he would be pulped under the weight of it.

He glanced up, his eyes blinking in the sudden dust storm.

The noise and shaking gradually subsided.

There was the hollow sound of plaster dropping off of the walls onto the floor.

Dillon could hear his own heart. Hear the air rushing in and out of his lungs. Feel the adrenalin in his blood stream being pumped to every part of his body.

He glanced right. A heavy timber purlin, hung down at a precarious angle from the partly fallen ceiling; dust was floating thick in the air and only then did Dillon realise that the blast had deafened him and his ears were ringing.

The villa's sprinkler system suddenly cut-in, a mist of water dampening down the dust.

Dillon eased himself to his feet, treading carefully over and around the debris, moving through to the living room that was like looking at a scene from a war-zone. All the windows and their frames had blown out. The furniture had been tossed around and turned into matchwood and the mess was everywhere, outside in the garden and even strewn around the beach. The walls had been stripped, large portions of the plaster ripped off and scorched and there were piles of rubble where the ceiling had completely collapsed...

The man who had been impersonating Ezra had been running for the beach...

Dillon moved outside, wiping cool sprinkler water mixed with brick dust from his face.

There were people running up the beach towards the villa, shouting and talking into two-way radios.

Dillon's eye caught sight of the imitation Ezra in the corner of his eye.

"Fuck you, Dillon." Hissed the man.

Dillon stepped off of the deck, and walked over to the prostrate body of the large man, who was lying on his back clutching his blood soaked leg. The long open gash running up through his left limb glistened, the wound bleeding freely, the flesh and muscle torn open by flying debris when the sphere detonated. A split second earlier and

Ezra's impersonator would have made it to the sanctuary of the beach and the protection of being a sufficient distance away from the blast.

Dillon grinned nastily. Putting the muzzle of his Glock in the man's face.

"Who the fuck are you?"

"I'm someone who has been paid a lot of money to impersonate Ezra."

"Well, no shit Sherlock. So who are *you*?" Dillon stabbed the Glock against the man's cheek. "Answer me - at least you're still *alive*..."

Dillon felt something across his left cheek.

His hand instinctively lifted, blood dripped from his fingertips.

"Shh-" He began as he hit the ground and two more bullets whizzed overhead. Dillon shimmied across to the cover of a large exotic looking plant, teeth gritted, shock starting to register in his system.

This sniper's bullet had carved a strip from his cheek, only just missing his eye.

Dillon breathed deeply, calming his racing heart.

Too close for comfort, he thought.

"Fuck!" He breathed.

"You got an answer yet, Ezra, or whatever your name is?" He said through the ringing in his own head.

The sniper's bullet entered the back of the man's skull, punching its exit through his right eye. Death was instant, the man's left eye staring unseeingly ahead, his body deflating, going limp as he slumped forward. And then he was still...

Dillon's face looked grim.

"Son of a bitch," he said out loud.

He crawled across the villa's garden, across the debris caused by the bomb blast, moving towards the entrance gate. He could hear sirens. The fire service and police. Could he trust the police? He doubted it.

And then he saw them - coming from the water. The small power-craft raced for the shore and beached, four Assassins jumped down onto the white sand and sprinted at speed towards the villa. Silenced Uzi mini sub-machine guns spat out their lethal payload in rapid automatic fire and Dillon found himself back inside the devastated living room of the villa, ducking below the trajectory of both the Assassins' and the sniper's bullets and - thankfully - a little shielded by the piles of rubble and upturned furniture.

He could sense them closing in.

Dillon tossed another sphere; the metallic globe bounced from the deck and rolled down the steps.

He heard a single gasp.

All four Assassins ran for it.

The explosion was silent, but the shock-wave re-arranged the garden. The whole world seemed to have gone mad as Dillon re-positioned himself by the open window. Dillon's sharp eyes spotted the Assassins. Steadying his hand on the ragged glass-edged sill, Dillon levelled the Glock and began to fire.

Three, four, five, six bullets.

When the dead man's click sounded, he switched magazines, and took a step back into the room, dropped a sphere into the middle of the room and leaped through the window.

Several things happened at once.

The sniper stood up from its cover on the beach and Dillon raised the Glock and placed two bullets into its chest.

Three more black-clad Assassins slid around the corner, carrying silenced Uzi mini sub-machine guns.

The sphere detonated.

Dillon was thrown violently against a wall as debris spat from the hole in the wall; even as the chaos erupted Dillon swung himself around and unloaded another full magazine towards the three Assassins.

Then he ejected the empty magazine and slotted a fresh one in. His ears were still buzzing as he slid under the deck and moved steadily along the full length of it, and after breaking through the screening, emerged onto the beach to the amazement of a few onlookers who were standing, mouths agape, staring at the blazing villa that he had suddenly vacated. Fire bellowed up into the air and thick black smoke started to drift across the garden and onto the beach.

Dillon glanced around, then sprinted for the nearest cover, an upturned rowing boat, switching magazines in the Glock as he ran. Seeing the automatic in Dillon's left hand, the onlookers fled from the area. From behind the wooden boat he saw the police squad cars and two fire tenders pull up on the service road fifty yards up the beach, sirens blaring and lights blazing.

Dillon ran up the beach, away from the emergency services,

shoved the Glock back into his waistband and walked as quickly as was possible, without bringing undue attention to himself, out of the hotel complex.

He was functioning on instinct now. All six-cylinders running at full throttle and turbo charged for good measure.

He moved past the 4x4 jeep that he'd arrived in earlier, deciding to return for it a little later. Quickly scanning the tatty old vehicle for any obvious signs that it had been tampered with. And then walked off along an unmade service road, keeping his demeanour casual and relaxed. It was then that he spotted the two large blacked-out SUV's turn into the road some distance away and start coming towards him. He dived over a low wall and watched the blacked out off-road vehicles go roaring past.

Bad, thought Dillon.

Really bad.

As the SUV's turned towards the hotel, Dillon started to run, boots crunching on the gravel, his intention was to move to a vantage point he'd noted on his arrival located on the other side of the resort. From there he could bide his time - he would wait and watch...

Two minutes later, pouring with sweat, Dillon was crouched on the edge of a rocky headland that afforded him an uninterrupted view of the hotel, burning villa and the ocean.

After three hours of laying prone on the rocky surface, he stood up and at a jog made his way back to the 4x4 jeep. He stood in the shadows at the edge of the small staff car park, watching and waiting.

After five minutes, he jumped in, gunned the engine and floored the accelerator. The powerful V8 roared and, as the tyres bit into the loose gravel, he wheel spun out of the car park and onto the main road.

The blacked-out SUV's were prowling, waiting, and searching. Their engines howled as they raced down the highway after Dillon's vehicle as it appeared; wolves hunting down a running lamb.

Both vehicles screamed around a large loop of tarmac, tyres smoking and suspension dipping as they veered round corners and ended back on the main road. They slipped past the oncoming police cars and Dillon, bent forward over the steering wheel, sweat dripping in his eyes, cursed his pursuers.

Dillon pulled free his Glock and looking at the weapon, said. "You've saved me before, my lovely."

He fired through the 4x4's rear window. Glass exploded in a shower and the two blacked-out SUV's veered, one mounting the pavement and sending a couple of pedestrians sprinting for cover, wheels churning over and through anything in their path into the ground.

They regrouped on the road and, then accelerated towards Dillon.

"Where's the cavalry when you need them?" He thought. Closely followed by; "I should have asked to borrow a much faster car!" He picked up the small two-way radio off the front seat, it squelched as he pushed the talk button, and quickly relayed what was going down to the others.

The lead SUV vehicle smashed into the back of the 4x4 jeep. Dillon was jolted in his seat, and almost lost the Glock. His foot slammed to the floor and suddenly he veered left, down a narrow slip road leading away from the Paradise Island resort.

The blacked-out SUV's followed in tight formation.

Dillon raced onto the Paradise Island exit bridge, followed closely by the SUVs. He fired another few bullets from the rear of the 4x4 and was immediately gratified when he took out a headlight. But that did nothing to stop the large SUV.

It's bullet-proofed, he realised. The panels have all been bloody bullet-proofed.

The lead SUV shunted him again.

Dillon fired the remaining rounds, emptying the magazine; there was a wrenching of metal from the engine compartment and the lead SUV veered off to the right and crashed out over the barrier and into Nassau Harbour. Dillon caught a glimpse in his mirror of the black vehicle shooting off the edge of the bridge, and then heard the sound of police sirens heading at speed towards him. The 4x4's wheels squealed at the extreme abuse that Dillon was giving the old vehicle as he powered off the bridge and onto the highway. Police cars screeched to a halt, officers jumped out, just as Dillon dropped a gear and pressed the accelerator to the floor and a split second later smashed two of the cars, like skittles, out of the way. The back end of the 4x4 slid out wide as he fought to keep control, swerving out around a bus load of tourists at speed and then straightening up. The remaining SUV was still perilously close behind him, and closing the gap.

Dillon pressed his foot to the floor. The engine growled.

Help, he thought.

The 4x4 sped through an intersection; there was a cacophonous blare of car horns as cars zipped insanely all around and Dillon closed his eyes for a moment and kept up the power. He no longer checked his rear-view mirror. The view in it only seemed to get worse.

Engines roared close behind him, shots rang out from the passenger side window, as the occupant leaned out and emptied an entire Uzi magazine into the back of the 4x4, the rear windscreen disintegrated as the bullets smashed into the tailgate. Once more he wrenched on the steering, feeling the 4x4 lose traction as worn tyres slid around on the tarmac, and once more he narrowly missed another vehicle - this time a heavy goods lorry. The horn blared at him and Dillon involuntarily flinched, half ducking down in his seat...

Focus, he thought. Must focus.

Meeting. Tatiana and Claudia...

And Vince, of course.

His gaze went up to the rear view-mirror, checking for the signs. He wrenched the steering wheel hard over and slewed into a right turn, then dragged the 4x4 over a grassy embankment and down onto an unmade road that ran parallel with the road he'd just left, and then forced a U-turn. Dillon floored the accelerator, tyres throwing up loose debris and clouds of thick dust as the heavy off-roader gained speed.

Dillon caught a flashing glimpse of the passenger leaning out of the open side window of the blacked-out SUV as it sped by in the opposite direction, a silenced Uzi pointing directly at him. And then the bullets ripping through the body work...

Dillon checked his rear view mirror again as he roared along the unmade road. He had managed, by some twist of fate, by some fluke, to get away from the lone SUV and the police cars. But moments later the SUV was again closing fast from behind.

Gunshots rattled.

He heard the dull *thump* of metal being punched a number of times. Dillon half tuned and fired the Glock through the open rear window, luckily hitting the driver's front off-side tyre and bringing the large vehicle to a gradual halt as the rubber shredded itself back to the rim.

Dillon swerved from side to side and floored the 4x4's

accelerator...

He drove for ten minutes, and had re-joined the main road, reducing his speed a little so as not to attract too much unwanted attention. He cruised back to the marina to meet with the others, constantly checking his mirrors for anyone following.

And there, way back in the distance, he could see three more blacked-out SUVs.

"No way," he said out loud, frowning. "How the fuck?"

He watched the large vehicles accelerating, still distant blobs, their polished chrome grilles like long teeth.

Smiling teeth...

Dillon's mood darkened. His foot hit the floor again and the 4x4 jeep surged forward, spun left down a slip road leading to the marina. He slammed on the brakes and the 4x4 screeched to a halt beside a brand new white Porsche 911 Carrera GT3.

Dillon leapt out.

"We've got trouble."

"Big trouble?" Tatiana asked.

"Oh yes."

As they walked along the pontoon to the boat, Dillon slotted a fresh mag into his Glock. "We need a much faster boat, that gin-palace simply won't cut it up against this lot."

"What do you suggest?"

"We haven't got much time. You round up the others and I'll sort out the transport." Dillon said, his gaze on the other side of the marina. He moved quickly, sprinting over the pontoons.

Dillon stood on the end of the pontoon, grasping the Glock in both hands, and pointed the gun.

The powerful deep-throated rumble of the in-board Penta engines became quiet, and a sleek thirty-six foot power-racer drifted to a halt alongside the pontoon.

"Hey man, you have got to be kidding!"

Tatiana and the others were now standing behind Dillon. "What are you doing?" hissed Tatiana.

"I'm acquiring faster transport."

Dillon met the man's outraged glare: he was young, wore a black bandana, Ray-Bans and no shirt, revealing heavily tattooed arms. When he spoke, he lifted them from the helm in emphasis.

"Get off of that boat."

"You mother -"

The Glock moved. There was a *thud*. A hole appeared in the windshield - and in the leather upholstery beyond. The man stared at the hole in the windshield, then at the seat. Then he leaped up out of the boat onto the pontoon as if he'd been stung by a hornet.

Dillon, Tatiana, Claudia and Vince jumped on board.

"You know how much this boat cost, man?"

Dillon met the man's gaze again. "I don't know, and I don't care," he said as he started up the in-boards, and engaged the power drive. The power racer's nose lifted as they left the marina, Dillon opened the throttles up fully; unleashing a beast that pinned them all back in their seats.

Dillon looked back over his shoulder, at the tattooed man standing on the pontoon, mouthing obscenities and shaking his fist at them.

The power boat became practically airborne with each wave as they raced forward past sailing yachts, larger power craft and cruise ships on their way into the harbour. Dillon slowed the racer, veering to starboard to miss another boat, and then increasing speed as he righted the craft back on course, the in-board Pentas roared with renewed vigour and the water beneath them became a blur; like a scene from a very bad drug-induced trip.

Tatiana stood up and leaned forward - both women had leaped into the power racer's cramped open cockpit. "Err, Dillon, how fast are you going?" There was an edge of fear to her voice.

"I couldn't tell you," he said through gritted teeth. "Can't you see I'm a little busy?"

"Are we in that much trouble?"

"Yes," said Dillon matter of factly.

"Did you see Ezra?"

Dillon looked at Tatiana from the corner of his eye. "No, Tatiana. I didn't."

"Oh, so it was a trick, after all?"

She sat back, completely deflated. Dillon wanted to say, *I told you not to get your hopes up, luv.* But he kept his mouth shut and concentrated on what was ahead, a high speed roller coaster ride of the deepest blue beneath the lighter shade of the sky.

"Who did you meet?"

"It was a set-up from the start. I'm afraid I blew up a luxury

5-star villa at the hotel..."

"With what?"

"A couple of sphere grenades."

"You maniac! What did they want - whoever *they* were?"

"It was Ramus' people and Assassins," Dillon said sourly. "And they wanted the optical disc with the Chimera blueprint on. Hold on," he snapped, spinning the helm, the power racer leaned over heavily to starboard, the side of the fibreglass hull lightly scraping across the reef lurking menacingly just below the surface. Dillon grinned like an excited child at the two women and Vince Sharp, who was looking worryingly green.

They didn't look impressed.

They'd left the pursuing police cars back in Nassau, along with the blacked-out SUVs. But now, two powerful jet-skis were fast approaching from behind, each with two black clad occupants on-board.

"Shit."

Dillon pushed the throttles as far they'd go, and the power racer surged forward, cutting through the water like a cheese slice, a wide grin on his face.

"Catch this baby, suckers," he muttered as they fell away behind him and he focused on the far distance.

"Tatiana, get a message to Matt Spencer to come pick us up on Grand Bahamas."

"But the minute the Learjet takes off from Nassau, the Assassins will tag it and then us..."

"So what? They already know we're here."

Tatiana pulled free her Ferran & Cardini smart-phone as Dillon concentrated on the water ahead; by late afternoon they had left their pursuers far, far behind..

* * *

The power racer cruised into Crab Cay on the north coast of Grand Bahamas; sailing yachts of all sizes gently rocked with the swell on their swinging moorings. Dillon lit a cigarette, Tatiana and Claudia climbed up onto the forward deck as the boat came to a halt at the edge of the beach. They all jumped down on the hot white sand and stretched their tense, aching muscles. No time to lose, they all moved off the beach at a slow trot towards the nearby airfield.

"You're a fucking lunatic, Dillon," said Claudia, jogging alongside him.

"We're still alive, aren't we?"

"What happened back there, Dillon?" Tatiana asked.

Dillon spoke as he jogged. "There were Assassins waiting for me; they wanted the optical disc and we had a bit of a lovers' tiff. There was a bit of body-slapping, hair-pulling and face-scratching and I had to make a rather hasty getaway..."

"You okay, now?" Dillon halted and turned to look at the beautiful woman. Tatiana stepped in close, the palm of her hand stroking his cheek. Dillon looked intently into her eyes then and smiled. He took her fingers, lifted them to his lips and kissed them.

"There was a sniper. Waiting for me."

"Bad..."

"I'm pretty sure I took him down."

The whine of the Learjet's engines reached their ears and Dillon gazed up into the afternoon sky. The under-carriage of the jet was suddenly above them as the pilot made his final approach, and then swooped down onto the runway. Dillon, Tatiana, Claudia and Vince collected up their backpacks and waited for the aircraft to come towards the apron, its suspension bouncing as the machine came to rest in front of them. Matt Spencer looked out from the cockpit and gave a thumbs-up.

Outside the noise from the jet engines was deafening. Dillon and the others started to walk across the apron to the open cabin door, Dillon suddenly halted as something unseen made him turn around involuntarily. His dark eyes peering out across the tarmac; towards the hangers and shadows and beyond to the beach, where they had come ashore only moments before. Something burned uneasily at the back of Dillon's mind. His head turned as he glanced around, eyes searching for the two jet-skis or anything that shouldn't be there... But there was nothing there.

Nothing out of place. Nothing *wrong*...

Something's not right though.

His gaze returned to the Learjet.

And then he could see it. A distant glint: like a silent scream from a 1920's movie...

Something definitely not right.

Dillon frowned. The whole world seemed to slow. The movement of the others whirled to a snail's pace, Dillon reached for his Glock and it seemed that his hand took ages to reach the heavy automatic weapon as his head was turning towards Tatiana and his lips formed the words. "Let's... Go..."

There was a distant *crack*.

Dillon's eyes caught the muzzle flash.

Something's wrong. The Lear started to edge forward and the noise from the turbines increased. A tiny hole appeared in the jet's windshield and Matt Spencer was punched backwards, falling slowly across inside the Lear's tight cockpit, a huge splatter of blood covering the back of his seat. Dillon's Glock 9mm automatic appeared instantly in his hand and he cursed the slowness and clumsiness of his own actions, cursed the sluggishness all around him and within him as his mouth opened to scream the words and both Tatiana and Claudia turned, their movements painfully slow, to gaze in confusion up at the Lear, the noise of the jet's engines roaring, the slumped figure in the darkened depths of the suddenly coffin like machine.

Dillon dropped to one knee, shifting and lowering his stance, the Glock kicking in his hand: one bullet; two bullets; three bullets and then he saw the black-clad figures detach themselves from the shadows and come racing at speed across the apron - they were Assassins, and a cold shiver ran through Dillon's body as the world suddenly slammed back into focus and reality.

"Oh, my..."

"Vince, get in the jet and prepare for take-off!" Dillon screamed, emptying the rest of the mag at the six identically black-clothed Assassins; they all carried Uzi mini sub-machine guns but did not return fire. Dillon hit two of them, taking both down with a clean shot to the head, but the others carried on sprinting towards him.

Tatiana was climbing, glancing back over her shoulder at the charging killers. Then her gaze transferred down to Dillon who grabbed Claudia and pushed her towards the Lear, keeping her safely away from the jet's exhausts and the awesome power of those reined-in engines...

Dillon ejected the magazine. Slotted another into the weapon and sighted on one of the killers running towards him. The Glock barked in his hand and the figure dropped instantly to the ground. Dillon's mouth was dry. He re-sighted and a moment later another shot rang out, and another Assassin went down onto the tarmac.

God, these fuckers are persistent...

He looked around at Claudia, his brain screaming. "Get up there!" He yelled. He fired several more rounds, the Glock a dark comrade in his grip, an extension of his body.

The remaining two Assassins, their Uzi's pointing, still did not fire. Dillon's gaze darted up towards Tatiana as Claudia reached up to the handholds. Dillon turned, swiftly...

...there came another distant *crack*.

Dillon felt a kiss of heat brush the side of his face for the second time that day, and as he spun round was just in time to catch Claudia's arms - which suddenly draped around his neck as she collapsed against him. Her face was the colour of a sheet, her eyes were wide, confused and innocent as her gaze met Dillon's stunned stare and her arms fell away from his shoulders. He grabbed her, his Glock forgotten, he held her around the waist and supported her sudden dead weight and looked into those deep intelligent hazelnut coloured fear filled eyes.

Eyes that held one simple question...

Why me?

Claudia opened her mouth to speak, to ask him. Blood trickled from her ears and nose, dripping onto Dillon's war-torn jacket. She shivered, head flopping back now and her beautiful face covered in blood. She tried to speak, but blood flowed out of her mouth and across her cheek. She sighed, exhaling air for the last time.

And then Claudia was dead.

"Come on, Dillon!" Tatiana screamed.

His gaze lifted and met the screaming panic-filled face of Tatiana, her eyes wide, her jaw dropped in despair.

"Dillon they're -"

He whirled round. The Assassins were only fifty metres away. The Glock *cracked* as the weapon kicked in Dillon's hand and lifted, as the lead Assassin took a bullet in the face.

And then Dillon was moving, leaping, the Glock kicking and blasting in his grip at the remaining Assassin. Gloved hands reached out for Dillon as he grappled his way to the handrail of the moving Learjet, and with each step closer he got the heavier his boots felt. He gripped the handrail and hauled himself up on the Lear.

Tatiana was above him and confusion gripped him as she was suddenly punched from the Lear's fuselage - a sudden violent lurching as blood splashed in a spray from her body and she spun above his head under the impact of bullets. Dillon could not understand and the sounds of the Assassin's Uzi firing washed over him and all noise was white noise and he reached out, fingers brushing Tatiana's hand as she fell but he wasn't quick enough and couldn't reach her and she toppled down on to the runway as the jet gathered speed to take-off. Dillon entered the cabin and held onto the airtight hatch, he didn't dare look down as the aircraft became airborne - Tatiana was dead...

"No," he said softly. "That should have been me."

Dillon started to close the door, his gaze looking down at the scene below on the ground to the lone Assassin standing over Tatiana's body; he swayed as the aircraft gathered altitude. He turned to Vince and screamed at him to go strap himself into the co-pilot's seat and make sure the Auto-Pilot was fully engaged. A moment later the aircraft climbed steeply up into a clear blue Grand Bahama sky. His gaze was filled with ice cold malice, his lips set tight, his face a mask hiding his anger and grief.

And he realised.

Realised the dreadful truth.

He was *alone*.

The Glock kicked in his hand; he swayed to one side of the still open hatch, his movements mechanical, his body running on adrenalin and reflex. The Assassin on the ground raised the Uzi to his shoulder. The Glock kicked again and now it was Dillon's only friend, only true friend, the only one he had left.

The bullet hit the Assassin between the eyes.

Dillon watched coolly as the life drained out of the black clad figure and it immediately went down onto the hot tarmac like a lead weight.

He dragged the hatch cover back in place and punched the large button to engage the automatic air-lock mechanism. He turned to see Vince sitting in the co-pilot's seat with his head in his hands and sobbing.

The Lear climbed steeply, banking slowly with a roar of engines, Dillon stumbled, pulled free the dead pilot, and slumped down heavily into the seat next to Vince. He looked round at the big Australian who, like Dillon, had also lost a friend. Neither man spoke, no words seemed appropriate.

And on the ground, Tatiana was lost...

The Lear banked again, Grand Bahama falling away far below.

"Are we safe yet, Dillon?" hissed Tatiana.

Dillon blinked and looked over his shoulder.

But he was, apart from Vince, quite alone.

Tatiana was dead.

Dillon's eyes focused on the clear sky ahead of him, then at the daunting array of control switches and lights in front and above his head. He ran a hand through his unruly hair, glancing for a brief moment at Vince who was now much more composed, and nodded. The two men had known each other for the best part of ten years and, although very different, had immediately found a common ground from which to build an everlasting friendship.

"I hate to have to say it, chap. But you were right as usual, it was a trap, and they were waiting for us!"

"The fact is they knew our every move, right down to our escape route! So the question is, did they just get lucky or did they know in advance? My guts tell me that we were betrayed! But by who?"

Dillon sat pondering the question. He knew, deep down in his subconscious, that the betrayal ran throughout the Government and possibly through Ferran & Cardini International!

Vince was wearing the aircraft's headset and had connected his laptop to the Lear's computer system. His head snapped round, "We've got company, Jake."

Dillon quickly flicked switches and push buttons. The Lear's control panels and screens immediately changed to military style displays. "Well, we'd better go *kick-ass* then..." He pushed two switches, turned to look out of the cockpit's side screen, and watched as the wings were pulled back towards the fuselage and the jet changed from luxury aircraft to sleek fighter. "Arm the weapons' systems and activated all scanners."

Dillon's gaze flicked to the scanners that were now displaying directly in front of him.

Four small single seater jets were coming up fast behind them as they headed out over the Atlantic Ocean. His eyes narrowed and death sat with him like an old friend. He pulled a cigarette from the crumpled packet, lit it with the gold Zippo lighter that Tatiana had given him many years before, and inhaled deeply, keeping the slim white pencil-like stick held in the corner of his mouth as he went through a checklist in his mind. He wasn't afraid of dying, fear was his ally; not fear itself but a love of the fear that he was about to inflict.

Dillon flew the Lear like a pro. He had been fully trained by the RAF to fly the specially adapted aircraft like a pro, and was now bringing all that he had learned to bear as he banked to the left and simultaneously climbed steeply, levelling out at nineteen thousand feet. The four jets behind them maintained their distance and speed to match his, and made no attempt to close in or fire their weapons. Dillon was painfully aware of the tiny hole in the side screen where the bullet had smashed Matt Spencer's life from his body had penetrated the aircraft, and the reason for not flying any higher than their current altitude.

And he thought about Claudia.

And he thought about Tatiana.

He suddenly felt nauseas and sweaty.

"Tatiana..." He whispered in pure agony.

Machine guns roared behind him; rounds clattered against the Lear's fuselage and Dillon's mask of pain fell away to be replaced with something cold and sinister.

Hatred fuelled him now.

Hatred - and a need to kill.

Vince broke into his reverie of thought. "You'll be pleased to know that we are presently carrying 40 standard air-to-air missiles, 15 Stinger air-to-air missiles and enough rounds for the forward machine guns to flatten a small town..."

Dillon looked round and nodded. His gaze went straight back to the console, he reached forward, flicked switches, heard hatch motors whirring below them; he glanced at the scanners, then looked quickly to his left. One of the tiny black jets had drawn alongside him and Vince confirmed another was on the opposite wing tip. Dillon slammed on the air brakes, dropping the Lear with dipped nose through the skies, then with a surge of power and a steeply banking turn that snapped both their heads back against the leather seats; the jet veered, coming up behind the two small single seaters. Dillon engaged two Stinger and two standard air-to-air missiles - saw the glow from their tails as they detached and watched coldly as they hurtled into the evading black jets. Both aircraft exploded with a roar and fell dead and spinning from the skies to smash into the dark blue sea below.

Machine guns hammered, abruptly bringing Dillon's hypnotised stare back to fresh dangers. Red lights flashed on the scanners and the Lear fell from the skies, whining like an injured animal in pain, to twist and skim not more than fifty feet above the surface of the sea - so close that spray splattered against the windshield and Dillon could almost smell and taste the salt.

He flicked a switch and the aircraft started to lay thick black smoke from the tail.

Missiles plunged into the ocean behind them.

"You want to play as well?" Growled Dillon. He studied the scanners in front of him, examining the two targets and tracking information displays. He rammed the Lear forward, the jet-turbines screaming at the rear of the aircraft. The Learjet surged forward, and speed powered through Dillon's brain; waves crashed just below the belly of the fuselage and there, against the white capped waves was an enormous oil tanker!

Dillon remained low, the jet engines whining, followed by the two remaining single-seater jets and their black-clad Assassin pilots. Dillon gained a little altitude and banked the Lear in - low and tight, wing-tips almost skimming the waves. The black jets followed. Machine guns rattled against the huge ship.

The Lear lifted; howling over the ship's elevated bridge and the black jets followed flying in close formation to each other. The pilots were extremely skilled.

"Time to tune in," said Dillon softly.

He flicked several switches and engaged a digital readout. He smiled a smile that conveyed only a longing for death and destruction.

"And now it's time to party."

He hit the air brakes and pulled the control column back sharply. The power was re-applied almost immediately and the Lear screamed as its nose lifted and then shot straight up, the pilots of the two single seater jets veered, one on either side, in reflex response to his insanely dangerous manoeuvre. Dillon hurled the Lear up into the air, climbing, lifting to ascend like a rocket into a clear blue sky. Dillon gazed up into the vast expanse as the Lear vibrated, its jet engines roared and he prayed to a God he had never really believed in. Tears rolled down over his cheeks and hatred boiled up inside his mind. The scanners blazed at him with altitude and low-oxygen warning read-outs, he twisted the aircraft around in a tight arc and then dropped from the sky like a bullet towards the distant tanker far below - his marker - spiralling and twisting. The black single seater jets were distant targets as Dillon allowed the release of a single Stinger missile... A vapour trail appeared from the rocket as it headed straight for the heat emitting from the jet's tail-pipe, moments later a fireball exploded as the rocket ploughed into the fuselage of the aircraft, its cockpit and pilot vaporised as the wreckage was sent crashing into the Atlantic Ocean, which swallowed it completely.

"Burn in hell, whatever you are."

The Lear spun, twisting, howling, and its under-belly skimmed the sea, wing tips careening as Dillon fought to keep control of the aircraft, he pulled back on the control column and the jet climbed once more with the final black jet following close behind with machine guns blazing and spitting hatred...

Again they climbed towards the heavens.

Wind howled through the tiny hole in the side-screen of the cockpit.

Both Dillon and Vince were freezing from the rush of cold air blasting in at them.

And there, hundreds of metres above the sea, the Lear levelled out and rolled in a lazy arc. Dillon slowed the speed, until the aircraft was almost stalling, stationary; his head drooped, eyes looking at nothing but his feet. And then his gaze lifted and he stared into the brilliant blue sky ahead of them. His jaw set and he ground his teeth.

The last black jet came level, perhaps three hundred metres away.

Dillon flicked the switch to release the Stinger missile restraints.

His eyes narrowed.

"So you want to have a go, do you?" He whispered.

Hatred and adrenalin was driving him, his brain registering everything in slow motion. His reflexes became cat-like...

The black jet's engine howled; Dillon couldn't actually hear it, but rather knew what noise it made. It rolled as it powered forward with machine guns firing and Dillon growled and surged forward while rolling and returning fire with the Lear's forward machine cannon.

The two aircraft hurtled towards one another. In the blink of an eye they had closed at speed, machine guns blasting. Dillon wrenched the control column over to the right and the Lear responded by rotating ninety degrees, veering and twisting down and to one side, the pilot of the black single seater jet did exactly the same manoeuvre, but in reverse, the two jets only missing by a matter of a few inches as they roared by in opposite directions...

Dillon levelled out, rolled to the left and then back over in a wide arc. The Lear came out of the roll and Dillon was again hurtling towards the other aircraft at speed, bullets smashing the enemy's cockpit, turning it into dust and decapitating the pilot in the process.

The Lear veered sideways, away from its dark and bloody deed.

The black single-seater jet broke up as it spun, twisted and rolled towards the ocean far below. And was then gone.

Watchers on the deck of the oil tanker searched the white crested waves.

Dillon breathed. Slowly. Looked round at Vince, and said. "Well, that was nasty."

Vince had gone the colour of a sheet. "That's one way of looking at it. You mad fucker."

"Gratitude!"

Dillon adjusted the rake on the wings, taking them back to their normal flying position again. And at a more sedate pace, the Lear dropped to within a hundred metres of the surface of the ocean, the white tips of the waves clearly visible and shot like a bullet across the empty dark water.

* * *

The Lear flew on over the Atlantic.

Dillon glanced, every now and then, across the cramped cockpit at Vince, who he had forgotten was there, sitting next to him all through the turmoil of battle. Until now.

"You know she was the enemy; you know that she'd gone bad?"

"Leave it, Vince. I can do without that crap right now."

"Jake. She almost got us killed. That bitch didn't hesitate in signing our death warrants..."

Dillon licked his lips and guided the Lear down to within fifty feet of the waves, wing-tips almost skimming the surface. He had no destination in mind, just a need to fly, to run, to flee, to get away from the Assassins and the death they traded in, the *death* they represented... What to do now? He thought. Dillon sighed out loud. I'm tired, so tired. Tired of everything.

"Jake. Jake, are you listening, mate?"

"What?"

"I said. We need to think of a plan. Contact Alix, Lola and, the Priest - yes, the Priest will help us; he'll pull you feet first and screaming out of this brain-fuck melancholy - just because Tatiana is dead. You need to become strong again, Jake, and we need to find those three reprobates - fast."

Dillon pulled free his private smart-phone. He scrolled through the apps and opened the one he wanted, punched in the Priest's number and then his de-scramble code and waited. The slender device vibrated in his hand.

"Dillon?"

"Priest - Vince and I are in deep shit!"

"Where are you, Dillon?"

"Flying somewhere over the Atlantic Ocean. We were set up in Nassau and then half a dozen Assassins jumped us as we were exiting via Grand Bahamas. The pilot was taken out, also Tatiana and the computer programmer, Claudia Dax."

"Tatiana is dead?"

"She betrayed us all. You, me, everyone."

"Remember what Kirill said on that mountain in Scotland? He told us that Tatiana was one of them! He also told us that Ramus never stays in one place for long. That is what we have to find out, Dillon. You make your way back to the UK, and I'll ask a few questions."

The connection was broken.

Dillon smiled grimly.

And it sent a cold chill through his soul.

He chewed his lip for a moment.

"I need a cigarette."

Tatiana.

He remembered her pretty face.

A little part of his soul said: No.

But he knew; deep down. If she hadn't died from the gunshot, then they had her; there was no escaping. No escaping at all.

He felt like rolling over and dying. But this wasn't the time or the place. He had to be strong. He could get through this; thank God Vince was with him, all he needed was a little brotherly solidarity.

Dillon banked the Lear, there was a drone from the engines and they spun out across the Atlantic Ocean; beneath them the waves rolled and the sea seemed suddenly endless, a vast world of merciless beauty stretching out into oblivion...

Dillon's smart-phone started to vibrate, the Priest's number showed on the screen. "What you got, Priest?"

The Priest's voice sounded metallic over the loud speaker. "I spoke to my source at GCHQ. It's all very strange, Dillon. They've intercepted a lot of heavily encrypted chatter between Ramus and an organisation here in the UK."

"What's strange about it?"

"The company appears to be legitimate, but is nothing more than a shell, a front."

"Is that it?"

"No. The company's registered office is in Nassau!"

"Nassau?"

"Nassau. But, that's not all. Get this, Dillon; the UK address is on the south coast of England."

"Where on the south coast?"

"Dorset. To be precise, somewhere that you are very familiar with, are you not?"

"You must be mistaken, Priest." Dillon's voice sounded confused.

"No mistake. And, I don't believe in coincidences either. I think that this Ramus, whoever he *is*, is leading you there for some reason, but as yet, I haven't been able to work out why?"

"You mean to say, that this front company is based in Poole? Now that is strange..." Dillon's mind raced, trying to think, *who*, if anyone from his past could be involved?

"Dillon, are you still there?"

"Yeah, I'm still here, Priest."

"Lola, Alix and myself, are heading down to Dorset in the Apache, that is, after we've stopped off in London. I've been summoned by Edward Levenson-Jones at Ferran & Cardini HQ."

"I'll set a course for the UK, and contact you again when we're over British airspace. Oh, and good luck with LJ, you're going to need it."

"The Lord will protect, Dillon. See you in Dorset. The Priest terminated the call. Dillon nodded to himself and said softly. "Dorset again?"

Vince had listened to the entire conversation on the smartphones loud speaker. Turned to Dillon and said thoughtfully. "You know, that two-faced bastard Ezra stitched us up bad. He couldn't have done a better job of leading us into a trap, if he had been alive. And, how the hell he got past the security checks, heaven knows..."

Dillon simply nodded again and continued to re-work the

coordinates that would get them back to the UK. Taking into account the fuel stop they would have to make.

Dillon felt sick. Dillon felt cold. Dillon felt alone.

Somebody is going to have to pay, he realised.

Chapter 23

The Learjet limped over the Dorset coastline just as the sun was starting to rise in the east, warning lights flashing on the display and fuel gauges registering almost empty. Dillon spoke into the microphone of his headset; the air-traffic controller at Bournemouth International Airport giving him immediate clearance to land on the east runway, and to then proceed to the north-west side of the airfield and await further instructions.

Dillon disengaged the auto-pilot, and without ceremony made his first and final approach onto the runway. Landing with a squeal of rubber as the undercarriage touched the tarmac and he breathed a sigh of relief. He taxied the Lear to the far end of the runway and waited for a moment, before being escorted by airport security to the private hanger of Ferran & Cardini International.

Inside the cavernous space the Lear came to a halt alongside the Apache attack helicopter. Through the jet's windscreen, Dillon could just make out the single occupant seated inside the Apache.

Alix climbed out of his seat and stepped down from the helicopter.

Dillon released the main door and a moment later he and Vince came down the steps of the Learjet.

"How goes it, Dillon?" Asked Alix, grinning. The rugged looking man was standing, heavy leather flying jacket belying his muscular physique, hands deep in fur lined pockets, a smoking cigarette hanging loosely from between his lips. His hair was still short and spiky, his eyes dark-ringed and hooded but twinkling with an irrepressible inner humour tinged only with a hint of concern. "Thought you'd gone and got yourself killed down there in Nassau. When the Priest saw your number on his phone, he almost jumped out of his skin. And what the hell happened to this jet?"

"Assassins, there were four of them flying single-seater training jets that were packing an awful lot of punch!" Dillon sighed, wincing as he pulled on his jacket.

Alix noted the 9mm automatic that was now holstered under Dillon's right arm. "That Glock the only weapon you're carrying?"

Alix held the cigarette packet towards Dillon. "What's mine is yours, and yours is mine." Dillon's weary face brightened a little and he took a cigarette, lit it with his own gold lighter, and inhaled deeply, looking thoughtfully at the slender object he was rolling in his hand, passed the packet back and lifted the barrel of the Glock gently under Alix's chin. Alix blinked, hand outstretched to receive the packet of cigarettes. He coughed slowly.

"You seem a little on edge," he said at last, after a long brooding pause.

"Let's see both hands, Alix. Dillon said, and Alix could see there was no humour and no compassion and no give in the man he had called a friend for many years. Alix removed his other hand from the jacket pocket and spread his fingers wide. Dillon frisked him from head to toe, retrieving two automatic pistols, six hand grenades, three knives and a length of piano wire.

"So talk to me, Dillon. What's going on?"

"Where are Lola and the Priest?"

"Outside."

"Where, I didn't see them out front."

"Most likely skulking in the shadows."

"Let's take a walk; you first. And don't make me shoot you in the back, Alix. Because it would be a fucking bad ending to a really good long friendship. Unfortunately, recent events have conspired to fuck-up my sense of who I can and who I cannot trust. And that includes you, Alix. Assassins are everywhere."

"But, Dillon. We've gone to hell and back since Hereford," Alix said, his voice hoarse.

"I know, we did. And in a few moments we'll either be having a drink or you'll be on your way to hell, my old mate. I thought I knew Ezra, but a son-of-a-bitch who looked just like him still tried to kill me."

They covered the distance across the hanger quickly, moving out through the main doors to be confronted outside by a stiff wind blowing in from the south-west. Alix zipped up his flying jacket, Dillon walked carefully behind the other man, aware of how fast he could move and how deadly he really was. He might have a glib tongue and a wickedly charming way with the women, but he was a deadly killer. Very deadly.

They walked around the corner of the building.

The Priest was sitting on a stack of wooden pallets and Lola was leaning against the side of a rusting cargo container smoking a cigarette. They both turned as Alix, Dillon and Vince appeared.

"You okay, Alix?" Lola purred, moving away from the building, her hand straying towards her gun.

"No worries," said Alix softly, waving for the sylph-like young woman to relax.

Dillon holstered the Glock. Alix turned, gently placing his hand on the shoulder of his old friend. "You really can be a paranoid fucker sometimes, Dillon, you know that?"

"Sorry mate," said Dillon, moving over to greet the Priest and Lola.

"You pull a gun on him, Dillon?" Lola asked.

Dillon nodded.

She shook her head. "You're one mad dog - he's here to help."

"So he said. But when I saw him on his own in the Apache, I suppose I thought I smelt a rat."

"Dillon, you've known Alix years. Why think that?"

"Nassau. Had some joker impersonating Ezra who wanted to terminate my contract with life. The latex prosthetics were so good that I wouldn't have known, until he slipped up that is. Threw him a trick question just to make sure, then I knew. But that bastard very nearly succeeded in killing me. So forgive me for being paranoid, but these bastards will stop at nothing to get what they want."

"Wow. You're forgiven."

"Thanks."

Alix jogged back into the hanger and retrieved his weapons, reappearing moments later. "Right then - to business, now that Dillon has it clear in his mind that I am for real. I presume you know what's going on with Scorpion?"

Dillon nodded. "I know that the organisation has been destroyed, most of the field units have been murdered by Assassins whilst on assignment, which I find disturbing in itself. Why?" Dillon mused for a moment before continuing. "These highly skilled and well equipped killers are part of the Ramus group who had professor Kirill moonlighting for them. They now have the Chimera virus programme that is so powerful and so intelligent, that it's capable of taking control of any computer it enters, which in turn, would cause a global internet Armageddon within the blink of an eye. And, nothing or nobody would be excluded; military, banking and government computer systems - private individuals - anybody. No matter how sophisticated their protection, Chimera intuitively learns, adapts, and enters without even a trace of evidence, that it was ever there. And here we are now - Kirill, we know is dead because we were all there when he was blown up in Scotland, which leaves only Ramus roaming around and unaccounted for."

"Yeah, that sums up just how bad things are," said Alix, grimacing. "They've certainly shown the world what they're capable of and what is likely to come. But what I don't understand is - why? What is it they want? After all, they've not even made a blackmail demand, so what do they want? What we do know is that they've used Chimera to hack into a number of mainframes, including; Scorpion, the UK Government, and the Bank of England. They've already got the world's most powerful governmental administrations sitting up and paying attention. The world's media are already reporting on this and it won't take long before some clever-dick journalist works out how all of these events are linked." He took a breath and his eyes were wild, sparkling with fury. He lit a cigarette, then pulled out a pack of rations from his backpack, and ripped open the packaging from a bar of chocolate.

"Yeah, we found out much the same with the help of one of my sources at GCHQ, and the Priest had one of his Whitehall spooks do the same. Ezra worked with Kirill, way back, in the early days of what was to become the Chimera project - although no one seems to know much about this stage of the research and development. Ezra pulled out, but Kirill carried on his work until the Government started talking about the withdrawal of funding and moving him from Scotland back down to London. But in the meantime, Ezra had joined Ferran & Cardini International as a station co-ordinator, although his real role and sole purpose was to develop counter-intelligence and covert ops software for the Government. The facility he had on Santorini was ideal because it positioned him in a perfect geographical location for any covert ops being carried out over in that neck of the woods by the SAS. So, there it is..."

"So where did these Assassins spring from and why are they involved?" Dillon spoke the words softly.

"Well, we've been talking to Interpol and they've been on the trail of an extremist occult group calling themselves, The Black Dawn.

And get this, from the case file that Interpol sent to me, these really are Assassins." Alix lit another cigarette, inhaling deeply.

"And..." Dillon prompted.

Alix grinned nastily. "We started to work on finding out just where they've run to."

"But?"

"Yeah, there's always a but, Dillon." Alix said, blowing smoke. He grinned at Dillon; the two men held each other's gaze for a brief moment, smoke trailed from Alix's nostrils.

"MI6 have been tracking you since you left England with Tatiana. Apparently they had a special interest in you - fucking spooks poking their noses in where they're not wanted. They initially used satellites and Tatiana's F&C smart-phone to keep tabs on your position, but then they lost the GPS link and that was that. But credit to you, Dillon. You always kept them one step behind you - they had trained squads chasing after you, but you kept them guessing. They turned up in Nassau to find dead Assassins everywhere and total devastation.

"What else did they find in Nassau?"

"Apparently you stole a power boat from one of the nastiest drug dealers on the island. Man, you've got a big pair of balls."

"Did the spooks go up to Scotland?"

"Yeah, they found a whole lot of mess: the remnants of the research facility. But no Kirill."

"You watched me shoot him. His body would have been burnt to a cinder with all of that explosive he'd planted."

"But there was no sign of his body. Even though he was in the middle of the explosion, they had a full team of CSIs and these guys were using state-of-the-art scanners. There were no genetic traces - in fact, no traces at all. *Somebody*, Dillon. Somebody must have gone back for his corpse."

"Why do that?" Dillon said incredulously.

Alix Shrugged and the Priest stepped forward. "I know what you're thinking, Dillon. What use is a char grilled carcass? But that's not for us to waste time debating. What you might not know is that MI6 lost you completely after Nassau, that is, until you powered up your smart-phone. I was glad you remembered to use the encrypted scramble code." The Priest walked around the group, and then strode off back inside the hanger, halting for a moment, then walked towards the Apache attack helicopter, and stood looking at it. The others watched him from the hanger doorway in bewilderment. After a minute he turned on his heel and came back towards the doorway, his long leather coat whipped around him as he walked.

Dillon watched the religious man walk towards him, the Priest's Bible held firmly in his right hand. He motioned for Dillon to walk with him.

Together they walked out to the edge of the apron and stared out across the airfield. The wind howled around them, buffeting them; nothing to shelter them from it.

"You ever been down here before, Priest?"

"You mean Dorset?

"Yeah."

"Never. You?"

"Fell in love with the place while on assignment down here, and have been here a few times since. Funny thing though. Every time I come back, some bastard tries to kill me..."

"Well, you're lucky that they have all failed, Dillon. Because, whoever they were. Someone is obviously looking kindly down upon you."

The two men shared a moment of silence.

"What are your plans now?" Dillon asked.

"This Ramus character has a stealth ship. He thinks he is going to take over the world or something like that, and it's our job to stop him."

"Our?"

The Priest turned and grasped Dillon's shoulders. "You're a part of this now, Dillon. You also know this area and the waters hereabouts like the back of your hand; we need you."

"I have my own war to fight."

"And what war would that be?"

"A war with my conscience."

"In my capacity as a fully ordained priest, Dillon. I'd say you were long past that point."

Dillon scowled.

"How long have we known each other?"

"Too long, Priest."

"It's nineteen years. That's how long. And in that time I've seen and heard many things about you, mostly how you always survive! I also know that when you attended your post assignment assessment interview with the shrinks, you used to always demonstrate that you had a consistently stable mind. But you have a secret, and you've kept it well hidden for a very long time, my friend."

"Which is?"

"Oh, come now, Dillon. Don't be coy. It's not your conscience you're at war with, is it? It's your subconscious."

"Only God knows what you're talking about, Priest. But you make sure you keep that very safely to yourself. Do I make myself clear?"

"Transparently. But I didn't mean to disrespect you, Dillon."

The two men stood in silence, until Alix walked out to join them.

"I've just had a call from Levenson-Jones," he took a long pull of his cigarette. "The sanction has been authorised. Ramus and these Assassins have to be found and terminated. LJ has just come out of an emergency meeting with the Prime Minister at Downing Street, the outcome of which, gentlemen, is simple. There is no time to lose in locating Ramus and his stealth ship... The Americans, Russians, NATO and virtually every other fucking government and their respective intelligence agencies around the globe are already experiencing problems with their Command and Control IT mainframes. They're all reporting exactly the same, that their systems keep crashing - going off-line and dumping its own data... It looks like Ramus' plan is starting to roll-out. I think we need to fuck-up his strategy good and proper. Now come back into the hanger, it's warmer in there, not much, but at least we'll be out of this freezing wind. We can sit down, talk tactics, and have a drink, I packed a bottle of Jack Daniel's especially for my old mate. And you can bring us up to speed on what exactly happened in Nassau."

Dillon smiled; the expression felt very strange on his face. "Jack Daniel's, you say?"

"The one and only Jack Daniel's." Alix winked. All three men walked back into the hanger, where Lola and Vince were huddled over his primus stove brewing a pot of tea. Alix bent down and drew out a full bottle of JD from his backpack and some small plastic cups.

"Drink, anybody? A toast to us winning against all the odds?"

Dillon laughed then, like a schoolboy, grinned. "You going to pour that whisky or simply wave the bottle around in the air? Because I need a drink, badly!"

* * *

Alix, the Priest, Vince and Lola were all crashed out in the main cabin of the multi-million dollar Lear jet. They were all sprawled, sleeping in the luxurious reclining seats, Vince was snoring loudly at the rear of the aircraft, Alix and Lola curled up next to each other and the Priest, eyes closed, sitting upright in one of the front seats. And that left only…

…Dillon. He sat at the front of the hanger, to one side of the partially closed doorway, staring out into the night, mulling over thoughts of catamaran stealth ships and Assassins. He could not understand; could not understand, how they could move so fast without making even the tiniest sound, could not understand, why they were so good at killing. Because he knew that even at his age, *he* was pretty good, if not one of the best. And, that if he was totally outclassed by these black clothed creatures.

"What the hell do you do that makes you like that?" He mused as he lit a cigarette, and blew smoke into the cold night air. "What is the connection with Ramus? And why did Ezra really pull out from Kirill's team, all those years ago?"

He watched the smoke as it was snatched by the wind and dispersed.

That's what you're about to do, isn't it? You're going to *snatch* away the world's feeling of security.

And then he remembered Tatiana, the look of shock and pain on her face as she fell away from the aircraft in Grand Bahama.

Dillon shook his head.

Shit always happens to the good people, he thought. It's just the way it goes.

A low drone came from the other side of the airfield.

And then in a burst of landing lights the JetRanger helicopter loomed from the darkness, hovering into view, and climbed slightly, then dropped smoothly, rotors throbbing, towards the apron in front of the Ferran & Cardini International hanger. Engines screamed. The rotors whined in deceleration. Then there was just the sound of the wind and hot metal cooling.

Dillon shaded his eyes against the glare of the JetRanger's powerful forward spot lights, climbed to his feet and walked out across the tarmac.

A familiar face met Dillon's scowl, a tall angular man with neatly groomed fair hair stepped down from the executive helicopter. He was wearing a long black overcoat, unbuttoned, that as he walked across the apron, flapped open to show a navy blue wide pinstripe suit. The tall man held a slim Cuban panatela cigar between the fore and centre fingers of his right hand, the tip glowed as he drew on the cigar. "Ah, Jake. Good of you to join the real-world at this time of trouble."

Dillon blinked.

"LJ - what the hell are you doing here?"

"Moral support, old son. Moral support."

Dillon raised an eyebrow, "Oh well you'd better come inside the hanger, then." He led the way inside the cavernous space, the others had all awoken and were stood around Vince and his tiny camping stove on the far side, next to the battered Lear jet.

"I say, Jake. So much damage in such a short time! I see you've not lost your touch, old son." LJ said, casting his eye over the black, bullet riddled, fuselage of the Ferran & Cardini Learjet. "It's good to see you've still got your sense of humour, LJ!" Dillon said smiling. He pulled a cigarette from the packet and lit it.

Edward Levenson-Jones walked over to Vince Sharp, who handed his boss a steaming mug of tea. He turned to face the small gathering, "I've dropped in, to tell you personally that the Prime Minister's order has now been issued and giving you carte blanche on this extremely arduous assignment. Needless to say, you have the full weight of No 10 behind you. Anything you want, just ask."

"Anything? Well, that's reassuring." Alix blurted.

LJ went on, "Your assignment is simple - to stop Ramus from launching a fully functioning Chimera virus programme. Jake, you have managed to halt this up to now, by ensuring the optical disc remained out of his reach. But the latest intelligence reports indicate that Ramus has been busy, he's had some of the best hackers on the planet writing the missing elements to the Chimera scripts and is now only hours away from causing global chaos."

"Where is Ramus now?" Lola asked.

"His last known location was somewhere off the coast of South America. But, the CIA has been tracking him with their newest satellite. Apparently, even a stealth ship can't hide anymore. It turns out that he's heading our way to collect something so vital to his plan, that he's willing to jeopardise everything by doing so."

"What about the Anthrax canisters the Priest found on the abandoned Chinook in Norfolk? Do you think Ramus is planning a bio-attack as well as Chimera?" Dillon asked, exhaling a plume of cigarette smoke.

"It wasn't Anthrax, turned out to be pure cocaine, old son. The street value of that single canister has been estimated to be at least fifty million sterling. The Anthrax labels were just a ruse, Jake. What better way to transport Class-A drugs, than in such a *deadly* container."

"Ramus is a cocaine trafficker? Well, that's a relief..."

LJ shot Dillon a look of exasperation, dropped his cigar butt onto the floor and stubbed it out with the sole of his expensive hand-made leather shoe. "Sit tight here until the CIA confirms exactly where this lunatic Ramus is. Oh, and Jake, please keep me in the loop, old son." He turned and walked out through the hanger door, a moment later the JetRanger helicopter lifted off the apron.

* * *

And wait they did...

Alix took a seat on a stack of empty wooden crates.

"Lola, what's new, girl?"

Lola glanced down at him.

"Tea, love."

She handed him a mug filled with steaming tea.

"Lots of sugar, Alix, just how you like it."

"Cheers, luv." He took a sip and stared out across the vast hanger, the end of his cigarette glowed in the gloom as he pulled hard to get the maximum hit.

"You okay?"

"Yeah," he sighed, wrapping his leather coat around him. "Just tired. Tired of all the shit."

Lola sat beside him, putting her arm around his shoulder, and he looked at her, surprised. She pressed her lips against his unshaven face and the smell of her hair filled his senses.

"Hello?"

"Mmmm?"

"You feeling horny, luv?" He grinned his boyish flirtatious roguish grin.

Lola met his gaze. His cheeky grin disappeared when he saw the seriousness there. "You've always been an insolent fucker, Alix. But I have really enjoyed working with you. I feel - I don't know - I have a very bad feeling about what we're about to do."

Alix nodded. "It's what we do, though," he said softly. "Ramus, and Kirill - they're about to bring this planet to its knees. And what will evolve, is a world of uncertainty and fear of the like of you and I have never seen! If we don't stop this fanatic from launching Chimera. Well, the alternative is unthinkable."

"Yeah, I know. But... not everybody is going to make it back."

She licked her lips. They gleamed in the light from Alix's cigarette. She reached up, suddenly, and kissed him, a long lingering pressing together of lips, and Alix felt lust rush through his body with a ferocity that he had forgotten.

She pulled away.

Alix smiled at her. "Wow, would you like to do that again?"

"If we come through this, I'll think about it. Maybe..."

Alix nodded. "Thanks, luv. I'll hold you to that." They both stood up and walked across the hanger to the Lear, and a few hours of sleep until dawn.

* * *

As the tendrils of light crept over the airfield and into the hanger, Alix rose bleary-eyed, stretched the sleep out of his aching muscles, thinking of what lay ahead. He rubbed at his eyes, then at his stubble, lit a cigarette and went over to where Dillon, Vince and the Priest were drinking mugs of steaming hot black coffee. Outside, the sound of helicopter engines screaming and rotors beating the cold morning air could be heard...

"What's all the noise outside?"

Dillon looked up and said. "Security Services. Three helis, courtesy of MI5, along with nine experienced tactical assault field officers as company."

Alix walked outside to a hive of activity.

There were three Bell 206B-3 JetRanger helicopters, filling the apron with their metal menace. Each had engines screaming, rotors hissing through the cold early morning air, waiting for the instruction to go, glinting in the glorious dawn sunlight.

Alix's jaw dropped.

He didn't need to be an expert, although he was, to see that these hover-birds were brand new and adapted for the security service, armed to the teeth with the latest weapon systems.

The Priest came out through the hanger doors and stood beside him, quoting from the small leather Bible, a look of wildness in his eyes. Alix's gaze roved across the three helicopters, scanning the occupants inside the cockpits, some of whom he would have worked with on ops in the past.

Moments later, the helicopters' engines were shut down and whirling rotors slowed to a gradual halt. All of the occupants got out and came over to where the Priest and Alix were standing. Alix immediately recognised the attractive Italian intelligence officer named Sophia Mazzaro, who had been seconded to MI5 for the past six months, her speciality, assassination.

The Priest led the nine new-comers into the hanger where, Dillon, Vince and Lola met them and everyone took a moment to get acquainted.

Alix followed them all inside and climbed up onto a fifty-gallon drum. A torrent of strength rushed through him and drowned his despair.

"Can I have your attention!" he bellowed.

Voices trailed off, and slowly all the intelligence officers along with the others turned towards this man who hadn't had a shave or a bath for over a week and looked like he'd been to hell and back. His gaze met with that of the Priest, who gave him a quick glance and a nod.

Alix took a drag on his cigarette. "Ladies and gentleman, and men of God," his words rolled out on a cloud of smoke, "You all know why you're here and what this assignment will involve. Our job is to ensure that the threat to the UK and Global security network is eliminated, and that Ramus is liquidated at the earliest possible opportunity. This man, if allowed to roam freely around the planet, will change the way we live our lives, if he is actually allowed to launch the Chimera virus programme. For those of you who are not familiar with Chimera, let me tell you; it is the most advanced piece of viral software that has ever been written. A silent attacker - undetectable - devastatingly aggressive - intuitive and most of all - infinitely adaptive. It reacts to the environment it has invaded, in the blink of an eye - a Chameleon. Once it's in, it can extract every piece of data from the hardrive, send it to a remote server and literally take over the system, whether it's a single computer, a corporate or government mainframe, military networks or *any* computer that is connected to the Internet. It can get past anti-virus software, firewalls and protected networks, no matter how many layers or encryptions, they have. Am I painting a graphic enough picture for you all?"

The intelligence men and woman all nodded.

Alix continued, "Ramus is the man who has systematically destroyed Scorpion and has murdered many good people, some of whom were *friends* as well."

More nods from around the gathering.

Alix's wide-eyed gaze roved over the small, yet, elite group. He exchanged glances with Dillon, Lola, Vince and the Priest. Sophia Mazzaro gave him a tiny smile, the sunlight catching her mane of auburn hair, and her dark eyes flashing bright with a sort of inappropriate flirtatiousness, and Alix beamed her a huge smile: they had got together from time to time. His gaze took in the eight MI5 officers: all were ready, all had weapons primed, all were ready to do their duty for Queen and country against the evil that was attempting to change the world and change it bad.

Alix smiled slowly.

"Intelligence reports are that the virus programme is not ready to be launched, the Chimera version the enemy possesses - is missing some of the vital script. The optical disc with it on is locked inside a safe on board the stealth ship that Ramus uses as his mobile operations centre..."

Dillon stepped forward, turned and stood in front of the group.

"And this," he held up his hand holding the optical disc that Claudia Dax had given him. "Is the disc that contains the vital script. In fact this is a copy that has been modified, so that anyone trying to merge this version with the one that Ramus has, will automatically erase both. Rather cunning, really."

"But, it would appear that Ramus has had some very capable people working on Chimera and is now very close to cracking these last vital elements. Once that happens, he will be unstoppable... So, it's lucky for us that the Americans have located the stealth ship using one of their newest spy satellites - and now we know where he is - *we* are the only ones who can make a difference." Alix said, and jumped down off the fifty-gallon drum. "And we will win," he said, his words soft as he tossed his spent cigarette down.

"We will be given a sat-link assignment briefing by Edward

Levenson-Jones at 14.30 this afternoon; be ready people, we move out at sunset. We have a madman to kill."

* * *

Dillon walked slowly around the hanger, looking up at the battered fuselage of the Lear and the Apache, both looked worse for wear. He knew how they felt! He suddenly needed to be in the daylight. Outside, he walked over to take a closer look at the three JetRangers on the hard-standing; red fuselage gleaming in the sunlight, heavy calibre machine guns and air-to-air missile launchers attached to the underside of their airframes. Inside the cockpit more fire-power; Heckler & Koch MP6 carbines, grenades, cases of ammunition and high-explosive. "Impressive." Dillon said out loud, and thought that these men were supposed to be the best. Although they were all travelling under the auspice of MI5, Dillon and the others knew that everyone of them had been hand-picked from the elite regiments and security agencies, and that they all knew exactly what was expected of them.

Sophia Mazzaro was something quite different. A contract liquidator for hire; Interpol, MI5 and MI6, Mossad and the CIA all having employed her special talent, and all having lost good agents to the Assassins and those who were behind the Assassins - and on behalf of them all, she wanted a slice of the payback cake.

Dillon halted. The Priest had followed him outside, was quoting from the Bible and reciting mantra-like phrases akin to a man possessed. Dillon turned and looked into the tall man's dark eyes. The Priest was muscular; one of the most muscular men of God he had ever seen.

"Can you *fuck off* and leave me alone," Dillon said.

"I see, Dillon. That you are annoyed by my intrusion," said the Priest closing his Bible slowly. The book looked small in his hands. "But I seek merely to make light of your pain, to fill your soul with joy in this most stressful of times, to fill you with light before we embark on our quest to eradicate this evil Satanic God-mocking heathen. from the face of this planet..."

"Well don't - just don't. I need to collect my thoughts on my own. I need calm. And you know, because now you're the only one who does know, why I need to collect my thoughts."

"Ah yes, of course. Tatiana was the only other person who knew,

369

wasn't she?" He held up a hand, "No need to answer, I know that is so. I'm still wondering, though, how the hell you have kept such a secret from the shrinks, for so long."

Dillon looked at the Priest for a few long moments. "You're wondering, aren't you how I keep the secret of my psychosis, my psychopathic alter-ego? Well, it only comes to the surface during moments of extreme stress. And lucky for me, I don't find a forty-five minute post-assignment assessment with a shrink, that stressful! That's how…"

"I see. Thank you for being so candid, Dillon. I know that you have suffered great loss at the hands of Ramus. The Lord will pay back this evil man with bolts of lightning from Heaven; the Lord shall smite down our enemies. He shall fuck him up real bad." The Priest grinned then, "Dillon, put your trust in the Lord and he will surely guide you."

"I'll put my trust in my Glock 9mm, Priest," said Dillon, smiling.

"It's worked wonders on Kirill, and it will work wonders on Ramus today."

The Priest's smart-phone sounded. He took a moment to decipher the encrypted message and read it, twice. Frowning, he looked up, his face filled with confusion and anger.

"Kirill still has to be punished."

Dillon shook his head. I shot Kirill in Scotland, Priest; I killed that son-of-a-bitch myself and left him to be fried by his own fucking bomb."

"You are wrong, my friend. By some perverted fluke of injustice, he somehow escaped a fiery death".

"How do you know this?"

"The encryption I received just a minute ago was from GCHQ. They intercepted a bounced transmission, a video. He had sent a message to Ramus; their arrogance is colossal, they actually think we are as nothing. They think they can flaunt themselves with impunity. But Kirill *is* alive, Dillon." The Priest handed his smart-phone to Dillon, who read the intercept and watched the video clip.

Dillon's jaw dropped. "That fucker just will not die."

"There is more."

"More?"

The Priest nodded. "They have Tatiana on the stealth ship. You saw her shot and then fall from the aircraft, yes, but she did not die;

she was mentioned in Kirill's message to Ramus."

"Tatiana! Alive?" Hope died as soon as it had flared. "Definitely not," Dillon growled.

"Well, it wouldn't seem bizarre that they would seek to save a bartering tool against you, their greatest proven adversary?"

"Me?"

"You scare them, Dillon. They know what you're capable of. There is a dark demon in your soul, and they can see that it's your protector."

"So what are you saying that they're reeling me in?"

"Like a lamb to slaughter," said the Priest softly.

Dillon moved back into the freezing cold interior of the hanger. He paced like a caged tiger, for what seemed like an age, his mind whirling, images of Tatiana flickering through his brain, sadness overtaking him, then anger, then frustration, and then utter disbelief.

If she was alive, then he had to save her.

And Kirill - alive, and using her as bait?

Dillon smiled a nasty grin.

"Our next meeting Professor, will be a sweet one, I'll make sure of that." He said softly.

* * *

The briefing was over. The intelligence officers were making final preparations for their departure; including the incorporation of a highly sophisticated software programme that Vince was uploading to the database of the three JetRanger helicopters to help them evade surface-to-air and air-to-air missiles.

From the airfield, they were to fly to the north west of the county, and then back down to the coast in the south. Flying at five hundred feet in tight formation with no filed flight-plan and total radio silence. Ferran & Cardini International had tracked Ramus using their world network of spies, their illegal (even by criminal standards) web of optical and digital communications, and good old fashioned leg-work by the intelligence men and women on the ground. That's how they found a one-hundred and fifty foot twin hull stealth ship. The powerful craft was a dull matt black and had no name. It was a huge vessel that would no doubt hold many surprises for those attacking it. But one thing was certain: all men and women involved were willing to lay down their lives to bring the enemies of the British Realm to justice.

Dillon stood watching the hive of activity, his Glock 9mm in his hand. Lola checked over the Apache and had refuelled her, ready for Dillon's part in the attack. Dillon did not care.

"Alix!"

Alix, now fully dressed, walked swiftly towards his friend.

"Yeah?"

"I need to ask a favour."

"Anything, man."

"I thought Tatiana was dead but the Priest has informed me that I was wrong. Kirill and Ramus have her; they have her aboard the stealth ship. I need time, Alix; I need time to get in there and get her the hell out before you start the carnage."

Alix stood up, mouth open. "What are you asking me, Dillon? To hold up this operation?"

"Yes. I really need this, Alix; I need the chance to get her out." Dillon ground his teeth. He stared into the eyes of the man he trusted most. "Come on, man, you can't let her die in there - I *know* what you've got planned... Come on, man, *please*," he said.

Alix closed his mouth. He frowned, glancing over his shoulder. Then he met Dillon's iron gaze.

"Just supposing I was able to let you do this, how will we work it?"

"We fly with the JetRangers, using them as our cover. You'll fly the Apache; I'll act as co-pilot and Vince will be your tactical weapons officer. When we get near to the stealth ship, you'll drop down, and I will make a house call on our friend, Ramus."

"But, you *do* know what I plan, don't you?"

Dillon nodded. "Bomb in a bag?"

Sort of. I like to think of it as a dirty-bomb in a small trunk, to be more precise. It's a home-made Molotov cocktail with a twist at the top. You will need to be well away from there, Dillon - because when this baby goes off, it'll send that ship down *big style*."

Dillon's face showed the strain of the last week.

"I'll be out, Alix, with Tatiana. If I'm not..." He left the sentence unfinished and Alix scowled, licking his lips.

"As long as you know the score, man. I can give you an extra few minutes... No more..."

Dillon nodded; he knew the score, all right. He knew the dangers, the risk, the hell that he would have to travel through before he could come out the other side and get his life back to normal. Normal? He laughed.

"So... Let's do it - and do it *now*," said Alix

* * *

Dillon looked up into a darkening sky full of heavy thunderous clouds, and a feeling of foreboding filled his soul with uneasiness.

He breathed deeply and walked over to the Apache helicopter now standing on the apron alongside the three JetRangers of the intelligence service.

Dillon settled into the co-pilot's seat alongside Alix, who was already flicking switches and turning dials as part of his pre-flight routine. A moment later the Apache's rotors started to turn, winding up to speed for take-off. He gave the thumbs up to the three JetRanger pilots, who confirmed with the same gesture, as no radio comms. would be used throughout the mission.

The four helicopters flew in tight formation; the noise of the engines filled the air around them. Alix focused on controls and weapon systems with Vince sitting behind him monitored the screens in front and on either side of him, revising the protocols. Dillon checked the Nav-Comp for the coordinates of the stealth ship. Their fuel tanks were full.

South of the Dorset coast, mid English Channel Alix flew the Apache, constantly checking the read-outs on the screen, and with each mile flown his confidence in operating the hi-tech machine grew: and he felt good.

No, he felt more than good. He felt *alive*.

Dillon gazed out across the landscape five hundred feet below them as they passed over. His brain running through the sequence of events that would surely take place as he entered the stealth ship and Ramus' lair... Alix took the lead, not out of choice, but because the Apache housed the most advanced detection equipment of all four helicopters. And now he knew what he had to do. He had to get Tatiana out. But more than that: this was about Claudia, Ezra and everyone who had died at the hands of the Assassins. This was about life and death. This was about finishing what others had begun. This was about finding the truth. And this was about …revenge.

Not for himself, no. For the innocents, the people who had died merely because they were in the way. Those individuals who had thought they had been working in jobs out of the firing line. Away from danger.

Dillon knew. Knew that he had to stop this thing and stop it fast.

"What can one man do?" Mocked his subconscious.

"One man can do enough," he replied calmly.

Alix dropped the Apache's altitude, flying low over green fields and large expanses of the woodlands west Dorset and then down towards the Jurassic coast in the south. They flew fast over small villages and towns; he even fancied he heard the ringing of church bells.

Dillon looked up. "It's Sunday, then," he said suddenly.

Alix checked the Apache's computer systems. "Yeah, Sunday. A day of rest and worship. We'll give them something to worship," he said grimly. "And boy, the Priest is not a happy-chappy." He chuckled.

Dillon checked himself: his body had taken a pounding over the last few days and he was now covered in bruises and scratches. He flexed his aching muscles, that weren't hurting quite so much now. His ribs didn't click as much when he moved, although the soreness was still a nuisance and his stomach still gave him twinges of pain. But the pain-killers and anti-inflammatory drugs he had dosed up on before leaving the hanger were now kicking in and now these irritants were fading... His broken ribs were still healing. The blow was just too much and he knew deep down that it was his weak point, his Achilles heel. To take another blow there? The pain would scream through his torso and physically paralyse him...

Primary location for maximum protection then, he mused idly.

The Apache and three JetRangers hummed over a huge swathe of sandy undulating terrain, a desolate battlefield landscape created by many years of training tank crews in the art of fast moving heavy artillery warfare. Their shadows tumbling across the land and then over a series of hills towards the coast. Dillon checked to make sure that they were not being tracked electronically or by other aircraft.

They needed the element of surprise, not a welcoming committee.

And *he* wanted the serenity of the sea...

The Apache, followed by the three JetRangers, came over the

brow of the hill and swooped down through the secluded bay of Lulworth Cove and out into the English Channel, just fifty foot above the waves.

Dillon, with a shock, thought his chances of survival were slim at very best. He realised that this assignment had tested him to the absolute limit, and that he was most likely going to die; so he would have to take this fight to Ramus and his Assassins, mess them up bad and sour their plans to hold the world to ransom and then die...

And Tatiana... well, Tatiana could already be dead.

So be it, he mused bitterly.

He forced himself to relax as the Apache flew out over the sea. Occasionally they passed fishing boats heading out to sea, and the fishermen on board would sometimes look up into the moonlit sky as they passed over, forcing Dillon to smile sadly.

What happy uncomplicated lives they lead, he thought.

What normal lives?

Why couldn't I have been normal? He thought...

Because you kill. Came the voice from deep within his subconscious.

Because you kill and you're good at killing.

You might not like it.

You might even loath it.

But you can't deny it. You're really *good* at it.

A natural- born killer.

* * *

The four helicopters skimmed over the English Channel heading towards their destination; the harsh, yet intensely beautiful cliffs of the Jurassic coastline on their port-side. The last bastion against a ferocious sea; constantly pounded by the severity of the elements over thousands of years.

The Apache flew low, staying in formation on the tail of the three Bell JetRangers as they veered away from the coast and headed out to sea.

Dillon shivered. Alix spoke into his ear through the closed comms link that all three of them were now wearing.

"Dillon, the final destination coordinates have just been uploaded onto the Apache's navigation system. Our ETA to target is four minutes.

Dillon checked the coordinates and Alix slowed his air-speed as he started to approach the estimated location of the stealth ship. The scanners still read zero: nothing. They flew. The Apache, despite having taken a number of hits over the last few days, was responding well and as long as nothing else slammed into the state-of-the-art helicopter, Alix knew the machine would get them all there in one piece...

A crazy thought careered into his mind.

The Priest was wrong.

They were all wrong.

There was nothing there; nothing but a lot of open water, and a bitterly cold easterly wind.

From under the blackened full-face visor, Alix laughed out loud. Both Dillon and Vince looked at him as the visor opened and Alix grinning face greeted them. "Sorry, just had a funny thought that we might have been sent on a wild goose chase." Then he saw it. A black dot moving at speed on the screen in front of him.   Dillon and Vince both saw it as well. Dillon said, "It must be the stealth ship, and it's heading straight for the entrance to Poole Harbour. But I still can't work out why Ramus has come to the Dorset coast?" All the time, Dillon was mentally preparing himself for what was to come; he would have to be totally focused, and without any fear...

The black dot started to grow; to materialise; to enlarge before Dillon's eyes.

The stealth ship was moving at a rapid speed for a craft so large; a churning wake of white foam followed it.

Dillon smiled nastily.

All I want, he thought, are answers before I die.

All I want, he thought, is to kill those involved - before I die.

He had resigned himself to meeting his maker, or whatever else was waiting for him on the other side. Kirill had asked him once if he was ready to die and now he understood; now he truly understood.

Dillon knew.

Knew that he wasn't coming back.

Alix reached over and tapped Dillon on the shoulder, pointing at the comm screen in front of them. The de-coded text told them that the Apache's on-board computer system had been remotely locked onto the CIA at Langley, along with the UK security service and Interpol. From this point forward, they were to have big-brother looking over their shoulder during the attack on the stealth ship, whatever the outcome...

* * *

The stealth ship, while not the largest catamaran ever built, was certainly the most menacing. Its dull matt black twin-hulls crouched low and it growled through the sea water, smashing the waves apart as it powered towards its destination. Dillon, like the other members of the hastily put-together team, had listened to Alix's briefing, based on information gathered by many hundreds of field operatives around the globe, including the Priest. Spy planes had been used without success, but an undercover CIA agent working as a docker in the Bahamas had seen the catamaran close up. He was able to get on board when it had made an unscheduled port of call at Nassau to re-stock with provisions.

The agent had reported back to Langley that the vessel was heavily armed with extensive weapons and guidance systems, far superior to those of even the most sophisticated military craft. As well as the standard surface-to-air and surface-to-surface missiles and large calibre machine guns, it had extensive anti-submarine sensors and weapons, and powerful radar giving complete coverage and able to track multiple targets simultaneously. It also had two heavily armed and armoured half-size remote controlled support helicopters. And the catamaran was nuclear powered. Unlike normal stealth ships, this state of the art machine had a top speed of 65 knots. And there had been no sign of any crew...

Alix hovered for a while at a distance, the Apache humming softly, the data-stream display inside his helmet screaming proximity warnings at him. Dillon and Vince were picking up the same information on their screens. Below them, the sea spun away in circular patterns, brushed aside by the down draughts from the four helicopters.

And yet, and yet the catamaran was not on the displays.

Chimera, Dillon thought.

Ramus has uploaded the programme to the stealth ship's computer system, and this was now acting as the 'originating' host. Chimera would automatically take over the existing operating system;

make it quicker, intuitive, and very dangerous. Chimera would re-write every script to its own specification and do everything in its considerable power to protect the host. Including; intercepting satellite, radar and scanner readings.

It's already found a way of enhancing the catamaran's stealth mode, but also of bouncing everything away from the catamaran!

Was he too late?

Behind, despite their agreed radio silence, Alix used his smart-phone to connect with the other helicopters. "You okay, Priest?"

"Yes, Alix. Are you ready?"

"Oh, we're ready. Vince and I are all set. Dillon is as ready as he'll ever be..."

"Stay close to him, Alix. May God be with you."

"I don't need your God, Priest." Snarled Alix, and terminated the link.

Grinning, Alix eased the Apache forward in step with the three JetRangers. They grouped closer now, machines flanking and leading the Apache to form a metal cloak around it... Dillon found himself suddenly tense, awaiting incoming fire, waiting for those large calibre machine guns to spit their welcome...

The matt black catamaran thrashed and growled through the choppy sea. Waves smashed against its twin prows. Seagulls cawed overhead. Small sailing craft, tied up to their swinging moorings were brushed easily aside by the stealth ship's ram.

Dillon grimaced.

It had started to rain, lightly at first, then a downpour of heavy droplets laced with sleet from a tumultuous cold night sky; clouds gathered and bunched, bruised and swollen.

The rain and sleet fell with increased ferocity.

The waters of one of the world's largest natural harbours churned, rain turning waves into prancing stallions.

Against the sky sat an inky blot that expanded and separated as the four helicopters loosened their formation.

"Okay, people. Let's do this thing." Came the crackle of Dillon's voice over the comm link.

As one, the four heavily armed helicopters advanced on the stealth ship, the Apache and the three JetRanger's stayed low, flying past the luxury Haven Hotel and multi-million pound prestigious mansions on the Sandbanks Peninsula as they entered the vast natural harbour. The men and woman aboard these high-tech machines were all armed with Heckler & Koch machine carbines and bombs, waiting to fight, waiting for what was surely to come.

In the lead JetRanger sat the Priest. His eyes flashed with fire behind the night-vision visor he was wearing. He pointed; he pointed at the catamaran, where a number of sliding panels on the black deck had been retracted to reveal heavy calibre machine cannons located on laser guided turntables. Two small black single-seater helicopters lifted from the lower stern deck, rotors screaming through the rain, guns and missiles armed and ready...

"Here we go," Dillon spoke softly, sliding the Glock's safety off. At the same time, Alix armed the Apache's weapons systems in a splash of coloured lights and flickering data streams on the monitors in front of them. Alarms started to sound all around them and through their headsets as, on the deck of the catamaran, one of the guns rotated smoothly, its laser guided sight locked onto its target. The large calibre barrels lifted, their angle of ascent adjusted; then came the massive concussive *boom* and the turret recoiled.

One of the advancing JetRangers was plucked from the sky and turned into a fireball of orange and yellow against the black sky, a ball of bright iridescence before it smashed down into the sea, rotors spinning screaming splashing into the churning waters where the blackened burnt out carcass disappeared swiftly below the waves.

From high above, one of the catamaran's single-seater helicopters came swooping from out of the low cloud and rain, its machine guns hammering.

The Apache returned fire and the dark sky was suddenly filled with a stream of tracer rounds.

Alix fired off two air-to-air missiles and allowed the Apache to gain altitude, rotors scything, while Vince was in the back, constantly making adjustments to the helicopter's weapon's systems. The Apache suddenly veered to the right as Alix reacted to the alarm screaming at him, the black single-seater helicopter only just missed them as it shot past at bullet speed... He allowed the Apache to drop - away and *down* towards the suddenly looming deck of the stealth ship: Ramus' mobile control centre...

Above them, both remaining JetRangers were engaged in aerial acrobatics with the black single-seater, bullets crackled across the storm filled sky.

And the heavens were painted crimson.

The command-room was devoid of any fitments, walls like a blank canvas, except for the three meter by four meter projection screen suspended at one end. A flickering glow from the myriad of screens within screens held; images, encrypted/decoded text, binary code and live news-feeds from around the world.

This was a control-centre built to withstand the heaviest of blasts, and designed so that this independent module could become detached from the main catamaran should the need arise. A self-propelled deep sea submersible.

Ramus stood in the centre of the darkened space, the flat tablet computer cradled in his left arm, long fingers tapped the virtual keyboard and hooded eyes stared into the void. His hand moved slowly, a sliver of ice down the spine of planet Earth... And then he gently pressed RETURN.

Nothing...

And then a quiet hum filled the command deck. The giant flat-screen monitor dimmed momentarily, as if bowing before some electronic divine being, and then brightened into life once more.

Script - Chimera script - sped across the display. Then, all of the screens disappeared and a virtual globe sprang into existence, a spinning manifestation of the earth. The tablet in Ramus' hand produced the virtual globe as a full Technicolor multi-dimensional hologram. He lifted his free hand and held it palm down over the spinning ball, a multi-coloured light that illuminated and deformed Ramus' facial features.

Ramus laughed a cold and sinister sound.

He reached out and pointed; the virtual globe spun, located its target, and zoomed in through layers of sparkling light to highlight Poole harbour. Ramus pulled back from this location; he typed in the coordinates of the central security services mainframe and smiled malevolently.

"So you come to destroy me, Mr Dillon. Like a lamb to the slaughter?"

He rapidly typed in the command sequence.

The stealth ship hummed from the heart of its massive mainframe. The black terminal that was now playing 1st host to the Chimera Virus Programme...

Chimera script locked on:
Initiation sequence engaged = threat = British Security Services
threat found = co-ords determined
Launch sequence armed = missile countdown set
Satellite request = granted = 40 hacked and armed
Chimera adaptive script = control logged = override all existing
controllers.

Chapter 24

The waves crashed and churned against the twin hulls of the stealth ship as it cut through the choppy waters of the natural harbour. Missiles detonated. There was a deafening roar of high-explosives from the catamaran's deck; the whole structure shuddered; one of the JetRangers released three air-to-air missiles that intercepted and destroyed the threat, smashed, burning insanely from the sky to die, extinguished in the waves. Guns roared, spitting and kicking across metal and flesh.

In amidst the furore Alix placed the Apache into a hover just twenty foot above the waves, and handed over the control of the helicopter to Vince Sharp.

Moments later, two figures wearing black wet-suits dropped into the water. Both were heavily armed and equipped with the latest power-fins that allowed them to swim the distance to the catamaran, effortlessly. Alix had the rucksack containing the dirty-bomb strapped to his back.

The two men climbed aboard, they gave one another the thumbs-up. Alix lifted his goggles for a second and stared into Dillon's eyes. Both men grasped hands, and Alix said:

"So, let's do this thing."

"Good luck, Alix."

"If I don't make it back... Tell Lola I love her."

Dillon laughed. "So touching coming from the king of all lady killers. And wasn't that the title of that song?"

"Possibly! A favour - for me."

"Of course. Anything for you, man," said Dillon, smiling kindly.

"Five minutes; then get the hell off this tub."

"Five minutes, it is." Said Dillon. He replaced his goggles and hoisted the Heckler & Koch MP6 machine carbine, glancing up at the fire-fight taking place in the sky above; at the turmoil of bullets and missiles and spinning rotors. Machine guns roared; the smell of cordite hanging heavy in the salt air.

"Good luck, Dillon."

"Luck's got nothing to do with it," said Dillon, grinning.

Alix checked the straps on the black rucksack, and then dropped backwards over the edge of the lower dive platform and was instantly swallowed by the churning black water.

Dillon sat for a moment, staring down at the few bubbles that reached the surface; then he concentrated on the task at hand, turned and looked up at the main structure of the catamaran, could feel the power emanating from its mainframe.

Dillon nodded to himself.

Retribution had to be served - and revenge was always best served cold.

* * *

The Apache banked low and hard, sweeping around the catamaran in a wide arc, so close that Vince could see the deck rails and the windows of the bridge. The Apache banked again, this time past the huge machine cannons, menacing and black, multiple barrels spinning, rotating, rising and falling as the laser guided system tracked and attempted to lock on to their target. The catamaran flashed past in a blur, the Apache roared just above the surface of the turbulent water. Alone on board, Vince flew the helicopter from his touch-screen linked directly to a virtual pilot that he had up-loaded to the Apache's flight management system. Vince dragged the tip of his forefinger across the screen, and the helicopter responded by swooping down, Vince tapped his finger once, the nose of the Apache lifted slightly and then dropped onto the deck with a *clash* of metal upon metal. The rotors howled as they continued to spin.

"Dillon, that was far too easy," said Vince calmly into his comm link.

"Like I give a shit," snapped Dillon.

Vince lifted the cockpit canopy and wind and rain lashed in, stinging his skin. He stood, climbed up onto the rim, then lowered himself and dropped onto the deck. His boots made dull thumps and he could feel the cold beneath him. "You've been bloody marvellous," he said, patting the Apache's fuselage. The wind snatched his words in an instant and swept them away in a tumble. The JetRanger helicopters were twisting and swooping, machine guns raging, missiles roaring. From within the stealth ship a missile shot skywards and sent one of the JetRangers tumbling, a flaming ball pitched into the freezing water.

Dillon turned; focused; orientated himself. His stare roved the dark surroundings lit sporadically by emergency lighting and he could see nobody as he gripped his battered Glock 9mm automatic - a small reassurance, but at least it gave him the certainty to deal out death to anybody who came near.

Tatiana.

Where would she be?

With Kirill.

"That fucker," growled Dillon. He moved quickly forward along the metal gangway, his gaze constantly shifting, scanning his surroundings for any unwanted company in the semi-darkness. This felt crazy, totally crazy and Dillon felt the burden of his life lift from his shoulders because it did not matter any more, truly nothing mattered and if he was to die, then so be it.

Dillon sprinted towards the nearest doorway. But then everything happened at once - there was a deafening *boom* from somewhere above him, and Dillon whirled, crouching, bringing the Glock up to see.

"*Nothing*," whispered the voice inside his head.

Behind him, Kirill slid from the shadows, from the darkness, like a ghost or a demon emerging from another plane of existence. He held a snub-nosed Smith & Weston handgun and his expression was almost serene.

Dillon turned and Kirill nodded slowly. He smiled, showing tobacco stained teeth. "Mr Dillon, we've been expecting you." Dillon fixed his glittering gaze on the muzzle of the gun that pointed straight at his heart...

He tried hard to conceal his shock at seeing Kirill.

"I left you for dead on that mountain in Scotland."

"No, Mr Dillon. You left me *dying*. There is a subtle difference. The pain I have had to endure at your hands - will make it a pleasure for me to finally kill you. Now, your weapon, please?"

"What makes you think I'll give it to you?"

An explosion rocked the catamaran. Kirill did not waver. But nodded to something behind Dillon. He turned. Behind him stood two black-clad Assassins, both bearing lethal looking Uzi mini sub-machine pistols. They blocked the corridor in silence, and to his shame he had not heard them creep up on him. These killers were subtly different to the others that Dillon had come into contact with; they seemed larger, broader, more athletic.

"Previously, you met Assassins who were smaller, slimmer, but equally capable of killing. These are different. These - well, they have been genetically enhanced."

Dillon licked his lips and smiled broadly.

"Is Tatiana on board?"

"She is. She has asked that you join her; she would weep and wail in your arms and seek one final kiss and your forgiveness before you both die. Please come this way, Mr Dillon. Let me show you exactly what we are creating aboard this ship..."

"And what might that be, Kirill. Armageddon?"

"On the contrary. What we are on the brink of is going to change this planet forever. When Chimera is launched, information technology everywhere will cease to exist in its present form," said Kirill softly. He gestured with his gun, and Dillon allowed the Glock to be taken from him. "This way."

Dillon stepped forward.

Towards the black door.

And the gaping maw of uncertainty beyond.

* * *

Kirill led Dillon through the dimly lit corridors, metal floors and metal grilles beneath their boots. As they walked, Dillon could hear the deep distant drone of the catamaran's massive nuclear powered engines.

Kirill seemed different; Dillon could see that something had changed. The back of Kirill's neck and head - it was scar tissue. Severe scar tissue, bright pink and painful looking; something about the hair, of course it was not his, instead he was wearing a wig. So he had been caught in the blast when the device had detonated deep within the top-secret facility in Scotland. Dillon smiled, the hair-piece had slipped to one side, *different*, he thought...

Dillon shivered, thinking. What the hell is going on?

He glanced behind him; the two Assassins were there, weapons trained on his back.

Dillon followed Kirill.

There was little else that he could do.

They descended; steep metal staircases that led down. The mustiness that hung heavy in the freezing cold air was all around them, and condensation on the metal handrail brought a chill beneath Dillon's fingers, and he felt his mind numbing, his sub-conscious stirring, coming into focus...

Good, thought Dillon.

They reached wider corridors and there were more Assassins, Dillon counted ten as he was led past them, some of them were without their hoods and Dillon could observe their faces for the first time. Each and every one of these young women had natural beauty and raven coloured hair.

"Kirill, where in God's name did you get all of these beautiful women from. And how come they're all so fucking dangerous?" Dillon asked softly.

"Quiet."

"Or what? You'll kill me?" Dillon laughed a sneering cold bark. Dillon looked Kirill up, then down. His smile was sickly sweet. "Come on, Kirill, answer my question."

Kirill halted. He turned and his gaze was burning.

"They are beautiful, aren't they, Dillon? And they are killers, very efficient killers. But do you mean to tell me that Ezra never explained about the Assassins? Kirill sneered. "We - Ezra, Ramus and I - found them, or rather, they found us. The Assassins you have encountered so far have all come from the same secret society in northern France. But these that you see before you are something completely different. All of the Assassins on this ship are true bloods, descendants of the first band of Carpathians that were collected by a clever fellow named Hassan, the *Old Man of the Mountains*, so called because he made Mount Lebanon his stronghold. These original Assassins were the terror of the world for two centuries, and then they were hunted down by Sultan Bibaris and almost eradicated. As a result, those who survived disbanded and scattered to all four corners of the planet, where they continued to ply their lethal skill from secret locations. You asked what makes them so dangerous. *Haschisch* or bang turned into intoxicating liquor and then enhanced and refined in the lab by Ramus. They use the liquor just before they go on a mission to kill."

Kirill turned and continued to walk. Dillon followed.

"Ramus - the creator of fear!" Kirill cackled, and the sound was cold; chilling; nightmare turned real.

Moving down the wide corridors now, Dillon felt the hairs on the back of his neck stand up. He kept thinking that he was passing through an area of the catamaran where perhaps unspeakable torture had taken place. There was something dreadfully wrong with this place, and with these Assassins who had been hunting him for so long, these killers who had wiped out a number of key Scorpion squads and the individuals they had been protecting... But he could not put his finger on it.

Kirill halted.

A door slid open and he gestured Dillon through and onto a massive control deck. Computer servers lined the walls, their status lights flickering incessantly. Display monitors were set up on benches, showing every global satellite position of every nation on the planet. And there, in the middle of the deck, was Tatiana!

"Tats!"

"Dillon!" She leaped to her feet, sprinted towards him and they fell into one another's arms. Dillon kissed her passionately, then pulled away and stared down into her tear-filled eyes.

"They took me, Dillon. Took me from that airfield and plucked me from the brink of death," she sobbed. "I haven't told them anything, Dillon; I promise... they said that I was their insurance policy, that you would do what they want as long as they could kill me..."

"So touching," snapped Kirill. He strolled over to one of the terminals and placed the Glock on an alloy bench. He flicked a switch; there was a whirring of fans and then a part of the front panel opened to reveal the optical disc drive. "Behold," said Kirill. "This is Chimera. Are you impressed, Mr Dillon?"

"The Master Copy on optical disc, wow. That's so not impressive."

"What it lacks in size and impressiveness, I can assure you it more than makes up for in ability. Thank your saviour, Mr Dillon."

"My... *saviour?*"

"Ask yourself this question - why did we take Tatiana and ensure that she stayed alive? Why didn't I simply shoot you back there? You think I give a flying fuck about your answers to these questions? You think I care about sparing your miserable life after what you did to me in Scotland? No... But Ramus is puzzled by you, Mr Dillon. You worry him, and that worries *me*. He thinks that there is something strange about you, Mr Dillon, something dark *inside* you that makes you uniquely dangerous. And he is going to tear that secret from you - even if it kills you."

Kirill smiled, and it was not a nice smile. "I, however, am

sceptical; I simply want you dead. But Ramus has other plans... He believes that he can play with your soul."

Kirill turned and ran his fingers over the top of the glistening processor housing.

All around them there was a gentle humming.

"So what are you waiting for?" Dillon said softly. "For me to shoot you again?"

Kirill turned; a fluid whirl. He smiled at Dillon. "Let me warn you, it is Ramus who wishes you alive, and not I. Do not antagonise me or you may push me beyond my limit. Now that we have Chimera operating at 100% effectiveness, that copy you have is no longer required. You've already witnessed what the programme is capable of - but soon, you and your sorry excuse for a government will see the full extent of our plans."

"What, to take control of the entire planet?" Dillon sneered.

Kirill laughed then. "You really are quite naive, Dillon. So very, very simple. In your world everything is in black and white; not so in mine. We systematically destroyed your government's secret weapon against terrorism - Scorpion. Well their time is well and truly over... It disgusts me that they had the opportunity to make a real difference, but all that happened was, nothing. Evil men walk the world with guns and bombs, and politicians become more and more corrupt. We live in a world that is warped beyond belief, Dillon. Scorpion was supposed to make a difference: once I actually thought that this highly trained task force would make a *difference* - allow ordinary people to sleep easy in their beds at night. But no, they were weak, Dillon - weak, because the politicians would not allow them to do their jobs properly and with a free hand. Now is the time for change... It is time for the strong to rule with an un-swervable belief that the world will then be a far better place - once we have erased every corrupt government and dictatorship from it. God will be proud of humanity for this."

He stepped away from the processor and picked up a tablet processor.

Kirill tapped his instructions into the device.

A hologram appeared suspended mid-air in the centre of the room. A spinning, almost perfect representation of the world; colours merged and flowed as land mass was separated by the deep blue of the oceans. Major cities appeared and around this virtual globe spun satellites.

Dillon glanced down at his Omega. Time was fast running out...

The door opened. A huge, athletic bodyguard entered, followed by a much smaller figure in heavy dark robes, its face hidden, its shoulders rounded. The bodyguard nodded to Kirill, who smiled once again. It was with unease that Dillon noted the hooded figure facing him.

"Mr Dillon, let me introduce to you, Ramus." The mysterious figure moved towards the virtual globe, took the flat tablet from Kirill, and skimmed his long fingers over the touch-screen. Satellites repositioned themselves, and the dark figure chuckled, a deep melodious sound.

"So we meet at last, Mr Dillon."

"We meet at last, Mr Ramus."

"Just Ramus, Mr Dillon. I have to say, that you have been an exceptional adversary."

"And you're the one in charge of this snapping terrier called Kirill."

"Yes. Let me show you what we can do here," came the voice of Ramus from within the robes.

Suddenly, one of the virtual satellites moved into position directly over Poole.

Ramus typed in new instructions and loud speakers all around them came alive with a live news stream.

"You are extremely privileged indeed, Mr Dillon, to witness this moment..."

Ramus rapidly typed in more commands, and script started to flow across the monitor screens of each terminal at lightning speed.

Tatiana gasped. "He's instructing Chimera to do it..."

Dillon watched coldly as - Chimera took control of the satellite weapons system; locked onto the target, initiated the arming sequence, confirmed the target, awaited the launch command.

Ramus tapped the screen once.

* * *

Outside, the fight in the air above the stealth ship was going badly. The JetRanger was holding its own, and the programme that Vince had up-loaded to each of the helicopters to evade the missiles, was working perfectly. But, it was running low on ammunition and missiles, and just when it seemed that things couldn't get any worse, the Priest and Lola looked up to see a bolt of white laser light shoot through the low cloud. Fire exploded from the heavens and hit the Royal Navy destroyer that was standing a mile off the Dorset coast in readiness. The laser cut through the mid-ships, blasting the ship into glowing splinters of steel that rained down into the English Channel.

The Priest swallowed hard. He blinked and crossed his chest.

And his faith was shaken.

Dillon watched the monitor closest to him in disbelief.

It showed the devastating power of the laser from the hi-jacked Chinese military satellite.

It showed, in High Definition, the Royal Navy destroyer with its helpless crew.

There was a flash of white light.

Followed by - death.

There had been no screams, no panic, and no time to know what was happening.

Death had been instantaneous for everyone on board.

Dillon's jaw tightened; he stepped smoothly away from Tatiana, eyes scanning the room: the Assassins, the bodyguard, Kirill and Ramus.

"You're running completely off rails," Dillon growled.

"On the contrary, Mr Dillon," said Ramus, as he turned to face Dillon. "We are quite sane. We only seek to do what is *right* - by our definitions of the term. You see that Chimera can take control of the most secure of military assets with ease. This virtual globe is merely my theatrical way of communicating with the programme, something to keep me amused - a pretty light show... But while you were watching one of Her Majesty's very expensive warships being vaporised, Chimera unlocked every single bank on the planet. *It* now controls them. *I* now control them. It has also taken control of every single satellite that circles the earth. Which means that it and I now control every single nuclear weapon in existence today? Shortly I will issue a statement to all the governments of the World Powers - they will surrender their position to me in exchange for their lives. And then... *then* we will start to re-design this wondrous planet to our liking."

Ramus' voice had risen in anger and, to Dillon's ears, in madness.

He tapped and dragged his fingers over the touch sensitive tablet screen. Suddenly, the light was gone and Dillon blinked...

Kirill walked towards the door, following Ramus. He was almost casual in his movements. His arrogance was total. His position of strength was clearly evident. He halted and turned to Dillon as Ramus disappeared with the tablet processor, the gateway to the Chimera Programme...

Kirill started to walk away, then turned and looked at Dillon.

"Mr Dillon, I feel duty bound to ensure that your last minutes before death; are the most painful you will ever have ever endured. That's why I'm leaving you in the most capable hands of Ramus' personal bodyguard. Azar will see to it that you - die."

The huge muscular man took a step forward and threw off his robe to reveal a heavily muscled torso. Dillon had to look twice at the man's disfigurement.

"What the hell happened to you?" Dillon said looking up at the huge man.

"He cannot talk, Mr Dillon. His tongue has been cut out, and the scarring on his torso was made by repeated and prolonged beatings with a large stick. Oh, you're probably assuming that we did these horrific things. But you'd be wrong; we rescued him from the Arab who owned him. And as we'd terminated his master's existence, he joined us, willingly. Now, if you'll excuse me, we have a world to take over. Goodbye, Mr Dillon."

"What about me, Kirill?" Tatiana called out.

Kirill glanced at her. "Tatiana, my sweetness. When my large friend has done with Dillon and sent him on his way. I have promised him his reward - *you*, my dear. Unfortunately, I doubt if you'll get any pleasure from this experience, but you can be assured of one thing - he will kill you afterwards." Kirill laughed loudly, a cold and callous laugh.

Dillon dropped his gaze. Something in his subconscious stirred, screaming inside his head. He glanced at his watch, at the seconds passing by. "*Time is running out, kill him, and kill him now and we'll be able to get off this stinking tub...*" His mind was racing ahead of itself...

Kirill stepped through the door and was instantly gone.

Leaving Dillon and Tatiana alone with the two Assassins and huge bodyguard. The Assassins already had a firm hold of Tatiana, who hissed a string of profanities at them and then everything happened at once. The huge muscled hulk of the bodyguard stepped forward with a mean smile and a deep throated grunt, tossing his gun aside where it clattered against the metal decking. The man's emotionless face under shaved head - serene and relaxed and ready to kill...

Dillon charged.

And the mute bodyguard leaped to meet him...

They clashed in mid-air with a rapid exchange of blows so fast that they were just a blur. They fell away from each other, both landing and whirling on to the grated metal floor of the control deck...

The mute man smiled nastily.

Dillon glanced at where the two Assassins had dragged Tatiana to the open doorway - but he was stuck, stuck without any form of escape route...

He looked back at the bodyguard. "Any chance you could get on with it, old son. Only a rather nasty bomb is about to be detonated under this tub, and I'd rather like to be some distance from it when it goes off." Dillon smiled back at the huge man.

The bodyguard charged, throwing a series of heavy punches at Dillon who blocked, dodged, blocked again and then landed a massive blow to the big man's jaw. Bone crunched as the head was knocked sideways. Then he lifted the toe of his boot and smashed it into the mute's testicles, causing him to immediately bend forward and grab his crutch with both hands and expel a sort of wincing sound. Dillon stepped back one pace, put all of his weight on his right foot, spun around and made contact with the side of the big man's head, snapping his neck with the full force of the kick. Dillon whirled round with incredible speed as the big man's carcass dropped to the floor with a thud, the two Assassins released Tatiana, and with cat-like movements advanced on him. They circled him like caged tigers, waiting for the moment to pounce.

"You are weakened, Mr Dillon. I guess, your age is catching up with you. Why not make it easy on yourself and let us bring your life to a swift end?" Said one of the Assassins, its voice soft and feminine.

Dillon laughed. "I don't feel dead yet."

"You will," said the feminine voice, its deep blue eyes gleaming.

"Don't you understand? I know what's about to happen. I'm toying with you; I am playing with you, Mr Dillon. You are *slow* compared to the two of us; you are *weak*. We are going to make you suffer as you made our friends suffer; we will send you to them and they will enslave your soul..."

"Could you hurry up then? I have to be somewhere else, you see." Dillon snapped.

They closed, slowly, warily.

Dillon went on the offensive, threw a complicated series of punch and kick combinations - the two Assassins blocked them all, and then moved in on him, as if as one being, with front kicks. Dillon dropped to the floor, sweeping his right leg around, knocking both Assassins off their feet. Like a street break-dancer, Dillon flipped over and spun round, leaping up with agility, that surprised even him. The Assassins recovered almost instantaneously, both delivering high kicks and punches to Dillon's torso, and suddenly a soft leather boot made contact with the side of Dillon's face. Luckily, he had been on his back foot as the blow came, lessening the impact and saving his neck from being snapped like a twig. Dillon went back down onto the hard metal floor with a heavy thud.

Dillon yelled, holding his hand to his ear, blood pouring from the long gash across his cheek bone.

"No!" cried Tatiana.

The Assassin landed in a crouch, then unfolded and stood. The black clothed figure walked forward. It looked down. Suddenly dropping, one elbow hitting Dillon in the chest with all its weight. The armoured body vest took the brunt of the blow, but Dillon still felt the impact. Dillon grunted - as his hands suddenly shot out, grasped the Assassin's hooded head and dragged it forward into the crunch of a head-butt - once, twice, three times until the Assassin's fingers prised Dillon's hands free and it scrambled, coughing and blinded, backwards, spinning and dazed, away across the metal grated floor.

Dillon, feeling sick, rolled to his knees, then to his feet, groaning. Pain raged through his head; he gasped, struggling to focus, his fingers coming up to his bleeding forehead. He glared across the room at the injured Assassin, who was shaking its head, a thin trickle of blood dripping through the black skin-tight hood from a broken nose.

The stealth ship around them rocked and shuddered. Distant screams could be heard as the first explosion ripped through armoured metal like a knife through butter. And then a low groaning rose as another distant explosion rumbled.

The Assassin stood, cobalt blue eyes fixed intensely on Dillon. And lunged.

Dillon readied himself; they punched, blocked, circled; the Assassin charged again, gaining momentum for a flying kick that Dillon barely moved away from. Again the Assassin came back with a quick

393

succession of punches, that Dillon blocked and counter-punched in response, and then Dillon struck with a kick to the Assassin's ribcage and the reassuring sound of bone cracking under the heavy blow. The Assassin staggered back for a moment.

They circled again, Dillon paining, sweat dripping from his brow. The Assassin seemed untouched.

"I thought you would be much faster," said Dillon.

"I am faster than *you*."

"Then show me, freak."

The Assassin charged. The blows were ferocious and Dillon found himself retreating, unsure about the outcome, under the insane barrage of punches and kicks. He barely managed to keep his footing as he dodged and blocked - a blow caught him in the side of the head and he staggered backwards, suddenly trapped against a bank of computer terminals.

The Assassin stood, watching the man in front of him as he struggled to get his mind sharp again.

"Dillon!" cried Tatiana. She was in the clutches of another Assassin, struggling with the thought that Dillon might not make it through this fight.

Dillon shook his head in an attempt to clear his mind. He looked up, looked up into the cobalt eyes of the Assassin; and at that moment he knew he had been out-classed; knew he was *dead*...

"Is that really the best you've got?" Dillon taunted. "I thought you were supposed to be a fucking killer - you're dead mate put up a better fight..."

The Assassin's eyes widened and the narrow smile disappeared. Dillon dodged and blocked a combination of punches and kicks, and then launched himself across the metal grilles, a full-on rugby style dive. As he hit the deck he rolled and sprang towards one of the benches and - the Glock 9mm automatic.

His fingers curled around the weapon, carelessly left by Kirill on the alloy bench and discarded in a fit of arrogance. Now his fingers curled around the heavy familiar weapon, around the sturdy grip of his 9mm defender and he rolled onto his back, gun up and pointing at the Assassin who suddenly halted and dropped to a crouch.

A laugh emanated from under the black hood.

Dillon squeezed the trigger.

The gun kicked and the Assassin moved with cat-light reflexes to the right, and the bullet slammed into a computer monitor on the other side of the control room. The screen exploded into a billion fragments, Dillon rolled, the Glock coming around for a second shot.

He heard the metallic click - and despite his injuries, he dived as the other Assassin holding Tatiana opened fire with the silenced Uzi. Dillon rolled behind one of the metal workbenches as bullets smashed into metal panels all around him. He waited a moment before breaking cover; heard the dead man's click, rolled, raised the Glock and squeezed the trigger. The bullet entered the Assassin through the right eye, Tatiana looked round as the black clothed figure released its grip on her and dropped dead to the metal floor.

Dillon watched momentarily as the bullet hit home, dropping the Assassin like a stone. He smiled with satisfaction, short lived; as the Assassin he had been fighting became fully aware of his position and moved towards him.

Dillon closed his eyes for a brief moment, he opened them - and a world in black and white prevailed.

"Now we finish this, once and for all," snapped Dillon's alter-ego. He slipped a long darkened blade from its hidden home in his boot. In a normal situation Dillon would shoot to kill, but this was no ordinary situation, and it called for the use of a blade... He was fast losing patience and *strength*. The remaining Assassin loomed above him and Dillon slammed the dagger up hard into its inner thigh, feeling the razor sharp blade part flesh and muscle with consummate ease. Blood flushed warm and crimson over his fist and he twisted the knife before pulling the blade out. The Assassin staggered, then slumped slowly to its knees. Dillon pulled himself up to his feet, bathed in the Assassin's blood, reached back and hurled the dagger across the control room. It drove into the neck of an Assassin rushing through the open doorway - without a sound it toppled forward onto its face and twitched as the life drained out of it and down through the metal grating. Bullets flew at Dillon, and he ducked as sparks kicked up around his head, and everything was suddenly quiet - except for the moaning, writhing form of the Assassin he'd stabbed.

Dillon got to his feet and checked around. He recovered his Glock and moved to where the back clothed figure was squirming. The Assassin's hands were coated in deep red glutinous liquid. Dillon pulled back the hood to reveal the Assassin's face. Cobalt blue eyes, naturally blond hair, the face of an angel...

And Dillon felt - sorrow. Not hatred, nor anger. Just sorrow for this poor wretched soul at his feet.   He lifted the Glock. Wiped his bloodied hand down the side of his combat trousers. And put a bullet in the middle of the Assassin's forehead, ending her pain.

Chapter 25

When the first explosion came, Vince climbed back into the cockpit of the Apache helicopter. The stealth ship shuddered and groaned as black metal was ripped open, Vince frowning to himself, checked his watch. Dillon had been gone far too long - far too long. He peered down from the cockpit, scanning the catamaran's deck areas for any unwanted company. He spotted two Assassins further along the deck, flicked a switch, and the forward cannon fired a burst of large calibre rounds directly at them.

"Great," he muttered.

There was more movement on the port side, six Assassins, all carrying machine-pistols. Vince fired another burst from the Apache's cannon and took down four Assassins, the other two scattered, he activated the cannon's heat seeking laser sight. Instantly, two short bursts erupted and one of the remaining Assassins was cut in half. The other one disappeared into the ship.

"Gone for reinforcements," Vince muttered. "Shit... Come on Dillon, you arse, *come on!*"

* * *

Dillon walked slowly across the control room where computers whirred and groaned to themselves. He took hold of Tatiana's arm and led her out into the corridor; he scanned the immediate area and found that it was completely clear of Assassins.

"Where is the real operation command room?"

"Level 1, but we won't get anywhere near it. Ramus has his elite guard protecting it and him."

"Let's see, shall we?" Dillon moved forward with Tatiana trailing behind him. They moved up through each level with a remarkable lack of confrontation, Dillon was amazed that there appeared to be no other Assassins on the stealth ship.

The corridor was wide with glass running along one side, and looking down Dillon could see a mass of activity; this was definitely the catamaran's bridge and command centre. Dillon could see Ramus and Kirill, the massive screen at one end showing the world laid out with live streams of information informing them as they directed their master plan for a New World Order. Tatiana looked down with disbelief.

"They really are arrogant fuckers," he said vehemently and slid the Glock's safety catch off. He checked the magazines stowed in various pockets of his armoured vest.

He had bullets. Lots of them.

Dillon smiled at Tatiana. "Now don't argue, But I want you to get to the Apache and wait there with Vince." He put his hand on her shoulder, leaned forward and gently kissed her on the cheek. He watched her go through the hatch that led directly out onto the deck, and then turned.

"Let's finish this Kirill," he said. And stepped warily along the corridor.

* * *

Further along the corridor, Dillon could hear heavy machine gun fire. There was also the incredibly loud whining of the laser-guided gatlin guns. Distantly, he could hear other explosions and the scream of engines.

"You're doing your work well, Alix."

Dillon touched the comm-link in his right ear and said. "Vince, are you there?"

"I'm here, chap. I've got the rotors spinning, but time is running out. Where the hell are you?"

"Corridor outside the main command bridge. Talk to me about the ship's damage."

"The JetRangers have knocked out the navigation systems; the ship cannot steer without the help of the Chimera Programme. The same goes for the stealth mode and weapon's systems. Chimera is controlling all of them."

"Thanks. I'll be along to you both shortly."

"You have exactly two minutes and thirty seconds before the big one goes off."

Dillon moved along the corridor, which was sloping down. He came to steps and carefully picked his way down their metal surfaces. He heard something behind him. Ducking into a service hatchway, he watched an Assassin rush past. The main doors to the bridge opened: Kirill stood there, a true blood Assassin to either side of him, and a look of anger and frustration on his face. Behind, a massive wall mounted monitor running streams of data created by Chimera as it went about its business of entering every computer connected to the Internet and taking electronic control of them - taking control of the digital planet...

Ramus was dictating a message to the heads of state and leaders of the world; Dillon caught phrases such as "ultimate destructive technology" and "total digital shutdown". He wiped the sweat from his brow with the back of his hand and gripped the Glock even tighter.

"Well?"

"The surviving intelligence service JetRanger helicopters, is as we speak, fleeing into the rain and gloom - but the Apache helicopter is still standing ready on the rear starboard deck. I would assume that they are waiting for Dillon. Why has it not been destroyed?"

"Ramus, believe me when I tell you that attempts have been made, but this helicopter is equipped with a sophisticated weapons system programme - that is definitely not standard." Kirill spoke softly.

"It is of no importance at this time. Ramus raised his right hand in a gesture of dismissal, a gesture of *arrogance*...

The sound of footsteps came from the corridor, and another four Assassins came into view. They came to a silent halt in front of Kirill. But Kirill could tell that something was wrong... Something was seriously amiss...

"What is it?"

"A bomb has been attached to the hull on the port side," said the Assassin calmly, eyes sparkling.

"What type of bomb is it?" Snapped Kirill. "Tell me, what kind of fucking device is it?"

"Our scanners have determined that it is a sophisticated dirty-bomb of unspecified yield, magnetically attached to the underside of the ship." The voice was soft and very calm.

Kirill's eyes widened. "We need to get a diver down there. Now! You hear me?"

The Assassin ignored him. "We must evacuate this vessel immediately."

"Won't the armour plating protect us against this?"

"No. This type of device creates extreme pressure at the point of detonation. The hull is extremely strong, but it will be ripped open by the explosion. Our armour is thick, designed for attack by torpedoes and mines. This device is different; when it detonates there will be no water to support the catamaran's weight. The ship will simply break itself in half."

Kirill stared, dumbfounded.

A million thoughts rushing through his brain.

Out of the corner of his eye, he could hear Ramus talking rapidly into the microphone of the comm link. A look of utter triumph at his defiance of the world, in celebration at bringing the world's most powerful administrations to their *knees*...

And all this through a virus programme.

Kirill lifted his gun; a single shot through the centre of the forehead ended the Assassin's report. He turned towards the other Assassins and smiled a thin cruel smile. "It would seem that Dillon and his friends had an ace up their collective sleeve. They're not running away like girls, they're getting free of this ship and the immediate blast zone." Kirill walked towards the main doors, and stepped off of the bridge.

Dillon stepped out from his hiding place behind him.

"Stop right there, Kirill."

Kirill turned, raised his gun and started firing, a mad smile creasing his lips, his brow furrowed in bewilderment. As Dillon had spoken, he had also stepped back into the shadows and concealment of the door recess. Sparks kicked up all around him, bullets ricocheting from the wall, one scorching a furrow across his right forearm - there was a moment when the wound was nothing but a narrow strip of red, and then blood started to gush out. Dillon clamped the wound with a silent curse and pressed himself tight up against the doorway. He tore off a sleeve of his shirt and bound it tightly about his forearm, instantly blood soaked through. Gripping the Glock 9mm, he stood shakily, his mind swam: loss of blood, constant pain, and a severe pounding at the hands and boots of Ramus' bodyguard had left him weak.

It's also left you slow, Dillon thought. He licked his lips, and stepped forward to peer along the corridor; he could hear a commotion on the bridge. His jaw became taught with the tension he felt, as he caught the fleeing form of Kirill who was once again cheating death.

And then he averted his attention back to the bridge and the processor containing the master copy of the Chimera Programme. Hell-bent on destroying the digital world as we know it.

"Damn it."

He strode onto the bridge, past two Assassins standing to one side of the doorway; each got a bullet in the head. He broke into a sprint as he heard Ramus saying arrogantly, "...we will spare the lives of millions of Americans..."

The Glock touched the back of Ramus' head.

Dillon could feel the bony skull through the muzzle of the automatic.

Ramus froze.

"But I won't spare your life," Dillon hissed as he squeezed the trigger.

The bullet smashed through Ramus' brain and exploded out of his right eye along with blood and gore.

Ramus collapsed.

The bridge became silent, except for the humming and whirring of the processors. Four Assassins turned their attention towards Dillon. He took a single step forward, glanced down at the processor unit with the Chimera optical disc and levelled the Glock directly at it.

"This is for everyone who has been murdered," he muttered. "Now it's pay-back time..."

He put six bullets into the processor as one of the Assassins behind him screamed a single word - "No!"

Bullets smashed the cold black casing into a billion tiny harmless fragments that blew violently outwards in a black mist.

All of the monitors around the bridge went blank. The master screen turned blue and all of the Chimera script disappeared.

"Now that's what I call terminal hacking!"

Uzi mini sub-machine pistols blasted.

Dillon sprinted, head low, as the Assassin, who had screamed - no, emptied a full magazine in his direction. Dillon raced into the corridor with bullets kicking up sparks behind him and bounced from the wall, groaning long and low to himself as his battered body seemed to gather up energy from somewhere deep within him. Spurred on by the thought of Alix's dirty-bomb, Dillon sprinted as if his life depended on it.

Which it did.

* * *

Dillon stumbled madly down the corridor in pursuit of a way out onto the deck. His alter-personality rose up through his sub-conscious to taunt him... "*You really are slow and weak, old man. You'll never get off this tub in time, you know. But I can get you off, Dillon. I have the strength you could never dream of - come on, Dillon, you'll never do this without me...*"

"Fuck off," snarled Dillon.

He stumbled forward, rebounding from wall to wall. His aching muscles felt like they were tearing with every jolt, making him want to cry out with each step forward. He halted; fell to his knees, his breathing laboured, the broken ribs, causing severe pain down his right side.

"*You're dying Dillon, and the clock is tick-tocking. Alix has done his job well, Vince is up there waiting for you with Tatiana, the blades of the Apache spinning. You have, roughly one minute and thirty-five seconds to get off this fucking death-ship.*"

Dillon steadied his breathing and stood up again.

Bullets kicked up sparks from the floor behind him.

He pushed on at a weary pace, stumbling, as the large catamaran was assaulted in succession by Alix's smaller explosive devices, shaking the very structure of the vessel as it made for deeper water outside of the harbour.

His boots thudded dully on the metal walkways, upstairs, and to the door that had allowed him entry. He wrenched the lever over and heaved it open.

More bullets came at him, striking sparks from the door's metal surround; Dillon dropped to one knee, the Glock kicking in his hand. Ramus was dead and Kirill was jumping ship like a rat, into a waiting black helicopter as rain pounded all around him.

Dillon stepped up and out into the wind and lashing rain.

And looked around, dazed.

The skies were filled with thick black smoke billowing up from the ravaged decks of the catamaran. The surviving JetRanger helicopter was fleeing and Dillon could just make out the Apache, blades spinning, and hovering twenty feet above the deck. Vince's outline was visible inside the cockpit, with Tatiana sitting next to him. The helicopter's forward machine cannons flashed as they spat out their lethal payload at each and every Assassin that came through the hatchway leading out onto the starboard side deck. As Dillon stood, mouth agape, an Assassin cut in half not more than ten feet away from him - closely followed by another who met with a similar end. Dillon started to sprint towards the Apache, all pain suddenly forgotten. Vince spotted him and opened fire on a small group of Assassins who were trying to cut him off, but who were mowed down instantly by the large calibre rounds. More bullets whizzed around him. Dillon growled, glaring at the helicopter up ahead. It jumped around in the sky and Dillon could see Tatiana's face looking down at him.

Dillon stayed low and sprinted for the Apache.

Two Assassins ran at him. The Glock's bullets knocked both of them from their feet, smashing through skin, bone and matter as their faces were pulverised. Dillon did not even break stride. As he reached the hovering helicopter, it was with despair that he saw the bullet riddled fuselage.

Vince brought the Apache down until he was hovering no more than twelve inches above the deck. Dillon clambered up and dropped into the cockpit. As he slipped into the co-pilot's seat next to Vince he noticed alarms were sounding and lights were flashing, .

The Apache's engines faltered under the increase of power required to lift the attack helicopter up into the air.

"I don't believe it!" Dillon growled.

Dillon took the controls, flicked a number of override switches and the twin engines burst into life again and the helicopter lifted quickly into a thunderous sky. It vibrated alarmingly, its engines howling. All around was a chaos of gunfire, flames and explosions; wind and rain streamed in through the cockpits shattered side-screen.

As the Apache veered to the right, Dillon spotted Kirill's small black helicopter in the distance. His stare locked on to the small black dot that was heading out low over the waves and he then circled a broad arc and gaining height momentarily to observe the stealth ship's demise.

Dillon powered the Apache forward.

The attack helicopter dived, howling towards Kirill's small black machine. Dillon armed the machine cannons, Vince and Tatiana tightened their seat harnesses, and then fired a short burst to make sure the guns were operating properly. Kirill had to *die*...

Lights flashed and a warning siren sounded on the console in front of him.

They had a fuel leak; he glanced at the levels and noted with despair that avgas was streaming from the Apache's fuselage. Dillon forced the helicopter on regardless.

Kirill saw him coming and banked his own machine aggressively, on-board machine guns opening fire. Bullets whizzed past to left and right, and scored a line up one flank of the Apache. Still Dillon urged the aircraft forward and something, some inner sense made him veer hard to the left as Kirill came at them head-on. Dillon fired the forward guns, as the small black machine went into a high wide sweep, sparks clearly visible as bullets struck the metal landing skids.

Machine guns hammered again.

Dillon suddenly realised there were two small black helicopters on his tail; he realised they must have been flanking Kirill, protecting this man who was their master.

The Apache took more hits.

"The fuel..." Dillon muttered, as avgas spray streamed away behind the battered helicopter.

The Apache lifted rapidly, gaining on Kirill's fast black machine as it made its way back towards the catamaran. And then everything happened at once.

There was a low, deep sound. And then the world seemed to shake.

The catamaran *staggered*, as if tripped, as the dirty-bomb that Alix had planted detonated. There was a weird underwater roar; a foaming cauldron erupted and light and fire danced beneath the sea, spreading out like tentacles of some giant octopus. The catamaran lifted and a rending, tearing and screaming sound of stressed steel ripped the airwaves - huge cracks appeared down both flanks of the stealth ship, the amidships of both hulls dipping and the prows rearing up into the sky on a gush of suddenly boiling water. The massive groaning structure thrashing around in the last throws of its life.

Foam and flames burst into the sky, like a geyser spraying skywards.

Bullets zipped past Dillon, and he launched the Apache down and under Kirill's machine. He rolled to the left and then right, before lifting the nose, reducing power, and firing the forward machine cannons.

Kirill's face held an expression of disbelief as the bullets ripped up through the fuselage and into his body. One of the bullets drove itself up into the Professor's groin and erupted through the back of his neck in a shower, spattering against the headlining of the cockpit. With the second burst of gun fire, Dillon hit the fuel tanks and Kirill's helicopter exploded into a spinning fireball, free-falling towards the nearby stricken catamaran, which was sliding beneath the water, settling below the waves like a dying dinosaur.

* * *

Tatiana tapped Dillon on the shoulder, making him aware of their unwanted aerial entourage and banked the helicopter in a wide circle, the two marauders following suit. Then he suddenly spun the aircraft and opened fire with the machine cannons.

The two Assassin helicopters attempted to evade the heavy-calibre bullets... And in doing so, collided in a sudden tangle of twisting metal and razor sharp rotor blades cutting through canopies and then came fire and explosions. They plummeted towards the sea in a ball of fury.

Tatiana smiled; she tried to calm her pounding heart but failed. Vince looked round and smiled, "You okay, luv? You look awfully pale."

"I'm fine, Vince. Really, I'm fine."

Dillon flew the Apache low over the sea. The helicopters that he had destroyed had sunk slowly beneath the cold waves of the English Channel.

Bringing the helicopter round in one last sweep of the area, Dillon's mood was lifted by the sight of the catamaran - sunk...

The rain and wind continued to lash down.

Before very long, it was all over and the damaged Apache helicopter limped back to the hanger.

Chapter 26

A bitterly cold north-easterly wind blew in off the water, rain lashed down, beating the smooth surface of the tarmac. The new BMW-7 Series saloon sped through the torrent of surface water, along roads that were as quiet as a graveyard; towards Baiter Park near to Poole Quay. Turned left at the bottom of the road and headed out towards the deserted car park by the slip-way

It was early. Four-thirty a.m. and not yet light.

The BMW stopped, engine ticking over, headlights beaming out over the water; one of the back doors opened and a bruised and battered Dillon, yet cleaned up and bandaged, feeling very nearly whole again - stepped out onto the gravel and breathed deeply of the salt laden morning air. The rain had stopped, he limped slowly across to the water's edge, wincing with every step, and halted, staring out at the black water lapping at the shore. He pulled free a packet of cigarettes, took one and lit the weed with his gold lighter.

Smoke plumed and danced on the cold damp air and Dillon sighed.

He turned at the sound of another car; the Porsche Cayenne cruised slowly past the luxury BMW and approached Dillon where he stood beside the water.

A cold wind whipped across the open space as the Porsche Cayenne cut its engine.

Dillon glanced in at the four suited men. One of the doors opened and two men stepped out; it was Edward Levenson-Jones and a man Dillon had never met before, and yet Dillon instinctively knew that he was part of the Whitehall machine; he was tall, had the air of authority, and was expensively dressed. Somewhere in his late fifties with neatly groomed sandy coloured hair, wearing a full length black overcoat of impeccable quality and tailoring.

"Jake." LJ smiled at Dillon.

The other man stood beside the chief operations director of Ferran & Cardini. "Mr Dillon."

Dillon shook the man's extended leather gloved hand.

Dillon nodded, drawing deep on his cigarette. "Good morning, gentlemen."

"Yes, I'm sure it will be later," said the stranger. "Come, walk with us."

They walked along the path at the water's edge, the wind blowing beneath their collars and making coat tails flap. An occasional seagull cried as it swept low in its quest for a breakfast...

"You know who I am?"

"No, I haven't got a clue who you are."

"That is probably for the best. But it has been brought to my attention that after your recent... exploits, shall we say, you have come to know rather a lot of things about Scorpion that maybe you shouldn't. And yet we cannot forget that you have sacrificed much, coming out of your retirement - leading us to the core of the Assassin network, and destroying this terrorist scum Ramus along with the traitor Kirill."

"Thanks. It's not often a field agent gets paid a compliment or words of thanks, I appreciate it."

The man stopped and gazed out across the world's second largest natural harbour. He then turned and gazed deeply into Dillon's eyes.

"Hmm," he said. And then Dillon spotted something in the man's gloved hand.

The man smiled.

"Here, this is our way of showing our appreciation. We thought it was the least we could do in light of your contribution."

Dillon opened the white envelope, and read the contents carefully.

Looking the tall man in the eye, he said. "Well I'll be... This is dubiously generous."

"Putting your castle in Scotland back together as it was, along with the impressive hi-tech security equipment, is the least we can do, Dillon. After all, if it hadn't been for your sheer determination and those extraordinary skills that you possess. We would all be in a very different place now. A dark place that one shouldn't think too much about as it's quite unthinkable."

"I had a *lot* of help from a few very good friends. They deserve to be rewarded as much as I do."

"Oh, they will all be suitably rewarded for the vital part they all played in averting the threat of a global meltdown."

Dillon smiled warmly, staring out over the water. "Did they ever find him?"

"No."

"Oh." Dillon scratched an imaginary itch on his chin. "Look, you can be assured of my loyalty and secrecy concerning the things that I have seen and heard during this assignment. I admit that I was maybe a little hacked off about being tricked back into service; only because I thought I had been targeted for a hit at the beginning of these... shall we say, adventures. But it soon became apparent that I was mistaken." Dillon's voice had turned somewhat cool. His eyes had a glint and his mouth had set into a grim line.

The tall man nodded. "Information is power, Dillon. Look what too much information did for Ramus and Kirill. You cannot tell everybody everything; as the best field agent that Ferran & Cardini has, you are still a tiny cog in the machine, only a small player in a very large game. Those two individuals were enemies of every state, who very nearly succeeded in bringing this planet to its knees because of information: their knowledge; their complete understanding: the things that they *shouldn't* have known."

Dillon ran a hand back through his hair. He flicked his cigarette butt into the water. The black waves took it and extinguished the glowing tip. The wind howled softly; Dillon shivered, remembering the beatings he'd endured over the last few days.

"I have questions..." said Dillon.

The man held up his gloved hand. He shook his head in the negative, just once.

"Maybe another time, Dillon."

Dillon smiled sardonically. "You mean another time as in never?"

"It's for your own protection," said the man. He smiled then, but it was an uncertain smile, a smile without humour - a smile used by a face not used to the expression. "I want you to remember Dillon, that contrary to popular belief - people like you are not expendable." He lit a slim Cuban cigar. Held it delicately.

Dillon met the tall man's gaze: greenish eyes, hooded from years of overworking and masking a thousand emotions. Their stares locked for a long time. Dillon held the man's cool look. Without another word, he nodded, turned and strolled leisurely along the path, admiring the beauty of the natural harbour.

LJ held back for a moment, both men staring out across the water, hands deep in pockets. "You did well, Jake. You did really well. The partner's want me to convey their eternal thanks and; I know this is not really the time, but that a situation has come to light that requires someone with special talents - the kind of talent that you possess. If you're interested, then come and see me when you return from your holiday." The two men shook hands. LJ turned and strode off to the waiting luxury 4x4. He climbed back into the Porsche Cayenne which started its engine, turned, and was gone.

Dillon turned back, staring out over the black waves. He shivered, pulling the collar of his coat tighter around his neck. He lit another cigarette. He heard the footsteps approaching and did not turn. Tatiana came and stood beside him, staring out across the water and Brownsea Island. They remained there in silence and then she looked up at him. "You alright, Dillon?"

He nodded.

"They want you to join them?"

"They?"

"You do know who it was you were just talking to?"

"Haven't the foggiest. All I know is that my home has been fully restored to its former glory. So who was he?"

"Let's just say that you're a very lucky man, who has ingratiated himself with one of the most powerful men in England." Tatiana took his hand; their fingers entwined and squeezed.

"You are a lucky man, Dillon," she said. "Lucky to be alive."

"Listen luv," said Dillon grinning. "Lucky is my middle name."

"Come on; let's get back to the others. We have a party to go to."

"What. At five o'clock *in the morning?*"

"Well, it's the tail end of a party. You know what Alix and Lola are like. They'll still be drinking."

"Where are they?"

"Sandbanks. LJ took out a short rental on a place named, Emporio, it's one of the most amazing properties I've ever seen, Dillon. And it has the most breath-taking views overlooking the harbour."

Dillon nodded. "Yeah, I'm game," he yawned. "Unless..."

"Yes?"

Their gazes met.

"I thought you would want to drink and sleep, in that order?" Tatiana smiled.

"Oh, I'm not *that* tired. And the Champagne's already on ice at my place!"

409

"Really. But isn't Scotland just a little too far away?"

"What. Oh, not Scotland. Here, out on the peninsula."

"Are you kidding, Dillon. You own property down here."

"I've always loved the place, Tats. Decided to invest about a year ago when I left Ferran & Cardini and the prices hit an all-time low."

"Oh, well in that case. I'm impressed Dillon."

She moved away, and Dillon stood staring out across the water as daylight started to break over the harbour. The cold breeze reminded him of Scotland.

From the pocket of his overcoat he removed a small object: a metallic looking disc. It rested in the palm of Dillon's left hand and he stood staring at it for a moment, wondering at the secrets it held. The only surviving Chimera script in existence, and whoever possessed it, also held the most destructive power on the planet. And he was holding it in the palm of his hand...

"Time you didn't exist," he muttered.

Reaching back, he threw the silver disk as far out into the harbour as he could. There was a tiny *splash*. The last copy of Chimera sank without a trace in the deep water.

Dillon smiled softly.

"Thank God, it's finally over," he breathed. He walked back towards the BMW thinking about LJ's offer of another assignment. Climbing into the warmth of the plush heated interior next to Tatiana, he made a mental note to call his old boss when he returned from a much needed holiday. The gleaming vehicle turned with a crunch of tyres on the gravel and headed smoothly for the Sandbanks Peninsula...

THE END

Until the next time...

Made in the USA
Charleston, SC
21 January 2013